African Students in East Germany, 1949–1975

Social History, Popular Culture, and Politics in Germany
Kathleen Canning, Series Editor

Recent Titles

Moderate Modernity: The Newspaper Tempo *and the Transformation of Weimar Democracy*
Jochen Hung

African Students in East Germany, 1949–1975
Sara Pugach

The Arts of Democratization: Styling Political Sensibilities in Postwar West Germany
Jennifer M. Kapczynski and Caroline A. Kita, Editors

Decolonizing German and European History at the Museum
Katrin Sieg

Spaces of Honor: Making German Civil Society, 1700–1914
Heikki Lempa

Bankruptcy and Debt Collection in Liberal Capitalism: Switzerland, 1800–1900
Mischa Suter

Marking Modern Movement: Dance and Gender in the Visual Imagery of the Weimar Republic
Susan Funkenstein

Anti-Heimat Cinema: The Jewish Invention of the German Landscape
Ofer Ashkenazi

Dispossession: Plundering German Jewry, 1933–1953
Christoph Kreutzmüller and Jonathan R. Zatlin, Editors

Sex between Body and Mind: Psychoanalysis and Sexology in the German-speaking World, 1890s–1930s
Katie Sutton

Imperial Fictions: German Literature Before and Beyond the Nation-State
Todd Kontje

White Rebels in Black: German Appropriation of Black Popular Culture
Priscilla Layne

Not Straight from Germany: Sexual Publics and Sexual Citizenship since Magnus Hirschfeld
Michael Thomas Taylor, Annette F. Timm, and Rainer Herrn, Editors

Passing Illusions: Jewish Visibility in Weimar Germany
Kerry Wallach

Cosmopolitanisms and the Jews
Cathy S. Gelbin and Sander L. Gilman

Bodies and Ruins: Imagining the Bombing of Germany, 1945 to the Present
David Crew

The Jazz Republic: Music, Race, and American Culture in Weimar Germany
Jonathan Wipplinger

The War in Their Minds: German Soldiers and Their Violent Pasts in West Germany
Svenja Goltermann

For a complete list of titles, please see www.press.umich.edu

African Students in East Germany, 1949–1975

SARA PUGACH

UNIVERSITY OF MICHIGAN PRESS
Ann Arbor

Published in the United States of America by
the University of Michigan Press
Printed and bound by CPI Group (UK) Ltd, Croydon, CR0 4YY

First published September 2022

A CIP catalog record for this book is available from the British Library.

Library of Congress Cataloging-in-Publication data has been applied for.

ISBN 978-0-472-07556-0 (hardcover : alk. paper)
ISBN 978-0-472-05556-2 (paper : alk. paper)
ISBN 978-0-472-22057-1 (ebook)

To Scott, Catriona, and Saskia Frey,
and in Memory of Joseph Pugach

Contents

Digital materials related to this title can be found on the Fulcrum platform via the following citable URL: https://doi.org/10.3998/mpub.12077279

Preface and Acknowledgments

I first began research for this project in December 2010. I spent about ten days at the University of Leipzig Archives, poring over documents about African students who had come to the German Democratic Republic (GDR) between the 1950s and 1970s. When the workday ended, I wandered around Leipzig's *Weihnachtsmarkt*—the Christmas market. I thought about the students, almost all of whom had arrived in Leipzig to take German classes before fanning out to other destinations in the GDR, and how they had perceived the city. It had been very different when they lived there, as I knew. I spent some time in Leipzig during the mid-1990s, when the city was undergoing a transformation from its recent socialist past—the landscape that would have been most familiar to the students—to its approaching capitalist future. The ubiquitous construction cranes of the early post-*Wende* era dotted the sky, and West German and American businesses were moving into the downtown. The *City-Hochhaus*, a skyscraper that locals referred to as the *Weisheitszahn* (wisdom tooth), was still part of Leipzig's Karl Marx University (KMU), as it had been from the early 1970s. By the time I went back to Leipzig in 2010, the building was privately owned and housed various companies, including the local German television station, MDR.

Cold War Leipzig, and the GDR more generally, have often been depicted as cold, grey, bleak places. That is not the impression you get, however, from the stories of African students. Instead it was the gateway to an education that they hoped would improve their lives and those of their families. Their experiences were ambiguous: they had close, affective relationships but also experienced horrific racism and the ideological pressure to conform. In some ways they had advantages that their East German peers lacked; while the mobility of East Germans was extremely restricted, especially after the Berlin Wall went up in 1961, for the most part Africans were free to come and go as they pleased, traversing the boundaries between the communist East and capitalist West with ease. Yet their lives in the GDR were also marked by a keen awareness of their own difference, and of inhabiting a society that would never entirely accept them.

Leipzig was my starting point for this study, and I returned to the city many times to conduct more research. I also continued my work for this book elsewhere, primarily in Berlin, but also in Dresden, London, and Accra, with detours to Cologne and Dakar. Most of it was written in Los Angeles. I owe a major debt of gratitude to all the people who helped me along this journey, wherever I met them. In Leipzig, the staff at the University Archives assisted me in locating a wealth of long-untouched material that proved invaluable to reconstructing the students' lives. I especially thank Jens Blecher, director of the Archives, Petra Hesse, and Sandy Muhl. I have known Adam Jones, Professor Emeritus of African History at the University of Leipzig, for approximately twenty-five years. I met with him on most of my Leipzig trips, where we discussed all manner of things concerning African studies in the GDR. He also graciously opened his home, a 220-year-old farmhouse on the outskirts of Leipzig, to my family and me on one of our visits. I thank him for his continued support of all my projects.

I was fortunate to receive funding from the National Endowment for the Humanities (NEH) and the German Academic Exchange Service (DAAD), which enabled me to travel to Berlin and conduct most of the research for this book, and I thank them for it. Their generous support enabled me to spend the summers of 2013 and 2014 working at the Federal Archives, Political Archives, and Stasi Records Archives in Berlin. I thank the staffs of all these archives, especially Bärbel Bartel at the Stasi Records Archives, who helped me find invaluable material about students who were monitored by the Stasi or approached as potential collaborators.

I owe many other debts in Berlin, including to Bernhard Debatin and Patricia Stokes, who sublet their apartment to me both summers, and their friend, Christiane Seiler, who helped my family get acclimated to the neighborhood. I could never have gotten my work done without the help of Sebina Maseela and the staff of INKAS, the summer camp that my children attended not only in 2013 and 2014 but additionally on a return visit in 2018. My research would also not have been possible without my mother, Eleanor Heumann-Pugach, who accompanied me to Berlin, or my husband, Scott Frey, who was with us for part of the time. My friends and colleagues Katrin Roller and Holger Stoecker were there for me as ever, whether to discuss German and African history or simply to hang out and have long dinners. I shared other wonderful meals and conversations in Berlin and elsewhere in Germany with

Cäcilie Engelmeyer, Karin Goihl, Cora Granata, Chad Kea, Priscilla Layne, Sheryl Oring, Stephanie Neumann, Heather Perry, Philipp Prein, Jake Short, Quinn Slobodian, and Nicole Thesz. I had the pleasure of speaking to Adama Ulrich, and of interviewing Ginga Eichler, Yvonne Kolagbodi, and Mohamed Touré. I thank them all.

There are many other people from all over who supported me in various ways as I worked my way through the project, and I want to thank them all here. Matthias Lienert, archivist at the University Archives of the Technical University Dresden, provided access to files illuminating the lives of students at that university. The late Jürgen Kunze invited me to an event hosted by the reconstituted Deutsch-Afrikanische Gesellschaft Leipzig (DAFRIG). The National Archives and the British Library were instrumental in helping me find information on the Nigerian students I discuss in chapter 1, and the Zambian students I talk about in chapter 2. Indeed, I could never have had access to the files concerning the Zambians without Jody Butterworth, Robert Miles, and the Endangered Archives Programme, which is housed at the British Library. Mulenga Kapwepwe provided indispensable assistance by translating letters from the Zambian language of Bemba into English for me. In England, Alex Cobbinah, Daniel Hodgkinson, Friederike Lüpke, and my former student Andrea Jean Sutterfield were all also extremely helpful. Jojo Cobbinah, Michel Dormont, Akosua Darkwa, Heather Heckel, Abdulai Iddrisu, Nii Markwei Marmah, and David Tette provided tremendous assistance during and in preparation for my trip to Ghana. Desmond Aryee-Boi, Jeannette Aryee-Boi, Kobina Bondzie, Robert Quansah, and Alfred Quaysah all kindly allowed me to interview them while I was in Accra. At the Public Records and Archives Administration Department in Accra, Botwe Bright, the managing director, went out of his way to help me find the documents I needed for chapter 3, and Paul Elisha took me on a fascinating tour of the archives. Unfortunately, I never had the opportunity to visit Kenya, but Alfred Anangwe, a researcher who has voluminous knowledge of the Kenya National Archives, found documents there for me that ended up being crucial to chapter 2. In Dakar, Mbye Cham and Ousmane Sene were kind enough to let me slip away from an unrelated faculty development program to interview a former Senegalese GDR student. I also thank the former student, who wished to remain anonymous.

Back in Los Angeles, where most of this book was written, I also received support from many directions. Cal State LA granted me a sabbatical that allowed me to complete much needed writing, as well as faculty funding for several courses off in other semesters that let me do the same. I was a fellow at the Center for the Study of Genders and Sexualities at CSULA in spring 2012, where I developed ideas and drafted talks for what would eventually become chapter 5. The Department of History at Cal State LA was incredibly encouraging of this project from the start, and I want especially to thank Choi Chatterjee, Christopher Endy, Eileen Ford, Cheryl Koos, Kittiya Lee, and Afshin Matin-Asgari. My many students at Cal State LA inspired me to ever greater heights. The Wende Museum of the Cold War and its staff, including Cristina Cuevas-Wolf and Joes Segal, was an invaluable resource on all things GDR in the LA area. Paul Lerner, who runs the Los Angeles German Studies reading group, let me present drafts of two of my chapters to the group, and members including Elizabeth Drummond, Ann Goldberg, Cora Granata, and Marjan Wardaki all provided excellent comments and suggestions. Marjan Wardaki also read the draft of this book, and her advice was crucial for helping me make substantial improvements to the manuscript.

Many, many other people also read parts of the draft; invited me to speak at conferences, workshops and other venues; gave me leads on sources; or helped me talk through my ideas. They include Edna Bay, Paul Betts, Adam Blackler, Eric Burton, Kirsten Fermaglich, Tiffany Florvil, Veronika Füchtner, Alyssa Goldstein Sepinwall, Paul Grant, Anne Hartmetz, Julie Hessler, David Hoyt, Kevina King, Eljana Lang-Djanteu, Brittany Lehman, Stephanie Lovett, Patrick Malloy, Omon Merry Osiki, Laura Mitchell, Nick Ostrum, the late Stephanie Patton, Katherine Pence, Alix Pierre, David Pizzo, Vanessa Plumly, De Anna Reese, Marcia Schenck, Elizabeth Schmidt, Kathleen Sheldon, Jake Short, Levar Lamar Smith, Edward Snyder, Aaron Sonnenschein, Lauren Stokes, Evan Torner, Didem Uca, Anna von der Goltz, Valerie Weinstein, and Tamara Zwick.

The University of Michigan Press has done an excellent job of shepherding this book through the publication process, just as they did with my earlier book. I especially want to thank my editor, Christopher Dreyer, and the Press's executive editor, Ellen Bauerle. The two anonymous outside reviewers also provided excellent feedback that helped me revise the manuscript.

Good mentors are always very important, and I have been lucky to have several: Ralph Austen and Michael Geyer, who were my advisors in graduate school, and more recently Nina Berman and Sara Lennox. They have all helped me throughout my career, and I cannot thank them enough. Good friends are also crucial in this crazy world, and Kirsten Fermaglich, Dana Mendez, Nancy Polutan, Galit Rich, Rachel Schuldiner, and Alice Segal are the best there can be. I thank them for all of their constant support and camaraderie as I worked my way through this book. Art Pugach is still the best brother in the world, bar none. My parents, Joseph Pugach and Eleanor Heumann-Pugach, have encouraged and been there for me throughout my life, and their love has carried me always.

On the same first trip I took to Leipzig in 2010, my older child, Catriona Frey, was three. The end of the trip was a comedy of errors, complete with a lost passport and canceled flight, and I got home a day later than expected. They were not happy but somehow forgave me. They are now fifteen. Since then, my husband, Scott Frey, and I have welcomed a second child, Saskia Frey, who is ten. They struggled with me through the many stages of this book, including the two (!) times when an earthquake struck Southern California and I happened to be away in Europe on research trips. I love them, and it is to them that I dedicate this book.

My father, Joseph Pugach, passed away on November 28, 2021, while this book was in the final stages of copyediting. The loss has been devastating, but tempered by the memory of his support of and enthusiasm for all of my endeavors. He had a doctorate in chemistry, which he obtained in 1964 despite hardships. His example inspired me to pursue my own doctorate in history, and so this book is also dedicated to his memory.

• • •

An earlier version of chapter 1 was published as "Eleven Nigerians Students in Cold War East Germany: Visions of Science, Modernity, and Decolonization," in *The Journal of Contemporary History* 54, 3 (July 2019): 551–72.

Portions of chapter 4 were published as "Agents of Dissent: African Student Organizations in the German Democratic Republic," in *Africa* 89, Supplement S1 (January 2019): S90–S108.

An early version of chapter 5 was published as "African Students and the Politics of Race and Gender in the German Democratic Republic, 1957–1976," in *Comrades of Color: East Germany and the Varieties of World Socialism*, edited by Quinn Slobodian (New York: Berghahn, 2016).

• • •

A note on anonymization: wherever I was unsure about whether an individual was deceased, I have tried to anonymize their names. The exceptions are for people who explicitly gave me permission to use their given names, or were officials in government institutions, for example ambassadors, and were as such public figures.

Sara Pugach, Fullerton, CA, May 31, 2021

Abbreviations

The following is a list of abbreviations that appear in this book:

ABF—Worker's and Peasant's Faculty, Leipzig
AESM-RDA—Association des Etudiants et Stagiaires Malians en République Démocratique Allemande (Association of Students and Trainees in the GDR)(Mali)
AfD—Alternative für Deutschland
ANC—African National Congress
BStU—Archives of the former State Security Service (Stasi)
CAF—Central African Federation
CMB—Ghana Cocoa Marketing Board
CMLN—Comité Militaire de Liberation Nationale (Military Committee for National Liberation (Mali)
CPP—Convention People's Party
CRO—Commonwealth Relations Office (UK)
CUT—Committee of Togolese Unity
DAfriG—German African Society
DHfK—Deutsche Hochschule für Körperkultur (East German School of Fitness)
EAP—Endangered Archives Programme
FDGB—Free German Trade Union Federation
FDJ—Free German Youth
FRG—Federal Republic of Germany
FRN—Federation of Rhodesia and Nyasaland
GDR—German Democratic Republic (East Germany)
GYP—Ghana Young Pioneers
IM—Unofficial Collaborator (with the Stasi)

KADU—Kenya African Democratic Union
KANU—Kenya African National Union
KMU—Karl Marx University
KNA—Kenya National Archives
KPU—Kenya People's Union
KSA—Kenyan Students' Association (GDR)
KSU—Kenyan Students' Union (GDR)
MfAA—East German Ministry of Foreign Affairs
MfS—Ministerium für Staatssicherheit (Stasi)
NCNC—National Council of Nigeria and the Cameroons
NHG—National Hochschulgruppen (National College Organizations)
NLC—National Liberation Council (Ghana)
NNFL—Nigerian National Federation of Labour
NPD—Nationaldemokratische Partei Deustchlands (National German Democratic Party, GDR)(Neo-Nazis)
NRC—National Redemption Council (Ghana)
NSU—National Socialist Underground (Post-Reunification Germany) (Neo-Nazis)
PAAA—The Political Archive (Berlin)
PEGIDA—Patriotic Europeans against the Islamicization of the Occident
PRAAD—Public Records and Archives Administration Department, Accra
SACP—South African Communist Party
SAPMO—The Archive of The Foundation for East German Parties and Mass Organizations
SED—Socialist Unity Party
SWANU—South West Africa National Union
SWAPO—South West Africa People's Organization
TANU—Tanganyika African National Union
TNA—The National Archives (UK)
TUC—Trade Union Congress (Nigeria)
TUD—Technical University Dresden
UAL—University of Leipzig Archives
UASA—Union der Afrikanischen Studenten und Arbeiter in der DDR (Union of African Students and Workers in the GDR)
UAD—University Archives Dresden
UNIP—United National Independence Party (Zambia)
UPC—Union of the Peoples of Cameroon

USRDA—Sudanese Union-African Democratic Rally (Mali)
VAS—Vereinigte Afrikanische Studenten in der DDR (African Students in the GDR United)
ZAPU—Zimbabwe African People's Union

Introduction

In the waning days of the German Democratic Republic (GDR), sometime around 1988 or 1989, a Ghanaian student named Desmond Aryee-Boi had one of the scariest experiences of his life. Walking down the street in Berlin, a group of young East German men approached him. They demanded to know whether he was African or African American. When he replied that he was from Ghana, the men became agitated. They accused him of taking a valuable university spot from a GDR citizen. Things turned violent as the East Germans began to beat up Aryee-Boi. He defended himself and then slipped away, running off in the direction of the nearest police station. When he got inside, the police had to barricade the door against the growing mob of East German men pounding on it, demanding that the police let Aryee-Boi out. Eventually they dispersed, but only after several hours milling around outside.[1]

Jeannette Aryee-Boi, Desmond Aryee-Boi's wife, also had frightening memories of the GDR. Her situation, however, was a little different. Jeannette Aryee-Boi was born in the GDR in the early 1960s. Her mother was East German, and her father, Jacques Latta, was a Cameroonian student who was in that country's opposition, the Union of the Peoples of Cameroon (UPC), and had fled from legitimate threats against his life. Later in the 1960s, he was able to return but was not able to take Jeannette, her mother, or her brother with him. Because her mother had been a member of the GDR's ruling Socialist Unity Party (SED), they were unable to get visas to relocate to Cameroon until 1970. Jeannette Aryee-Boi remembered East German citizens frequently levying racist slurs against her family and above all her mother, whom they accused of being a race traitor. They were relieved when they got to Cameroon.

Years later, at her father's behest, Jeannette Aryee-Boi returned to the GDR to study medicine. This might seem counterintuitive, but she explained that her father had loved East Germany, despite the fact that he knew all about the racist proclivities of some of its citizens. When he was picked for a scholarship in the GDR, he had already departed Cameroon and was living in a slum in Accra, the

Figure 1. Jacques Latta at his desk in Karlshorst, Berlin, where he studied economics. Undated (Jeanette Aryee-Boi, Private Collection).

Ghanaian capital. The future seemed grim, and the GDR saved him, providing him with an education and comfortable living quarters. From his perspective, some racism was an acceptable tradeoff. For his daughter, though, it was too much. She met and married Desmond Aryee-Boi while they were both studying in the GDR. They were there at the time of reunification in 1990. But ultimately, the couple did not want to raise their children in a place where they believed ill-treatment could be expected, and they resettled in Accra.[2]

The attack on Desmond Aryee-Boi in the late 1980s and the memories of Jeannette Aryee-Boi from the 1960s *and* 1980s undercut one of the central tenets of GDR mythology: that the GDR was an antiracist, anti-imperialist state. From its inception, the GDR was envisioned as a partner to people struggling for independence against the evils of colonialism. The politicians who were architects of the GDR envisioned the neighboring Federal Republic of Germany (FRG)—West Germany—as the inheritor of the racist, Nazi past. Meanwhile, the concept of solidarity with the Global South became so predominant in the GDR that it was incorporated into the state's constitution in 1974.[3]

Figure 2. **"1970, Bringing Simo to Airport," Jacques Latta and Jeanette Aryee-Boi at Schönefeld (Jeanette Aryee-Boi, Private Collection).**

Figure 3. Jacques Latta dressed in "traditional" regalia in procession with other Cameroonian students, front row, center. Undated (Jeanette Aryee-Boi, Private Collection).

When I first began conducting research for this book, I wanted to know whether the antiracist proclamations of the SED were more than just lip service and had indeed reshaped East German society along antiracist lines. The SED claimed the mantle of antiracism not that many years after the fall of the Third Reich, which was the definition of a racial state—one hierarchically organized by the principle of racial difference and founded on a racist ideology. On the face of it, antiracist principles seemed impossible under such circumstances—on the ruins of a viciously racist state—yet the SED nonetheless claimed to embody antiracism.

But in undertaking research on Africans who lived, studied, and worked in the GDR, I was interested in more than just the German context. I wanted to find out how the African students' history was molded by the dual, overlapping contexts of the Cold War and decolonization, and how these ongoing global events influenced their lives before, during, and after their sojourns in the GDR. East Germany, with its antiracist policies but continuing struggles with entrenched anti-Blackness, certainly shaped the experiences of those Africans who studied there. However, so did the nations or colonies that the students called home, the places they visited on their ways to and from the GDR, and the broader shifts in the power dynamics of the Cold War.

Viewing student experience in terms of these wider contexts helps explain attitudes like those of Jacques Latta, who tolerated racism in exchange for relief from political violence and poverty in Cameroon during decolonization. The East Germans supported his party, the UPC, at a time when Cameroon was achieving independence under a government that was extremely friendly to the French, to the extent that it was considered a French puppet.[4] Further, the United States, with which France was allied, had a vested interest in keeping newly decolonized states in the capitalist orbit and not allowing left-wing parties like the UPC to rule. The intersecting politics of France, Cameroon, and the wider interests of both the Eastern and Western Blocs therefore all had an impact on Latta and other students.

These two themes—the dynamics of racism and antiracism in the GDR, on the one hand, and the significance of the Cold War and decolonization to the lives of African students, on the other, are the main subjects of this book. I will address the impact of the GDR's antiracist proclamations on the growth of phenomena such as solidarity and humanitarianism, but also look at how racism was an everyday fact of life for African students in the country; East German attitudes toward race were contradictory, and the students' history shows how these attitudes reflected both welcome and bias. In addition, I will explore the multifaceted ways in which the Cold War intersected with decolonization across Africa to influence the students as they moved from their home countries to East Germany, where they pursued educational goals that were sometimes individual and sometimes driven by political equations dictated either by their own governments or those of the GDR and other Eastern Bloc countries. African students were always independent agents who made their own decisions, but they were nonetheless affected by prevailing historical currents.

In what follows in this introduction, I first address the long history of Germany's connection with Africa, together with the equally extensive history of anti-Blackness and antipathy toward People of Color in Germany and German-speaking regions. This provides a necessary backdrop to the story of East German encounters with Africa. Second, I turn to the issue of how the Cold War and decolonization were determinative for the students' experiences and shaped their impressions not only of the GDR but of the Soviet Bloc more generally. Third, I review the extensive and continually expanding literature on the GDR's relationship with the Global South. Fourth—and finally—I outline the chapters that will follow in the rest of the book.

Racism and Antiracism in Germany and Europe before 1945

Interactions between Germany and various parts of Africa have a long history. While much of the scholarly focus on German connections with Africa has centered on the colonial era (1884–1918), documentation stretches much further back. Despite their small population, Blacks appeared in German medieval and early modern iconography and literature.[5] Africans were slaves at princely courts from the thirteenth century, functioning as *Hofmohren* (Court Moors).[6] Once the transatlantic slave trade opened around the beginning of the sixteenth century, African slaves became more readily available even to those German sovereigns who did not directly participate in the trade. Having an African at court became a sign of prestige, and Black servants were often integrated into royal social structures, even marrying German women on occasion. Yet assimilation did not mean that African otherness disappeared. Instead Africans were marked by difference, exoticized and described contrarily from whites who supposedly had the same social standing.[7] African agency also existed; conversion to Christianity, for instance, offered opportunities for social advancement.[8]

Germans became actively involved with the transatlantic slave trade beyond simply having African slaves serve at court. Even those Germans who lived far from the ports where the slave trade occurred could be implicated, either directly or indirectly, through business with slave traders from countries such as Britain and France. The economic relationships that the trade engendered in turn shaped impressions about Africans and factored into the popularization of beliefs in African animality.[9]

The othering of Blacks in the medieval and early modern worlds was not the same as it would be after the advent of scientific racism in the eighteenth and nineteenth centuries, since it was not grounded in the same sense of biological difference.[10] Instead, as Sara Eigen and Mark Larrimore have maintained, it was around the end of the eighteenth century that "the word 'race' was adopted in remarkably similar forms across Europe as a scientific term denoting a historically evolved, quite possibly permanent, and essentially real subcategory of the more inclusive grouping of living beings constituting a single species."[11] German intellectuals such as Georg Wilhelm Friedrich Hegel, Immanuel Kant, and Johann Friedrich Blumenbach, among others, were deeply enmeshed in these evolving discourses on race.[12] Their thoughts on race were multifaceted and grappled with defining the concept in relation to religion, culture, language, biology, and color. I do not believe, though, that German prominence in the creation of racial ideologies means that there was a German *Sonderweg* on ideas about race; anti-Blackness was a Pan-European project, with information about race and difference exchanged fluidly across national borders, and German ideas about race and Blackness were largely consistent with those of other European nations.[13]

With the nineteenth century came increased German involvement in colonial ventures, even before formal German colonization in the 1880s and 1890s. Recent scholarship has made clear that German involvement in Africa and elsewhere in the non-Western world was not predicated on formal colonization, and that notions about categories such as Oriental or Black did not require the active participation of a German nation-state. Itinerant Germans such as Emin Pasha (Georg Schnitzer) regularly represented other empires and contributed to their store of knowledge. The German impact was often felt keenly in Orientalism, owing to a German fascination with the Middle East and India.[14] Meanwhile the work of Wilhelm Bleek, a German linguist and anthropologist who migrated to South Africa in the mid-nineteenth century, was critical to the construction of ethnic and racial narratives about indigenous South Africans.[15]

After acquiring its own colonies, Germany continued to be involved in transnational conversations on race and Blackness, including those with the United States, as Andrew Zimmerman has demonstrated in his work on knowledge transfer with regard to labor practices and racialized identities in Germany, West Africa, and the American South.[16] My own work on German Protestant missionaries who labored for the British Church Missionary Society (CMS), as well as Jeremy Best's studies on the ecumenicalism of German missionaries, demonstrate that German nationality did not necessarily equal fealty to a German empire.[17] German anthropological and linguistic research on Africans was similarly transnational, since linguists like Carl Meinhof were intimately involved in developing theories about African difference that had impact far beyond German borders.[18]

Once Germans began moving to the colonies, and especially to the empire's designated settler colony, German South West Africa, their concern with race became more charged. The question of racial "mixing" was never far away for settlers who lived in close proximity to Africans. German missionaries of the early to mid-nineteenth century somtimes married African women with the hopes that their unions would ingratiate them more with local communities and encourage conversion.[19] Missionaries such as Carl Büttner, who worked in Namibia in the mid-nineteenth century, indeed favored mixed marriages on grounds that they would more closely bind colonizer and colonized.[20]

By the early twentieth century, however, consensus on intermarriage had shifted, as colonial governments enacted bans on the practice, as "miscegenation" was now generally regarded as unacceptable.[21] The first law against German-African unions was passed in German South West Africa in 1905, with similar prohibitions following later in German East Africa and Samoa.[22] Questions of marriage intertwined with those of citizenship, since Black spouses acquired German citizenship, as did their children, before the bans were enacted. As whiteness had come to be considered a requirement for German citizenship and nationality, these marriages had to be made illegal and their offspring had to be reclassified from citizens to subjects,[23] lest the German nation and "race" be polluted.[24] Whiteness and Blackness were now considered intractably incompatible, and upholding the purity of the white race was tantamount.

Over time, perceptions of Blackness thus underwent a series of shifts. The idea that Africans were somehow intrinsically different from Europeans, however, remained even as the exact characteristics comprising that difference changed. Many aspects of this difference stayed centered on sexuality, gender, and reproduction. This is especially important to note, since racism in the GDR was often embedded in discourses of African sexuality and lasciviousness. In the late nineteenth- and early twentieth-century imperial period, German colonial officials often portrayed African men as hypersexual and unable to control themselves. Germans—similarly to other European colonizers, including the British and French–[25] believed that if African males lived in Europe they would be unable to harness their baser impulses and be easily tempted by loose white women. This would have dreadful effects on their behavior when they returned to Africa, where they would see every white woman colonist as a potential sexual partner and target of sexual violence.[26] Further, Africans who did live in Germany in the same time frame, such as Swahili lecturer Mtoro bin Mwinyi Bakari, were shunned and made outcasts if they entered into relationships with white women, as Bakari did when he married the German Bertha Hilske.[27]

Anxieties about race mixing and the introduction of "impurities" into the German *Volk* also ran high during the Weimar era, coalescing around the issue of "the Black horror on the Rhine." This myth that France's colonial African troops had raped and sullied white German women and girls during the early Weimar occupation of the Rhineland was again rooted in a fear of uninhibited African sexuality and the associated birth of mixed-race children. The specter of immoral German women having sex with African men unleashed a firestorm of propaganda against the French occupation.[28]

In the Nazi era, fear of miscegenation extended beyond hysteria at the thought of German-Jewish relationships to encompass concern for African-German romance. The threat of a new generation of Afro-German children following those who were born to German mothers and African fathers during the occupation of the Rhineland so disturbed the Nazis that they sterilized some Afro-Germans.[29] However, at the same time Nazi policies toward Afro-Germans were also not uniform. As Eve Rosenhaft has argued, the Nazis devised antimiscegenation policies to concentrate on Jews and not more "visible" racial others, such as Gypsies or Blacks, because of a conviction that most Germans would not mix with these groups of their own accord. The Nazis thus relied on preexisting racial prejudices and beliefs toward Afro-Germans—ones that predated Hitler's rise to power—to prevent any "mixing" with the German population.[30]

The Cold War, Decolonization, and Race

Considering this long and complicated history of anti-Blackness in Germany and the rest of Europe, the answers that I found to my question about antiracism in the GDR were inevitably complex, rooted both in historical precedents and the contemporary context of Cold War and decolonization. Racism and antiracism inhabited the same space, not only in the GDR but across the Eastern and Western blocs and beyond. East German antiracism surfaced in a world still reeling from the horrors that racism had wrought, with six million Jews dead as a result of Nazism. The United Nations, which was founded in 1945, worked to establish a framework of human rights that would put a stop to future atrocities by drafting agreements to which member nations would adhere.

The UN Convention on the Prevention and Punishment of the Crime of Genocide of 1948 indeed declared that the world would no longer tolerate genocide, a crime that was defined as "acts committed with intent to destroy, in whole or in part, a national, ethnical, racial or religious group, as such."[31] Thus crimes against race, which I define as a socially constructed category that has had a profound impact on how biologically indistinguishable groups of people have been treated over time, would theoretically be policed by the UN and all the signatories to the Convention. Two years later in 1950 the UN issued the Universal Declaration of Human Rights (UDHR), which outlined the fundamental rights to which all human beings were entitled, including freedom and equality, which were available "without distinction of any kind."[32] Theoretically, people of all races were now to enjoy the same set of privileges.

The same world that declared "never again" with regards to the crime of genocide, and purportedly defined all people as equal regardless of race, gender, religion, or ethnicity, was however still organized according to a hierarchical, racial logic, especially in the West. As Mark Mazower has argued, Europe in 1945 was on the precipice, and Western Europe could have easily sunk further into authoritarianism and violence rather than turned toward democracy. The line between liberty and barbarity was razor-thin, and in the postwar years arced in the direction of democracy largely because of war fatigue and economic prosperity.[33]

In the Global South, meanwhile, violence continued. Fading empires such as the British and French clung desperately to their colonies. Trying to hang on, the British committed mass murder during the Mau Mau Uprising in Kenya (1952–1960), slaughtering thousands of Kenyans fighting for their independence. One million Algerians lost their lives during the Algerian War for Independence (1954–1962), as France tried to preserve control over the country. The UDHR seemed not to apply in Africa, and indeed Bonny Ibhawoh cautions against reading too much into its impact there; he argues that since the European colonial powers monopolized the UN, and Africans had no representation at all, the latter regarded the document with suspicion. The UDHR was, in any case, not legally binding.[34]

From its inception in 1917—well before the Cold War—the Soviet Union was already positioning itself as the antiracist foil to the US, with the latter country's long history of racism going back to its roots and the era of the slave trade. Welcoming African Americans to their shores in the 1920s and 1930s, and publicizing the horrors to which they were subjected at home, highlighted Russia's open-mindedness while simultaneously foregrounding U.S. perfidy.[35] The Soviet Union continued to present itself as a bastion of egalitarianism during the Cold War, as Africans from across the continent arrived to attend its universities. There were Africans who prized their experiences of the USSR and what they learned there.[36] The Soviet Union, GDR, and other Warsaw Pact states also provided invaluable support to liberation movements across the continent with economic aid, material assistance, and military training.[37]

At the same time, Africans and African Americans undeniably experienced racism in the USSR, both on the street and at the universities they attended.[38] There was a disconnect, or gap, between the policy statements of the Soviet government and the behavior of some Soviet citizens.[39] This was also true for the GDR. SED rhetoric was antiracist, and the country provided support, monetary and otherwise, for nonaligned African nations and independence movements. Heartfelt solidarity existed, but so did pronounced xenophobia and vicious racism. Tanja R. Müller's book on the East German School of Friendship, which was attended by Mozambican children and teenagers in the 1980s, encapsulates how contradictory attitudes about race in the GDR could be. She points out that in the students' memories, the GDR was like a "paradise." Yet the murder of one student by a group of German youth in 1987 considerably darkened this Eden.[40] Stories like this—of being embraced like brothers but also suffering racially motivated violence—are woven throughout the broader history of African students in the GDR. This contradiction between acceptance and hostility is suggested both by Müller's work and tales such as those of Jeanette Aryee-Boi and her father.

This book is therefore concerned with the slippage between the rhetoric of the SED and the lived reality of African students in the country, primarily in the first two and a half decades of its existence. That reality was complicated, incorporating experiences of blatant and sometimes violent racism, but also deeply felt affection for the GDR and the honest solidarity of many East Germans. This means that I address questions of continuity and change between the pre-1945 and postwar eras. I argue that many of the racist assumptions and beliefs of the Imperial, Weimar, and Nazi eras carried over into the GDR, as much as state rhetoric tried to deny this fact. The persistence of racism was not lost on the African partner states that worked with the GDR and other Eastern Bloc countries to send their students abroad. For instance, S. W. Kumah, Ghanaian ambassador to Yugoslavia in 1963, commented that although the Soviet Bloc showed "support for the liberation of colonial peoples from imperialism" and "great desire to win the friendship of the people of Asia and Africa," their "official policy . . . does not rule out the possibility of individuals in these socialist states exhibiting a racial contempt and discrimination towards coloured (sic) persons."[41] In other words, the gulf between rhetoric and reality was large, in Yugoslavia but also in other Eastern Bloc nations like the GDR.

At the same time, African students undeniably integrated themselves with East German society. They made friends, had romantic relationships with East German women, married and had children who became citizens of the GDR. When the family of a young woman engaged to a Togolese student welcomed him into their home and lives in the late 1960s, and tried to find a way for him to remain in the country even after he was supposed to go home, it demonstrated that some East Germans, at least, were open to Africans.[42] The students' everyday histories, caught between violent rejection and cautious acceptance, tell us much about the dynamics of life in East Germany, a state that, as recent scholarship has noted, was far more connected with the rest of the world than has often been presumed.[43]

African Students and the Age of Multipolarity

The students' story also goes well beyond their experiences of East German amity or animosity. It is enmeshed in the dual, overlapping contexts of the Cold War and decolonization, which are vital for understanding the evolution of the relationship between the students and the state, and the students and ordinary East Germans. There were vast, invisible networks linking the students to the GDR as well as to points beyond. These networks, which were imbricated in a worldwide flow of students from the Global South, were determined by anticolonial struggles and patterns of decolonization as much as they were by Cold War competition, and they flowed through cities such as Accra, Conakry, Bamako, Dar es Salaam, Nairobi, Lusaka, and Cairo.[44] The book is therefore not only about Cold War German history but about postwar African history and the history of transnational migration in the latter half of the twentieth century.

All of the involved players—the GDR, newly independent African states, independence movements, and the students themselves—had different reasons for promoting student exchange. The East German interest in attracting African and other non-Western students was wrapped up in its ongoing rivalry with the neighboring Federal Republic of Germany (FRG), especially after the establishment of the Hallstein Doctrine in 1955. The Doctrine stipulated that the FRG would not maintain diplomatic relations with countries that recognized the GDR. It hamstrung GDR efforts to forge connections with decolonizing countries through its retraction in 1972.[45]

The GDR's involvement with student exchange programs was additionally linked to the interests of the Soviet Bloc. The USSR, the GDR, and many of the other Soviet satellites competed with the United States and its allies for students from the Global South. From the late colonial period through the era of decolonization and independence, there was recognition that new states would require many kinds of aid. That assistance included cash and goods to build infrastructure on the ground, but also university education and vocational training. The blocs envisioned this aid as a possible mechanism to bring emergent nations into their ideological spheres of influence, and thereby expand either Soviet or American predominance across the globe.[46]

The governments of African and other Third World countries were very aware of the fierce competition for their favor. The Non-Aligned Movement, which solidified at the Bandung Conference of 1955—and was strengthened during the Tricontinental Congress in Havana in 1966—was made up of states whose governments rejected both Soviet and American ideologies in favor of a third path. African leaders such as Ghana's Kwame Nkrumah and Guinea's Sékou Touré subscribed to the philosophy of nonalignment and accepted aid and influence from both the American and Soviet sides in the Cold War. They recognized the significance of receiving support from all directions, including other states not firmly aligned with either bloc, such as China, Israel, or India.

Government functionaries in new African states were particularly keen to have students trained in scientific or technical subjects. This would have the benefit of speeding development and complementing other kinds of aid. Indeed, in 1960, a Ghanaian committee tasked with choosing candidates for scholarships in the GDR, Czechoslovakia, and Yugoslavia issued a memorandum mentioning that, "The Ghana Co-operative (*sic*) Society has arranged to set up quite a few factories from Eastern Germany and it is necessary to send some technicians and other people to be trained in advance for the operation of these factories."[47] During a Cabinet Meeting in the same year, it was further decided that the awards the GDR and other Soviet Bloc countries had offered could only be used for programs in agriculture, science, or technology—which were the clear priorities of the state.[48] Official agreements between the GDR and countries like Ghana, Guinea, and Mali stipulated what the students' major fields would be, and they were most frequently scientific or technical.

Independence movements and trade unions from countries that were not yet decolonized also forged agreements with the SED and other governments that allowed members of their organizations to study abroad. Parties such as South Africa's African National Congress (ANC), which had an alliance with the South African Communist Party (SACP), maintained strong ties with the Soviets.[49] The ANC's connection with the SACP made some in the West suspicious,[50] though a robust anti-apartheid movement ultimately took root in the United States and its allies too, often driven by Black American and British communities.

The GDR also developed substantial relationships with movements like the ANC,[51] the South West African People's Union (SWANU), the South West African People's Organization (SWAPO), and the Zimbabwe African People's Union (ZAPU). In 1960, the GDR founded the Committee for Solidarity with the Peoples of Africa, which was later renamed the Solidarity Committee of the GDR.[52] This committee had a fund to provide aid to liberation movements throughout Africa, and it largely raised money through the Free German Trade Union (FDGB), which collected the cash annually from its members.[53] The fund was partially used to provide scholarships for students. For instance, in 1960 Wera Ambitho, secretary of the Kenya Office in Cairo, corresponded with an FDGB official about funding for Kenyans to attend the FDGB's Trade Union College in Bernau.[54] Kenya would not become independent until 1963, and at the time Ambitho was coordinating liberation activities in Cairo, which included finding money to finance Kenyan educations. Francis Meli, a procommunist member of the ANC who later became a historian and editor of *Sechaba* (Nation), a party journal that was published in the GDR,[55] was also educated at the Karl Marx University (KMU) in Leipzig with a scholarship from the Solidarity Committee.[56] Support came as well from the Deutsch-Afrikanische Gesellschaft (DAFRIG), run by KMU historian Walter Markov and founded in 1961.[57] On behalf of the SED, the DAFRIG promised that the GDR would back the ANC in its struggle against apartheid, eschewing any connections with South Africa's National Party and its racist policies and making clear its allegiance to the Black African cause.[58]

Political entities on all sides—whether they were Western or Eastern Bloc governments, recently decolonized African states, or independence movements still involved in the struggle—had vested interest in the students, and in co-opting them for different national interests. But what of the students themselves? In the pages that follow, I unpack their reasons for going abroad, beginning with the first students to arrive in the GDR, eleven Nigerians who came in 1951. It is often difficult to gauge motive, since many of the sources relating to the students, such as *Lebensläufe* (curriculum vitae) and letters from the students to East Germans, can be interpreted in a variety of ways. *Lebensläufe* were written with a particular audience in mind, one that was often comprised of professors, university administrators, and other students.[59] The students knew what university management wanted to hear, and so their *Lebensläufe* often included mention of loyalty to communism or a penchant for left-leaning causes. Their letters probably went through similar filters; those I have looked at were most commonly sent to university or technical school workers, or in some cases bureaucrats at the East German Ministry of Foreign Affairs (MfAA). *Staatssicherheitsdienst* (Stasi) reports on meetings with students often contain similar biases, since the Stasi targeted those students it thought most receptive to Marxist-Leninist ideology to recruit as *Inoffizieller Mitarbeiter* (unofficial collaborators, or IMs) and asked leading questions about their political positions.[60]

Despite the obstacles that the research materials present, definite patterns of student motivation emerge. Some students came from countries where opportunities for higher education were almost nonexistent at the time of decolonization. Those who came from formerly British colonies without institutions of higher education, like Zambia, had once gone to England to study; those from Francophone countries without western universities, like Mali, went to France.[61] With decolonization, however, they had the potential to study abroad elsewhere. Decolonization opened up new vistas of educational possibility, and students seized them. Many were concerned with individual advancement, and with elevating their individual and familial social status. They were less interested in the development platforms of their states. Some had little intention of returning to Africa and preferred to stay in Europe, whether they remained in the GDR or left for the West. Remaining in Europe provided them with a better chance for social mobility. Additionally, many students developed affective relationships with East Germans and did not want to leave their partners or the families they had created. There were also instances when going home could be genuinely dangerous, as was true for Cameroonians like Latta in the late 1950s and early 1960s, or for Congolese students in the early to mid-1960s.[62]

The sources concerning the students' lives are many and varied. University archives have proved a particularly rich lode, especially those of the University of Leipzig and the Technical University of Dresden. They contain lists of the African students who attended from the 1950s onward, along with *Lebensläufe*, information about African national student organizations, academic performance and grades, student theses and dissertations, complaints to university officials from African students, and complaints about African students from East Germans. A sense of the texture of the students' everyday lives emerges from these documents, tracing everything from the arcs of their relationships to the bonds they formed with East German students, to their frustration with East German racism.

Other archives also afford glimpses of student lives, often along with detail on SED policy regarding student exchanges and internal bureaucratic discussions about the same. Both the Foundation Parties and Mass Organizations of the GDR in the Federal Archives (SAPMO) and the Political Archive of the Federal Foreign Office (PAAA) have proven invaluable in this respect. They demonstrate that many different departments within the East German government had vested interests in the students, including the Central Committee of the SED, the Free German Youth, the Free German Trade Union, the Ministry for Foreign Affairs, and the National Front of the GDR.

Because the Stasi was so interested in recruiting African students to become IMs, there is in addition a wealth of data in the BStU, which houses the records of the Stasi. Beyond the files on potential recruits, the Stasi documents contain information on student delegations from specific countries, trips students made to West Berlin and elsewhere, intercepted love letters between African students and East German women, reports of alleged crimes committed by African students, and incidents of racism directed against African students on the part of GDR citizens. Stasi files contribute to our understanding of how the students interacted with each other and with East Germans as we see them doing such mundane things as smoking Western cigarettes, studying late into the night, developing close relationships with their neighbors, and receiving short visits from friends.[63]

Archives outside Germany also feature prominently in this study. The Public Records and Archives Administration Department (PRAAD) in Accra, Ghana; Kenya National Archives (KNA); and the United National Independence Party (UNIP) of the Zambia Archives (now digitized and available at the British Library) all provide vital insight into how African governments negotiated with the GDR and other Soviet Bloc and Western governments to send students abroad. They show how students were chosen for scholarships, and what they had to do in order to reach Europe. The National Archives of the United Kingdom (TNA) house documents on how the British and colonial Nigerian governments struggled over how to prevent Nigerian subjects from taking up studies in the GDR, as is detailed in the first chapter.

I also conducted a handful of interviews with former students and, in two cases, their children. It was difficult to locate individuals who studied in the GDR during the time period covered in this book. Many of the students who were in the country during the 1950s and 1960s have died, and others have left no historical traces outside the archives, for instance on the Internet. It is especially difficult to find female students, since some likely married and changed their names. The students that I did interview were mostly in the GDR later, in the late 1970s and 1980s, and sometimes straddled the period between the end of the East German dictatorship and the beginning of the Reunification era. Still, their experiences—good and bad—go a long way toward demonstrating how the expression of racism in the GDR did and did not change over time, as some, like the Aryee-Bois, reported increased racist incidents the closer it got to the *Wende*, while others saw little change in their level.

Taken together, these sources demonstrate that African students were a visible presence in East German lives, both at universities in large cities like Leipzig, Dresden, and Berlin, as well as in smaller towns where they went for vocational training. They detail students both struggling to fit in and blending into East German society. Their experiences are a chronicle of East German ambivalence toward questions of race: there were individuals who were hostilely racist, others who were blatantly ignorant of non-Western races and cultures, and yet others who genuinely welcomed the students into their home and lives. The sources additionally prove that Africans were not particularly passive in their dealings with East Germans or their state. They had power that few East Germans did, such as the ability to cross back and forth between East and West Germany. Piles of requests for permission to visit different states in the West are preserved at the University of Leipzig Archives, and these requests were regularly stamped approved.[64]

The Transnational GDR: A Critical Review of the Literature

This work makes interventions in several key areas. I cover issues relating to solidarity, ideology, humanitarianism, multipolarity, and alternative, late twentieth-century Cold War modernities. Research on students, whose lives were affected by all of the categories above, ties these discourses together and sheds new light on areas of the Cold War that are only beginning to be discussed in the same critical framework.[65] My approach, which involves overlapping microhistories of numerous students interspersed with analysis of key moments in the history of the Cold War and decolonization, is rooted in the archival material discussed above. It reflects how such broad historical currents impacted the history of the everyday, what in German is called *Alltagsgeschichte*. I argue for the primacy of a transnational view of the Cold War and decolonization, one which parses the conflict on a global plane instead of within a national framework. At the same time, however, I believe that the global, local, and transitional—that is, the space of movement between spheres, such as Africa and Europe—must be interwoven with an evaluation of quotidian experiences that lifts these seemingly mundane, everyday events to the same level of significance as the realm of high politics.

This book therefore contributes to and extends different historiographic literatures that are not often joined, but which I think need to be: histories of postwar Germany, postwar Africa, and the global Cold War. In terms of modern German history, my work on students adds to a mounting body of research on the GDR as a global actor. When I began this study in 2010, research on postwar German connections to the wider world tended to focus more on the FRG. Books by Heide Fehrenbach and Maria Höhn, for example, addressed how West Germans and their government dealt with race through investigations of African American GIs and their relationships in the early FRG,[66] and there was a steadily growing literature on Turkish and other guest workers in West Germany.[67] This is unsurprising, since East German documents were only opened to historians from outside the Soviet Bloc in 1990, after the *Wende*.[68] Before this time, there were indeed studies of the GDR's Africa policies—by, for instance, Ulrich Post, Frank Sandvoss, Ernst Hillebrand, Hans-Joachim Spanger, Lothar Brock, and Gareth Winrow—but since these authors did not have much access to East German sources, they remained incomplete.[69] They were also very much traditional political histories, rooted in the area of diplomatic relations on a high level, and did not really take individual life stories into account.

Some of the first treatments of the global GDR in the post-*Wende* era were by East Germans who had earlier access to the sources, including Hans-Georg Schleicher, Ilona Schleicher, and Ulrich van der Heyden. In the 1990s, the three of them produced two edited volumes on the relationship between East Germany and Africa.[70] These works were also problematic. The books' editors are historians with doctorates earned in the GDR, but most of the contributors were not. Instead they were East Germans who had worked in politics, journalism, and other fields related to the books' subject. The content of the volumes was not necessarily scholarly, then, but focused on highlighting the positive aspects of the GDR's relationship with Africa for a post-*Wende* audience. While the books are extremely important as a first foray into the subject of East German transnationalism in Africa, they are still biased toward the GDR and may obscure the more negative or ambivalent aspects of its transnational politics. The Schleichers themselves were not only historians but also East German diplomats in southern Africa—Zimbabwe and Namibia—and thus had a vested interest in the GDR's success in the region during their earlier careers. Van der Heyden is a prolific academic, who has spent a good deal of time defending East Germany, the place where he grew up, against what he sees as slights from the West.[71] He has been especially vociferous in maintaining that racism was not a significant problem in East Germany,[72] despite ample evidence to the contrary, as this book and much of the literature discussed below demonstrate.

More contemporary scholarship, produced at a remove from the events being analyzed, incorporates a critical, cultural approach to German transnationalism, both with regard to Africa and elsewhere. Quinn Slobodian, Young-Sun Hong, Jennifer Hosek, and Katherine Pence, among others, have brought new dimensions to our historical understanding of the GDR and reframed its position within the Cold War world.[73] Research on students, workers, diplomats, and anyone who moved across the boundaries between decolonizing Africa and the "second world" of the Soviet Bloc has been a crucial element of this new spate of literature. Following the lead of Julie Hessler and Maxim Matusevich, who wrote pioneering studies of African students in the Soviet Union,[74] scholars like Marcia Schenck, Eric Burton, Immanuel Harisch, Jason Verber, Constantin Katsakioris, Nedžad Kuč, and Thom Loyd have addressed actors such as students, workers, and diplomats who traversed both realms. They have looked at pathways to the GDR, Yugoslavia, and in Loyd's case to Ukraine.[75] There have, moreover, been studies that look at the traffic of African students and workers to Bulgaria, Czechoslovakia, and Romania.[76] Individually and jointly, these authors have illuminated the pathways students took to the Eastern Bloc, as well as the conditions they encountered once there.

Recent literature on East Germany, including that on migrants, foregrounds the role that socialist Europe, as opposed to the USSR or the United States, had in the Cold War relationship to Africa, Asia, and Latin America. It also reminds us, as Slobodian does in the introduction to his 2015 edited collection *Comrades of Color*, that from the vantage point of the Global South, the GDR was relatively privileged and more similar to the neighboring Federal Republic of Germany than countries in Asia, Africa, or Latin America in terms of quality of life. The ideological divide between East and West may have been wide, but the economic gap was not as glaring as it was between either Germany and that of regions emerging from colonial domination.[77]

Student experiences indeed bring the extent of the economic disparities between the comparatively wealthy GDR and its decolonizing African partners into sharp relief. African students in the GDR had access to products and services unavailable to them in countries recovering from or still mired in colonial economic exploitation. Higher education, or in many cases even secondary education, was itself elusive to most Africans. Burton, who discusses different routes that East Africans took in their journeys toward higher education in both blocs, emphasizes this point;[78] so does Schenck in her study of Lusophone

African migrations to the GDR.[79] European colonizers had ensured that education was mainly available to a small, elite stratum.[80] In the postcolonial phase, the experience of study abroad was thus that much more critical to the few who had it.

While most African students were concentrated in large cities like Berlin, Leipzig, and Dresden, others, especially trainees in various industries, fanned out across the country. This meant that even in villages and rural areas, East Germans had the opportunity to meet these visitors, undermining the idea that East German citizens were backward or had little contact with the outside world. In general, the burgeoning historiography on East German transnationalism has also had the effect of further deprovincializing the GDR and recasting it as a society that was less insular,[81] inward-looking, and uncosmopolitan than has often been imagined.[82] In their 2008 edited volume *Socialist Modern: East German Everyday Culture and Politics*, Katherine Pence and Paul Betts contested the idea that the GDR had been "backwards" or "unmodern" in comparison with the capitalist West. Drawing on a wealth of literature that refutes the notion of the GDR as a "shut-down" society,[83] they argue for a reassessment of the GDR as representative of an *alternative* modernity. Taking a cue from postcolonial studies, Pence and Betts contend that the term modernity is too often defined in a hegemonically liberal, Western sense that negates the existence of other meanings for the modern, be they non-Western or socialist. The GDR, in their view, was thus not modern in exactly the same way as the FRG or United States, but had its own form of modernity, characterized by the desire to present a socialist alternative to capitalist development.[84]

I make a similar point about alternative modernities in this book. Africans who studied in East Germany did not perceive their education as "backwards." They instead saw it as vital to their future careers. Again, the "second world" of the GDR was still more technologically and economically advanced than African countries that had been devastated by decades of colonialism and a lack of access to schooling. Moreover, at the beginning of the Cold War, it was not yet obvious which "side" most African nations, struggling to decolonize, would ally themselves with in the global conflict once they achieved independence. Ultimately, many African nations, like Ghana, Guinea, and Mali, became part of the Non-Aligned Movement. Some, including Kenya, Cameroon, Ivory Coast, and Senegal, affiliated themselves with the United States. Others, such as Tanzania, embraced socialism, but the Maoist model,[85] not the Marxist-Leninist one espoused by the GDR and Soviet Union. In the end there were only a handful of states that aligned themselves firmly with the Soviet camp, and they did so at different times, with for instance Somalia in the 1960s, and Ethiopia, Angola, and Mozambique in the 1970s and 1980s.[86] In 1949, the year that the GDR first invited a group of Africans from Nigeria to study in Leipzig and Dresden, it was anyone's guess which—if either—Cold War "modernity" would prevail.

GDR connections with the Global South played out on other levels as well, for instance in terms of solidarity and development. Both older and newer studies of GDR solidarity foreground the role that it played in countering the Hallstein Doctrine, as well as the general significance of solidarity to SED diplomacy. Ulf Engel and Hans-Georg Schleicher's 1998 study underscores the role of the SED's ideology of solidarity, arguing that it was central to GDR diplomacy in Africa through around 1972, when détente made Africa policy less of a priority.[87] If the GDR could not fight the Hallstein Doctrine economically, it could chip away at it ideologically.

More recent work continues to untangle how the GDR used solidarity to counter the economic might of the FRG. Pence has demonstrated how the GDR used the rhetoric of anti-imperial solidarity with the Arab world to make non-Westerners question the FRG's commitment to their independence and well-being.[88] Heike Hartmann and Susann Lewerenz address how the GDR not only presented itself as the anticolonial Germany but also emphasized the idea of the FRG as a fascist, imperialist state that had collaborated with the apartheid regime in South Africa to keep the Black population down.[89]

In his work on GDR relations with the Namibian SWAPO, Toni Weis has further illuminated how the concept of solidarity was central not only to diplomacy but to East German identity, and remained so even after the Hallstein Doctrine fell out of effect in 1970. The GDR was able to join the United Nations in 1973 and thereafter took an increasingly prominent role through its backing of socialist governments in Mozambique and Angola, continuing to justify its activity through the prism of solidarity. East German support for liberation movements in the Global South was enshrined in Article Six of the GDR's 1974 constitution, and so solidarity was its watchword even after relations with the FRG had begun to thaw.[90]

As much as the GDR pushed its message of solidarity, the experience of African students demonstrates that East German solidarity had its limitations. There were indeed legitimate expressions of solidarity with independence movements and political parties across the African continent. Groups like the Free German Youth (FDJ) were, in addition, especially involved with solidarity and development projects in the Global South.[91] Yet as I show, solidarity was reserved for some Africans and denied to others. Those students who came from countries considered socialist or nonaligned were favored, whereas those who were from capitalist-oriented states were shunned. Indeed, for much of the period covered here African students could only enter the GDR if they were from nations that had concluded educational exchange agreements with East Germany.

Solidarity intertwined with another, similarly vital issue: humanitarianism. Financial and material assistance, often couched in terms of development aid, were critical for newly decolonized states. African governments and resistance movements worked with actors from across the West, the Soviet Bloc, and beyond in the quest for assistance. The frameworks under which states like the GDR and FRG offered aid were distinctly ideological. In her work on humanitarianism in both nations, Hong has discussed several instances when the GDR and FRG provided relief at cross purposes.[92] For example, while the GDR, in accordance with its anti-imperialist principles, was one of the first nations outside the Middle East to support Algeria's National Liberation Front against France, the FRG supported and enforced French embargoes on humanitarian aid.[93]

Hong also maintains, however, that whether they were looking to the capitalist or communist worlds, Africans and others from the Global South encountered relatively similar discourses on development from the two Germanies, which framed the West as the superior civilization with respect to its ability to offer support. She holds that German involvement in Third World development was anchored in a paternalistic vision of North-South dichotomy that cast European civilization as the savior of those in the benighted South, and that this was so on both sides of the Iron Curtain. Humanitarianism was therefore structured by the schism between Global North and Global South.[94]

Hubertus Büschel's arguments about German developmental aid on both sides of the Cold War conflict complement Hong's. Comparing development projects undertaken by the GDR and FRG in different parts of Africa, Büschel concludes that they failed because of East and West German refusals to listen to the people they purported to help. For Büschel, this also means that the GDR's highly touted concept of solidarity was essentially the equivalent of the West German concept of *Hilfe zur Selbsthilfe*. It can be equated with development aid in exchange for the acceptance of a new political and economic system to replace the "primitive" ones already in place. The developmental paradigm in both East and West Germany emerged from the same discourse on European "uplift" of the Global South, one that was rooted in the earlier colonial economic programs of the British and French.[95]

The burgeoning corpus of literature on the GDR and the Global South reveals the ambivalence of East German attitudes toward non-Western "others" and exposes the similarities between East German and West German understandings of race, and their approaches to diplomatic and humanitarian states in Africa, Asia, and the Americas. Newer research has also highlighted how East German citizens interacted with non-Westerners in their everyday lives. My book, along with work by scholars such as Schenck and Burton,[96] complements and extends our understanding of East German interactions with the Global South. It does so in large part by further integrating the perspectives of the students themselves—an action that foregrounds the voices of those whom scholars have mostly ignored in histories of the GDR. During the colonial period, Africans often appeared in written documents but rarely composed them. We learn about them at a remove, when they show up in European texts. That is frequently still the case with material from German and other European archives from the early Cold War. Where African voices appear in files at the Federal Archives, it is often to provide testimonials to the greatness of the GDR and condemn the West in comparison. These documents must be carefully picked apart and read with the knowledge that they were constructed with a specific audience in mind—their East German professors, university administrators, and often foreign office officials. Yet student opinions are still present, for example in letters they wrote to East Germans after leaving the country, or in complaints they lodged with various authorities. Combined with sources from various African archives and personal interviews, a much more rounded picture that incorporates African and East German vantage points begins to emerge.

The literature on the GDR in the Cold War world is very much in conversation with a broader historiography that aims to reposition the Cold War entirely, and to question its fundamentally Western framework. Odd Arne Westad has been key in shifting the debate on the conflict by suggesting that it was a multipolar struggle in which the "Third World," long considered peripheral, figured prominently.[97] Heonik Kwon has also destabilized standard beliefs about the Cold War as a period of tense peace, pointing up the multiple wars and extreme violence that enveloped much of the Global South during this time. Kwon has eschewed the more typical national or superpower perspectives and telescoped in on the local, micro context, commenting "that it is misleading to think of the Cold War as a unitary historical reality," as it "took diverse forms across territories."[98] I agree but argue that it is also crucial to look at how the Cold War played out in the interstices between territories, and at the lives of the individuals who crossed them. The competition for non-Western students between and beyond the blocs produced a steady, global flow of individuals who experienced different facets of the Cold War on deeply personal levels.[99]

This book also contributes to the historiography of postcolonial Africa, and especially of Africa during the Cold War. This literature has also grown substantially in recent decades. It includes work on the scope of the conflict across the continent, as well as a large and varied body of scholarship on how the Cold War impacted individual countries and their inhabitants. Because most of Africa decolonized during the Cold War, the United States and Soviet Union, but also the former European colonial powers, East and West Germany, Cuba, China, and others took a vested interest in the continent.[100] Westad and Elizabeth Schmidt have both addressed the deleterious effects of outside interference. For example, Schmidt demonstrates how multiple actors, both foreign and local, shaped African trajectories and spurred violence and underdevelopment. The Cold War severely hampered African independence, even as external powers paid lip service to promoting it.[101]

In general, bipolarity as a framing device is insufficient for understanding post-1945 global history, as Matthew Connelly has suggested.[102] The Cold War geopolitical concerns of the Soviet Union and United States were not always relevant to the interests of other nations or nongovernmental actors. Sue Onslow has persuasively argued that people in Southern Africa were less concerned with the Cold War than they were with local issues.[103] While the United States and USSR played significant roles in the region, apartheid South Africa was more influential in conflicts like the civil wars in Angola and Mozambique. Moreover, Cuba played a major part both in those wars and in other African independence struggles. Cuba's impact on the region was substantial, given the amount of material and military aid that it provided, as both Pierre Gleijeses and Christopher Saunders have shown.[104]

Even so, Cold War ideologies undeniably had a major impact on Africa, if not necessarily in the way one might think. Western and other forces attempted to disseminate these ideologies across the continent, calling for Africans to embrace imported ideals of capitalism or communism. Yet Africans either transformed Western ideologies in ways that Europeans would not have expected or put forward their own, competing beliefs about the past and how the world should be restructured in the second half of the twentieth century. Africans supported African socialist and Pan-Africanist principles that were not always welcome in the Western or Soviet spheres,[105] and which shaped postcolonial trajectories in ways that could not be captured in terms of a bipolar Cold War framework. African intellectuals like Leopold Sédar Senghor, the first president of Senegal, argued that African societies were naturally socialist and organized around concepts of family and community, which inherently promoted the equal allocation of resources.[106] The idea of class conflict, so central to Marxism-Leninism, was thus alien to Africa and had no place there. Pan-Africanism, which was first introduced in North America and the Caribbean by figures such as W. E. B. DuBois and E. W. Blyden, advanced the unification of all peoples of African descent. In the postwar era, among other things this meant trying to unify African states across borders in experiments such as the Mali Federation, which ultimately failed.[107]

The independence of the paths that African nations took during the Cold War—even as they were subject to Western interference and cultural impositions—are elucidated in a number of recent works addressing how the Cold War impacted specific countries such as Tanzania, Ghana, and Guinea. Priyal Lal examines *Ujamaa*, Tanzania's project of villagization that both resembled and deviated from experiments with collectivization elsewhere;[108] also focusing on Tanzania, Andrew Ivaska looks at how the country's first leader, Julius Nyerere, embraced socialism but also rejected Western values as immoral and un-African.[109] Meanwhile, Seth Markle's study of Pan-Africanism in Tanzania highlights the transnationality of the movement, which drew African Americans and Afro-Caribbeans to the state.[110] Tanzania was a laboratory of political experimentation, where leftists from all over gathered to exchange ideas and imagine new world orders.

Ghana and Guinea did not become hubs in the same way, but they still embodied African political principles and could not be neatly slotted into Cold War hierarchies. Jeffrey Ahlman emphasizes the uniqueness of Nkrumahism, named after Ghana's first leader, Kwame Nkrumah, to defining Ghana's early postcolonial period.[111] Jay Straker turns to how the concept of youth became critical to shaping a distinct Guinean nation state, one that would ultimately suffer horrifically under Sékou Touré's authoritarian rule.[112]

All of these works consider emergent African states in situ, within specific national contexts, even as they also demonstrate how they were impacted by broader, global dynamics. This study is different, since it follows African students from various countries as they traveled north, west, and east. Even so, it still looks at how Africans shaped their own, unique political and cultural identities when confronted with demands to conform intellectually to European—in this case, East German—norms. Some students accepted the brand of Marxism-Leninism endorsed by the SED and taught in their classes. Others challenged the GDR's Marxist orthodoxy, arguing for the superiority of African Socialism or Pan-Africanism. And many—probably the majority—were ambivalent to Cold War ideology, primarily interested in achieving economic success for themselves and their families, and only secondarily in improving the fortunes of their nations. They pursued individual goals while negotiating the divisions of the Cold War in ways that were sometimes advantageous, but could also have tragic consequences.

African students, like the countries they came from, were thus architects of their own fates, working with or against Western and Soviet forces depending on their interests. Their movements across continents corroborate Westad's argument about the multipolarity of the Cold War world. Power was not vested in two particular nodes; it was far more diffuse. The students created connections across and around the supposed Cold War divide as they negotiated their way through the GDR and beyond.

The Structure of the Book

The history I chronicle here covers the first two and a half decades of African student exchanges with East Germany. It begins in 1949, with the invitation of eleven Nigerian students to attend university in the GDR, and largely ends in 1975, when the calculus of the Cold War in parts of Africa was beginning to shift. Under the FRG's SPD chancellor Willy Brandt, a more moderate *Ostpolitik* replaced the hardline strictures of the Hallstein Doctrine, which was first weakened and then dissolved between 1969 and 1972.[113] *Ostpolitik* meant that the FRG acknowledged the GDR as a separate nation, paving the way for African countries to recognize it and establish their own embassies in the early 1970s.[114]

This change in the diplomatic relationship between the GDR and FRG was followed by political shifts in Africa that occurred through 1975. In April 1974, the Portuguese dictatorship, the Estado Novo, was overthrown, and Guinea-Bissau became the first Portuguese colony in Africa to gain independence, which it achieved later that year. Guinea-Bissau was followed by Mozambique, Cape Verde, and Angola, all of which decolonized and became independent in 1975. Moreover, in 1974 the pro-Marxist Derg overthrew Emperor Haile Selassie in Ethiopia. These events signaled a marked change in geopolitical configurations, as left-leaning, Marxist governments emerged in the former Portuguese colonies, which aligned themselves with the USSR and Soviet Bloc. The Derg, too, aligned themselves with the Soviets, while their Horn of Africa rival, Somalia, associated itself with the United States. This was a switch from the pre-1974 era, when Ethiopia was in the American camp and Somalia in the Soviet.

Such changes in Cold War geography altered which students were most prominently represented in the GDR, as well as its African diplomacy. Ethiopians, who had hardly been represented before, began to make up a large part of the student population. This was especially true after 1979, when five hundred to seven hundred began to come each year.[115] Angolan and Mozambican students also became more prominent; many received military training in the GDR.[116] Further, by 1987, 18 percent of African students in East Germany were from Mozambique.[117] This was in addition to the thousands of Mozambican guest workers who came to the country as a result of agreements between the GDR and their own government during the 1980s.[118] Other shifts included a movement from accepting only students whose governments had concluded educational exchange agreements with East Germany to the admission of increasing numbers of private students who applied to its universities without going through official political channels. These students were self-pay and did not have scholarships; such admissions were rare in the 1960s and early 1970s.[119]

Scholarships were, indeed, crucial in allowing African students the opportunity to study in the GDR from the beginning. The first African students to come to the GDR had East German financial support: these were the eleven Nigerians, who were invited in 1949 and arrived in 1951. Chapter 1 addresses why the SED first invited them to East Germany, the various paths they took to reach the country, and what they experienced once there. Their story is embedded not only in the context of postcolonialism but that of late colonialism as well. In a time when Africa's colonies had yet to achieve independence, Africans were interested in acquiring the scientific and technical knowledge they needed to develop their states once decolonization finally happened. They looked both to the East and West for this knowledge, since at this point scientific progress was considered relatively equal across the blocs, and the Soviets had the advantage of being viewed as anti-imperialist and antiracist. The GDR took advantage of this and offered Africans both the promise of anti-imperialist support and technical know-how. At the same time, the students continually confronted racism in the supposedly antiracist country.

The Nigerians who arrived in 1951 did so under the auspices of their national labor union. Many of the students who followed in the 1950s and early 1960s were also affiliated either with labor unions or in some cases with national independence movements. This included Kenyans and Zambians, whose paths to the GDR I trace in chapter 2. Before they were decolonized, in 1963 and 1964 respectively, Kenyans and Zambians were happy to send students to the Soviet Bloc and accepted all help fighting imperialism. After decolonization, though, a divide grew between African leaders who leaned to the left and those who tended to be more centrist or right wing. Reaching the East became trickier, as postcolonial governments like Kenya's aligned themselves to the capitalist West.

Chapter 2 further shows how difficult it could be for Africans to make the trek to the GDR from a sheer physical standpoint. For Kenyans and Zambians, the route usually went through Dar es Salaam and Cairo and could take over a year as they stopped and waited for placements in foreign universities and plane tickets to take them onward. In West Africa, this same journey could lead from hostile regions to socialist-friendly Ghana, Guinea, or Mali. Although their nation had technically been decolonized in 1960, Cameroonians like Jacques Latta, who found themselves in the opposition, were also still fleeing to cities like Accra and Conakry before getting scholarships to the GDR or elsewhere.

For students from independent nations with socialist leanings, the process of reaching Europe was less onerous but still required a grueling selection process that could make travel uncertain, as archival evidence from Ghana demonstrates. Chapter 3 provides an in-depth look at the process through which Ghana selected students to go to the GDR between 1957 and 1966, and how their fortunes were affected by the changing political constellations of the Cold War. When Ghana decolonized in 1957, its government was willing to consider accepting scholarships from the GDR and other Soviet Bloc nations, but it was also leery since substantial links to its former colonizer, Great Britain, remained. As the Scholarships Secretariat in Accra received increasing numbers of offers for university placement, they appeared to take most of them, whether they came from the capitalist West or the communist East. Once Kwame Nkrumah, the first president of Ghana, was overthrown in a coup in 1966, though, the new government of the National Liberation Council (NLC) immediately suspended all scholarships to the GDR and its allies. This had a lasting effect on the Ghanaian students already in the GDR, as well as on those waiting to leave.

Once students finally arrived in the GDR, the FDJ and other governmental bodies attempted to shape their experiences and beliefs. The students took classes on Marxism-Leninism and visited East German factories and farms. Starting in the late 1950s the FDJ also organized national student clubs to represent students from each African country, as well as an umbrella organization for all African students and workers. GDR authorities envisioned the clubs having mainly a ceremonial purpose; they were to arrange independence day celebrations for their respective nations, with speeches and "traditional" dances. Yet the clubs soon became much more: They turned into sites of protest, where students would object to the policies of their own governments or to racism in the GDR. In chapter 4, I look at how Africans turned their clubs into political forums and how East German officials struggled to suppress them. The SED did not have the ability to punish Africans as they would East

German citizens, because there were no agreements preventing them from leaving the country or from broadcasting their displeasure abroad. This gave the students considerable leverage over their own organizations, and left GDR bureaucrats scrambling for a means of control.

From the arrival of the Nigerian students in 1951, relationships between African men and East German women became a fact of life. Ten of the first eleven Nigerians were men, and most married East German women. Thereafter many African students entered relationships, which often led to children. Chapter 5 looks at these relationships and public and governmental reactions to them. Much of the racism reported in archival documents stemmed from East German male reaction to interracial couples. African men were targets of anger over the sexual appropriation of "their" women. The women they dated also became objects of ridicule and derision, particularly from GDR authorities, which blamed these couplings on "loose" German women, rather than their African partners. The state additionally laid claim to children resulting from these unions, maintaining that they were German citizens. This was very different from the situation in the 1950s FRG where, as Fehrenbach and Höhn have shown, attempts were commonly made to remove interracial children from German mothers and, in some cases, send them to the United States for adoption by African American families.[120]

In the book's conclusion, I return to the questions posed in this introduction and argue that understanding the complex history of the GDR's confrontation with racism is vital for analyzing events in reunified Germany since 1990. The GDR's anti-imperialist policy both masked a racialized undercurrent in East German society and reflected the struggle of both government and citizens to come to terms with the recent Nazi past. Ambivalent student experiences from the 1950s through the 1970s continued in the 1980s, 1990s, and through the turn of the century. Yet many students remained in the GDR, rather than return to collapsing governments and social and economic insecurity, or to the specter of being in the political opposition, often a dangerous proposition. They had the same fears as Middle Eastern and African immigrants today, who cannot return to their home countries but are commonly discriminated against both publicly and privately in Europe.

Chapter 1

Between Colonial Nigeria and Socialist East Germany: The Story of the First Eleven African Students in the GDR, 1949–1965

In 1951, eleven Nigerians arrived in the German Democratic Republic to begin studies at East German universities. The Free German Youth (FDJ), the youth wing of the SED, had extended the invitation to the students through an institution called the National Scholarships Board in December 1949, only two months after the GDR itself was founded.[1] They were among the first of thousands of exchange students who would study in the GDR through its dissolution in 1990.[2] The invitation came after a British colonial massacre of twenty-one striking workers at the Iva Valley Coal Mine in Enugu. The slaughter followed years of labor disputes among African union representatives, African workers, British mine management, and the British colonial state.

While the significance of the events at the colliery has been thoroughly and expertly detailed by Carolyn Brown and others,[3] I am the first to situate them within the wider framework of East-West competition during the early Cold War, and to tell the story of how it intertwined with the history of African students in the Eastern Bloc. For East Germany's SED, the massacre in Enugu provided an ideal opportunity to create ties with Nigerian nationalists. This included establishing links with Nigeria's Trade Union Congress (TUC), as well as with the Zikists, a short-lived but influential group affiliated with the National Council of Nigeria and the Cameroons (NCNC) party and named for Nnmadi Azikiwe, one of its leading politicians.[4] To say that the British were unhappy with this development is an understatement. Nigerian governor Sir John Stuart Macpherson reported that, "the Council of the Free German Youth (FDJ) in the Soviet Zone of Berlin has sent a cable to the Nigerian National Federation of Labour (NNFL), expressing their solidarity with the miners of Nigeria and stating that they proposed to offer scholarships in German institutions to Nigerians."[5] He expressed alarm at the prospect of British colonial subjects in communist East Germany and sought to prohibit Nigerian travel to the Eastern Bloc. He was desperate to stop any potential “communist indoctrination.”[6]

That these students would find themselves in GDR, which had belonged to a country that only six years earlier was ruled by the Nazis, appears nothing short of extraordinary. The year 1945 is often posited as a radical break in world history—and the presence of the Nigerians in East Germany seems to confirm it. But does it? What did the Nigerians experience in the GDR? What did they hope to get from an East German education? Moreover, how did the various, intricate features of the unfolding Cold War shape both emerging GDR policy toward Africa and the Nigerian encounter with ordinary East Germans?

For the Nigerians, and many of those who came to the GDR after them, the decision to go to East Germany was a complex one, driven primarily by the promise of social and economic advancement and secondarily by ideological considerations. The FDJ extended invitations to the Nigerians as a means of opening up a cultural, intellectual front in the Cold War that would pit its socialist ideology against that of American and West German capitalism. Welcoming the students marked the first stage in a long effort to participate in the political and economic growth of the emerging Third World. Yet this attempt to curry favor was only partially successful, both because the Nigerians experienced racism in a country whose government claimed it had been expunged and because the students' attitude toward Marxism was ambivalent. While SED officials expected that the students would absorb Marxism-Leninism and bring it back home, the students themselves were more pragmatic. They were chiefly interested in learning professions—medicine, engineering, architecture—that would increase their social standing once they returned to Nigeria.

This chapter buttresses the book's main arguments through an analysis of how individual African actors became embroiled in Cold War politics, as the GDR tried to co-opt them in an effort to influence the ideology of Nigerian political parties like the Zikists. Further, the Nigerians' story shows that racist assumptions and attitudes were still normalized in East Germany, reinforcing long-standing anti-Black tropes of the “primitive” and “childlike” African. Moreover, the chapter demonstrates that issues of gender were crucial from the GDR's earliest encounters with African students, following on but also shifting narratives on interracial unions from earlier periods in German history.

While in the GDR, the Nigerians also became enmeshed in East German culture, cementing ties of friendship and intimacy. Archival documents provide a rare window into their experiences. The chapter thus explores the students' immersion in everyday East German life. Their acceptance by some and rejection by others show that the SED's proclamations of solidarity and equality—

which were central to its policy because of how the SED positioned itself as an antiracist, anti-imperialist champion—ran aground when confronted with persistent racism among the East German population.

The Nigerian students were significant not only as the first Africans to attend university in the GDR but as representatives of a rising world order in which opposing visions of the postwar future—Soviet and Western—contended for their allegiance. As Westad has shown, the Third World was the terrain upon which much of the Cold War was fought, with both blocs struggling to bring it into their respective folds. Often figured as peripheral to the Cold War in the past, the non-Western world was instead central to the conflict.[7] Both the United States and the Soviet Union claimed that they would "modernize" the Global South and raise it to a par with the nations of Europe and North America. The terms "modern," "modernize," and "modernity" are notoriously difficult to define, since they contain not only notions of progress grounded in the Enlightenment but, as Adelheid von Saldern has pointed out, the threat of barbarism.[8] For the purposes of the chapter, I define postwar modernity as a state of economic, technological, and developmental progress that the United States, USSR, and their allies hoped to bring to the Global South.

The Cold War was shaped not only by the superpowers but by actors across the globe. It was informed by a complex interplay between imperial collapse and the emergent postcolonial order. The potential power of the Global South as presenting a third path between the United States and the Soviet Union was evident in events such as the 1955 Bandung Conference, which brought together leaders of decolonized and decolonizing countries to discuss the promise of nonalignment, or the succeeding Tricontinental Conference of 1966.[9] In this context, Africans had authority to negotiate with the Cold War superpowers and their proxies. They were active agents dictating the terms of transnational relationships even before the decolonization process was complete.

What did the Nigerians expect to get from the GDR? On the face of it, they were primarily interested in acquiring pragmatic, scientific knowledge. Why go to the GDR then? For much of East German history, scientific development was closely yoked to the purpose of building a socialist society, and the restrictions and policy goals this entailed meant that, by its collapse, the GDR lagged significantly behind the West in terms of technological advancement.[10] In the 1950s, however, Soviet and Eastern European technology were not yet considered backwards.[11] For Africans whose economies were underdeveloped after years of European exploitation, and who had had little opportunity to study advanced science at home—in the colonial era, most Africans who went to university did so in the metropole—the GDR offered similar educational possibilities to those of the West.

This scientific modernity was very much *developmental*—rooted in the concept that technocrats were the answer to the ills of the Global South. As David Engermann and Corinna Unger observe, while economic modernization has often been associated with the United States and considered "an American export," it was more aptly a "global phenomenon that was hotly contested between blocs."[12] Developmental modernity was scientific and focused on transforming economies hampered by colonialism. But it was not only imagined in the context of Western democracy; it could be achievable through capitalism, socialism, or a mixture of both. Development was one of the central terrains on which the Cold War played out, as nations from both "sides" funneled aid to non-Western countries as part of the broader battle for their fealty.

Hong has maintained that despite competition between the two Germanys, Germans from both nations sometimes treated non-Westerners similarly, with a large degree of condescension, paternalism, and racism.[13] Despite official professions of antiracism and solidarity, the Nigerians' experience in the early 1950s bolsters her argument. They encountered racism and disdain from their arrival in 1951 onwards.[14] Tracing the history of the Nigerians' lives in the GDR thus shows strong continuities between Nazi and postwar "Modernity." Nazism, as Jeffrey Herf has shown, was an eminently modern movement, foregrounding the Third Reich's advanced technology even as the Nazis also rejected Enlightenment ideals.[15] While the GDR claimed to embrace a postwar ethics of equality that denounced the Nazis, the experiences of African students demonstrate that the state struggled with a citizenry that had complex attitudes toward race. The microhistorical, *Alltagsgeschichte* focus on eleven individuals in an unfamiliar setting therefore exposes the contradictions the state faced as it adapted to its position as a champion of Third World causes and developmental modernity.[16]

Travels to the GDR and Early Experiences

According to Damian Mac Con Uladh, when the eleven Nigerians arrived in 1951 they were among the first international students admitted to study at universities in the GDR.[17] This predated the arrival of students from elsewhere in Africa or Asia.[18] Who were they? The amount of information concerning their lives varies. Some of their *Lebensläufe*—short autobiographies—have been preserved; others have not.[19] The *Lebensläufe*, which are in German, are narratives describing where the students came from, their educational background, how they came to the GDR, and their future hopes. Most of the students also filled out a questionnaire, which provided similar information. The *Lebensläufe* also address politics, though it is best to read them against the grain and in context of the students' position in the GDR.

In addition to the *Lebensläufe*, other crucial sources include an interview with the daughter of one of the students and an autobiographical novel written by another. Yvonne Kolagbodi, who lives in Berlin, is the child of a student named Mayirue Kolagbodi who went on to become a leading member of the labor union movement in Nigeria.[20] She supplied many details about her father's life; for example, she maintained that he was the only one of the students who remained involved with socialist causes after departing the GDR.[21]

A. E. Ohiaeri, another of the first students, published a novel entitled *Behind the Iron Curtain* in 1985. It examines the travails of a fictional student named Anyanjo as he traveled from Nigeria to the GDR in the early 1950s. While Ohiaeri claimed the book was purely fictitious,[22] many details correspond with archival records in England and Germany. Moreover, while he went by the name of "Alex" in the West, Ohiaeri's own birth name was "Anyanjo."[23] The tale of Anyanjo in *Behind the Iron Curtain* is useful for corroborating features of the students' story. Its plot closely mirrors the students' real-life journey: it starts with the offer of the scholarship and the difficulties the students encountered in trying to get from Nigeria to the GDR, follows Anyanjo as he arrives in the GDR, then details how, while away from the GDR on a short vacation to the United Kingdom, the British confiscated his passport and refused to let him return.[24] All of the students had a similar scholarship offer followed by trouble getting to East Germany. Moreover, Ohiaeri was indeed detained in England in 1959.[25]

Since the novel traces the students' tale from its origins, it is also a convenient place to begin a broader, more detailed reconstruction of their experiences. In the book, Anyanjo traveled from Lagos to London to the GDR, where he and ten others had received scholarships. The group consisted of "ten boys and one girl." Originally, the scholarships were meant exclusively for the children of Iva Valley's fallen miners. However, few of the slain miners had children old enough to accept them, so only one student actually had a father who was killed at Iva Valley.[26] The British constantly placed roadblocks before the students, trying to stop them from getting to East Germany. Yet despite these colonialist attempts, all reached Leipzig with the help of the Nigerian trade unions, British Communist Party, West African Students' Union, and Soviet and Czech embassies.[27] Key in this endeavor was Edward Onowochei, a Nigerian member of the British Communist Party.[28] While some features of the book diverge from the archival record—in Ohiaeri's novel it was the "East German Trade Union known as the Land and Forestry Union" offering scholarships, not the FDJ[29]—many elements dovetail with historical accounts. There were really ten men and one woman—Agnes Yetunde Bankole, who features prominently in chapter 5—in the group. Further, there was only one student whose father died at Iva Valley.[30]

Behind the Iron Curtain describes Anyanjo as "one of the lucky winners of the German scholarships" but does not explain how he was chosen.[31] The scholarships were in fact negotiated through the Nigerian Scholarships Board, which was headed by left-wing union leaders F. O. Coker and Nduka Eze.[32] Coker and Eze were Zikists, members of the staunchly anticolonial, nationalist movement that drew on NCNC leader Azikiwe's ideas. The Zikists, who emerged in 1946 and were banned in 1950, called for immediate independence in West Africa and the creation of a West African Union across multiple colonies. The Zikist demand represented a radical departure from previous, more conservative political movements that were willing to work with the British toward the goal of independence.[33] That Eze and Coker formed the leadership of the Scholarships Board affirms its connection to the Zikists. The Board appealed for students to apply for the scholarships in newspapers like the pro-independence *West African Pilot*,[34] which Azikiwe had founded.[35]

British officials were uncertain about how to handle the scholarships. They argued over whether it was legally possible to refuse passports to British subjects wishing to travel to the Eastern Bloc when "becoming indoctrinated—whether in communism or anything else—is not . . . a criminal activity." One bureaucrat believed they needed to tread lightly; another disagreed and claimed that Macpherson had the authority to deny passports for any reason he saw fit.[36] However, although Macpherson was originally uneasy about the scholarships, Jim Griffiths, Secretary of State for the Colonies, alleged that he later changed his mind and said there was no real concern. The Scholarships Board would not, in Macpherson's opinion, be able to raise enough money to send anyone to the GDR.[37] In a letter to Griffiths, Macpherson mentioned that the GDR would pay for the students' tuition, room, and board as long as they could find a way to get to East Germany. Eze had requested travel funds from the Nigerian government, but Macpherson said it would be easy enough to reject his request.[38]

Student autobiographies correspond with Ohiaeri's novel in suggesting that getting to the GDR was complicated. Travel to East Germany could not be direct and meant a stop for an indeterminate time in England or, in one case,

Paris and Prague.[39] In *Behind the Iron Curtain*, the students' arrival in the GDR was staggered,[40] as it was for the actual Nigerians, who entered the country at different times during 1951.[41] The *Lebenslauf* of a student who graduated with a degree in civil engineering from the TUD shows that he spent six months doing manual labor in England before continuing to the GDR.[42] The student never mentions how he finally made it to Leipzig, but Hajeem Tijani has shown that England's communist party played a role.[43] During another student's sojourn in London he met with members of the party and joined it.[44]

After these stops, the students entered the GDR as attendees at the 1951 *Weltfestspiele* in Leipzig. Of the thirteen Nigerian festival delegates, only two did not belong to the student group.[45] Perhaps the British thought that the students, like other colonial participants, would simply return home after the festival. Instead, the eleven remained behind. Once the students reached the GDR, they enrolled in a German language course through the Arbeiter- und Bauernfakultät (Worker's and Peasant's Faculty) (ABF) of the UL. The ABF had plans for what the students would do after language training, which included integration into the political, cultural, and social life of the East German state. The students would be incorporated into sports teams and clubs, allowed "uninhibited participation" in all FDJ activities, and full membership in the organization. They would register at East German universities, specifically the UL and the TUD.[46]

While the students' *Lebensläufe* often correspond with the details provided in Ohiaeri's novel, they may still have been composed under pressure from their GDR hosts, an impression that is reinforced by the formulaic quality of the narratives. It may be best, then, to read them less as "true" stories and more as expressions of a larger desire on the part of Nigerian labor leaders, GDR officials, and the students themselves to craft an image that mirrored a desire for a specific kind of modernized, scientific, and socialist future. The *Lebensläufe* share commonalities that support a reading that reflects a specific kind of African past—marginalized, downtrodden, oppressed by the British—and belief in a technologically advanced postcolonial future. They tell of coming from modest backgrounds in worker or peasant families and encountering difficulty raising funds to attend school.[47] Some students mention a friend or relative assisting with tuition.[48] Despite these obstacles, most finished secondary school. The *Lebensläufe* further demonstrate a slow, steady growth of interest in socialism and an increasing commitment to workers' struggles, culminating in union membership.[49]

The students described personal difficulties they experienced under British imperialism and capitalism. One complained that his dreams of attending

Figure 4. Nigerian students and participants in the III Weltfestspiele der Jugend und Studenten standing in front of the entrance to the workers' and peasants' faculty at the University of Leipzig. ADN-ZB Donath - Vorbereitung zu den III Weltfestspiele der Jugend und Studenten Berlin, July 1951 (Bundesarchiv).

Figure 5. Chukwuma Ozoani (center) and other Nigerian students are welcomed to Leipzig with gifts of flowers. Illus Detlof, July 6, 1951 (Bundesarchiv).

university were at first dashed because, "Money decides whether or not we study, not ability; only few possess both." Given these conditions, he had been forced to work as an assistant in the pathology laboratory of the United Africa Company. He said that, "Here I became acquainted with the labor relations of the 3000 workers of this massive, exploitative corporation. This was determinative for my future development, which led me to the party of the working class," the Zikists.[50] Another student had to attend a "cheap mission school" and get teacher training, although he had no interest in teaching. It was through his work, however, that he joined the "Nigerian Union of Teachers," which positioned him to receive the scholarship.[51]

A pattern emerges from the students' descriptions of their lives. It includes accounts of birth in humble circumstances, economic woes, patchwork schooling, unsatisfactory work experiences, and conversion to socialism. In addition, students often addressed the Iva Valley massacre, British racism, and support for socialist states like the GDR. The final element in the *Lebenslauf* focused on what the students hoped to achieve in East Germany. This is where the interest in modernity comes to the fore. The students tied professional objectives to building an independent, socialist Nigeria through technology. The student who railed against the injustices of colonial education hoped to study electrical engineering so that he might return home and, "help . . . in (the) struggle for independence and freedom, and also assist in the organization of (our) own strong (national) industry."[52] Among the first eleven Nigerian students, nine received training in a natural science area.[53] The preference for subjects such as engineering, medicine, veterinary medicine, and pharmacy remained fairly consistent among African students in the GDR throughout its history.[54] Later, countries with socialist-leaning governments—such as Ghana, Guinea, Mali, and Tanzania—would forge student exchange agreements with the GDR stipulating that a certain number of students be trained in scientific areas.[55]

The interest in natural sciences merged with the alleged student commitment to building a socialist, industrialized Nigeria. Subjects like electrical and civil engineering or architecture were a means of modernizing the country's infrastructure,[56] as well as creating state-run industries. As Hong has pointed out, Western medicine was deemed crucial to the development of a healthy socialist state and healthy socialist citizens in the GDR. This was also true for the decolonizing peoples of Africa and Asia. The emphasis on healthy, able-bodied individuals working together to build the socialist nation was reflected in the health care training programs the GDR offered.[57] In the 1950s, the Nigerian students may have harbored similar sentiments about the significance of Western medicine. Four of them became medical doctors, including Bankole, the only female student in the cohort.[58]

Being "modern" in the GDR meant more than achieving technological sophistication, however. It included adopting a particular secular and moral mindset. Some East Germans considered the students woefully lacking in this regard. Shortly after they arrived, the ABF assigned them a tutor. He gave them a poor progress report, which began by discussing how the students' *Bewusstsein*—their consciousness—was underdeveloped. According to the tutor, the students were heavily influenced by both pre-Christian animist religion and Christianity. This made it difficult for them to accept a scientific, rational, and socialist education. They were unable to separate Christianity from imperialism, even though it had been introduced by the latter. Instead they believed Christianity could be a weapon against the British.[59]

The tutor also criticized the students' emotional maturity, drawing upon a catalogue of stereotypes Europeans had long used to denigrate Africans. He said that they lacked a "precise understanding of time and were incapable of planning ahead," which led to poor work habits. They were extremely sensitive: "They require tender care, a markedly open affection of the kind we are used to showing our elementary school students. Clear, sober demeanor hurts them, and they easily collapse in a jumble of feelings." The Nigerians considered a "criticism about arriving too late to lecture as a severe insult."[60] The idea that Africans had no sense of clock time and were "lazy" was widespread in the colonial era;[61] so was the conception that Africans were oversensitive and childlike.[62]

The tutor worried that the students also lagged behind their East German counterparts in terms of political education and understanding of social class. Their sentiments were "utopian" and "had formalistic emphases," which made them ignore the big picture. They were socially organized as they might be in Africa, with one student acting as the "father" of the group. Everything was achieved through constant "palaver" and decisions came at a glacial pace. The students claimed to be from peasant or worker families, but this was only half-true. Some had *kleinbürgerliche* (bourgeois) backgrounds, and their education, though acquired through struggle, differentiated them from the working class. The tutor insisted that they were more a native intelligentsia than a true proletariat.[63]

The issue of race and the relationship between Blacks and whites also arose in the tutor's report. He complained that the students' treatment under the British had so demoralized them that they were unable to recognize that not all whites were the same. He remarked that, "Owing to their experiences with whites in their own country, they are still skeptical of people with our skin color." The Nigerians overreacted to the "cumulatively harmless, stupid, heavy-handed attempts at conversation by Leipzigers, such as 'you have it good, you don't need to wash yourself,' or 'is your color real, or does it come off?'" He complained that, "despite all our discussions, they still see these insults as carefully thought-out, conscious, and deliberate." The students saw all criticism of their classwork as racism, when the critiques were designed to enhance their personal and collective development. They lacked "political maturity," and it was only "Marxism-Leninism that would be able to overcome the barrier of race through concrete, hard-fought legwork." The tutor's "avowals about equality between the races" would mean nothing before the students absorbed the lessons of Marxism.[64]

Others at the ABF were also concerned that the students simply expected East Germans to be racist. A member of one Nigerian's study group submitted a report on his progress to the ABF that reflected East German anxieties about the Nazi past and its correlation to the socialist present. The author observed that his Nigerian colleague originally retained a cool distance from his classmates. This was "understandable," and, "the Nigerian friends are critically watching our relationship." The author continued, noting that, "in the time of fascism Black people were also victims of awful race-baiting. And there are often still subconscious relics of this imperialist ideology. This is what gives our Nigerian friends pause, and this is what we must help them to overcome."[65] In this instance, the author placed the onus on two parties. He chided the Nigerians for not distinguishing between Nazi Germany and its socialist successor, while acknowledging that racism was still a problem for East Germans, if in his mind only a residual one.

The acting director of the ABF also reproached the students. His remarks chastising them for their romantic relationships with East German women constitute an early instance of a kind of criticism that became common in the GDR.[66] He argued that ABF students as a whole were to dedicate themselves either to the establishment of socialism in their own country or the struggle for independence if they were still under "the colonial yoke." Deviation from these goals was unacceptable, and he worried that "our friends" from Nigeria did not recognize this. The prospect of marriage between Nigerian students and East German women raised the "national" question of what citizenship and loyalty a Nigerian-German couple might hold. Such uncertainty could only complicate each partner's resolve to prioritize nation-building.[67]

The director never couched his objection to intermarriage in outwardly racial terms, drawing instead on national and political arguments. This kind of justification jibed with the antiracist, anti-imperialist rhetoric of the GDR.[68] He also shifted blame away from Nigerian men and onto East German women. By pursuing the students, women "challenge(d) the moral posture of our Nigerian friends, and tarnish(ed) our good relations with them." He claimed that the Nigerians were clear about their responsibility to the national interests of a future independent Nigeria. The women were a distraction, and would tempt the men away from the proper moral and political course.[69]

At the turn of the twentieth century Bertha Hilske, the working-class wife of Mtoro bin Mwinyi Bakari, a Swahili lecturer at the Berlin Seminar für orientalische Sprachen, was impugned as morally corrupt for pursuing the relationship.[70] Critiques of gender and class were interwoven, as the morals of Hilske, a woman who traveled from the far reaches of Eastern Germany to find work in Berlin, were questioned when she married an African man. Such attitudes would not have been out of the ordinary during the imperial era, when concepts of class and race intertwined and poor Germans and colonial subjects were often identified with each other and considered similarly depraved.[71] Although class was supposedly disappearing in the GDR, the women who had relationships with the Nigerian students were similarly coded as morally suspect, reflecting a sense that they were somehow "fallen" in the same way that lower-class women had been in earlier periods.

While he criticized the students' love affairs, the ABF director added that he did not want to diminish the good relationship Nigerians had established with locals. The students had made a positive initial impression, and he did not want to damage it. Yet their general popularity in the community was also problematized. The tutor's words are again instructive. He claimed that the Nigerians attracted large crowds wherever they went. They were celebrated as heroes in the press and at social gatherings. This constant festivity was disruptive and sidetracked them from their real, scholarly purpose. The East German public's admiration lacked any knowledge or critique of the students' actual development. The "friends" were thus "spoiled" without having merited their star treatment.[72]

The students' own actions, however, undermined the tutor's assertions. For instance, he criticized the students' continued adherence to Christianity. It is true that all but one of them came from southern Nigeria,[73] which was heavily Christian,[74] and their interactions with Christian East Germans show that they had been raised as Christians. But they were also very suspicious of the religion. In May 1953, three of them contacted the directorate of the ABF to discuss their recent interactions with a group of theology students. The theologians had approached the Nigerians at a university conference, then dropped by unannounced to visit their dormitory on successive weekends. They offered the Nigerians bibles, invited them to church, and suggested they check out the university's theology department. The Nigerians refused their advances and told them not to return.[75]

When they spoke of meeting the theologians, the Nigerians recounted arguing about politics and ideology. A Nigerian medical student had asked whether the visitors belonged to the FDJ, and was told they did not. They were against Marxism, "because it was based on false precepts" and "could not be reconciled with the church." The Nigerian answered that he was a member of the FDJ and a communist, and thus had nothing to discuss with them. He told them that he did not believe in God and presented copious examples of the church collaborating with imperialists. This angered one of the theologians, who responded that he was against socialism and in favor of Adenauer and the capitalist politics of West Germany. The theology student said that communists—now including the Nigerians—thought of Stalin as their God. The medical student tried to calm him down and convince him of the rightness of communism. He remarked that the theologian had probably not yet distinguished the "true path," but that once he did he would turn to socialism.[76]

Figure 6. "Students from Nigeria demonstrate arm in arm with their German friends," May 1, 1951. This photograph demonstrates the supposed unity in socialism between Nigerians and East Germans (University Archives, Leipzig).

Here we see how a Nigerian student—whose tutor said was mired in traditional and Christian ways—tried to persuade a religious East German of the benefits of socialism. Far from being backwards or antimodern, the student presented himself as a politically advanced Marxist who understood the ravages of colonialism. In reporting the theologians to university authorities, the Nigerians also behaved in what the SED would have recognized as a "morally" modern, upright manner. They were informing the state of possible conspiracy, and protecting it against capitalist forces.

The *Staatssicherheitsdienst* (Stasi) was also impressed by a Nigerian student whom it had briefly recruited as an informant. The agent who recruited him remarked that the student and his peers had successfully silenced the theologians. When they came to the dorm, the Nigerians shocked them by quoting and interpreting lengthy biblical passages. Their skillful analysis proved that they knew more about the Bible than the theologians. The informant had explained that in Nigeria, 80 percent of education for natives revolved around the Bible.[77] Although he and his colleagues were steeped in Christianity, their experiences with the colonizers and belief in socialism led them away from

Christianity and to Marxism-Leninism. Religiously, the Nigerians were *more* modern in GDR terms than Christian East Germans.[78]

Stasi reports on the Nigerian informant were glowing. They described him as an ideally modern man. Stasi agents viewed him as intelligent, charismatic, affable, and well-informed about the GDR and Marxism. He was an exemplar of socialist awakening and growth. When he first learned that he would study in East Germany, the student wanted to pursue medicine. This had nothing to do with the working class or the quest for independence; he thought only of himself and his desire to be rich. Once in the GDR, however, that changed. He recognized the necessity of fighting for his country's future, and in consultation with his collective—the other Nigerian students—he altered his career path and resolved to study engineering. Nigeria was not industrialized and had little electrification. All the engineers currently in the country were either English or American. They cared little for ordinary Nigerians. By contrast, the student understood everyday Nigerian struggles. The town where he had studied lacked electricity. He had read by petroleum lamp, almost destroying his eyesight. The student said, "I wanted to help my people get out of this miserable life." Upon his return from the GDR, armed with knowledge of electrical engineering *and* socialism, he would be able to fulfill his dream of modernizing Nigeria.[79]

Through the admiring gaze of the Stasi report, two points become clear. First, the student was modern—primarily because of his experiences in the GDR. His GDR education lifted him above the general Nigerian populace. He was now more advanced than the Nigerian petite bourgeoisie, from which the tutor claimed he had come. Second, the student was modern, but his home, Nigeria, was not. Nigeria needed the students to modernize it by electrifying its cities, industrializing its economy, healing its sick, and preparing it for socialist revolution. Training in the GDR was thus key to Nigeria's imagined socialist future.

The Nigerian *Lebensläufe* indeed present the East German state as a savior from imperialism. Yet *On the Tiger's Back*, the autobiography of Aderogba Ajao, a student who came to the GDR after the original group, is markedly different.[80] Ajao's account highlighted the evils of the Soviet Union and GDR when compared to the West. The work was likely fabricated, and its publication possibly funded by the CIA.[81] Nonetheless, the book provides a contrasting vision of modernity, in which the Soviets and their East German allies emerge as brutal but ineffective taskmasters, whose static vision of society developing through specific, scientifically observable stages is resented by a captive populace. Ajao's writing represents the Western side of the struggle for the future, a counterpoint to East German arguments about the superiority of socialism.[82]

Ajao—also known as Adelani—claimed that Russian and East German agents abducted him in 1952 and forced him to study and work alongside other foreign students at a camp in Bautzen.[83] Later, he transferred to the TUD, and then finally to the UL. Ajao's tale is grim. He speaks of a GDR under complete Russian dominance. The citizenry is oppressed and would like nothing better than the dissolution of the GDR.[84] Attempts to indoctrinate Ajao are constant.[85] As his disgust grows, he turns against communism, even though he had once belonged to the British Communist Party.[86]

Even the technological modernity that the GDR offered students was a ruse. It covered their real intention, which was to train them to be political agents and spread propaganda.[87] Statements prizing the technological superiority of the Soviet Bloc were a sham. They included bald-faced lies like "the steam engine was invented by the Russians, and . . . Lenin . . . personally invented the tractor," which Ajao claimed an East German professor had told them.[88] Moreover, those Africans who became delegates to the 1957 World Festival of Youth in Moscow and "were familiar with the very simple forms of agriculture practiced in their own countries," soon recognized that in comparison, "the Russian village appeared as unmistakably and unarguably backward."[89] The mighty Soviet Union was thus not modern at all.

Ajao's story reads like an adventure tale. He tries to escape the GDR in 1954 with other disgruntled international students but fails.[90] He receives military training, which he is meant to use to subvert the Nigerian government by "join(ing) the armed forces of the bourgeois regime in power (to) try to destroy it from within."[91] A German woman named Anneliese, who was probably an SED operative, attempted to seduce him.[92] His involvement as a delegate at the 1957 Festival in Moscow leads to sharp disagreements with other Nigerian students from East Germany and results in his expulsion from the University of Leipzig.[93] Finally, after seven years "in captivity," Ajao is able to leave the GDR only because his son becomes ill. He is allowed to travel to a hospital in Potsdam, where he abandons his wife and child and crosses the border into West Berlin.[94]

After leaving the GDR in the late 1950s, Ajao told the story that would be published as *On the Tiger's Back* in interviews with West German radio and the BBC. His interviews got attention back in East Germany, since the president of the Union of African Students in the GDR, who was also Nigerian, wrote a scathing response to Ajao, entitled "The Fairy-Tales of Aderogba Ajao alias 'Adelani' and the Truth." His comments reached a wide audience through publication in an FDJ journal. The student president's purpose was to denounce Ajao and his claims but also show how good life was for Africans in the GDR. He extolled "studies in the universities and colleges of the German Democratic Republic" as "a combination of the best in the traditions of German universities and . . . advancement in modern science and technics." Students were always learning, even outside the classroom, where they applied what they had gleaned from their lessons in practice. It was impossible for Africans to get this practical knowledge in the racist Federal Republic, where a Ghanaian medical student had for example been prevented from observing operations on German women to protect them from his lecherous gaze.[95]

This diatribe against Ajao highlighted the modernity of the GDR and condemned the fascist, imperialist, and war-mongering FRG. According to the union's president, there was no racial discrimination in the GDR. African students had generous stipends and access to the same academic facilities as East Germans. This included full use of the "most modern instruments, books, (and) libraries." Further, he asserted that while the GDR spent 130 marks per person on "scientific purposes," the FRG expended only 15.[96]

In addition to praising the GDR, the student union president offered a point-by-point rebuttal of Ajao's claims. Russians had not kidnapped Ajao. He had arrived in East Germany of his own free will in 1953, requesting political asylum. Ajao told East German authorities that he was an orphan, the only surviving member of his family. He was cheated out of his father's farm and stowed away on a ship to Europe. When he came to the GDR, he was placed in a camp for asylum seekers in Bautzen.[97] Starting in 1951 such a camp indeed existed. Over the years it housed two hundred asylum seekers, mainly deserters from NATO armies. There was a school at the camp, and its inhabitants worked at factories.[98] Ajao too had described political indoctrination in Bautzen, alongside factory work. Otherwise, the student union president intoned that most of what Ajao said was fictional and served as a cover for his poor academic performance.[99]

In his writings and interviews, Ajao accused the Soviet Union and GDR of gross crimes against his person. He rebuked them for their lack of modernity and scientific expertise. The president of the Union of African Students did the opposite, praising the GDR and its people as noble partners in the struggle against imperialism, which included the provision of scientific education to aid in the modernization of African states.

The eleven Nigerians who came to the GDR in 1951 were the first in a long line of African students who attended East German universities. Throughout the 1950s more Nigerians arrived, including Ajao and the president of the

Union of African Students. Toward the end of the decade they were joined by students from Kenya, Ghana, Guinea, and elsewhere. The Kenyans, who will be discussed in more depth in the next chapter, were in a similar situation to the Nigerians. They too journeyed to the GDR prior to Kenya's official decolonization in 1963 and had difficulty getting there. A Kenyan who arrived in 1959 told of having first gone to England, where he was promised admission to a university. When he got there, the opportunity evaporated, and he ended up working at a glass factory and studying at night. When this became unsustainable, the Kenyan Student Organization in London advised that he and a colleague try their luck in the GDR, which had scholarships for Kenyans. After a detour through Hamburg—he commented that Britain's Black subjects were systematically denied visas to the Soviet Bloc and had to pass first through West Germany—they reached East Berlin. The student went on to study in Halle and at the Hochschule für Ökonomie in Karlshorst.[100] The situation with the Ghanaians and Guineans was different, as will be detailed through the example of the Ghanaians in chapter 3. They arrived after their countries officially decolonized, in 1957 and 1958 respectively. The GDR crafted agreements with the governments of Ghana and Guinea regarding how many students they would send to East Germany, as well as whether they were to be educated in a technical school, at a university, or enter an apprenticeship to learn a trade.

GDR policy on the future of the African students after they completed their degrees was clear: they would leave East Germany and return home, where they would put their knowledge to use in factories, on farms, in hospitals, and for trade unions, building industrialized and socialist states. The director of the ABF had emphasized that relationships between African students and East German women were for this reason undesirable—a man would not want to return home if he had intimate ties to the GDR, and the GDR did not want women to leave. Even so, over the years many students either stayed or tried to get permission to stay, whether or not romance was involved. This was a vexing issue to university and government officials. They wanted students to go, but the students hoped to stay—in order to get more education, continue a relationship, or escape poor, even frightening, conditions at home.[101]

Complete information on what happened to all of the first eleven students after they finished their studies is not available. Still, it seems that most did return to Nigeria, if sometimes only after a protracted stay in the GDR. For example, while Ohiaeri appears to have eventually gone back to Nigeria permanently, he was in the GDR on some basis at least through the mid-1960s, well after completing his medical degree.[102] He returned to Nigeria at some

Figure 7. Nigerian student Igbokwughaonu Unamba-Oparah (holding flowers) celebrates his successful dissertation defense with friends in Leipzig, 1964 (University Archives, Leipzig).

point after graduating in 1958,[103] but then must have come back to East Germany, since in 1965 he became an advisor and chaperone to a new generation of African students in Leipzig.[104] Another student, who completed his engineering degree around 1960, left shortly thereafter and by the late 1960s was employed by the Western Nigeria Water Corporation in Ibadan.[105]

It is unclear whether most of the students were ever committed socialists. While their 1950s *Lebensläufe* reflect an attachment to socialism, their professed allegiance may have been dictated by self-interest, because they knew what the ABF wanted to hear, or because ABF officials prompted them to write specific things. The students were fairly young when they arrived in the GDR, ranging in age from fourteen to twenty-nine.[106] Further, it is difficult to tell if and when the students turned away from socialism.

There were at least two dedicated socialists among the students: Mayirue Kolagbodi and Modilim Achufusi. Moreover, there is evidence that Bankole and perhaps another former member of the original group were involved in an organization called the Nigeria-GDR Friendship Society, which was formed in order to pressure the Nigerian government to provide diplomatic recognition to the GDR. Kolagbodi, who was the most active Marxist of the eleven and remained committed to communism throughout his life, was also involved with this society.[107] Yvonne Kolagbodi has further related how her father returned to Nigeria soon after finishing his degree, along with her mother, who is East German. He remained devoted to socialism for the rest of his life. She said that his political activities and socialist position caused him problems with the Nigerian government; he was never paid the salaries he was owed for union work and her mother had to support them.[108] Mayirue Kolagbodi also wrote extensively on Marxism and the effects of the different stages of Marxist history as they related to Nigeria, as well as on how workers and union leaders should organize for the coming struggle.[109]

Achufusi, another of the original students, was still in East Germany as of 1961. At the time he espoused communist beliefs, as his published works demonstrate. In a 1960 book on African history, he fretted that African communists viewed the central struggle as one of an African proletariat against a European bourgeoisie, and that, "Such a trend leads to playing down the class conflicts inside Africa."[110] In the early 1960s he was active at Soviet Bloc conferences on African history, giving the opening lecture at the 25th International Congress of Orientalists in Moscow in 1961.[111] Achufusi later became professor of history and deputy vice chancellor at the University of Nigeria in Nsukka.[112] From 1980 to 1981, he was in the United States because he held a Fulbright Scholarship at Northwestern University, where he did research on the "Land and Labor Situation in West Africa."[113]

Yvonne Kolagbodi did not remember Achufusi. She did, however, know most of the other former students—both those in the original eleven and those who followed later in the 1950s. She remembers them gathering at her father's house in Lagos when she was a child. Among this group, she maintained that he was alone in continuing to embrace socialism. In her memory, the other students became capitalists when they returned to Nigeria; they had to take care of their families, and in postindependence Nigeria this meant looking out for their own interests, not those of the working class. She also remembers one of them telling her father that all communists should be prosecuted. At the same time, this man stayed friends with him as well as with their entire family, even giving her money on occasion. Ironically, Mayirue Kolagbodi was also close to Aderogba Ajao, the student who wrote the scathing memoir of his life in the GDR. Yvonne Kolagbodi explained that a certain conviviality remained among the students, regardless of political or economic orientation.[114]

For the GDR, African students became a front in the effort to portray East Germany as an appealing alternative to the West, with claims to offer both ideological superiority and advanced technology. It is important to remember, though, that the students, labor union officials, and other Nigerians had a critical role in deciding what was modern and what would best benefit their emergent nation. The students were born into a world of British subjugation, and the GDR offered both technological expertise and a path out of unhappy circumstances; the latter included not only physical removal from colonial Nigeria but also a potential alternative ideology—socialism. Science stood out as the most prominent means of bringing progress home, but socialism also provided a possible means to defeat the British and elevate Nigerian nationalism. This would change, but at this stage socialism differentiated the GDR from the FRG and the British more than technology, which could theoretically be obtained on either side of the Cold War divide.

While SED officials and Nigerian trade unionists like Nduka Eze dreamt of a time when Nigeria itself would become a socialist state, this was not to be. The Zikist movement, which represented the greatest hope for socialists in Nigeria, garnered a lot of interest in the mid-1940s when it was founded during a period of labor unrest. While the Zikist movement was originally affiliated with Azikiwe and the NCNC, it came to be seen as a distinct political entity that threatened them both. The NCNC hoped to negotiate with the British to ensure a transfer of power that would benefit their party, and they believed that the Zikists undermined them. Azikiwe thus shunned the movement that bore his name and helped the British put it down.[115] In April 1950, as plans to get the students to the GDR were already underway, Zikism was banned.[116]

The enthusiasm that had bolstered the trade unions and the socialist movement when the students left Nigeria in 1950 may well have evaporated by the time they returned in the later 1950s and early 1960s. For most, their East German education became a means to an end, not something that would burnish their credentials with parties such as the NCNC. The GDR's interest in a partnership with Nigeria had also declined by the 1960s. The Nigerian Breweries African Workers Union requested spots for students in 1966 but were turned down because there was no intracountry agreement governing student exchanges between the GDR and Nigeria.[117] By this point, the GDR primarily admitted students whose countries had completed such agreements.[118]

The radical break of 1945, which was supposed to herald a new dawn of equality and racial tolerance in East Germany, was furthermore not that radical after all. GDR modernity was still firmly rooted in Western science and Western philosophy and drew on general European technical advancement in addition to Marxist doctrine. Further, while the SED held that East Germany's solidarity with Africa and rejection of racism made the state an ideal partner for long oppressed nations, the Nigerians' experiences showed otherwise and pointed to the persistence of a different, uglier kind of modernity. The students found a state that provided them with educations that promoted social mobility, but also an East German citizenry steeped in a racial prejudice not unlike that of prior eras. It was this tenacious racism that would continue to haunt the history of African students in the GDR through the state's dissolution in 1990 and complicate its relationship with postcolonial Africa, as we shall also see in the succeeding chapters.

Chapter 2

Bumps in the Road: Uncertain Journeys to the GDR and Beyond, 1959–1964

On December 30, 1961, French authorities detained two Zambian women, Anna P. and Sabrina M., for twenty-three hours at an airport in West Berlin. They were traveling that day because they had received scholarships to study in Quedlinburg—a small city in the GDR. But since representatives of Zambia's United National Independence Party (UNIP) did not realize that there were several airports in divided Berlin, they had procured tickets to what was probably Tegel airport in the West, rather than Schönefeld in the East.[1] For the two women, this could have easily proven disastrous. At the time, Zambia—then known as Northern Rhodesia—was still under British colonial control. It was in addition part of the Federation of Rhodesia and Nyasaland (FRN), also known as the Central African Federation (CAF), a semi-independent state largely under white settler rule. Zambian student Michael B. thus noted that, "it gave us (an) international headache to extract them from the colonizer," presumably since the women's status was that of colonial subject, not independent citizen. The French had, indeed, been very close to turning the women over to British authorities. As it was, Michael B. was tasked to negotiate with the French to acquire the women's release to the GDR's border police. Since he was on Christmas holiday at the time, this also meant that he had to drive more than 150 miles from where he was spending vacation to get back to Berlin.[2]

Anna P. and Sabrina M., who found themselves trapped in an unfamiliar place just before New Year's 1962, and Michael B., who had traversed a rural East German landscape to retrieve them, were all at the end of what had been a much, much longer journey. That journey began after they had received scholarships to study abroad. It started in Zambia, either in Lusaka, the capital, or another part of the country, depending on where they lived; Michael B., for example, had likely traveled from Kitwe in the north of the colony, where he worked for the UNIP, to Lusaka in the south, before venturing further.[3] After some period of wait in Lusaka, students like him journeyed on by truck to Mbeya, a city just over the border in neighboring Tanganyika, which had gained independence earlier, on December 9, 1961. They probably stayed in Mbeya until they were issued air tickets for a flight from Dar-es-Salaam to Cairo. At that point they took another truck to Dar-es-Salaam and then flew to Cairo. Once there, they almost certainly waited again for the tickets that would take them onward. The women's flight went to West Berlin, while Michael B. took a more circuitous but safer route to Prague and then Schönefeld in East Berlin. The entire trip may have taken several months, a year, or even more. John M., another Zambian who later studied at the GDR's Hochschule für Ökonomie in Berlin, spent nine months in Mbeya alone, where he assisted the UNIP representative and others with a local fishing project while he waited for his ticket to arrive. His trek to the GDR took nineteen months in all.[4]

This chapter is a story about movement, whether that movement was across colonial borders, international boundaries, or even internal frontiers. It is also the tale of a vast network that developed in sub-Saharan Africa in the 1960s, an era of ongoing decolonization across the continent. This chapter only covers a short period—1959–1964, the time during which Zambians and Kenyans, who are featured most prominently here, were active travelers in the network. However, as Eric Burton has shown, networks connecting the Soviet Bloc, in particular the GDR, to what he calls "hubs of decolonization" in Africa lasted longer and had other nodes that rose to prominence as time went on—for example in Algiers, Rabat, and Brazzaville.[5]

The chapter confirms further that while Cold War politics, combined with the politics of decolonization, did shape the students' lives, they were also active in determining their own fates as they negotiated pathways north. Questions of race and anti-Blackness also emerge, as officials from countries such as Zambia complained about racism in the West. From their vantage in cities such as Dar-es-Salaam, however, the officials usually did not have similar criticisms of the GDR. While stories of racism directed against African students in the GDR are plentiful in the archives, it was not known for anti-Blackness globally. Reports of racist behavior occasionally emerged in the international press, but they were rare.[6] This suggests that the SED was successful in suppressing such accounts, but also that its overtures to solidarity and humanitarianism likely had some positive impact among those involved in independence movements; the Zambians and Kenyans trying to procure scholarships for their countrypeople seldom complained about the GDR the way they did about other countries in the capitalist West or communist East.[7]

The networks that the students took consisted of multiple routes to Europe,

North America, and Asia. One set stretched from central, southern, and eastern Africa to points north, while another, more limited network linked states in West Africa. Students left home with the intention of receiving a scholarship for study abroad, often under duress as they escaped colonial violence or the violence of postcolonial African regimes. Their trips were often arduous and required extra planning, as in the case of a Namibian who had to have two separate tickets issued, one from Dar-es-Salaam or Nairobi to Cairo, and the second from Cairo to Berlin, so that the gate agents in Dar-es-Salaam or Nairobi would not know that the GDR was his final destination.[8]

How were these networks constituted? Where did they start, and where did they end—if they indeed ended? How did they contribute to the shaping of alternative Cold War geographies? My argument is that the students created a mobile formation all their own, one which traversed and transcended Cold War divisions, as well as national space. Sebastian Conrad has summarized the concept of "following" as a transnational term that allows the historian to focus not on traditional boundaries but rather on the circulation of people, things, and ideas over vast distances.[9] If we think of the students this way, and follow their movements from place to place, it helps us understand how extra-African national and political differences collapsed as educational opportunities superseded grounding in any specific national or political context. The goal of knowledge acquisition could displace ideological considerations, with students striving for scholarships anywhere they could get them.

At the same time, we should be aware that the students came from particular locales, and had varying experiences depending on the distinctive struggles in their countries. In the Kenyan case, local politics are as important for understanding student pathways as the broader Cold War context.[10] Burton has further suggested that understanding the trajectories of specific actors can illuminate what the Cold War and decolonization meant in different times and places on a greater scale.[11] Moreover, once students reached their new homes, they became involved in the politics of their host nations, whether they wanted to or not. In the case of the GDR and other Soviet Bloc nations, that sometimes meant participating in courses on Marxism-Leninism, and sometimes opposing East German policies regarding their native lands.

Student Networks in and beyond Africa

Burton has recently written about some of the same networks I discuss here, maintaining that African students "were crucial in expanding the 'repertoire of migration,'" that is, the range of the destinations, practices, and customs of mobility" during the Cold War.[12] He zeroes in on "non-state initiatives" that propelled educational migration and how students transformed scholarship policies across and beyond the blocs, opening up new vistas of possibility and movement. He investigates how parties with different interests—students, European (primarily British) state actors, and African officials—reacted to the routes, as the British tried to block movement, nonaligned leaders like Egypt's Gamal Abel Nasser encouraged it, and students agitated for the education they wanted, which did not necessarily suit the expectations of the leaders in their independence movements or opposition parties.[13]

I employ a different set of sources than Burton in the research for this chapter. Thus, while I agree with Burton's arguments about the significance of African students in creating and maintaining Cold War pathways to education, the sources I examine add new dimensions to the history of these networks. For example, based on his studies of British East Africa, Burton concludes that almost no women traveled the "Nile Route" through Uganda and Sudan to Egypt, and then to socialist Europe or other destinations.[14] However, viewing archival evidence from Zambia, which is usually grouped geographically with Central African countries, demonstrates the significance of women to Africa-based networks. Zambian officials were extremely interested in finding scholarships for women. In October 1961, a representative for UNIP's education secretary wrote to Robert Makasa to discuss recruitment of new female candidates for scholarships in the Copperbelt, since there were not enough women with the level of education needed to fill the ones on offer.[15]

That same month Makasa also wrote a letter to a Zambian woman named Monica C. who was studying in Yugoslavia. He commented that "On 25th October I sent 7 students to Cairo, to our shame, all of them are young men, there are no young women. Currently we do not have any applications from young women at all. However, we are hopeful that in the days to come, perhaps we will receive some. That is why, it is only you that we Zambians have outside the country."[16] Monica C. was not, in fact, the only Zambian female student in Yugoslavia at the time; there was also a woman named Catherine P., with whom Makasa was also corresponding.[17] Further, while there may not have been many Zambian women outside the country in late 1961, that would soon change as Makasa found increasing numbers of women applicants to go to Eastern Europe, including the GDR, as well as to other nations in Africa, including Tanganyika and Ghana.

It is not surprising that Makasa had such a difficult time recruiting female candidates. The lack of adequate educational opportunities in Zambia during the colonial era was probably even starker for women than it was for men, given that boys in sub-Saharan Africa were more likely to be sent to school than girls. In the specific Zambian case, colonial powers had suppressed girls' education especially severely, as they were most interested in training boys to work in the copper mines and did not believe that women belonged there.[18] Hence UNIP officials were particularly keen on sending women overseas; when negotiating for scholarships to Poland, a Zambian official emphasized that he wanted both men and women to fill them;[19] another time, a different official asked that girls be considered for bursaries in North Korea.[20] Zambian women were still always a minority among students going abroad, as were African women in general, a topic I discuss in more detail in chapter 5. Nonetheless, male-dominated independence movements and political parties did agitate for women's education, often in fields that were seen as appropriately "feminine," such as nursing and teaching.[21]

The route that Zambians, including women, took was one that could intersect with the Nile Route that Burton describes, but also went around it after Tanganyika decolonized and Dar-es-Salaam became a central hub for students and other travelers. These networks began in central and southern Africa and then reached up in the direction of eastern and northern Africa. Prospective students from colonies such as South Africa, South West Africa (Namibia), Northern and Southern Rhodesia (Zambia and Zimbabwe), Nyasaland (Malawi), Mozambique, Angola, and Bechaunaland (Botswana) were constantly traveling in the direction of Dar-es-Salaam and Cairo, where they hoped to receive papers that would allow them to continue to countries as diverse as the GDR, the FRG, the Soviet Union (Russia, but also other SSRs such as Georgia), Yugoslavia, Czechoslovakia, Poland, North Korea, China, India, Israel, Egypt, Ghana, Liberia, France, England, and the United States. During their journeys students occasionally took detours to other nearby African countries, such as Uganda and Sudan, and sometimes settled there. Those traveling further than the Zambians, for instance the Namibians, also established branch offices in other cities on their own, more extensive routes; for example, Namibia's largest liberation movement, the South West African People's Organization (SWAPO), set up an office in Francistown (Gaborone), Botswana, to aid students in the middle of their long treks.[22] Moreover, once it became clear in 1963 that the Central African Federation would dissolve and that Zambia was headed for independence,[23] Lusaka became another important stop on the northward march for Africans whose countries would take much longer to decolonize.

Kenyan students traversed the Nile Route, which went through Cairo but not Dar-es-Salaam, since it lay to their south. Instead students like Hassan

Wani Ali Kamau (also known as Hassan Wani), who would later become president of the Union of Kenyan Students in the GDR, transited through Sudan, one of the countries that Burton notes was on the route. Wani's journey began earlier than most of the others I discuss in this chapter. He was arrested in Juba in 1954 for entering the country without a passport but managed to get out of prison, reach Khartoum, and find employment as a bookkeeper with the Blue Nile Brewery. Eventually though, Wani found his way to Cairo, where he worked as a shopkeeper from 1956 to 1959, when he left to study agriculture at the KMU in Leipzig.[24] Like Wani, most Kenyans tapped into the route heading for Cairo. Kenyan students may even have walked from Nairobi to Cairo, a distance of approximately 5,301 kilometers over arduous terrain.[25] Godwin W. Wachira, assistant secretary of Kenya's Kikuyu Union, wrote to the president of the Deutsch-Afrikanische Gesellschaft (DAFRIG) in early 1964 and reminisced that, "(For) (S)ome of us it is still fresh in our minds, how we, in the colonial days, walked from Kenya to Cairo on foot, just to reach (the) GDR."[26] Kenyans like Wachira clearly considered the GDR not only a place to get an education but also a political safe haven. Many other Kenyans had to travel through London before they could reach the GDR.[27] This adds another layer of complexity to their distinct story, and had much to do with ethnic politics in Kenya, as we shall see below.

Cairo, however, was the first definitive hub to emerge in the Cold War. Burton has detailed how Nasser purposefully worked to make the city a capital and refuge for Africans from throughout the continent. Nasser, a leader in the Non-Aligned Movement (NAM), saw Egypt not only as a bastion of Pan-Arabism but also of Pan-Africanism. He believed that as Egypt was part of Africa, it was his duty to bolster its anticolonial liberation movements. Cairo thus became a center where independence movements and opposition parties from various African states established offices in exile to coordinate their activities abroad.[28] In addition, Nasser brought Egypt into the socialist orbit and strengthened ties to the Soviet Union and its satellites, including the GDR, which also positioned themselves as anti-imperial defenders against the brutality of Western colonialism.[29]

For students who traveled the network that reached from south to east, Dar-es-Salaam (after Tanganyika's 1961 decolonization) was also a significant stopping point. In the 1963 article "Dar es Salaam: Where Exiles Plan—and Wait," Harvey Glickman described the city as "the political mecca of the 1960s" for members of outlawed parties and independence movements from across the region. Students were one of a number of groups seeking refuge in Dar-es-Salaam, alongside political escapees fleeing violence and migrant

Figure 8. Hassan Wani (center), president of the Union of Kenyan Students in the GDR, giving a speech at "Kenya Day," an event held in solidarity with Jomo Kenyatta and others who were then imprisoned by the British. Wani had undergone a long, circuitous journey to reach the GDR. Among those in attendance was future Ugandan president Miltion Obote (far left). Zentralbild Schaar Koch, October 21, 1960 (Bundesarchiv).

workers. Glickman emphasized the significance of the students in the city, calling it a "clearinghouse for scholarships" to universities in countries across the political spectrum.[30] He mentioned, too, that many were taking these scholarships in Soviet Bloc countries, and that those who did traveled on to Addis Ababa, Ethiopia, where most of the Eastern scholarships were tendered.[31] According to Glickman, this did not mean that the students preferred to study in communist nations, only that they wanted to study abroad, and not in Africa. In any case, while the students stayed in Dar es Salaam they were supported not only by TANU but by the offices that their own parties had set up in the city.[32]

The central and southern African travelers—together with the Kenyans—belonged to a late colonial wave that was distinctly different from the flows of students arriving in the GDR from independent African states, especially if those states were socialist-friendly. Nations like Ghana, Guinea, and Mali did not have embassies in the GDR, but they did conclude educational agreements with the Socialist Unity Party (SED) stipulating that certain numbers of students would study in the country each year, as I will discuss in more detail in the next chapter. The two flows overlapped—students from independent states and colonized ones were both coming to the GDR in the late 1950s and the 1960s. However, the ease of reaching Europe could be determined by the relationship a state had to the GDR and other socialist nations.

Earlier student exchange agreements with independence parties or trade unions were, indeed, decidedly more haphazard than contracts worked out with sovereign nations. Staff at Zambia's UNIP offices in Cairo, Dar-es-Salaam, and Accra scrambled to find placements for the students who sometimes showed up on their doorsteps with no idea where they might ultimately be headed, usually without any means to support themselves while they waited. Robert Makasa, UNIP's representative in the Tanganyikan capital, often complained of having to feed and house students for varying lengths of time because officials back in Zambia sent them to him before he was ready for them to come, that is before he had secured them placements or, in some cases, air tickets.[33] Makasa and his field office colleagues worked assiduously at securing offers of university scholarships or vocational training from around the world. They solicited offers as well, writing letters to contacts in an effort to secure further placements for Zambians.[34]

Where they could, the British—and the Portuguese—also tried to prevent Africans from reaching the Soviet Bloc. The home office in London and the colonial regime in Nigeria had struggled to find justification for denying permission to travel for the Nigerians who had received scholarships to the GDR in 1949–1950. In the early 1960s, British colonial governments were still trying to thwart students who wanted to go east. For example, in 1963 four Botswanan students who were members of the Bechuanaland People's Party applied for university admission in unnamed Eastern European countries. The Refugees' Advisory Committee in Dar-es-Salaam, which was comprised of representatives from independence movements throughout central and southern Africa, maintained that this was impossible. The colonial government in what was then the Bechuanaland Protectorate would not issue passports for their travel, though they would provide them for study in Western countries.[35]

The network of routes in western Africa served a similar function to the ones in the east. Students from countries such as Cameroon transited through Accra in Ghana or Conakry in Guinea as they attempted to reach the GDR and its allies. There were, however, some distinct differences. For instance, from January 1960 the Cameroonians in Accra and Conakry came from a nation that was decolonized, but under very calamitous circumstances. Many of the students who reached the GDR were members of the populist Union of the Peoples of Cameroon (UPC), which was formed in the late 1940s and driven into exile in 1955. Meredith Terretta has discussed how Accra became a haven for thousands of Cameroonian nationalists forced to leave their own country.[36] They included students, whom Terretta says were particularly attracted to scholarships from China or the Soviet Bloc.[37] Jeannette Aryee-Boi remembered that her father, Jacques Latta, spent time in a poor area of Accra while anticipating his eventual departure for the GDR.[38] Moreover, in 1961, Aloys-Marie Njog of the executive committee for the Democratic Youth of Cameroon Overseas noted that twenty Cameroonian students were waiting in Accra for plane tickets that would take them to the GDR.[39] In addition, Cameroonians commonly returned to Ghana or Guinea rather than Cameroon after completing their studies.[40]

Cameroon's situation diverged from that of countries such as Kenya and Zambia, in that Cameroon technically was independent in 1960. However, Cameroonian independence was tightly controlled by the French. Its first president, Ahmadou Ahidjo, was a staunch French ally who cracked down on dissent, and especially on UPC sympathizers. This effectively made the UPC an independence movement, but one that never succeeded in toppling the neocolonial regime that emerged in its country.[41] Indeed, the UPC continued to send students through their offices in Accra, Conakry, and Cairo before they received final approval to travel to the GDR; they never came directly from Douala or Yaoundé.[42]

Togolese students had similar difficulties reaching the GDR from their West African home, despite their country's independence in 1960. In 1961, the administration of the Deutsche Hochschule für Körperkultur (DHfK), East Germany's premier sports academy, held a meeting with three Togolese students to find out how it was that they had come to Leipzig. The students explained that they had not gone through Togo's government to get the scholarships but, rather, had procured them through membership in a progressive Togolese trade union with assistance from the *Guinean* government. No one from the Togolese government knew that they were in the GDR. If their sojourn in East Germany was discovered after they returned to Togo, they could face serious repercussions.[43] The postindependence government of Sylvanus Olympio had become increasingly authoritarian after independence in 1960. It is likely that the students were members of Juvento, once the youth wing of Olympio's Committee of Togolese Unity (CUT) but by 1961 a political party in its own right, and one that was aligned against Olympio.[44] The students claimed that they were planning to return to Togo anyway to help develop sports programs, as the DHfK desired, but were clearly nervous about doing so.[45] From the perspective of students like the ones at the DHfK, whether their country was technically independent or not made little difference; like their counterparts in Kenya and Zambia, they struggled against political repression and faced the threat of persecution, imprisonment, or worse upon reentry.

Members of independence movements also converged in West Africa, with Accra as the primary hub. Kwame Nkrumah, Ghana's first postcolonial leader, made Pan-Africanism a central aspect of his politics. As Burton, Jean Allman, and Jeffrey S. Ahlman have all noted, Nkrumah thus supported freedom fighters from across the continent and also invited students from nations struggling against colonialism to come to his country.[46] Among them were members of independence movements from countries in eastern, central, and southern Africa.

Zambian members of UNIP were among those who gladly traveled to Accra, and their number purposefully included both men and women. S. Kalulu, later a minister in Zambia's first postcolonial government, wrote M. Sipalo at the Bureau for African Affairs in Accra to discuss possible scholarships for Zambians in Ghana, and intoned that in addition to finding positions for "boys" in Ghana, "Girls should also be considered for such things as Nursing, Teaching, Welfare Work, etcetera."[47] In this remark, Kalulu stressed that scholarships for women should mainly be in certain fields coded as female, as was usually the case when women were sent for education abroad. Nonetheless, Kalulu wanted them to go to Ghana, as did Sipalo. Indeed, in one instance Sipalo sent a woman named Mary N. to study at the women's branch of the Kwame Nkrumah Ideological Institute in Winneba,[48] which provided a socialist education emphasizing Nkrumah's ideas.[49]

Sipalo's decision to send Mary N. to the institute may have dovetailed with UNIP leader and future Zambian president Kenneth Kaunda's developing principle of Zambian humanism, which Kristen Ghodsee says was "an egalitarian ideology that proposed that African societies needed to be organized to prevent economic exploitation and discrimination on the basis of race, ethnicity, religion, tribal affiliation, class, or sex."[50] The philosophy was grounded in a mix of African socialism and Christianity, in which God gave land to the people and it was then held for them by the state; in this sense, it was the collective property of all Zambians, both male and female.[51] Kaunda imagined an active role for women in the party, and many became involved with the UNIP Women's Brigade and later members of the UNIP Women's League.[52] Zambian women thus also had a place in Accra, and if they were mostly shunted toward "female" professions, some received an additional political education to bolster their activism and strengthen their role in Northern Rhodesia's independence movement. They could do so as they traveled the routes to Accra, Dar-es-Salaam, Cairo, or sites throughout the Soviet Bloc, including the GDR.

Politics on the Road

Wherever the networks led, the students who traveled them continued to maintain and cultivate contacts long after their paths diverged. Burton has commented that the networks did not appear out of nowhere and could not be maintained without individuals bolstering them.[53] Archival records make clear that students were rarely abandoned or cut off from those who had helped them reach their destination. For example, there were strong ties between the Kenyan students in Leipzig and their counterparts in London.[54] In addition, officials from the Kenya African National Union (KANU), the primary political party negotiating for independence, periodically visited the GDR to meet with students. Oginga Odinga, KANU's vice president, and his secretary, Paul Naboth Mwok, were the most prominent to make the trek.[55] Guineans in the GDR had strong connections with Guineans elsewhere in Europe, particularly those in Paris, as we will see in chapter 4.[56] Students even formed supra-European student organizations to collaborate the activities of students who studied in different European countries.[57] The networks linking the students from Africa to points abroad continued to impact their lives well after they had arrived at their destination.

As we have seen, international students were key to the GDR's foreign relations. Unable to establish diplomatic relations with emergent nations because of the Hallstein Doctrine, educational agreements became one of the key ways for the GDR to make connections with African governments. Once students were in East Germany, they could be subjected to Marxist indoctrination. On the East German side there was a sense that those who wound up in the GDR already had socialist proclivities, given that they were often members of trade unions or appeared to have other socialist bona fides. Countless reports on the students, often from their professors or university administrators, noted their attitude toward Marxism and whether it needed adjustment or improvement. Reports on students who were considered politically suspect are the ones that stand out, but those that note a students' ideological conformity are more common.

Yet as noted previously, students were probably more ambivalent about socialism than ardently in favor of it. For them, the primary goal was still education—where they received that education was less significant. From the African perspective then, the GDR recedes in importance, becoming one more node in a network of intellectual possibilities. For East Germans—and indeed for Soviets, Americans, and other Europeans—ideology was crucial, and they hoped to influence their exchange students. But in countries such as Zambia—which had no universities before independence—getting accepted to a university, wherever it was, was key.[58]

In order to speed up development, young governments and independence movements commonly strove to improve their citizens' technical knowledge and create "technocratic" regimes.[59] By the 1980s, technology in the Soviet Bloc in general and the GDR in particular lagged significantly behind that of the West. In the 1950s and even 1960s, the scientific achievements of states such as the GDR were as much a lure as those of their Western neighbors. Indeed, right around the time of independence in 1964 the organization of Zambian students in Poland argued for an increase in scholarships to Eastern Bloc countries thusly: "Whether or not all students in the East are communists and whether or not communism is bad, is indeed, a very debatable subject. But the worry of Zambia should be to have lots and lots of engineers, doctors, geologists, chemists, physicists, etc., etc., not tomorrow but today, and this is possible here."[60] Eastern European universities appealed to African technocrats; African students and political officials alike were above all pragmatists.

Nonetheless, we cannot completely discount the role of ideology either. Parties like Zambia's UNIP, South Africa's ANC, Zimbabwe's ZAPU, and Namibia's SWAPO and SWANU were left-wing oriented and sought and received support from the GDR. Moreover, some African politicians were more associated with socialism than others. In 1962, politicians Oginga Odinga and Daniel arap Moi had a dispute over sending students to the Soviet Union or its allies that played out in the Kenyan press. The GDR was very interested in courting Odinga,[61] the most left-wing of the Kenyan political elite and a proponent of African socialism and Fabianism.[62] Officials saw Odinga as the key to giving them an opening in Kenyan politics as the country decolonized. He visited East Germany in early 1960, right after attending the first Lancaster House Conference, which was designed to negotiate the terms of Kenyan independence.[63] While in the GDR he met with SED officials to discuss the proceedings of the conference and to visit with Kenyan students already in the GDR. The officials commented that although Odinga came from a "wealthy family," he seemed very open to their political positions.[64]

The ebbs and flows of students from southern, central, and eastern Africa were dependent on the regnant political situation in their home territories and rapidly shifted as various nations gained independence. The Kenyan example continues to be illustrative in this respect. Politicians who would later split along ideological lines joined together to fight the British. Jomo Kenyatta and Oginga Odinga, the most prominent, were the country's first president and vice president, respectively, after Kenya finally gained its independence in 1963. Their political differences would ultimately drive them apart, however—Odinga leaned toward the Soviets and Chinese, while Kenyatta embraced American and Western European capitalism. Their divisions ultimately drove Oginga into the opposition and marked the beginning of a political breach that remains today.[65] Moreover, this breach ran not only along political lines but ethnic ones, as the Kikuyu, Kenyatta's ethnic group, came to be more associated with his party and the West, and the Luo, to whom Odinga belonged, were seen as affiliated with him. While Kenyan students headed for the GDR and its allies in the years leading up to independence, movement would be increasingly toward the West, not the East, from 1963 onward.[66]

Zambia was also in flux. In the short period from 1960 to 1964, the emergent nation underwent enormous changes that impacted student journeys. As the decade opened, Zambians—not to mention Zimbabweans and Malawians—struggled to dissolve the CAF (FRN), which consisted of Northern Rhodesia, Southern Rhodesia, and Nyasaland. The CAF was founded in 1953 and was mainly under the control of Southern Rhodesia's infamously racist white settlers, and had been established mainly for their economic benefit. Additionally, Zambians were politically divided between the Zambian African National Congress (Zambian ANC), headed by Harry Nkumbula, and UNIP, under the direction of Kenneth Kaunda, who would ultimately become Zambia's first president and stay in power from 1964 to 1991. They fought among themselves as well as with Roy Welensky, the racist white governor of the CAF.[67]

UNIP refugees, whether they were students or not, thus fled to Tanganyika, not only because it was a waystation on the path to overseas education, but because of the very real risk that they would be detained and jailed by CAF forces.[68] Dingiswayo Banda, director of the Zambian Youth Movement, told a man named Henry, who was a former vice chairman of a youth brigade in Ndola, to flee Zambia for Dar-es-Salaam because there was news of his impending arrest. Henry, who reached Dar-es-Salaam circuitously, via Nyasaland—Malawi—hoped to study engineering or something similar once he was out of Northern Rhodesia.[69] Edward L.'s case was not much different; he was a vice constituency chairman for UNIP in Solwezi and, upon being told that there was a warrant for his arrest, left for Dar-es-Salaam via Malawi. He said he intended to study agriculture once he was out of Zambia.[70] The main reason for both trips, however, remained personal safety, since Henry and Edward both had to abandon their positions within UNIP under considerable duress. In the years leading up to independence, Zambia was generally wracked by violence, particularly in the north, where arson was common.[71] Flight was therefore sometimes the best option.

Once the CAF was dissolved in 1963, Zambia was granted self-governance and was well on its way to independence by 1964. At this point, Lusaka itself became a stop for other student refugees fleeing colonial brutality. Zambian students continued to go to the GDR and other Eastern Bloc states,[72] but the arduous trek was no longer necessary. Other liberation movements from countries that would not become independent until later—Namibia's SWAPO and SWANU, Zimbabwe's ZANU and ZAPU, South Africa's ANC—would take the route to and from Dar-es-Salaam for much longer.

The rest of this chapter will focus on the pathways of two groups of students—Zambians and Kenyans. Both faced challenges specific to their national or local situations but also became entangled in the wider field of Cold War politics. For the Zambians, this meant contending with the last vestiges of CAF authority in Northern Rhodesia, as well as internecine struggles between the country's two main political parties, UNIP and the Zambian ANC. It also meant pursuing scholarship opportunities wherever they might emerge. The Kenyans had to deal with divisions between political parties and additionally navigate regional ethnic rifts. They, too, looked for educational placements across the globe, but specific politicians, such as Odinga, had connections to the East, while others, most prominently Tom Mboya, built extensive ties to the West.[73] The stories of both the Zambians and the Kenyans demonstrate how the global and local intertwined in considerations of where students would go, and how they would get there.

"Everybody who comes here is to be fed":[74] Zambian Students on the Road and out of Place

Tanganyika was celebrating its independence in mid-December 1961 with parties held almost every night, but M.S., the UNIP representative in the border town of Mbeya, could attend none of the festivities. Instead he was hard at work processing a steady stream of Zambian students and other refugees pouring into the city. M.S. explained the situation to the TANU provincial secretary:

> Sir, I think you know that my party . . . in Mbeya has embarked upon a massive and crash student programme (sic). All these students pass through Mbeya on their way to Dar-es-Salaam, where they are despatched (sic) to colleges abroad. This exodus of students was at its apex during the Independence Celebrations. This coupled with the unearthly hour of arrivals of Rhodesian buses in Mbeya made it very difficult for me to attend to those students and at the same time keep up my date with the committee. . . . I had to arrange accommodation and victuals for these students and afterwards had to go through the formalities required by my party. . . . By the time this came to an end it was rarely before 9:30 p.m., and so impossible for me to come.[75]

It is difficult to tell exactly how many students and others fleeing Northern Rhodesia passed through Mbeya between 1961 and 1964, when Zambia achieved independence. The town was certainly a major transit point on the way to Dar-es-Salaam and beyond, where students like John M., mentioned at the beginning of the chapter, sometimes waited for months to receive word on where they would travel next.

The rush of students across the border reflected a fear of brutal colonial repression and reprisals for political activism, but also an eagerness for long-denied education. All students fleeing their colonies had limited access to higher education at home, but the educational offers in Zambia were especially grim. When the University of Zambia first opened in 1966, Kaunda gave its inaugural address. In it, he said that, "as far as education is concerned, Britain's colonial record in Zambia is most criminal. The country has been left by her as the most uneducated and most unprepared of Britain's dependencies on the African continent."[76] Indeed, the level of education in what had been Northern Rhodesia was extremely low, even by colonial standards. Gatian F. Lungu has explained that a lack of unified governmental structures, systemic racism, elitism, distrust of missionaries by the British South Africa Company when it was in charge of the colony, and the increased presence of European settlers after World War I meant that few Zambians who were not royalty had the opportunity to achieve higher education. Where there was education, it was mainly industrial.[77] Women were, moreover, almost completely shut out of colonial education, since they were not deemed fit for work in the copper mines, and a lot of the training in Northern Rhodesia was geared toward this.[78]

Among higher up Zambian officials like Makasa, who ran UNIP's Dar-es-Salaam office, the situation in Mbeya may have been understandable, but it was still a challenge. There were various problems. Not everyone who showed up in Mbeya was a student or even eligible for refugee status. Makasa believed that some of the border-crossers were merely trying to escape their duty to fight for independence. In theory, all members of UNIP were to stay in Zambia unless they were specifically designated for study abroad or were in danger of being imprisoned by Northern Rhodesian authorities and thus needed to get out of Zambia fast. He ordered the Mbeya branch to turn away anyone who appeared to be a deserter and without a legitimate reason for being in Mbeya.[79] Makasa's colleague Masaiti, the representative in Mbeya, additionally feared that "federal agents" might infiltrate the camp, presumably disguised as refugees.[80] In 1958, UNIP had broken away from the Zambian ANC, and by the early 1960s UNIP members were fighting ANC members in the vicinity of Mbeya. Thieves reportedly lurked as well, and yet another UNIP representative had to write warning his colleagues to turn away a man who had assumed multiple identities and would try to con them into thinking he was a student.[81] Who was supposed to be in Mbeya—and who was not—was thus a central concern for UNIP authorities.

The question of how to feed and house the students also worried UNIP's field representatives and presented a constant challenge. In Mbeya, Masaiti never had enough money to supply the many students and refugees in his charge. At their next stop, Dar-es-Salaam, Makasa also struggled to meet student needs. He said, "The position is we haven't got money. We have got many boys and girls here waiting to go to school, (and) we have to feed them. Everybody who comes here is to be fed." Makasa had explained the crisis to colleagues in Zambia and suggested they give ten pounds to every student they sent to Tanganyika.[82] No one followed his suggestion, and more students appeared in Mbeya each day, impoverished and requiring assistance. An organization called the Refugee Advisory Committee in Dar-es-Salaam did send fifty pounds to Mbeya, which Makasa had held by a priest, who would dispense the money as needed.[83] Lack of adequate housing and clothing only compounded the matter and increased the urgency to either move the students more quickly or raise more money. UNIP leaders begged students coming to Dar-es-Salaam to stay with friends or relatives if they had them,[84] but few did. Students sometimes left home without the clothing they would need if they wound up in cold climates—one man "left without anything except his briefcase"—and UNIP had to pay to dress them, too.[85]

The issue of provisions and accommodations was not unrelated to the overarching subject of exactly who was crossing the border to Tanganyika. Simon Kapwepwe, at the time national treasurer for UNIP and later independent Zambia's first vice president, complained that the issues with food, accommodations, and even the long waits students experienced in their travels or the staggered nature of their arrivals could be attributed to lack of coordination within UNIP's National Education Committee. Students were being channeled to Mbeya and Dar-es-Salaam from at least three separate sources, none of which had information about what the other was doing. Further, the students were not being vetted properly, which led to individuals who were unqualified for scholarships traveling long distances to receive them. When that happened, the universities granting the scholarships could rescind their offers, and UNIP would lose those placements. In addition, sometimes Kapwepwe and his colleagues in the Dar-es-Salaam or Cairo offices would expect one student to arrive and wind up having someone entirely different show up.[86] S. Kalulu, UNIP's national chairman, suggested that the delays themselves were responsible for last minute substitutions; students who had applied earlier and been on long waiting lists gave up and took jobs at home. When the scholarships eventually did come through, replacements had to be found.[87]

The organizational problems were not surprising when you consider the pressure under which UNIP officials abroad and students wishing to leave worked. UNIP's offices were scattered across Africa, with headquarters in Lusaka, but regional bureaus in Mbeya, Dar-es-Salaam, Cairo, and Accra, along with smaller stations throughout Zambia and Tanganyika. Communication among these offices was slow, with various UNIP representatives making decisions to send students away without the ability to notify their colleagues elsewhere. Bureaucracy and red tape further hampered official work, and thus student progress; for instance, Wilted Phiri, the UNIP representative in Cairo in early 1964, could not pass information on student travel dates to a colleague because he had no cholera vaccination, and he was detained for days at Cairo airport with no access to his files until one could be arranged.[88]

The delays, the disorganization, the lack of funds all demonstrate the haphazardness and uncertainty that beset students on the road. Students and officials had to strategize the paths they might take, be ready to leave on a moment's notice, and end up at destinations other than the ones they originally envisioned. The experience of Jonah S. is illustrative. He eventually made his way to the GDR but not before his journey had taken many twists and turns. His travels started in 1960 in Uganda, where he tried to gain admission to a school—likely Makerere College, as he was staying with one of the school's faculty while in the country—and was almost sentenced to ten months in prison for not having a passport. He asked Kapwepwe to find him something else, preferably either in Ghana or Sudan.[89] Whether Jonah S. made it to either is unclear, but by late 1961 he was in Cairo, where Makasa wrote him and urged that he continue studying.[90] In 1962, Jonah S. finally received a scholarship to the University of Rostock.[91] By 1964, he was secretary of the Central African Students Association in the GDR.[92]

Once they were in Europe, the students' journeys were not always over. Students were sometimes dissatisfied with their placements and either requested a move from the Party or got other scholarships themselves and left of their own volition. Those who did so defied UNIP authority, angering party officials. Student choices were understood as personal insults and political acts. In April 1963, Makasa and Humphrey Mulemba, the UNIP representative in Accra, exchanged a heated set of letters involving students in Yugoslavia who, claiming to be dissatisfied with the level of education there, had accepted scholarships offered by Western embassies in Belgrade without UNIP approval. According to Mulemba, the students then turned around and denounced UNIP itself in the Western press.[93] The student exodus came at a difficult juncture for UNIP. The CAF was in the process of being dissolved, and home rule and independence were virtually assured. As Zambia tried to position itself within the framework of the Cold War, politicians did not want to give the impression that they were alienating the Soviet Union and its allies.[94] Student insubordination was the last thing they wanted. Further, such defiance demonstrated that once they were in Europe, students were less bidden to follow the dictates of the parties that had sponsored them. They essentially became free agents. Deciding on where to go also gave them a measure of control that was lacking during their difficult journeys from Africa to Europe and beyond.[95]

The situation in Yugoslavia obliged Mulemba to consider the question of student selection, always a thorny issue for UNIP. Finding students who were both qualified to attend university and had the proper ideological slant for countries "in the East" was difficult. Makasa, Kapwepwe, and their colleagues were in a bind: they needed to educate as many Zambians as possible in preparation for independence, but colonial era negligence of African education in Northern Rhodesia left them with few well-qualified students. Masaiti expressed the frustration well when he told William M., who applied for a scholarship abroad in early 1963, "Your educational qualification will not make it possible for you to further your education outside Zambia. . . . It is and it has been impossible for us all."[96] Yet the clamor for scholarships, and UNIP's desire to create an educated work force to speed national development, meant that Makasa, Kapwepwe, and their colleagues still continued to hunt for scholarships wherever they could find them.

The UNIP also pursued scholarships for women, and here they had even more trouble finding qualified applicants, since the British had neglected education for girls even more so than they had for boys. Most of the scholarships for women were in stereotypically "feminine" subjects such as domestic science or nursing. Anna P., one of the two women stranded at Tegel Airport that I discussed at the beginning of the chapter, was headed to Quedlinburg to take a course in domestic science.[97] Before aiming for the GDR or elsewhere in the Soviet Bloc, UNIP tried to locate nursing scholarships closer to home, for example in Dar-es-Salaam's Princess Margaret School of Nursing.[98] Whatever the situation, the low level of educational achievement among Zambian women complicated the quest for candidates.

In general, the interest in finding scholarships for women was intense, as they were considered both integral parts of the independence process and the development of the postcolonial state. Indeed, Makasa's view about the significance of women in a future postcolonial Zambian society was similar to that of Kaunda, UNIP's president. Kaunda embraced Zambian humanism to explain why he believed there should be equality between the sexes. This line of thought is evident in Makasa's correspondence with Sabrina M., the other woman who had been trapped in West Berlin with Anna P. Sabrina M. was also studying in Quedlinburg, where she was enrolled at a *Medizinische Fachschule* that trained nurses and medical paraprofessionals. In one letter to Sabrina M., Makasa explained, "In Zambia we have not forbidden women who want to advance themselves where ever they may be. That is why we believe that you will fight (for what you want) until you succeed."[99] Makasa and the other men pressing for women to go abroad followed Zambian humanist principles in support of an egalitarian ideal; it was also an ideal that privileged the "indigenous" over white colonizers and highlighted the significance of Black women to the national project. They were eager to send Sabrina M., Anna P., and other African women to university, but they rejected the applicant Stella C. because, although qualified, she was a white Southern Rhodesian.[100]

Such professions of gender equality were, to be sure, undercut by the reality of a strongly patriarchal Zambian society. Agnes M., who was technically qualified for a scholarship, was unable to take the opportunity to study abroad in 1961 because her parents forbade it. She wrote a letter to Makasa to let him know that it might be possible for her to take the bursary the next year, but that "many things are not straightforward," and she could not be entirely open in her correspondence about the difficulties she faced.[101] In another case, the father of a woman named Mercy M. wanted to stop her from accepting a scholarship to the University of California, Berkeley. Mercy M. appears to have reached Dar-es-Salaam but was then sent back to her family home in Zambia because "her father in particular is against her going to school."[102] Yet another woman, Lizzie C., was denied a scholarship because her brother was already studying overseas, and UNIP wanted to distribute the scholarships equally among families.[103] When deciding which child to send to school in a central or southern African context, boys have traditionally been given preference over girls, as Tsitsi Dangarembga discussed in her renowned autobiographical novel, *Nervous Conditions*.[104] This could explain why the brother was tendered the first scholarship, and not the sister.

UNIP officials were, moreover, concerned with girls' behavior and the impression they might make when abroad. In August 1961, Kalulu, national chairman of UNIP, exhorted Makasa to keep close watch over the women in Dar-es-Salaam who were waiting for scholarship placements. "I am making special appeal to you Mr. Makasa over care for our girls in Dar-es-Salaam. You are the man at the head. Kindly see to it that girls keep under your personal elderly care and orders. I do not want silly stories about them because over their success hangs our reputation here at home. Our aim is education and no more."[105] While Zambian men abroad—indeed, specifically in the GDR—were also instructed to behave themselves so as not to embarrass their country in front of potential allies,[106] the paternalism evident in Kalulu's letter was lacking in similar correspondence to the men. Instead of addressing the women directly, Kalulu turned to Makasa as their putative father figure, who was charged with keeping them in line and making sure that they comported themselves correctly. This made sense in the context of Zambia, a country where despite the push for women's education and professions of equality under Zambian humanism, women's status was generally low. Patriarchy was deeply embedded in both the family and the state during the precolonial period, and patriarchal structures were upheld through the colonial era under the authority of both white and African men.[107] Even those Zambian women who were involved in the politics of independence early, from the 1950s, were seen as subservient to their husbands. Gisela Geisler notes that one female political activist "recall(ed) that her male party colleagues carefully questioned her husband for his approval" to be involved in politics.[108] Although UNIP emphasized the importance of women's education, their stance toward equality was more ambivalent than Zambian humanism suggested. Women's political and intellectual participation in society was blunted by both familial and state repression.

Gender obviously became a factor for Zambians on the road, as the UNIP struggled to find female candidates with high enough levels of education whose families would not prevent them from taking scholarships. Racial discrimination was also an issue. Kapwepwe doggedly petitioned for scholarships from the United States. However, although there were Zambians in the country at institutions such as Roosevelt University in Chicago,[109] Kapwepwe believed that American relations to the colonial establishment in Northern Rhodesia permeated all decisions on funding for Zambians to attend American universities. In a 1961 letter to UNIP's office in Los Angeles, Kapwepwe said, "About the Scholarships for our boys, it is now very (clear) that the American Government is not prepared to offer Scholarships or any assistance to our students, simply because the white settlers in our country are against this move."[110] Questions of decolonization were intertwined with questions of race, broader Cold War struggles concerning the eventual alignment of states like Zambia, and potentially even the wider political crisis in Congo that enveloped central Africa in the early 1960s.[111]

Bias was not only a problem in the United States. Students also claimed discomfort in Eastern Bloc countries. Kay Sifuniso, who studied in Yugoslavia around 1963, wrote an article for the Zambian *Mail* in 1964 complaining both of the poor educational standards and lack of cultural awareness in Belgrade. Sifuniso wrote that she lived down the hall from a Guinean woman in their dormitory, and that their Yugoslavian peers were astonished by the fact that they spoke to each other in Serbo-Croatian and not in a common African language. She also said that Zambian and other African students were escaping to Western Europe whenever the chance arose, which jibes with UNIP officials' own reports on students fleeing Yugoslavia for the West.[112] It is also consistent with the protests that African students mounted in the Soviet Union, and their exit en masse from Bulgaria in 1963.[113]

The leaders of UNIP were generally impressed with the GDR, though, and it did not come in for the same kind of overt criticism as the United States, Soviet Union, Yugoslavia, or Bulgaria. In late 1961, Kapwepwe visited Berlin and was extremely happy with his reception. He claimed that he had "very strong impressions about the general set up of (the East German) Government, its ideology, the people's realisation (sic) regarding the dignity of man and his associates."[114] Further, Amos Ndyamba, who had studied economics for more than two years at the FDGB Trade Union College, countered Sifuniso's article about Yugoslavia in a follow-up piece for the *Mail* that detailed his experiences in the GDR. In his article, entitled "Former Berlin Student Replies to Kay Sifuniso: Eastern Europe is not that bad," Ndyamba maintained that he had heard of no other African students who had "complain(ed) of ill-treatment at the hands of the Communists." He argued that those Africans who left the GDR primarily did so because they were too steeped in Western colonial ideals to adapt to a socialist environment. While Ndyamba would not say that he preferred socialism to capitalism—he held to the nonaligned stance that "Africa's policy is one of positive neutrality . . . (and) it is up to us in Africa to evolve our own systems of government suitable for our needs and conditions"—he refuted Sifuniso's claim that the Soviet Bloc was not welcoming of African students, and he praised the GDR.[115]

Kapwepwe and his colleagues were more concerned with how Zambians studying in the GDR presented themselves to the East German public than with how the GDR was treating the students. After meeting with Zambian students in the country during his 1961 trip, Kapwepwe wrote to tell them that "(GDR officials) told me without any flattery that so far you are the best students, well-seasoned and well-disciplined, that they have ever received from Africa. . . . I am sure you will realise (sic) the importance of this prestige you have built for yourselves and your country. It is very difficult to build (a) good reputation, but very easy to destroy it if you are not careful. . . ."[116] Only a few months later, however, another UNIP representative, M. Sokoni, wrote in sterner language that suggested students were not comporting themselves as they should. He reminded them that "money paid for your fare and the money you are using now has been contributed by the poor man in (the) Zambian street who has been shot dead in cold blood, who has been looted, who has been raped, who is languishing behind prison bars and who is, as I say now languishing in the bush under heavy rains, all in the struggle for our freedom." Sokoni claimed that since the students now lived in comfortable circumstances, far away from colonial violence, they had forgotten how dire the situation was at home. They represented the hope that Zambia would be able to rebuild itself once decolonization was finally complete, but to do so they needed to behave well, respect their hosts, and not sully their country's good name.[117]

While Kapwepwe and Sokoni seemed most concerned with student demeanor and were outwardly admiring of the GDR, there are still signs hinting at some measure of dissatisfaction with how students were treated. In April 1963, James C. and Joseph M. had scholarships to study in the GDR and were supposed to travel to the country by ship.[118] This was after Zambia was assured independence, since the British had announced that the constituent parts of the CAF could secede in March of that year, effectively meaning that the Federation would be dissolved.[119] This should have meant that travel for the two aspiring students would be less difficult than it was for students before 1963. Yet instead the captain of the *S. S. Stralsund* almost denied them passage on his liner. The details of why he tried to prevent their access are unclear, but the captain did not seem to believe that they had license to be in the GDR. Finally, after D. M. Lisulo, another UNIP representative in Dar-es-Salaam, pled with him to take them, the captain grudgingly allowed the students on board. But Lisulo did not seem convinced that he would let them stay for the entire journey; the pair were traveling via Lourenço Marques (Maputo), Mozambique, and Durban in South Africa, and Lisulo worried that they would have a difficult time remaining on the ship unless letters explicitly certifying their status as students were sent to the *Stralsund* while it was at sea. He said that the letters would "help . . . avoid any un-called for hardships the boys are likely to encounter" on the voyage.[120]

This incident does not definitively demonstrate discrimination. The men had tickets—but no passports, as the CAF had never issued them ones—and could have been turned away for this reason. Lisulo's language, however, hints at resistance to the idea that James C. and Joseph M. were actually bound for the GDR or had a legitimate reason to be there. GDR authorities were eager to bring students from Africa to their country, but ordinary citizens, such as the captain of the *Stralsund*, may have been less enthusiastic, or not even known about the scholarship program. The general uncertainty of the time—confusion over the future of Northern Rhodesia, who would run the government once independence came, and the position the new Zambian nation might take within the Cold War—also possibly contributed to the East German captain's behavior.

The long waits, the organizational miscommunications, and the ambiguity about where they were going or how they would be received once there, factored into an overarching sense of unease among student travelers in the years leading up to decolonization. But these difficulties did not end once a country achieved independence. Instead there were ongoing shifts in how African politicians approached offers of scholarships, and whether certain destinations, particularly in the Eastern Bloc, became unpalatable to leaders trying to reposition themselves in the fast-moving circumstances of the Cold War. In Zambia, Kaunda made a firm commitment to nonalignment, attempting to forge a space between the United States and USSR that would allow him to negotiate with both.[121]

While Zambia technically embraced nonalignment after independence and had embassies in capitals such as Moscow and Peking, Kenya was more closely associated with the United States and its allies.[122] It did, however, have a sizeable socialist-leaning minority, which Odinga represented. The divide between U.S.- and Soviet-inclined politicians thus caused conflict over where Kenyan students should attend university, both before and after Kenya's actual independence. It also shows that the fault lines between them, which would harden once Kenya was decolonized, were all visible in the late colonial phase.

I will now move into a discussion of the disagreement over communist bloc countries and their treatment of Kenyans that sprung up in the early 1960s between Odinga and Daniel arap Moi, who would later become Kenya's second president. Their disagreement demonstrates how political considerations could shape student trajectories, but also how ethnic divisions, which split political parties across the continent, played a role in determining student pathways.

Kenya: Stranded in Cairo?

In November 1961, Jomo Kenyatta, the future first president of postcolonial Kenya, landed in Cairo for a brief stopover on a trip back to Nairobi from independence negotiations in London. Kenyatta had spent seven years in prison, and had only been released a few months prior. This was therefore a rare opportunity to see him. Three members of the GDR's Solidarity Committee were in Cairo and rushed to the airport hoping for an introduction. They were not the only ones clamoring to see the newly freed Kenyatta. The Kenya office in Cairo (hereafter Cairo office) bused in forty Kenyan students who were waiting in Egypt for the plane tickets that would eventually take them to various destinations in Europe and elsewhere. Kenyatta had little time for the East Germans or others in the crowd, but he was very interested in the students and addressed them directly. He told them that the struggle against imperialism had to go on and that their role was to study diligently, as he needed each and every one of them in the fight.[123]

Two years earlier, in 1959, there were already a handful of Kenyan students in the GDR, most of them studying at the KMU. None of them were women, although a handful of Kenyan women did study in East Germany during the early to mid-1960s.[124] Like the Zambians, the Kenyans usually transited through Cairo. Some—like the aforementioned Hassan Wani Ali Kamau, who worked in Cairo for three years before finally getting a plane ticket to Leipzig—remained for long stretches.[125] For the Kenyans, however, the Cairo stop became a significant point of contention in a way that it never was for the Zambians. Views of the Cairo office were indeed ensnarled in Kenya-specific politics. Joseph Murumbi, who was briefly vice president of Kenya in 1966, recalled that the Kenyan African Union (KAU) opened the Cairo office in 1953, and that it closed after independence in 1963.[126] During the decade in between, Murumbi claimed that Kenyans were walking to Somalia in order to be airlifted to Cairo and the possibilities that existed there. He said that Nasser, in collaboration with the Somalian government, had personally arranged for their travel. While they waited, the Kenyan students worked, likely at jobs that Nasser procured for them.[127]

The politics of the Cairo office—who ran it and how they chose which students to send abroad—was at the heart of the conflict between Odinga and Moi, as well as between Odinga and other Kenyan politicians, such as Mboya,[128] whose politics were oriented toward the United States and clashed considerably with Odinga.[129] Murumbi referred to the Cairo office as being run by Odinga, or rather by two Luo students who were followers of Odinga.[130] As it turns out, their ethnicity was a key issue, which shows that the problems in Cairo were not only about Cold War rivalries and ideological differences. They were about much more local political concerns and questions of national versus "tribal" identity, which became complicated with transnational conflicts.

Norman N., a Kenyan studying in London who visited the GDR in 1960, indeed claimed that the leadership of the Cairo office put non-Luo students at a serious disadvantage. He had traveled to the GDR with two other Kenyans from London, both of whom gave him "nasty looks" when he mentioned ethnic divisions in conversation with GDR officials, and thereafter retreated into their "tribal tongue," shutting him out. Norman N. was Kikuyu and the other students Luo. They dismissed his allegations and held that Norman N. was interested first in his "tribe," and only then in the Kenyan nation.[131]

Norman N. continued to cultivate connections in the GDR after he left and kept up his claim that the Luo were prejudiced against other Kenyans. In a letter to Heinrich Eggebrecht, secretary general of the GDR's Solidarity Committee, Norman N. commented that he "remembered an Indian . . . in Prague who only helped Indians from the state of Punjab to take the scholarships and other amenities," and suggested that the Kenyans working in Cairo were similarly biased toward the Luo.[132] Further, he remarked, "To clear any confusion that we may cause by cross information . . . there is some unfair game being played on Kikuyus and other small tribes by Luos both in Kenya and abroad. This sort of thing will only create more trouble for Kenya, and however much you may wish to help us, you will fail by helping (only) one tribe."[133] Norman N. indicated that even after leaving Cairo the students were held up in London, ostensibly because the GDR needed approval from the Cairo office to let them into the country. This created one more stop on the way to their final destination and another barrier to reaching the GDR.

Norman N. was not the only one to accuse the Cairo office of favoritism. Thomas G., a student who had studied in Bernau and Leipzig during the early 1960s, made inflammatory remarks about the "tribalist" nature of the office.

Thomas G. had presented Eggebrecht with a list of eight students living in London who wanted to come to the GDR,[134] but whose names never came up in a discussion of scholarships between Eggebrecht and Kenyan Cairo staffer Oliver O. Thomas G. wrote a scathing letter to Oliver O. and accused him of having injected the issue of "tribalism" into conversations with Eggebrecht, thus embroiling an outsider in private Kenyan matters.[135] Thomas G. also believed that Kevin I., another student hoping to come to Leipzig, was delayed because he was Kikuyu, and implored Eggebrecht to help get him to the GDR.[136] For his part, Oliver O. dismissed Thomas G. as a troublemaker known for stirring up controversy.[137]

The conflict between the Luo and the Kikuyu is well-known. The Kikuyu are the largest ethnic group in Kenya, and the Luo are the second largest.[138] Rok Ajulu has addressed how the Kikuyu, Luo, and other Kenyan ethnicities originally came together in Kenya's first political organization in the 1920s but were increasingly driven apart in the struggle for resources and power that marked much of the colonial period. Nationalist movements and parties emerged when it was expedient—as with the creation of the KANU in 1960, when the country was negotiating for independence—but splintered thereafter.[139] These fractures could run along both ideological and ethnic lines, as Odinga himself made clear in a 1960 meeting with GDR officials. He told them that he believed Mboya, who was also Luo, was a corrupt puppet of the Americans and British, but that he was working alongside him anyway toward the shared goal of independence.[140] Ethnic loyalties therefore only went so far and were dispensed with when it became necessary.

Ethnic identity was, indeed, only one part of the dispute over the Cairo office. It was wrapped up in the broader struggle among different members of the Kenyan elite, most notably Odinga, Mboya, and Moi. The history of the "Airlift," Mboya's program sending Kenyans to the West, is fairly well-known. This is due in large part to Barack Obama's father, who came to the United States under its auspices. However, there is much less information about Odinga's considerable drive to procure scholarships in the Soviet Bloc, even though more Kenyan students actually went to Eastern Europe and the Soviet Union than to the United States in the late 1950s and early 1960s. Branch notes that Odinga—despite his reputation for leaning left—originally reached out to the United States for help with scholarship funding. When he was rebuffed, Odinga successfully turned to the USSR and its allies.[141] Like many African politicians, at this stage Odinga was fundamentally nonaligned and willing to work with either Cold War power.

It was not Mboya, however, but Moi who condemned the Cairo office run by Odinga's affiliates in late 1962. Moi had just returned to Nairobi from a visit to Egypt and said that he had met individually with many of the fifty students who were "stranded" there. He claimed that Odinga was personally responsible for twenty-five of the students and "ha(d) never done anything to help them." Moi further accused the Cairo office of keeping money that the Egyptian government had provided for the students, as well as of holding their passports indefinitely so they could not leave the country.[142]

B. F. F. Oluande K'Oduol, Odinga's personal secretary, responded forcefully and angrily to Moi's allegations. K'Oduol said that if Moi were to go to Odinga's office in Nairobi, he could read letters from students in Cairo that attested to the excellent care and respect that they had received while there. None of the students under Odinga's charge were "stranded"; they were merely waiting, and briefly at that. Any student who was experiencing problems had either arrived in Cairo with a different program or come on his own. The fact that other Kenyans had become stranded after trying to transit through Congo, Sudan, or Somalia on their own was, K'Oduol maintained, testament to this. Moi also knew that none of the students in Cairo had passports, and so there were obviously none to confiscate. Finally, the Cairo office had never withheld funds from students. Indeed, every bit of what the office received went directly to their upkeep.[143]

Moi's denigration of the Cairo office could be read as ethnically charged, given that he belonged to the minority Kalenjin, and he may have shared Norman N. and Thomas G.'s concerns that the Luo were stalling other Kenyans as they tried to go abroad. But this is too simplistic and leaves out the more complicated, overlapping interests at play in the early 1960s. David Anderson's work on the Kenya African Democratic Union (KADU), of which Moi was a leader, is instructive here. KADU was a regionalist party that briefly rivaled KANU, and which brought Kenya's smaller ethnic groups together as a front against the stronger Kikuyu and the Luo. KADU was fundamentally conservative and for a time aligned with Kenya's white settler population.[144] K'Oduol knew this. In addition to suggesting that Moi had lied about the students' situation in Cairo, K'Oduol therefore reproached him for his conservatism. He wondered whether Moi would be able to understand the plight of students desperate for scholarships, given "KADU's well known hatred for assistance from communist states."[145] Regionalist and geopolitical considerations merged in Moi's rebuke of the Cairo office. Since, according to K'Oduol, Moi was not in favor of the Soviet scholarship scheme in the first place, his aggravation with the office may have been rooted in ideological grievances, while Norman N. and Thomas G. viewed it through an ethnicized lens.

In a press statement entitled "Truth is Bitter and Hard to Swallow but Let it be Known: A Reply to Mr. arap Moi," however, Wera Ambitho, secretary of the Cairo office, criticized Moi on different grounds. Ambitho commented that he had visited Moi at the Nile Hilton and that the subject of students had never come up. Ambitho continued, claiming that Moi knew full well what was going on with the students who were stranded, since it was his party, KADU, who had provided them with passports to travel to Egypt. Twenty of them remained, waiting for their placements. This was not Odinga's fault, Ambitho maintained, but Moi's, and rooted in his party's regionalist platform. KADU had sent the students abroad without "even elementary verification about their prospective institutions of study" as a "political gimmick by a KADU cabinet to please the people of the Coast, Kibera, and some parts of Kenya."[146] Once again, it was ethnic—or more so regional—considerations that came to the fore, this time with the promise of scholarships for Kenyans from a specific area. Moreover, the back-and-forth accusations between Moi and Odinga's supporters demonstrate the intense jockeying for power that was occurring among the Kenyan political elite at this time.

Conclusion

The Kenyan case illustrates how geopolitical, ethnic, and regional considerations shaped student routes to the GDR and elsewhere. KADU's traditionalism made it at least somewhat hostile to socialism. Kenyatta never embraced socialism and it is debatable whether Odinga did, but global Cold War ideologies were employed to advance the agenda of specific individuals and political movements. Odinga and his allies accepted Soviet and Eastern Bloc support to move their own interests forward, and they accused Moi of thwarting what was best for Kenyans because of KADU's antipathy for socialism. When K'Oduol commented on KADU's "well known hatred . . . for communist states," he was drawing on the transnational rhetoric of the Cold War to challenge an opponent on a national, or even regional, level.

Local and global concerns also merged to impact Zambian travels. The lack of education in the country prior to independence compelled students to seek opportunities to attend school wherever they presented themselves, regardless of ideology or Cold War alignment. UNIP officials in Dar-es-Salaam worked tirelessly to find scholarships abroad for both men and women. In addition, the Zambians were caught in a web that connected them not only to the Americans, Soviets, and their allies, but to Africans in other countries and beyond. They had to navigate a diverse political and economic terrain in order to one day return home and fulfill national or local needs. Moreover, whether or not the American government truly was reluctant to provide Zambian students with scholarships out of fear it would upset Rhodesia's white settlers, as Kapwepwe maintained, it is clear that he and his colleagues were quite conversant with the racial politics of the United States and the barriers they presented. Overlapping contexts—local needs, Cold War divisions, inter-African relationships, heightening racism during the American civil rights movement—all played a role in where and when Zambians finally attended university.

In the history of student travels along the road, we can see how different considerations that echoed on local, regional, national, and transnational registers shaped the progression of this "following" as it crossed multiple borders. Once students had arrived at their last stop—in the GDR or elsewhere—they continued to be influenced by a blend of Cold War and national, particular politics. In the next chapter, we will see how similar political considerations played out in a very different context: that of Ghana, which became independent in 1957 and whose government forged an early educational agreement to send students to the GDR. Ghanaians first arrived in East Germany after independence, which meant that their story diverged from those of students who came during national struggles to decolonize.

Chapter 3

Getting In: From Ghana to the GDR, 1957–1966

In July 1965, I. R. O. Neequaye, Ghana's registrar of scholarships, wrote a rather mundane memo to the office in charge of administering the country's passports and exit permits. A new round of Ghanaian students was heading to Eastern Europe—including the GDR—and he wanted to "(get) their papers cleared in time to enable them to fly as early as possible."[1] The memo is unremarkable, except when the relative ease Ghanaians experienced receiving passports is compared to the arduous struggles detailed in the last chapter. Those journeys were taxing, to say the least. For students from newly independent, nonaligned and socialist-friendly countries, however, the process of procuring scholarships was more straightforward. From the late 1950s to the mid-1960s, this included the West African troika of Ghana, Guinea, and Mali, all of which were nonaligned and socialist-leaning. Later in the decade, Julius Nyerere's socialist Tanzania became more prominent. All four countries eventually cemented educational exchange agreements with the GDR. These agreements stipulated how many scholarships were on offer, and whether they were for university or vocational studies. Frequently, the agreements also included the majors that the students would take, which tended to be in technology or in the natural sciences.

Just because the process of arriving in the GDR was relatively easy for Ghanaians, Malians, Guineans, and Tanzanians, however, it could still be demanding—and in some instances tentative and provisional. Ghana, known as the Gold Coast when it was under British colonial rule, was the first sub-Saharan African nation to decolonize in 1957. Kwame Nkrumah, the country's first leader, was a staunch proponent of Pan-Africanism and the nonaligned movement. In addition, he espoused aspects of both Marxism and "traditional" African socialism. Nkrumaism, the ideology Nkrumah propounded and which guided Ghanaian development during his nine-year administration, drew on Marxist, Pan-Africanist, and Gandhian principles, and had the end goal of African unity.[2] Nonalignment, that is remaining above the bipolar divisions of the Cold War as a "third force" and working with those on either side of the divide, was also key.[3] It meant that from 1957 through Nkrumah's ouster in 1966, Ghana accepted scholarships for both university and vocational training from Soviet Bloc nations, including the GDR,[4] as well as from Western, capitalist states like the FRG.

Using Ghana as the primary example, in this chapter I will address the methods employed to choose students for scholarships abroad in the late 1950s and 1960s. I argue that political concerns in many nations across the African continent made student admissions uncertain, as relationships with the GDR and the rest of the Soviet Bloc were subject to political instability and rapid governmental change. This bolsters one of the central tenets of this book, that the students were both independent agents *and* subject to the ever evolving, ever-shifting, parameters of the Cold War and concomitant decolonial process.[5] In the case of Ghana, when the National Liberation Council (NLC) overthrew Nkrumah with assistance from the U.S. Central Intelligence Agency (CIA) in 1966,[6] it set off a chain of events that disrupted the lives of students intending to go to the GDR, as well as those who were already there.

Plainly, histories of decolonization, the Cold War, and postcolonial politics intersected and overlapped. The manner in which a nation decolonized, and the people who wound up in charge, originally determined student trajectories, but these could reverse rapidly as new governments rose and Cold War allegiances shifted.[7] The fragility of many new African democracies meant that student existence was often liminal. In addition, even within Nkrumah's government there was division over whether students should go to the GDR. Exactly why is unclear, but it probably had to do with three things: British influence even after decolonization, wariness of potential Marxist-Leninist indoctrination, and the need to accept development aid from both the GDR and substantially richer FRG. Ghana sent students to both countries during the Nkrumah era, when the Hallstein Doctrine was still very much in force.

We cannot, moreover, discount the significance of individual agency on the part of the students. While political changes at the top did impact students' fortunes, they were also very much in control of their own destinies. Students were not shy when complaining about their experiences in the GDR. They blamed both the Ghanaian and East German governments for failure to provide them with enough economic support and faulted the SED for its inability to control racism in the country.

Students still sometimes felt that they were subject to the whims of their government. Despite the educational agreements signed between Ghana and the GDR ensuring the students scholarships, the process of application, admission, and enrollment was often very haphazard, in ways that did sometimes mirror the experiences of the Kenyans and Zambians. This was true not only in terms of questions of economic support but in the amount of information provided to the students on what they would be learning. Indeed, many thought they were going to a university and instead found themselves as trainees in various industries.

Since there were few if any impediments to leaving the GDR or other Eastern European countries for the West, some students who were dissatisfied did so with little impunity. Racism did play a role in a few of the student departures, as we will see below, highlighting another theme of the book in showing that student experiences sometimes undermined East German antiracist dogma. On the flip side, there were also "defectors" who later crossed back over the border from the FRG to the GDR if what they found in the West was not to their liking. Movement, and the ability to traverse permeable Cold War boundaries, was again a crucial part of the African students' history and demonstrates that what was an iron curtain for some was easily lifted for others.

While the GDR was significant as a partner in educational exchange, it was also only one of many socialist and nonsocialist states offering scholarships. Again, students had little preference for where they traveled, and if they did it had little to do with ideology. A student named Aaron N., for instance, said he was applying for a scholarship to study medicine in the FRG, DDR, or "any other foreign government," and only mentioned the two Germanies because he already knew German and thought it might help his case.[8] In any event Ghanaians submitted only one application for study abroad, which was then considered for scholarships in one of several countries, including the GDR, FRG, USSR, Poland, Yugoslavia, Bulgaria, Romania, and Czechoslovakia. As we shall see, prominent members of the Ghanaian business and political communities chose where each student would study based on the fields available in various nations, and they gave little thought to where a student might land.

Admission and Rejection

The GDR first offered scholarships to Ghanaians a few months after the nation became independent. The SED acted quickly, just as it did with the Nigerians in the wake of the Enugu massacre. The details of these scholarships are sketchy, but they were extended to five Ghanaians who were already studying in England at the University of Hull. Although Ghana was no longer part of the British Empire, the British continued to exert considerable influence on Ghana's postcolonial government in this transitional period. According to a Hull student named Acquah, who claimed to have contacts with British and Ghanaian government officials, there were forces in his new government that would not look upon the East German scholarships favorably. Acquah said that he would speak about the scholarships personally with Ghana's minister of education and smooth the way for them to be accepted over any protests.[9]

Acquah was probably correct that scholarship offers from the GDR might not be entirely welcome in newly independent Ghana. His suspicion was indeed shared by another Ghanaian student, Mohamed R.. In November 1957, the nineteen-year-old student approached an East German named Kupferschmidt while the latter was on a trip in Egypt. Mohamed R., then a student at Cairo's Al-Azhar University, told Kupferschmidt that he wanted to continue his education in the GDR. Kupferschmidt replied that Mohamed R. could only do so if the Ghanaian government allowed it. Ghana had celebrated its independence earlier that year, on March 6. Still, Mohamed R. replied that his government would never grant such permission. He said that he planned to go anyway. Kupferschmidt referred Mohamed R. to the GDR's Trade Mission in Cairo, and the thread of his story ends there.[10]

Indications are that there were already discussions in Ghana about sending students to the GDR in 1957. These talks were, however, likely greeted with such prudence and skepticism that Mohamed R. thought his government would refuse to let him study in East Germany. This political ambivalence is testimony to the uncertain nature of Ghana's emerging position in the Cold War world. The new state needed to seek aid wherever it could be found and not upset any of its potential donors in the process. Wanting to be co-opted by neither West nor East, and recognizing the economic benefit of placating the FRG, the Nkrumah government had to be extremely cautious when considering scholarships from the GDR. This was also true for institutions such as Ghana's Trades Union Congress, which worked with international trade unions in broad networks of exchange and cooperation and did not limit itself by choosing sides.[11]

While waiting to see whether their official offer of scholarships would be accepted, the GDR sought other means of recruiting Ghanaian students. A man named Krause, who was the representative for East Germany's department of international organizations, met with Gerald O., a spokesperson for the Ghana Cocoa Marketing Board's (CMB) Scholars in Europe program, to discuss the prospect of expanding the program to the GDR. The CMB was a powerful organization that was founded during the late colonial era, in 1947, and regulated sales of cocoa,[12] Ghana's most significant crop. The CMB program was headquartered in Stuttgart, and Gerald O. was presumably looking to increase its presence in Europe and send students to different countries.[13] Krause's efforts with Gerald O. were likely in vain. It does not appear that any Ghanaians went to the GDR through the CMB.

By 1958, however, relations between the GDR and Ghana had warmed. The East German Ministry of Foreign Affairs (MfAA) formalized its plans to invite Ghanaian students in that year, with an agreement stipulating that the GDR would cover the costs of their tuition, room, and board.[14] It was the first such educational agreement that the government of postindependence Ghana would conclude with another country.[15] Once the government had decided in principle to take the scholarships, it originally wanted to accept only three or four of the fifty academic and vocational scholarships the GDR had allotted.[16] A flood of applications may have later compelled the Ghanaians to change their minds and take them all, though this is unclear.[17]

Concerns that the Ghanaians were indisposed toward sending students to the GDR continued, however. East German representatives at the Trade Mission in Accra considered it a triumph when they admitted the son of Ghana's minister of health, J. H. Allassani, to study television and film in Potsdam in 1959. Allassani wanted his son to become a cameraman and director for a fledgling Ghanaian television station and had been assured that East Germany had the technology to provide a top-flight education. Alfred Muhlmann, who worked at the Trade Mission, was optimistic that admitting Allassani's son would lead to the selection of further candidates for study in the GDR.[18] At the same time, when several Ghanaians in England allegedly gave up their jobs for scholarships in the GDR but received no confirmation on when they were to travel to Berlin, fear that the fragile relationship between the two countries might break increased.[19] Officials at the MfAA lamented that they were dealing with a very delicate matter, as there was still reluctance in Ghana about students going to the GDR.[20] If the Ghanaians heard that this group was in an indefinite holding pattern, so to speak, might they just decide not to send their students at all, especially when they had other options?

East German officials complained further that the Ghanaians did not fulfill their responsibility of sending the number of students stipulated in exchange agreements concluded with the GDR,[21] although Ghanaian sources contradict this, indicating that the positions were at least provisionally filled.[22] Nkrumah's commitment to nonalignment and working on both sides of the Cold War divide may, in any case, have continued to prompt his government to be vague about commitments made to socialist nations that had less development aid to offer than their capitalist counterparts.

British influence also contributed to Ghana's reluctance to fully embrace the GDR. The idea of scholarships for Ghanaians in the Soviet Bloc troubled the British, who wanted to keep their former colonies firmly in the U.S. fold. The Commonwealth Relations Office (CRO) was clearly worried about Ghana's relationship with East Germany. In 1959–1960, the CRO was closely following the activities of GDR representatives in Ghana and took careful note of the scholarships being offered in East German universities. In July 1960, a flurry of messages between Accra and London indicated that the British were anxious about Ghanaians traveling to East Germany. The British were especially alarmed that Gerhard Mehnert, a professor who was a member of the East German Academic Council for Asiatic and African studies, had visited Ghana and tried to convince the minister of education to accept all fifty GDR scholarships for 1960–1961.[23]

The U.S. Embassy in Accra also provided the British Embassy in Bonn with information about the upcoming visit of Z. B. Shardow, deputy organizer of the Ghana Young Pioneers (GYP), to the GDR.[24] The GYP was the youth arm of Nkrumah's CPP[25] and essentially equivalent to the FDJ. A confidential telegram from British officials in Ghana to the CRO followed the report about Shardow and mentioned that "[d]elegations from the Central Council of Free German Youth and the Union of Co-operative Societies have been visiting Ghana. They have been lavish with gifts, offers of scholarships, expressions of solidarity and invitations to visit East Germany."[26] The competition for African students was fierce, and covert data-gathering on the scholarships reflected continuing British—and American—fears that communist indoctrination in places like the GDR would swing some African and Asian states toward the Soviets. In this sense, British suspicions about what might happen to Ghanaians in East Germany were similar to those they had earlier harbored about Nigerians.

In the midst of this back-and-forth about how many East German scholarships to take, in 1959 the Ghanaian government created a Scholarships Secretariat in Accra. A scholarships registrar was then appointed to consider candidates for both vocational and university scholarships in the USSR, the GDR and the FRG, and several Soviet Bloc nations. At the same time, two selection boards to vet candidates were established, one in Accra and the other in London, to accommodate those Ghanaians living in the United Kingdom.[27] The boards were comprised of government and business officials, including a member of the CMB. Scholarship candidates came from various walks of life and ranged in age from thirteen to the thirties and even forties.[28] After the scholarships were advertised in various newspapers, such as the *Daily Graphic*,[29] applicants would submit their credentials and go to London or Accra for an interview. These credentials varied widely, but in 1959 the students usually needed to have at least a Middle School Certificate.[30]

One thing that students probably did *not* need was to come from a particular region or belong to a specific ethnic group. Evidence suggests that as opposed to Kenya, ethnic and regional favoritism was strenuously avoided. The issue of ethnicity in determining who should receive scholarships arose on several occasions in meetings of Ghana's National Assembly in the late 1950s. The discussions of scholarships in the assembly concerned secondary students and university applicants for institutions of higher education in Ghana and overseas, and reflected a strong bias against judging students by their ethnicity or place of residence. For instance, in October 1957 an MP named Edward Ago-Ackam asked the minister of education how many scholarships were allotted to students from the "greater Accra region," including "Ga, Shai, Great Ningo, Prampram and Kpone" for the year 1957–1958. Nkrumah answered him by saying, "The Government's policy is to award scholarships strictly on merit to Ghanaians, irrespective of their 'regional' origins," with the exception of one "scheme" that was reserved for northern Ghanaian students.[31]

On another occasion, in December 1958, MP J. P. Blay questioned how many scholarship holders identified as Nzima, an Akan-speaking group from southwestern Ghana, near the border with Côte d'Ivoire. Once again, Nkrumah maintained that "tribal" origin was never taken into account, because "as the Honourable (sic) Member knows it is not the policy of Government to perpetuate regional or tribal differences." He continued to say that there was "no record kept of the tribe or region of the scholarship winner."[32] The National Assembly, with Nkrumah at its head, hewed to Nkrumaist principles when selecting scholarship holders, emphasizing Pan-African unity over ethnic division.[33]

Despite continued reservations on the part of the Ghanaian government, interest in studying in the GDR or one of its allies continued to grow. In 1961, the GDR's Trade Mission in Accra reported that the Ghanaian government had already received an excess of applications for scholarships from socialist countries, well more than the number of scholarships available. For this reason, they had begun to restrict applications to students living in Ghana and to refuse Ghanaian applicants living overseas. The Scholarships Secretariat claimed to make this decision because experience had shown that students abroad were more likely to be "troublemakers," while those in Ghana were apt to be "grateful and well-behaved."[34] With surplus applications, Ghanaians in the United Kingdom and elsewhere in Europe were no longer eligible, and the Selection Board in London was probably dissolved.

All students had to apply directly to the Scholarships Secretariat if they wanted to study abroad. Not everyone saw the official scholarships announcements, however, and some turned to the GDR directly to inquire about educational opportunities. Ernest O., a nineteen-year-old student who was studying to be an electrician in Kumasi, was among them; he wrote to the East German Ministry of Foreign Affairs (MfAA) in June 1959. A friend had told him that the GDR was offering grants, so he turned to them with the request that he be able to complete his studies there and receive financial support. Ernest O. was poor and had no means of paying his way abroad. His parents had died in a car crash in 1953, when he was a schoolboy, and he maintained that "[y]ou would cry if I told you more about the sad, difficult life that I lead here in West Africa."[35] Another Ghanaian, Charlie A., wrote after visiting an East German traveling medical exhibition in Accra, saying he was impressed enough to want to study medicine at an East German university.[36]

Appeals like those of Ernest O. and Charlie A. were in vain; for the most part, the GDR would not consider candidates who did not first go through the Ghanaian government. Scholarships were not even necessarily reserved for members of prominent families. When Ago-Ackam asked whether special scholarships could be created for the descendants of Tetteh Quarshie, a farmer whom some recognize as having introduced the cocoa crop to Ghana,[37] he was rebuffed and told that while Quarshie's relatives could apply for scholarships available to other students, they could not have one solely for their family.[38] Nevertheless, despite protests to the contrary, nepotism could indeed play a role, as it did with the son of Health Minister Allassani. Moreover Atta Mensah, the general secretary for Ghana's National Council of Associations, asked that his brother George be allowed to study in the GDR. George was duly admitted.[39]

Such admissions were politically motivated but also occurred because wealthier students and students with connections could often pay for themselves and did not need to utilize scholarship funds. Samuel A., an employee in the Ministry of Works and Housing, wanted to go to the GDR in 1960 and "learn the German way of cattle breeding and milk production." He addressed his original request to the East German Department of Agriculture and Forestry in Potsdam and assured them that his family had agreed to pay for his expenses. Further, if he earned money working on a farm in the GDR, that would supplement his income. Since Samuel A. would not be taking a scholarship and met the minimum requirements for study, he was admitted for a training course.[40] Throughout the period spanning the 1950s to the 1970s, East German officials continued to insist that they would not accept students who were self-funding. Cases like Samuel A.'s, however, sometimes still occurred. The GDR denigrated students like the Nigerians for being "bourgeois" and not true members of the proletariat. Yet the East German government was very willing to take affluent students when it suited national needs and would offset the cost of paying for other scholarships. Policy implementation was thus uneven at best.

Unlike those who had connections or money, most candidates who saw the scholarships announcement and applied for a spot had to undergo an interview that tested for students' "mental alertness, aptitude, and suitability for the course they have chosen."[41] Once the interviews were complete, the selection boards would make their decisions based on a students' educational background and experience in a given field, as well as chosen field of study. In 1959, scientific, technical, and medical fields were the primary options—enrollment in these areas was a condition of the scholarships "scheme" under which candidates were considered—so that students who requested studying art, music, or drama were usually turned away. In general, the boards preferred any field that could contribute to national development. This meant that the terms scientific, technical, and medical were broadly interpreted, and vocational candidates in areas such as building, carpentry, surveying, automotive engineering, telecommunications, fire prevention, and electronics had an edge. So did those who worked on the technical side of media. For example, the boards recommended candidates who wanted to train as cameramen,[42] as well as someone in a field called "television operation."[43] In the intervening years, not much changed. In 1965, the year before the coup against Nkrumah, the Office of the Planning Commission requested that the Scholarships Secretariat draw up a report detailing which fields should be given highest priority when considering candidates, and with the exceptions of actuarial studies and accountancy, all were scientific and technical.[44]

Once students arrived in the GDR, many seemed uninterested in what they had come to East Germany to study. This was especially the case among those designated for vocational training. In 1961, an MfAA official named Hasler indicated that many of the Ghanaians were under the false impression that they would be attending university; instead they found themselves either at technical schools or in positions as trainees for various industries.[45] Hasler said that the GDR was happy to accommodate some of the disappointed students and recommended that several be given scholarships to study engineering at universities. Not all could be reassigned, though, and many remained discontented with their lot.[46]

Student frustration demonstrates that they must have had significant tension with the members of the selection committees that chose them for scholarships. The businessmen and bureaucrats who sat on the selection boards were concerned with having Ghanaians trained in areas that would suit the needs of the state, not ones that would satisfy personal interests. There was a clear lack of communication between the two sides. When choosing students for scholarships, the boards relied mainly on academic qualifications and paid no attention to individual requests. Even after scholarship decisions were announced, many students had little idea about what sort of education they would get in the GDR.

We Have Some Problems in the East: Racism, Political Tension, and Economic Insecurity

Circumstances that had little to do with academics were sometimes key to the success of scholarship applicants. For instance, in 1959 the Selection Board in London urged that an auto mechanic named Daniel Y. receive a scholarship even though he lacked the required Middle School Certificate. Its members argued that Daniel Y. had adequate training in his field, but more importantly that he "(had been) in the army during the war and holds an excellent discharge."[47] Although Daniel Y. ultimately did not get the scholarship, his status as a veteran obviously held weight.

Meanwhile, Emmanuel K. fell out of consideration in the 1959 selection round for reasons that were potentially related to racial and gender bias. He was married to an English woman from London and had two children with her. According to the board, this would make it "difficult for him to undertake training in Germany," though its assessment gave no indication of why this conclusion was reached.[48] Would Emmanuel K. be unable to bring his wife, a British national, or their children? Did members of the board worry about the reception of a mixed-race family in the GDR? While many Afro-German children would be born in East Germany over the course of its existence, in 1959 there were likely only a few,[49] and thus not much information available on how Blacks were integrated in the GDR. Further, as I will address in detail in chapter 5, the GDR frowned on international students bringing their spouses and children with them to East Germany.[50] The Ghanaian records may be silent on exactly why Emmanuel K.'s family made him an unsuitable candidate for study in the GDR, but it is obvious that their existence was germane to the selection process.

Questions of race and racism in Eastern Europe and its impact on the scholarships emerged in various ways. In 1963, S. W. Kumah, the Ghanaian ambassador to Yugoslavia, wrote a memo entitled "The Future of African Students in Eastern European Socialist Countries."[51] Kumah's memo, which I briefly mentioned in this book's introduction, was composed in response to a series of hostile, racist attacks on African students in Bulgaria that ultimately led to their leaving the country.[52] He began by attributing the violence less to racial bias than to economic and political factors. He claimed that attempts at "communist indoctrination" among the African student population, combined with resentment on the part of Eastern Europeans at the "very generous nature of the scholarships," were the main reasons for the conflict.[53] As the memo continued, though, Kumah obliquely started addressing the role of race. He criticized the Ghanaian government's practice of sending the students abroad "shabbily clothed" and letting their hosts buy what they needed after arrival. According to Kumah, this habit enhanced "the degradation of the Black man whose prestige in Europe is already very low."[54] He went on to suggest that the Scholarships Secretariat needed to keep more in touch with Ghanaians in Eastern Europe in order to understand the specific hardships they faced.[55]

Kumah's own experience was with Yugoslavia, where he said that people approached Africans to call them "monkeys" or "(men) with tails," and asked if they ran around naked in the jungle when they were at home. He saw the issue resting not in the sincerity of Eastern European governmental commitment to antiracism but in local resentment of the Africans' government stipends and police failure to do anything about racist remarks or attacks. For Kumah, the problem was not only one of Yugoslavia and Bulgaria but an issue that extended across the Soviet Bloc—and it was getting worse.[56]

While Kumah did not mention the GDR, this sort of racism certainly existed. The persistence and strength of racism in East Germany, despite denials from the SED, is a theme that echoes throughout this book. In the Ghanaian case, there were early complaints of racist treatment. The Committee of African and Asian Students in Leipzig lodged an official complaint with the East German Ministry of Foreign Affairs in June 1961 after an especially disturbing incident involving two Ghanaian industrial trainees. A car had come to pick them up and take them to their place of work, where German colleagues rubbed cream on their heads. The cream was some sort of depilatory and removed all of their hair, so that

> the men were completely bald. The Ghanaians went to a doctor who prescribed a salve, and they were each given 10 DM to compensate for their lost hair. The Committee was outraged and wrote that "We were invited here to study, not to be exploited and abused by German fascists and mili-

tarists . . . this kind of racism should be immediately purged from (any) socialist country."

Ideology factored here as well; the Committee believed that they should not have to be treated like "apes, dogs, and mice," just to receive goods in their home countries, and hinted that there was a capitalist element behind the GDR's socialist veneer that drove not only racism, but also the very relationships that the SED had with non-western nations. The committee ended its complaint by saying that it would report the episode to politicians and newspapers abroad, including those in Ghana.[57]

Hidden or suppressed capitalism was not the only political dynamic prompting racist behavior. To Kumah, the Ghanaian ambassador in Belgrade, the minimal status that Africans held in Europe was also closely bound up with the issue of Marxist-Leninist indoctrination. He explained the problem as one emanating from the most radical and "zealous" Marxists among the "indigenous"—used here to describe Eastern European students, perhaps an intentional inversion of the common Western practice of labeling Africans as such. The "indigenous" leaders of communist student organizations would greet new arrivals with an excess of kindness, which often puzzled African students. This kindness was intentional, probably fake, and meant to encourage the students to join an international student club, which naturally fell under the purview of the communist student organization. Most exchange students had little interest in this club and came to see the forcefulness of their Eastern European hosts as "a sign of underrating their intelligence and maturity."[58] The ideological fervor was itself interpreted as racist, inasmuch as Europeans appeared to believe that Africans would not understand Marxism on their own. It had the further deleterious effect of distracting the students from the lessons of their own, African brand of socialism—Nkrumaism—which was what they would experience after returning to Ghana.[59]

In addition, Kumah linked the attempt to control the African students' organization in Bulgaria to the racist violence in that country, as well as to the Africans exiting Bulgaria en masse. He claimed that Bulgarian students had tried to prevent Africans from forming their own groups, and they had gone to the authorities to report that African political motives were suspect. Consequently, the Bulgarian government stepped in and the tumult began. Kumah applauded the students for holding firm to the conviction that their treatment was unjust, and for their exodus from Bulgaria. He explained that there was a "trend among African students towards Unity (*sic*) in those parts of Europe," which was "growing stronger from day to day," and that "any attempt to stop (it) (would) only lead to serious explosions."[60] Kumah's words echoed Nkrumah's Pan-Africanist conviction that African unity was a major political, economic, and social goal for the postcolonial world, as well as a means for introducing cohesion and community to Africans living in Europe.

Nkrumaism and Pan-Africanism were also considered important for African student unity elsewhere in Eastern Europe. In 1962, E. Ako Nai, the Ghanaian ambassador to Poland, visited Lodz to meet the eleven Ghanaians studying there. He found that there were eighty African students overall studying Polish in Lodz, with approximately forty different "nationalities" among them. He invited all of them to an open conversation at his hotel, and about fifty attended the event. They were delighted at the opportunity, since it was the first time they were able to gather as part of their newly established African Union and as what they called "a body of the same blood" or "one body of the same stock irrespective of their nationality." The students in Lodz emphasized the significance of cooperation among Africans across borders for achieving the goal of African unity, which was their "ultimate aim." They also considered Pan-African unity key to demonstrating their worth to the white, Polish population.[61] Pan-Africanism was thus a central organizing principle not only in Africa itself but for those Africans living abroad, linking Ghanaians in a state like Poland to other Africans, regardless of national origin.

Socialist states such as the GDR viewed Pan-Africanism warily, since it was a force that they could neither manage nor mold. First, tensions grew between the SED and FDJ on one side and the African students on the other, as the latter formed their own student groups with political positions contrary to the East German party line, as I will discuss more in the next chapter. Second, as Slobodian has commented, the GDR was hostile to Pan-Africanism for precisely the reason Kumah noted, because it was a power that they could not direct.[62] There was similar antipathy toward Nkrumaism, which an FDJ report contemptuously described as "an ideological mishmash of Marxist-Leninist theses, Christian dogma, and primitive African communism . . . linked to a cult of personality that compares Nkrumah to God."[63] This out-of-hand dismissal of an African ideology as confused and unsophisticated was yet another manifestation of the racism that underlay the SED's assertions that the GDR was an antiracist, anti-imperial state. Any form of socialism that was not "pure" Marxism-Leninism was suspicious and thus inferior.

At the same time, the Kwame Nkrumah Ideological Institute (KNII), which Nkrumah had inaugurated in 1961 in Winneba, arranged for several students and faculty to study in the GDR, as well as in the USSR and Poland. This

Figure 9. Dr. J. K. Nsarkoh, who worked at the KNII, also received a degree in law from the GDR; he is seen here defending his dissertation, "Local Organs of State Power in Ghana." Also pictured is Miss Middell, reader in English. Zentralbild hochschulbildstelle Leipzig, February 24, 1964 (Bundesarchiv).

included J. K. Nsarkoh, who worked at the KNII and received a law degree from the KMU in Leipzig in 1964.

As Matteo Grilli has shown, Nkrumah believed that the Institute would become a vital force for African nationalism in Ghana and beyond. It would promote Nkrumaism throughout the continent, emphasizing the significance of Pan-Africanism and African unity to the struggle, decolonization, and the postcolonial era.[64] The Institute planned to send advanced students to the GDR and other socialist states, where they were to concentrate in fields such as political science, philosophy, economics, and history.[65]

The courses that the students took in the Soviet Bloc would ostensibly have a Marxist-Leninist framework, which often clashed with Nkrumaism. Yet there were aspects of Marxism-Leninism that Nkrumah and his followers clearly wanted to incorporate into their political system. Ghanaian officials believed, for instance, that there were lessons to be learned from the GDR's implementation of structures such as a planned economy. In 1961, members of Nkrumah's Convention People's Party (CPP) met with representatives from the Deutsche Notenbank, the central bank of the GDR, to discuss the possibility of bringing students to East Germany for a course in socialist banking. Kwasi Akwei, speaking for the CPP, commented that since "Ghana was developing towards the goal of becoming a socialist state . . . it is important . . . to have cadres who are not only conversant with the banking principles of debit and credit, but who have studied the socialist banking system (planning, the fundamentals of socialist credit, questions on the issuance of securities) in socialist nations, and at the same time become knowledgeable in the different stages of socialism."[66] The idea, according to Akwei, was to restructure the bank on a fundamental, ideological level.[67] Further, even though Nkrumaism diverged from Marxism-Leninism, it was unlikely to faze Ghanaians from the Institute, who were advanced scholars. They were primarily members of the CPP, had strong backgrounds in Nkrumaism, and were prepared to confront ideological difference.[68] In other words, they were well-equipped to merge the lessons they had learned at the KNII with Marxist-Leninist principles.

The students from the KNII were to be well-supported through Ghana government subsidies.[69] Other students were not so fortunate, and many met with economic uncertainty. Technically, per the educational agreement with Ghana, the GDR was supposed to provide the students with food, housing, and tuition, though not necessarily money for travel.[70] But the stipend that some students received from the GDR could be insufficient or not provide for all the students' needs. In 1960, for example, two Ghanaian vocational trainees wrote a memo entitled, "For and on behalf of the Scholarship Holders in the GDR." The memo noted that they had paid their own way to Thüringen. After arrival, it became clear that they would be unable to remit money back home to their families as they had hoped. Not wanting to leave their relatives in dire financial straits, they requested that the families of all Ghanaian students in the GDR receive an allowance to help support them until the students came home.[71] The East German Ministry of Foreign Affairs did look into getting more support for the students, possibly through the Deutsche Notenbank, but it is unclear whether anything came of this.[72]

There was generally confusion over who was paying for what in these early years, reflecting a haphazard, incomplete understanding of what was included in the German-Ghanaian educational agreement. Günter Fritsch, in 1960 the primary East German trade representative in Ghana–[73] the equivalent of ambassador—commented that students who had received scholarships to study in the GDR were coming by his office every day, asking questions about how they were going to pay for their travel to the GDR and back.[74] Furthermore, there were two students who came to Fritsch to say they were unable to raise the funds to go, and he immediately informed the Ministry that it needed to pay for their tickets.[75] Yet it was apparent that not everyone on either the Ghanaian or East German side knew whether travel was indeed funded.

The pressures students faced were substantial—from racial slurs, to attempted indoctrination, to late or nonexistent stipends. It is thus not surprising that some, fed up with their lives in the GDR, "defected" to the West. For many, issues with ideology were key. Yet the students who left were not necessarily Nkrumaists. Instead they were disenchanted with both Nkrumaism and Marxism-Leninism. George Sapara-Arthur entered the GDR in 1960, where he received technical training in Schwerin and worked at the Schwarze Pumpe power station in Spremberg. He left one year later for the London Polytechnic University.[76] From London, Sapara-Arthur gave withering interviews that depicted the GDR and USSR unfavorably to the Western press, including the West German newspaper *Die Welt*. According to Sapara-Arthur, African students throughout the Eastern Bloc were unhappy, since unless they were communists they were poorly treated.

The GDR dismissed Sapara-Arthur's report, claiming it was full of lies. In his interviews, Sapara-Arthur said he had been a student at the KMU, when he had really been an apprentice in the building industry. There was undeniable concern that Sapara-Arthur would threaten the GDR's anti-imperialist image with the Ghanaian government, as an agitated letter from the GDR's Department of Vocational Training to the Office of the High Commissioner for Ghana in London attests.[77] They were probably right to be concerned; *Windward Islands' Opinion*, a paper published in the Netherlands Antilles, picked up Sapara-Arthur's story from the *Daily Telegraph*, meaning that the news had traveled a long way. The piece in the *Windward Islands' Opinion* said Sapara-Arthur held that "African students were expected to attend lectures and films with 'anti imperialist (sic)' and anti-Western slants and they were expected to give up their week-end (sic) to attend 'voluntary' study groups."[78] Like the Nigerian Aderogba Ajao, Sapara-Arthur broadcast unseemly images of the GDR that were, in their way, very small salvos in the Cold War.

Sapara-Arthur may well have been lying about some things in his interview with *Die Welt*. Evidence from Ghana and Germany affirm that he was indeed an apprentice builder, not a student at the KMU—where he tried to get admitted but was continually rebuffed.[79] He also wrote to the Scholarships Secretariat back home in Accra to ask whether he could transfer to a school in

West Germany, indicating further displeasure.[80] Sapara-Arthur's conversation with Western reporters tells us that he saw more opportunity and options for study in the West. Sapara-Arthur also indicated another cause of African discontent when he mentioned the treatment of noncommunist students in the USSR, and said that only the communists were "happy." For while overt racism was critical to the disillusionment of African students in the GDR, another kind of prejudice also existed: the bias against "capitalist" students.

Sapara-Arthur was not the only Ghanaian dismayed with East German politics. In February 1963, twelve Ghanaians reportedly left their universities in Rostock and Leipzig for the FRG.[81] A letter from the East German Ministry of Foreign Affairs commented that, "According to the Ministry for Higher and Technical Education, their exodus is in part related to their opinion of current Ghanaian development, since not all of (them) approve of the path that President Nkrumah is forging, and feel that they will be more secure studying in West Germany." Like Sapara-Arthur, two of the "defectors" had spoken with the West German press and taken the further step of appearing on television to condemn the GDR.[82] Socialist politics—whether Ghanaian or East German, despite the differences between the two—were at the root of the students' displeasure. Their frustration with the GDR may have also mirrored that of the Ghanaian politicians who were reluctant to accept the East German scholarships in the first place.

Ideology was, of course, not the only reason students left. As usual, the causes were more complex and multifaceted. The group from Rostock claimed dissatisfaction with the local food and referenced skirmishes with Rostock natives. Rumors had also circulated that the Ghanaian government had provided extra money for their stipends, and the students believed the GDR had withheld it from them.[83] Jeffrey B., a student from Kumasi who attended the TU-Dresden in the early to mid-1960s, had yet another rationale for wanting to leave. He was a religious Catholic and used to attending church every Sunday. He could not do so in the GDR. In addition, he fell ill and seemed generally miserable with his lot; records suggest that he dropped out of school and relocated to West Berlin.[84] Political pressure and racism were thus only two possible factors driving Ghanaians away; more subtle problems, including cultural and religious differences, could also have compelled their departure.

While Sapara-Arthur, Jeffrey B., and the others left East Germany several years before Nkrumah's ouster, their exit demonstrates, on a micro level, how Cold War ideology could impact student pathways. When they left Ghana for the GDR or other socialist countries, they had little choice about where they were going. The lack of any agreement concerning their mobility, however, opened up multiple options once they were abroad. If they were unhappy in the GDR because they disagreed with its politics, or with Nkrumah's—or for any other reason, for that matter—they were free to leave. Once the students exited Ghana, the world was open to them, provided they could figure out how to fund their travels.

Another Option: Staying Home

Despite issues of racism, political pressure, and economic insecurity, no one ever suggested that Ghana should withdraw from its educational agreement with the GDR or other socialist nations before the coup in 1966. Still, while scholarships from the GDR and elsewhere in Eastern Europe came to be accepted, the government clearly considered them a second choice to study in Ghana itself. There were many highly educated young Ghanaians all over the world, but Ghana reserved the best for its own growing universities.

Ghana had a long history of robust Western education at the primary and secondary levels. Basel and Wesleyan missionaries set up dozens of secondary schools in the region during the nineteenth century.[85] Interest in establishing European-style universities in British West Africa emerged in the same period. Between 1924 and 1927 the British built and opened Achimota College, a coeducational secondary school that would later form the kernel of the University of Ghana. The University College of the Gold Coast finally came into existence in 1948.[86] It was transformed into the University of Ghana in 1961.[87] Colleges in Kumasi and Cape Coast also gained university status in the early 1960s.[88]

National education was key for Nkrumah and his supporters. They were dedicated to expanding access to primary, secondary, and ultimately higher education in Ghana.[89] Kojo Botsio, in 1961 Ghana's minister of agriculture and chairman of a commission on university education, made this plain when he said, "It is not realised (sic), outside Ghana, how much university education means to us in this country. Of all our national investments, education is one of the most crucial and the pace of our educational progress is the pace of our national development."[90] This emphasis on the university was also imbricated with Nkrumah's Pan-Africanism. He hoped to make national universities hubs of Pan-Africanist knowledge through, for instance, the establishment of an Institute of African Studies at the University of Ghana or the KNII in Winneba. As Jean Allman has pointed out in the case of the Institute of African Studies, Nkrumah was interested in creating an Afrocentric discipline that broke through colonialist models and emphasized African unity.[91] Nkrumah's CPP government conceptualized the university as a draw for students from throughout the continent; while the Ghanaians were accepting scholarships for study abroad, they were also developing schemes for students from other parts of Africa, such as Zambia.[92] Nkrumah and his colleagues believed it was their mission to provide education for the entire continent, and to make up for the dreadful, demeaning nature of colonial schooling.[93] It was natural, then, that Nkrumah would want to keep the top Ghanaian students at home, where he hoped that they would come to embody his Pan-Africanist vision and contribute to the country's development at the same time.

Ghana's push for development thus included sending students abroad for university while at the same time strengthening tertiary options inside the country and making them more valuable. In 1957 and 1958, immediately following independence, there were approximately three times more scholarships available for tertiary studies in Ghana than there were for study abroad.[94] Further, those who had already been admitted to a Ghanaian university or other institution of higher education were barred from applying for overseas scholarships.[95] Thus in 1963, when the USSR offered Ghana 150 medical scholarships, the Selection Board only filled forty-one, owing to a weak scientific background among those applying.[96] Those with stronger profiles had likely already been matched with a Ghanaian university and were unable to apply, leaving mainly less suitable students. Indeed, a report on overseas scholarships from 1965 confirms that the best students were being reserved for Ghanaian universities. The report states that the students under consideration for foreign awards were all individuals who had graduated with a Higher School Certificate a year or two before and were not attending local universities. None of the students graduating in 1965 were slated for scholarships outside of Ghana; instead all "except for the failures" would be enrolled in Ghanaian schools.[97]

The desire to promote higher education in Ghana did not necessarily conflict with the interest in sending students abroad for college. In 1961, an act of Parliament created the Ghana Institute of Languages, which offered courses in not only several African languages but in German, Russian, English, French, Spanish, Portuguese, Chinese, and Arabic. Kersuze Simeon-Jones has characterized the Institute as a Pan-Africanist project, inasmuch as the languages offered were meant to facilitate communication primarily among Africans with different native and national languages.[98] Making Pan-African connections was indeed the primary function of the Institute, but it was also concerned with cultivating links outside the continent.[99] Students bound for either the GDR or the FRG studied German at the Institute before leaving precisely to prepare them for what lay ahead. For instance, Edwin P. was offered a scholarship to study agriculture in the GDR for 1966–1967. In a letter addressing how the coup had upended his plans, he mentioned that he had already been taking German at the Institute for several months.[100] Higher education in general was perceived as a Pan-Africanist project, as those who went abroad could both contribute to Ghanaian development and strengthen Ghana's ties to their host countries.

Scholarships Lost: The NLC and Political Reversal in Ghana

The Scholarships Secretariat continued to function as a clearinghouse for Ghanaian students going to Eastern Europe until February 24, 1966, when the NLC overthrew Nkrumah while he was abroad. Thereafter the NLC suspended scholarships to both the Soviet Union and the GDR, and it put other scholarship offers from Eastern European nations under review. In principle, the department of education would now favor scholarships from Western countries over those from Eastern ones, ostensibly because of linguistic considerations,[101] but probably also for political reasons; the United States had been involved in the NLC's takeover and Ghana's realignment toward the West.[102]

This reversal was extremely challenging to those students who had already been selected to study in the GDR for 1966–1967. Deadlines for applying to Ghanaian universities had mostly passed, and the students were "stranded" at home. The Scholarships Secretariat sent several letters to the University of Cape Coast on behalf of affected students, explaining their unfortunate situation and asking that they be granted late admission.[103] When the students could not get into a Ghanaian university, the Scholarships Secretariat tried to find them work, writing letters on their behalf to various organizations, but mostly in vain. The Volta River Authority sympathized with Jack D., who asked to work for them because he could not take his scholarship, but had no job for him;[104] the Modern Ghana Builders Ltd. had similarly negative news for Edgar A., another displaced scholarship holder.[105] Even when the students got interviews for jobs, the jobs themselves were not always ideal. The Ghana Broadcasting Station interviewed a few of the abandoned students, including Edwin P., for positions with the organization. The only available posts were clerical and in remote locations, however, and he refused to accept employment that he considered below his educational level.[106]

Paul O., another stranded student, even wrote an impassioned plea concerning the direness of his situation to Major General J. A. Ankrah, chairman of the NLC. He asked whether the NLC believed that he and the other scholarship holders were acolytes of Nkrumah's, and as such in a position to "further (his) Eastern ideology." Paul O. assured the NLC that if its members believed this, they were wrong. He and the others could "humbly (declare) that we have not the least interest in the false political ideology and godless atheism of Kwame Nkrumah." Indeed, they welcomed the change in government, which Paul O. claimed had ushered in intellectual and academic freedom.[107] Yet his appeal fell on deaf years. The NLC did not secure Paul O. the admission to a Ghanaian university that he desired.[108] However, his letter provides more evidence that many students had few political allegiances and were above all interested in education, not a specific ideology.

In addition to rescinding the scholarships for students planning to go to the GDR, the NLC demanded that those who were already in East Germany depart immediately for the FRG.[109] The Union der Afrikanischen Studenten und Arbeiter in der DDR (UASA)—the Union of African Students and Workers in the GDR, an organization that we will learn more about in the next chapter—wrote a letter to Nkrumah at the time, expressing their support for him and condemning the NLC's order for the Ghanaians to leave.[110] Even so, at least some of the Ghanaian students followed the NLC's instructions and ended up in a camp in Wickrath, near Mönchengladbach. The camp had existed as a haven for students fleeing the East from around 1963.[111] Students received two-month stipends from the Ghanaian Embassy upon arrival and were supposed to wait briefly in Wickrath before being reassigned to universities and technical schools in West Germany.[112]

It seems that many were unhappy in Wickrath and frustrated by how long it was taking to get their reassignments. News of this frustration is why, several months after the coup in July 1966, the Stasi approached a Ghanaian medical student whom they gave the code name "Ali" to ask him about working for them as an IM. The Stasi hoped to gauge whether there was interest among the departed Ghanaian students in returning to the East. At first the Stasi had qualms about taking Ali on, since they considered him "bourgeois" because he was reluctant to discuss anti-imperialism.[113] Yet the relationship continued, as a Stasi official named Seiler met with him several times to discuss Nkrumah's overthrow and how the GDR had sided with Nkrumah against the NLC. Seiler spoke about how important it was not only to bring wayward students back but also to root out any students still in the GDR who might have anti-Nkrumah or antisocialist leanings. For his part, Ali talked about how, while he was pro-Nkrumah, he did not want to turn any "African brothers" over to the Stasi and was thus unenthusiastic about continuing collaboration.[114]

The Stasi, however, was able to blackmail Ali into carrying on his work as an IM. When he first met Seiler in the summer of 1966, he had very poor grades and was close to failing out of school. Collaboration with the Stasi was appealing, because it would allow him stay in the GDR and complete his studies regardless of performance. He therefore traveled to Wickrath from August 24 to September 2, perhaps on the pretense that he was following the dictum of the NLC and defecting to the West, as he picked up his two-month stipend from the Ghanaian Embassy while visiting Bonn.[115] When he returned, he told Seiler that approximately 80 percent of the students in Wickrath wanted to return to the GDR but were unsure of whether they would be allowed back. Yet Seiler's report presents a more complicated picture. There were definitely some miserable students. Ali alleged that one was so downcast that he attempted suicide by throwing himself out a window, injuring his spine in the process. Another student, however, told Ali that he had returned to Potsdam for three days but had been arrested during his stay. Soured on the GDR, he went back to Wickrath. He was not the only one who was disappointed with East Germany. Another student in Wickrath left to return to Ghana, where he gave glowing reports of West Germany but entirely dismissed his years in the East.[116]

Some students did filter back into the GDR after the coup to resume their prior studies. Yet officially Ghana sent no more students to East Germany until 1973, when relations were normalized with official global recognition of the GDR, which was then able to open an embassy to replace its trade mission in Accra.[117] In 1972, Ghana also experienced another coup, which brought down its Second Republic. Communications with the GDR were therefore reestablished under the military regime of General I. K. Acheampong and his National Redemption Council (NRC). The two governments reinstituted an exchange agreement, but the number of students admitted from Ghana was far lower than it had been during the Nkrumah years. Under Nkrumah, at least fifty spots were reserved for Ghanaian students and trainees each year; in 1973, only six or seven Ghanaians were able to come to the GDR.[118] Further, the agreement now required them to undergo extensive medical testing in Ghana before they could enter East Germany.[119]

Conclusion

In November 1968, there was a coup in Mali, another important partner of the GDR that had sent many students to East Germany. The coup removed Modibo Keita, a nonaligned socialist with close ties to the Soviet Bloc, and installed military leader Moussa Traoré as the country's new head of state. This was concerning enough to the SED that in mid-1969 they had a Stasi agent named

Schmidt make contact with Mali's primary student representative, who was given the code name "Präsident." He studied at the Institut für Mikrobiologie in Leipzig. Schmidt probed Präsident about the putsch and about the continuing prospects for socialism in Mali. Over the course of several meetings, Präsident expressed his own commitment to socialism and said he believed that Mali's new government would continue the country's socialist policies. He assured Schmidt that there was already a kind of *Urkommunismus* in Mali and its people were "born socialists."[120] At the same time, Präsident casually remarked that Traoré's government would probably be closer with the West—especially France—than Keita's had been, given that neither the USSR nor the GDR were in a position to provide as much aid.[121]

The attempt to establish communication with Präsident was intertwined with the fear that Mali would curtail or end its student exchange program with the GDR, as Ghana had essentially done. This did not happen. The Traoré government pursued socialist policies similar to Keita's through 1981,[122] and Mali's relationship with the GDR endured. Yet the experience with Ghana was proof of how much political shifts in postcolonial Africa could lead to profound reorganizations of Cold War geography and upend plans for education. Individual lives and fates hung in the balance as postcolonial governments rose and fell. The GDR's attempts to influence emergent states with their scholarships depended on the political inclinations of their leaders, and the extent to which they accepted socialism, whether of the Marxist-Leninist variety or otherwise. With each Cold War rupture, students already abroad or waiting to depart saw their fortunes change, as they moved westward to obey the dictates of a new regime or saw their opportunities for higher education melt away as it rose. Yet the students were also independent agents, who could forge their own paths across Cold War boundaries for reasons of ideology or social mobility. As we shall see in the next chapter, the students also challenged both the GDR and their home governments through political participation and protest that caught the leaders unaware.

CHAPTER 4

The Politics of Home Abroad: African Student Organizations in the GDR, 1962–1971

While they were in the GDR, many African students joined Nationale Hochschulgruppen (NHG) at their specific universities.[1] The NHG were organizations that represented students from specific countries. For the SED and FDJ, the latter of which originally established and oversaw the NHG, the main function of the clubs was to organize annual independence day festivities for the nations they represented.[2] NHG celebrations typically involved speeches on the evils of imperialism along with "traditional" dances or other performances from the country in question. They were well attended, with invitees including not only members of the club throwing the party but other exchange students, SED members, and FDJ representatives. The national clubs were complemented by an overarching organization representing all Africans in the GDR, whether or not they were students: the Union der Afrikanischen Studenten und Arbeiter in der DDR (UASA) (Union of African Students and Workers in the GDR). The UASA was theoretically where Africans could turn for assistance in all manner of situations, including affairs related to housing, acculturation to the GDR, and interactions with East German universities.

When the authorities did think of the NHG or other student organizations in political terms, they saw them first as rubber-stamps for GDR, and hence Soviet, viewpoints, and second as forums in which to inculcate Marxism-Leninism. Independence day speeches held at NHG celebrations addressed issues such as the ongoing struggle against the racist Ian Smith regime in Rhodesia, which reinforced the GDR's commitment to antiracism and anti-imperialism.[3] The FDJ was likewise hopeful that mentors assigned to the different African student associations would help promote discussion and acceptance of socialism.

Very quickly, though, the NHG took on a function that was both alarming and highly distasteful to the SED and FDJ alike: the NHG became sites of dis-

Figure 10. "On March 6, 1961, Ghanaian students and Ghanaian guests at the spring trade fair mark the fourth anniversary of their independence with a dignified ceremony. The leader of the delegation from Ghana, Minister of Agriculture Kojo Botsio, called on the students to use their East German socialist education wisely. 'Our future, the future of the entire world, lies in socialism.'" Native music played in the background." (caption text from Bundesarchiv). The emphasis on socialism in the speech and the Ghanaian music being played were typical of such national independence celebrations, which were normally sponsored by NHG. Brüggman, Eva (photographer)(Bundesarchiv)

sent, often at discrete moments when crises emerged in specific African nations, or during general power struggles inside these same countries. African students were emboldened to speak out—or even gather together to protest—in these instances. Student groups assumed concrete stances with regards to politics at home, especially in emergency situations. Protests also took place on an individual level, as they did for Angolan students that Schenck has addressed elsewhere, and the ability to use one's position as an invited guest to subvert authority was immensely powerful.[4]

Figure 11. A student from Ghana greets Ruth Botsio, wife of Kojo Botsio, Ghanain Minister of Agriculture, at the celebration of Ghana's Independence Day in 1961. (Bundesarchiv).

What the NHG allowed, though, was for select groups of students—usually, if not always, conationals—to come together and amplify their respective voices. Their political involvement—and its positioning within the intersecting contexts of the Cold War and decolonization—reinforce arguments about the significance of regional struggles to the broader Cold War, as well as to the Cold War as a multipolar, not a bipolar, conflict. The GDR took political positions toward events unfurling in decolonizing Africa based on the stance of the Soviet Bloc, and this influenced their treatment of student protesters. East Germany did not assume policies of neutrality in African nations but rather considered conflicts in various African states as central to their own interests, both in terms of relationships with the Eastern Bloc and with the African countries involved.

Africans often had more opportunity to make public grievances than East

Germans themselves, for whom the threat of punishment was generally much greater. This was, simply, because the GDR needed African students, both to help it combat the Hallstein Doctrine and to reinforce ties between their parent countries and the USSR. This meant that there was a strong incentive to keep African students in the GDR despite their political activity. The potential for retribution against protesters was thus dependent more on the judgment of the African state whose students were in the GDR than it was on the GDR itself. As long as students remained abroad, however, it was also difficult for their governments to enforce any kind of discipline without the cooperation of the GDR.

There were many occasions for African students to express their displeasure with political developments at home. In early 1962, Guinean students in the GDR joined with other Guineans across Europe to protest President Sekou Touré's harsh crackdown on striking teachers. At around the same time, there were early signs of discontent among students from eastern Nigeria, those who would eventually support the breakaway region of Biafra during its war with the federal government from 1967–1970. The officially sanctioned Nigerian NHG ultimately fractured, creating an expressly Biafran club that the SED scrambled to dismantle. Meanwhile, the Kenyan Student Club also divided along political and ethnic lines, with a new group emerging to challenge the organization that the FDJ sponsored. Malians protested changes in their government in 1971, and other cases of disgruntlement arose later in the decade. While these events all occurred between 1962 and 1971—explaining the chronology of this chapter—they thus were not the last such protests, as cases from both The Republic of Congo and South Africa in the later 1970s show.[5]

The SED attempted to squelch any protests that conflicted with their own policies. Slobodian has addressed international student protest in the FRG, arguing that foreign students galvanized their West German classmates into political action around events such as the assassination of Congolese leader Patrice Lumumba in 1961. In the FRG, such protests often took on a sense of opposition not only to unjust colonial and postcolonial regimes but to the West German state itself. Students saw the state as imperialist and reacted against what they believed was West German collaboration with the United States and its other allies to smash the political aspirations of those struggling for independence.[6]

The GDR, however, still saw itself as an anti-imperialist, antiracist champion. To the extent that students in the GDR were faithful Marxists—and again evidence suggests that not many were—they would have found it difficult to agitate against the GDR on some of the issues that motivated those in the FRG, including the death of Lumumba and apartheid in South Africa.[7] On the surface, the GDR's positions on both were in line with those of the wider anti-imperial community. The GDR not only denounced Lumumba's assassination; it also established a close relationship to his widow, Pauline. SED secretary Walter Ulbricht wrote her a letter of sympathy that was also a promise of political support after her husband's death.[8] The relationship to Pauline Lumumba continued to be a strong one, as she made a state visit the GDR in 1965,[9] and there is evidence that she later worked with the GDR to secure spots for Congolese students in East German universities.[10] In terms of apartheid, the GDR both condemned it as an institution and rebuked the FRG for its continued support of the South African government.[11] The GDR also provided refuge for dissidents from the ANC, often together with university study,[12] or political and military training.[13]

Yet as Slobodian has shown, African students also complained about the political hypocrisy of the GDR and questioned its anti-imperial credentials. The UASA's second congress, in 1961, featured tensions over a possible resolution against Egyptian president Gamel Abdel Nasser's suppression of progressives, which the Deutsche Afrikanische Gesellschaft (DAFRIG) ultimately thwarted to avoid upsetting the GDR's relationship with Egypt. The UASA elucidated further East German hypocrisy when it showed that all the Cameroonian workers whom the GDR was preparing to send back to Cameroon at the request of the Cameroonian state were also members of the opposition UPC. Therefore the GDR was putting them in considerable peril by acquiescing to the demands of the Cameroonian president, Ahmadou Ahidjo, who was considered a proxy for continued French domination.[14]

The relationship of the GDR to certain African regimes became, in this respect, a subject of growing contention. The increasingly authoritarian nature of countries such as Guinea, Mali, Kenya, and Nigeria produced sharp divisions among the African students in the GDR, as well as conflict between the students and the SED. Student dissent often undermined the GDR's fragile efforts to curry favor with African governments, or it ran contrary to the political positions that the Soviets—and the SED—endorsed. The protests thus provide a window on how student opposition functioned in the GDR. This opposition was not as open as that of foreign students in the FRG, where exchange students marched in the streets, had hunger strikes, and held sit-ins to demonstrate against various global injustices.[15] On rare occasions, students in the East did make their displeasure more public, such as when Malians occupied their own Trade Mission in East Berlin to protest the policies of Moussa Traoré, as we will see below. However, protest in the GDR more commonly meant writing joint letters, holding meetings not approved by the SED, or disrupting the gatherings that it did sanction. In this manner, African students took it upon themselves to turn their national clubs from organizers of annual independence day celebrations into loci of dissent and debate.

The First African Student Organizations in the GDR

The first umbrella organization for African students in East Germany was established on May 7, 1958. It was called the Vereinigten Afrikanischen Studenten in der DDR (VAS) and was comprised of students from Madagascar, Kenya, Ghana, Sierra Leone, the Gambia, Senegal, and Guinea.[16] With the exception of Ghana, at the time all these countries were still under colonial control.[17] Even at this early stage, there was conflict. The GDR's Nigerian students already had their own, exclusively Nigerian group and tried to stall the foundation of the VAS. According to VAS leader L.I.J., a student from the Gambia, the Nigerians were unhappy with the idea of a student organization that linked all the African students in the GDR together, regardless of nationality.[18] While L.I.J. did not say so explicitly in his letter to the Nigerian group, he implied that the Nigerians resisted an organization that would be arranged around Pan-African principles asserting the unity of Africans in the face of imperial oppression. For their part, the Nigerians hotly denied that they were responsible for any delay in the founding of the VAS.[19]

The Pan-African nature of the VAS was evident in its constitution. It was conceived as a forum where African students could meet and discuss Africa-related topics, as well as broader subjects of interest for Africa. The organization was to awaken the "spirit of unity, helpfulness, and cooperation among its members," so that they might "provide their best service to mother Africa." The group would fight for the independence of all Africa and function as the "mirror of Africa" in the GDR. Its activities would not be restricted to the GDR, since it would forge bonds with other "democratic" African organizations in Africa and beyond that were working toward the goal of independence.[20]

Why the Nigerians would have kept an umbrella organization from developing is unclear. In addition to having been the first African students to come to the GDR, Nigerians were still the largest contingent in 1958; perhaps they felt that, given their own numbers, they did not need broader representation. The Nigerians in this period may also have aligned their politics with that of the East German state rather than the Pan-African movement. As Slobodian has shown, the SED was leery of Pan-Africanism and its emphasis on African as opposed to national unity.[21] This explained the SED's reluctance to accept the UASA when it formed after the VAS ostensibly went defunct. The SED believed that the UASA, formed in 1960, was too independent and subject to make statements that contradicted official SED party lines. Even after East German authorities placed the UASA under control of the DAfriG, the UASA continued to resist attempts to censor its statements or yield to state pressures to conform. Since Africans were usually not restricted from crossing the border into West Germany or beyond, they could simply leave the GDR if they were dissatisfied, complicating state control of their movements and actions.[22]

Both the VAS and the UASA also had to contend with individual national groups, not all of which were friendly toward them. Just as the Nigerians had rejected the VAS, the groups from Ghana and Kenya also rebuffed the UASA in its early stages.[23] From the beginning, the groups representing individual African states existed alongside the umbrella African organization. Their memberships were exclusive to students from specific countries. As of early 1959, there were already national groups for Nigerians and Madagascans, along with the UPC in exile group from Cameroon. Bankole, the only woman among the first eleven Nigerian students, was president of the Nigerian group around this time, though as a rule there were few female leaders of national groups, and their membership was male-dominated as well.[24]

Besides the UPC in exile, which appears to have had its own, unique status, there were twenty-three other national student groups in 1959, encompassing students from any country with more than two individuals attending university in the GDR. The division of student affairs of the GDR's Department for Higher Education and the leadership of the FDJ were both responsible for overseeing the groups and their activities.[25] FDJ representatives were the most involved, since they acted as mentors to the international students, working to ensure that their guests understood and approved of Marxism-Leninism, and that they behaved appropriately during their stay in the GDR.[26]

Fissures inside the national groups existed from the beginning. For example, by 1960 a Sudanese group had formed, but it was a group in name only. The FDJ forced its cohesion from above. The Sudanese students were not politically unified, and their leadership was weak. Some students were in favor of Sudan's military regime, while others belonged to the country's communist party. One of the students was a staunch supporter of Egypt's Nasser. The members of the group did not discuss their political differences, and their head believed that each student's education was a personal affair, not a political matter.[27] Divisions among student groups at different universities appeared as well. The Malian students most dissatisfied with their nation's government in 1971 studied in Dresden, which caused relations between them and other branches of the Malian organization to fray.[28]

Given the early difficulties that both the umbrella student organizations and the individual national groups encountered, it is perhaps not surprising that many became involved in protest. Political activity either unified students behind a specific cause, as in the cases of Guinea and Mali, or divided them along ethnic or sectarian lines, as it did with Nigeria and Kenya. In all instances, the FDJ and other GDR authorities found it difficult to control student activism, and even when they did tensions within the groups and between the groups and the East German state usually remained.

Resisting Recall: Guinean Reaction to Forced Repatriation

In late 1961, only three years after Guinean independence, the Guinean teachers' union produced a pamphlet criticizing the government's lack of support for their profession. The teachers, many of whom had studied in Europe and had close bonds with communists in France, denounced the Touré government for being insufficiently communist, or indeed not communist at all. The union then went on strike, and five of its top leaders were arrested and imprisoned.[29]

While the Soviets and their satellites, including the GDR, had considered Touré a staunch communist ally, the strike would prove otherwise. Touré ultimately expelled the Soviet ambassador from Guinea for his supposed involvement in organizing the strike. Among the Guineans in Europe, however, were a core of ardent Marxists who were disappointed that Touré had not ushered in the revolution. Protests were spreading among Guinean expatriates across Africa and Europe, from Dakar, to Paris, to Czechoslovakia, to the Soviet Union, and also the GDR. Indeed, Guinean students in the GDR, in coordination with their counterparts in Paris, Moscow, and Prague, organized to voice their disapproval of Touré's rule.[30]

It might seem as though the GDR, a Soviet ally, would have backed the students, since they were proving more faithful to Marxism-Leninism than their president. Yet the situation in Guinea was shifting quickly on the ground, and the GDR's foreign office and university officials found it difficult to absorb all the new information coming from their Trade Mission in Guinea. They did not want to offend Touré, one of the African leaders who seemed most open to the East. Authorities also had difficulty containing growing student agitation. There was already some anxiety among the Guinean contingent before the strike; in

1960, six Guineans in the GDR were recalled to Guinea. When they gathered at the airport before the flight back to Conakry, one of the students was missing. It transpired that upon hearing the news that he was to return to Guinea, he fled to West Berlin, frightened of what might happen if he were to go home.[31] The Touré government had additionally asked the GDR to keep a close watch on its students and provide Guinea with reports of their activities.[32]

Touré's crackdown on the teachers' union provided sufficient motivation for Guinean students throughout Europe to press their government for change. Without GDR knowledge, forty-six Guineans studying in Leipzig and Jena sent a telegram to the Touré government, demanding the release of all political prisoners.[33] They had also gathered without GDR permission in Leipzig on New Year's Day, 1962, and held a series of other, secret meetings both before and after.[34] The group was also not unified in their criticism of Touré: the Dresden contingent sent a counter-telegram, supporting their leader and his position on the strike, though some in the Guinean NHG later claimed that the Dresdeners had only signed it under duress.[35]

The story of what happened to the Guinean students, and who the main players in the unfolding drama were, is convoluted and difficult to retrace. It certainly involved the Guinean ambassador in Prague, members of the Guinean NHG, representatives of the GDR's cabinets of education and international affairs, and at least one professor from the KMU in Leipzig. The ambassador had stolen into the GDR unannounced—also an infraction against East German rules—and demanded that all Guineans in the GDR proceed to a mandatory meeting in Prague.[36] This was in preparation for their being sent back to Guinea, where they would likely be "re-educated" and brought around to Touré's opinion, possibly at a camp called Alpha Yaya.[37]

The students referred to Alpha Yaya as "Guinea's Buchenwald."[38] It was a political prison, smaller than Guinea's infamous Camp Boiro, but apparently still notorious enough to strike fear in the students' hearts.[39] The use of the word "Buchenwald" was clearly meant to goad the GDR officials from the foreign office who heard the term, which came out at the only state-sanctioned NHG meeting on the topic. Images of violence dominated the meeting, as NHG members described demonstrations in Conakry and Labe being brutally put down, essentially in a bloodbath. They painstakingly described reports that two thousand young girls had been raped in the course of the demonstration.[40] In a later discussion with Katharina Harig, director of the KMU's Herder Institute, one of the students' leaders further insisted that the Touré government was expressly veering toward fascism, and that the Guineans inside the country lived in constant misery.[41] The students thus turned to memories of Germany's recent Nazi past and linked it to current atrocities in Guinea to make the case that Touré had become an abusive dictator.

The GDR nevertheless sided with Touré. The SED was likely convinced that upsetting him would foreclose the possibility of establishing actual diplomatic ties to Guinea. Consequently, the SED moved cautiously but deliberately to silence the students. The foreign office did allow them the one NHG meeting, and even provided a room for it. However, they quickly dismissed the claims of the movement's leaders and their contention that the Touré government had become so corrupt that the struggle was no longer between the people and the imperialists, but rather between the people and the authoritarian postcolonial regime. Harig labeled these students *Feuerköpfe* (hotheads) and argued that they did not understand how a socialist revolution was supposed to work or the students' role in it. She also described the student representative who met with her as the son of a wealthy plantation owner, which was meant to further discredit him as a member of the reactionary bourgeoisie. When talking to Harig, he had insisted that the students were the vanguard of the revolution and had the responsibility to lead, but she countered that the role of youth was rather to listen to the voices of their wiser, more experienced elders.[42] Characterizing the students as hotheads or malcontents was typical of the GDR reaction to exchange student activists, as was their categorization as bourgeois.

While the GDR tried to stifle the students, the Guinean state reacted by recalling forty-five of the protesters to Conakry. The ambassador to Prague maintained that if the students went home, they would see for themselves that everything in Guinea was calm and that Touré remained beloved. According to the ambassador, the students had merely been taken in by imperialist propaganda emanating from France,[43] and there were no problems whatsoever in Guinea.[44] Once the students had returned, the Guinean state would replace them with other students, ostensibly those who were more Touré loyalists.[45] Such a replacement was something the students had feared and addressed during their meetings; they believed that an international student council should be responsible for selecting students to go abroad, and not the government.[46]

Whether the students did return—or if the GDR compelled them to do so—is unclear. The Guineans in Russia refused their recall and consequently lost the stipends that Moscow had been issuing.[47] In the GDR, it may have been easiest for students to follow the one man who left for West Berlin in 1960, since even after the Berlin Wall was built in 1961 it was fairly easy for Africans to cross. While their specific fate is unknown, what is clear is that the students used the NHG, the organization that the GDR had given them, to protest the Touré regime's actions against the teachers' union. As Elizabeth Schmidt has pointed out, Guineans had ample experience with activism, since it was ordinary Guineans who propelled their colony to be the only one to vote for independence from France in the referendum it presented all of its African colonies in 1958.[48] The students' case makes plain that this activism did not cease with independence; on the contrary, it was used against Touré, a president who would become one of Africa's most brutal dictators during his twenty-six years in power and responsible for various crimes against humanity. The Guinean incident also shows how student protest took on different forms depending on location. In East Germany, where open, public demonstration against a supposedly friendly foreign government was difficult, students reshaped their national clubs to make them vehicles for politics.

Divisions at Home, Divisions Abroad: Nigerian Students and the Biafran Crisis

Following independence in 1960, Nigerians struggled to determine which of its many ethnic groups would have the most political influence in the newly formed state—the Hausa/Fulani, who lived in the north, the Yoruba, who lived in the southwest, or the Igbo, who lived in the southeast. The tense political climate during the early years after decolonization culminated in 1967 with Biafra's secession and the Nigerian Civil War, which ended in 1970, after Biafra was literally starved into surrender. During the conflict, the GDR threw its support behind Nigeria's central government, as did the rest of the Soviet Bloc. Meanwhile, those students who were Igbo remained loyal to Biafra, the region from which most had come. The division between the GDR and the Igbo students—not to mention the division among the Nigerian students themselves—ultimately led to the existence of two Nigerian NHG, one that was officially recognized and the other that was specifically Biafran and therefore illegal in East Germany.

If you will recall, the Nigerians who were asked to study in the GDR received their invitations following the 1949 British massacre of striking miners in Enugu. Enugu was the heart of Igboland and later became the capital of Biafra after secession. Perhaps owing to this early connection, the majority of Nigerian students in the GDR—approximately two-thirds—were ethnically Igbo. After rejecting the VAS, the Nigerians also became among the first to have their own national student club. An official Nigerian NHG, the Group of Nigerian Students in the GDR, then formed in 1960, when it was headed by

Bankole.[49] While the group briefly went defunct, it was revived in 1962 as the Nigerian Student Union, and thereafter had a continual presence.

In the GDR, Nigerian students followed the events in Biafra closely. As tensions in Nigeria grew, the students from the region of Biafra began to identify themselves more strongly with their home area.[50] Biafran students began to quarrel with non-Biafran students on campus and in meetings of the Nigerian NHG, and tensions exploded after the Civil War began and Biafra declared independence in 1967. In a report from the general secretary of the Nigerian NHG to the division of international studies at the KMU, the Biafrans were portrayed as thuggish radicals willing to use violence to get their way. The putative "ringleader" of the Biafran group is described as carrying a long knife under his jacket, which made him a menacing, frightening figure.[51] The university official charged with monitoring the groups concurred with the assessment of the general secretary of the Biafran leader, but he went further, putting all of the man's activities under a microscope. The official criticized him not only for his involvement with the Biafran cause but also for other unrelated behaviors, such as his supposed lack of cleanliness.[52] Attempts to discredit him were similar to those used to dismiss the Guinean students who spoke out against their government, and were again typical of GDR tactics toward student agitators.

The Nigerians who were not Biafran and were members of the officially sanctioned NHG used the GDR's endorsement of their political position to condemn the opposition and to ensure that their places as the authorized representatives of Nigeria in East Germany were secure. They did so by making clear that they were anti-Biafran and therefore stood with their own federal government, as well as with the GDR. They called attention to what they described as the disruptive, radical behavior of the Biafrans, which they claimed was in sharp contrast to their own upstanding demeanor.[53]

Both the president and secretary general of the Nigerian Union indeed used a GDR-sanctioned "Nigerian evening" in February 1968 to make their harshest attacks against the Biafran students. The secretary general described the evening as an opportunity for all Nigerians living in the GDR to join in polite conversation and to see if they might be able to work out a way to live peacefully together despite their political differences. Whether Biafrans—ostensibly Igbo—were actually invited to the event, however, remains an open question. On the same February night that the Nigerian Union held its meeting, the Biafrans had congregated upstairs in the same building for their own, separate gathering. The secretary general claimed that after the Biafran meeting broke up, two of its members purposely came down to the other meeting to provoke a riot. According to him, the two men were armed, and the threat of violence hung over the meeting. Yet the Biafran attempt to incite bloodshed ultimately failed because the other Nigerians refused to allow themselves to be drawn into a conflict. After the disruption, the rest of the evening went smoothly. Later, the Nigerian members of the Union drew on the language of unity to make the point that they strove to heal political and ethnic fissures, whereas others chose to provoke them.[54]

The endgame for the Nigerian students, like that of the Guineans, is unclear. The GDR, in coordination with the official Nigerian NHG, did manage to dissolve the Biafran club, though doubts over whether unity among the students was possible lingered. The leaders of the NHG spoke of trying to heal rifts and of attempting to reincorporate the Biafrans into their ranks. Whether this happened, or if conflict made it unfeasible, is debatable. Nigeria was an American ally. From the 1970s the numbers of Nigerian students in the GDR dropped steadily, until by the end of the decade there were only about twenty in the country; with such low numbers, the issue may have been moot.[55] The GDR does not, however, appear to have expelled the Igbo students or had any contact with the Nigerian federal government concerning their activities. Despite Nigeria's political stance, the SED may have retained hope that better relations with Nigeria would develop, and that continuing to welcome Nigerian students from across the country was the wisest course.

Kenyan Students: A Mirror of their Nation

Ethnic and political tension also shaped the history of Kenyan student organizations during the 1960s. The first Kenyan Students' Association (KSA) was established in 1960. The KSA's first chair was Owilla Ouma Olwa, a Luo student of political economy who remained in the leadership position until 1966.[56] Olwa had connections to the innermost circles of Kenya's political elite, and he caught the attention of the Stasi, which assigned an informant to him in 1963, after he had returned to East Germany from a trip home.[57] Both the informant and Gurke, an official from the Ministry of Foreign Affairs, developed highly positive opinions of Olwa and of his commitment to socialism.[58] The informant described him as *linksdrall*, very far to the left,[59] while Gurke, in a letter of January 1966, called him "highly intelligent."[60] In 1960, Olwa's politics jibed with those of the Kenya African National Union (KANU), which had been organized that year, just as the bloody Mau Mau Uprising was ending.

Troubles within the KSA did not begin until 1964, when it split and a new group, the Kenyan Student Union (KSU), emerged to challenge the original organization. By this point, KANU was also fracturing internally, as leading figures Jomo Kenyatta, the country's president, and Oginga Odinga, its vice president, were increasingly at odds with each other. They had come together at the grass roots during Kenya's struggle for independence, but even before independence came in 1963 there were sharp differences among KANU's leadership, as we saw in chapter 2. These differences were often couched in ethnic terms, since Kenyatta was Kikuyu, Odinga was Luo, and other politicians were considered representatives of their individual tribes.[61] Indeed, when discussing the breakup of the KSA, Gurke referred to the ethnic identity of the students involved. He mentioned that Olwa was Luo and that the student who had formed the KSU, future speaker of the National Assembly of Kenya Moses Kiprono,[62] was Kipsigis (Kalenjin).[63] Gurke thus implied that ethnic loyalty was responsible for the rift.[64]

Yet the place of ethnicity in causing ruptures within KANU and the KSA has been overstated, or rather ethnicity's role in galvanizing disunity is more complicated, and embroiled in other issues. As noted prior, in the early period after independence Kenyatta was in favor of capitalism, while Odinga leaned toward socialism.[65] Odinga ultimately broke with Kenyatta over their divergent economic beliefs, with Odinga founding an opposition party, the Kenya People's Union (KPU), in 1966. Olwa well understood the significance of the economic component behind Kenya's political divides. A Stasi informant reported that Olwa told him that the creation of the KPU "had nothing to do with tribalism; we can see that there are well-known and influential opposition forces coming from all tribes, and especially from Kenya's three largest tribes."[66] There was widespread discontent with Kenyatta's economic policies not long after independence, as those who had been promised an increase in their standard of living during the anticolonial struggle realized that they would really receive little material benefit, while elites divvied up the spoils.[67] Olwa stood firmly behind Odinga and hoped that his KPU would provide solutions for issues such as unemployment and landlessness, problems that he believed KANU had done nothing to address.[68]

The GDR originally seemed to prefer Odinga as a partner over Kenyatta. In addition to views that were seemingly more aligned with socialism, Oginga had ties to and had received funding from the USSR and China.[69] Gurke described Odinga as "Leader of the progressive forces in Kenya." His son, Raila Odinga—who would go on to become prime minister of Kenya between 2008 and 2013—even studied in the GDR, arriving in the country in 1962 and going on to complete an engineering degree at Otto von Guericke University in Magdeburg.

When KANU's National Secretary of Propaganda and Education visited the GDR in 1964, he tried to dissolve the KSA in favor of the KSU. The KSA would not yield, however, and chose Raila Odinga as their new president.[70]

Unity among national student groups was, however, very important to the GDR's Ministry of Foreign Affairs. While Pan-African unity across national borders was not desired, unity within a NHG meant political unity in the quest for a socialist future. There was concern that most Kenyans in the GDR were rallying around the KSU and that the KSA would isolate itself from the rest and ostensibly incur political problems for themselves and for the GDR. Moreover, Kenya was a one-party state, and the membership of the Kenyan national group was supposed to reflect that.[71] Gurke maintained that this was the case even as the cracks in KANU were increasingly evident; indeed, he discussed the factions developing among Kenyan students only two months before Oginga Odinga would leave KANU to form the KPU.[72]

As in the Nigerian case, Kenyan students used the fragmentation of their student organization as a means of expressing displeasure with politics in their own country. With Nigeria, the GDR followed Soviet policy in denouncing Biafra in hopes of extending socialist influence in the country. Kenya appeared no different. The GDR was inclined to push the students to demonstrate a superficial united front for its own political well-being. The Soviets were originally very interested in Kenya, and especially in Oginga Odinga's politics. They provided development aid in the first half of the 1960s. By the end of the decade, however, relations between Kenya and the USSR had worsened, as the Soviets grew uncertain of Odinga's position as opposition leader.[73]

There has been little research on the GDR's diplomatic position vis-à-vis Kenya; as with other African states, it did not officially recognize the GDR in the 1960s because of the Hallstein Doctrine. The Stasi's continued cultivation of Olwa suggests that East German interest in the country's politics, and in the possibility that it might lean further left, persisted throughout the 1960s. Olwa's Stasi file extends from his arrival in 1959 through 1969. Many of the conversations that informants conducted with him concerned Kenyan politics. The Stasi considered making Olwa an *Inoffizieller Mitarbeiter* (IM)(Unofficial Collaborator), believing that they might be able to use him to garner more information on the political situation in the country. But they also grew increasingly unsure about whether Olwa would be of use in this capacity, as it was difficult to tell whether the socialist opposition had any chance of success. In the end, the GDR had also been able to compel the KSA, Olwa's group, to dissolve and join the KSU, preserving the "united front." As a result, Olwa drifted away from the organization.[74] Although "unity" had been achieved, it was obviously done at the expense of GDR support for the more progressive student union. It also reflected a continued East German willingness to cater to the interests of the regnant power in an African country, regardless of its position in the Cold War world.

Mali: Sit-ins in East Berlin

Mali was decolonized in 1960, along with the majority of France's African possessions. It was also one of the first African states to embrace socialism, under the leadership of its first president, Modibo Keita.[75] Accordingly, Mali had one of the earliest educational agreements with the GDR. There was also at least one Malian student in the GDR in 1959, before official independence, a man named Omar P. He was a member of the French communist party, which meant that the SED took special notice of him and interest in his success.[76] The GDR and Mali finalized their more formal educational exchange program in 1961. It stipulated that the GDR would give roughly twenty scholarships to Malians.[77] The GDR and Mali renewed this contract annually thereafter.

Keita ruled Mali until 1968, when he was overthrown by a military coup and the dictator Moussa Traoré came to power under the Comité Militaire de Liberation Nationale (CMLN). Ghana's new government, the NLC, had immediately demanded that all Ghanaian students leave the GDR for West Germany in 1966, when Kwame Nkrumah was deposed. Nothing similar happened with regime change in Mali. Indeed, the GDR continued to renew its educational agreements with Mali under Traoré and to be cautious about upsetting him or the delicate arrangements they had made with the state. Traoré had not completely abandoned the socialist economic policies of the Keita years, which made it politically expedient for the GDR to maintain a cordial relationship. Mali did not establish formal diplomatic relations with the GDR until January 1973, a few years after the Hallstein Doctrine was relaxed. However, there was a Malian Trade Mission in East Germany from 1969,[78] and it was around this mission that tensions coalesced over opposition to the Malian government and its increasingly draconian policies.

The turmoil began in October 1970, when Tidiani Kanté, head of the Malian Trade Mission, returned to his offices in East Berlin from a visit with members of the FGDB at its academy in Bernau. Upon Kanté's arrival, he found that thirty to forty Malian students had occupied the building and refused to leave until they had presented him with a protest resolution. This resolution concerned a decision Kanté had made about visas that would allow them to travel to West Berlin and elsewhere in the FRG; he had recently announced that Malians would have to get approval from him for the visas, when before only the GDR's permission was necessary. The students said that this decree was "anti-social, anti-democratic, and reactionary."[79] Kanté told them that the GDR had asked him to take this measure. This turned out to be untrue. The Malian government did not want Malian students going outside the GDR, and it asked Kanté to assess applications for travel to ensure that they would not.[80]

The sit-in was likely about more than just visas. While the GDR's Ministry of Foreign Affairs dismissed claims that the protest really centered on the military's dismantling of Malian trade unions, other documents suggest that the intensification of military repression was in fact key. Not long after the sit-in, a congress for all members of the Association des Etudiants et Stagiaires Malians en République Démocratique Allemande (AESM-RDA), the Malian student group, met in Berlin. The congress produced a long political resolution, in which the participants spelled out their grievances and goals. Mali had not received the freedoms that the new military regime had promised. Instead the nation was now controlled by a *Kompradorenbourgeoisie*, which was moving ever closer to the West, and especially to Mali's former colonizer, France. The military had given assurances that Mali would experience economic revival under its stewardship, but contrariwise it had allowed the French to exploit Mali once again, as French firms moved in to monopolize the economy. Social programs were stagnating, health care and public education were in shambles, unions had been dissolved, and there were arbitrary arrests and imprisonments. Parents were being asked to cover the costs of their children's schooling, meaning that the cronyism and nepotism of the French era had returned.[81]

The mood in Mali after the 1968 coup had been one of hope. Economic and political conditions had deteriorated during the Keita years, as socialist policies did not have the desired effect of boosting production and employment, and Keita's government was also repressive. The hope that things would change soon soured, as Traoré's one-party state did not deliver on its promises and devolved into a despotism and authoritarianism that would last until 1991.[82] The Malian students' statements against their government reflected this deep disappointment. They also provided prescriptions for revolutionary change. The keywords were solidarity and unity, especially with other Malian students, whether they were abroad or at home in Mali. The students in Berlin concluded that as intellectuals, they were the vanguard of the revolution and were responsible for bringing back democracy and reinstituting a nationalized economy.[83]

Members of AESM-RDA were also unhappy with Kanté, the Malian representative in East Berlin, and demanded his removal. They referred to him as a corrupt demagogue and accused him of deliberately sowing confusion among the students in East Germany. Additionally, Kanté was trying to create a parallel Malian student organization that would undermine the power of the preexisting group. The students hoped to work together with the Malian Trade Mission, but could not as long as Kanté was still in power.[84] The students' targeting of Kanté made it clear that considerations of party and political position were critical to their activism. Many of the students had come to the GDR during the Keita years and were members of his Sudanese Union-African Democratic Rally (USRDA). As in the cases of Nigeria and Kenya, the Malian student organization was splintering along party lines, with those who belonged to the USRDA remaining loyal to the original organization and others aligning themselves with Kanté and the CMLN.[85]

Neither the Malian government nor the GDR were happy with the student agitation. Bureaucrats at the East German Ministry of Foreign Affairs were distressed because some of the students had claimed that they were helping with copying fliers that condemned the Traoré government. Ministry representatives feared that the Malians would break off relations, and they assured Malian officials that East German employees would never assist in the duplication of political materials relating to the internal affairs of another state.[86] In dealing with Malian officials, they needed to emphasize that the GDR wanted to distance itself from the entire affair.[87] At this critical juncture, the GDR did not want to upset the diplomatic relationship it had secured with Mali. The Malians quickly took advantage of the situation, and the GDR's weakness. A representative from Mali's Ministry of Culture visited the GDR in 1971 and informed his East German colleagues that the Malian government would likely disband the student group. As the organization in the GDR had been founded while the USRDA was in power, it was now outmoded and "did not fit into the current political landscape in Mali."[88] Clearly, the Malians hoped to synchronize international Malian groups like the AESM-RDA and to purge them of political malcontents.

Although Malian students massed at least one more time at their Trade Mission in Berlin—in June 1971, perhaps in response to news of a failed coup earlier that year[89]—there is no evidence that their protests continued beyond this point. However, as in the cases above, their activism inside a dictatorship like the GDR demonstrates that they were comfortable contesting their own government's policies and not afraid to make their voices heard. Unlike their East German classmates, they did not fear reprisals on the part of the GDR, as it had little power to coerce or imprison them. Moreover, once again the GDR supported its African partner state against the students, which was typical of the East German state's willingness to countenance repressive measures abroad in order to strengthen its own international position.

The UASA: Calling out Racism in the GDR

In 1965, a student rivalry exploded not within a specific, national group but in the UASA itself. Superficially, it appeared that the dispute was between the union's chapters in Leipzig and Rostock. The Rostock members accused the Leipzig branch of being "henchmen for the SED" and referred to it as an East German "puppet." Dissatisfied with what they considered corrupt representation, the Rostock contingent founded their own, alternative African student union. The Leipzigers complained and had a meeting to address internal divisions with various authorities in the city, including a party from the local FDJ.[90]

Below the surface, however, lurked the specter of racism. In addition to claiming the mantle of anti-imperialism, the GDR also maintained that it was an antiracist state. Any lingering racism was either a reflection of only a handful of retrograde, uneducated citizens,[91] or the result of an insidious influence coming from the West.[92] Yet the UASA alleged otherwise and described a much more pervasive racist presence—one that was growing, not declining.

While most of the NHG protests were tied to political events in specific countries, dissent in the UASA therefore stemmed from serious concern over matters in the GDR itself. The conflict between the students in Leipzig and Rostock arose when one student wrote a letter about East German racism. The letter was directed at Ulbricht and other leaders of the SED, presumably came from Rostock, and was signed "The Committee of African Students and Workers in the GDR." According to officials at the Ministry of Education, the actual writer was probably a Togolese philosophy student. The letter opened with a statement that tensions between African students and workers and East German citizens were on the rise. There was an upsurge in provocations on both sides, and these were increasingly resulting in physical hostilities. The writer warned that if something was not done soon, there would be a major confrontation that could lead to negative reports filtering out to the anticommunist, Western press. The GDR typically suppressed any news suggestive of racism inside the state,[93] but the student implied that stories about recent racist incidents were bound to get out. He believed, then, that it was in the best interests of the GDR to negotiate with the UASA and work on reducing such incidents.[94]

Like the Guinean students who had referenced Germany's Nazi past in their protests, the author of the letter did not shy away from discussions of the Third Reich and the continuing Nazi influence in the GDR. He said that a minority of African students were not conversant with postwar German history. Consequently, these students failed to recognize that there were "certain subversive elements in the GDR still associated with (the notorious) Hitlerism," and were more likely to be surprised, or provoked, by encounters with such regressive elements. Moreover, these Africans did not realize that the GDR was now committed to socialism, an inherently antifascist ideology, and perhaps saw isolated incidents of racism as reflective of wider state policy. These students were antisocialist because they incorrectly equated socialism with racism.

While he did not mention, the work of Francophone scholars such as Cheikh Anta Diop, Frantz Fanon, or Aimé Césaire explicitly, the letter writer's argument about African sensitivity to racism was reminiscent of theirs. These three were among the most significant Francophone intellectuals of the age.[95] All wrote copiously, and in the mid-1960s their work would have been widely available, if not necessarily to East Germans, then certainly to Africans who had more geographic mobility. French-speaking Africans such as the Togolese author of the UASA letter would probably have been even more familiar with these intellectuals, given the Francophone link.[96]

The letter writer's suggestion that colonialism had such a negative impact on Africans that they were now wary of any whites, including those with good intentions, would have been especially evocative for Francophone intellectuals. Diop had contended that Europeans convinced Africans of their inferiority and that this had caused generations of irreparable psychological harm.[97] Fanon argued that whites had ingrained the idea that Blacks were evil or depraved so deeply that the only way for Blacks to survive was to put on "white masks" that hid the shame of their Blackness.[98] Césaire famously discussed how colonialism had destroyed African cultures.[99] In addition, Césaire broke with the French communist party over the persistence of racism in countries that now claimed to be socialist, European socialists' fundamental misunderstanding of the complex differences between the struggle of European workers against capitalism and that of Blacks against colonialism, and their refusal to address the atrocities and prejudices of Stalin.[100]

Following the Francophone intellectuals, the Togolese writer stated that

East Germans understood neither the depth of Black psychological angst nor how simply "poking fun" at Africans could awaken deep-seated anger against whites. There were some who were blatantly racist and had never broken with the Nazi past or accepted the antiracist, anti-imperialist message of the GDR. Of these, the most devious were those who pretended to be antiracist, only later to reveal their true nature. Their foul intentions were bound up in the broader struggle between capitalism and communism, insofar as they made Africans doubt the solidity of socialism in the GDR and the morals of the SED. These individuals baited Africans in the hope that the news of racism in the GDR would get out and damage its image in the West. Cold War politics were, in effect, the motor behind much of the racism members of the UASA had encountered, and the African reaction was natural given the hardships they had experienced under colonialism.[101]

Racist behavior was not limited to teasing. The writer held that groups of East German men had recently come together to beat up Africans; two students had been assaulted the week before and almost died from their injuries. The African community was understandably outraged. What was to be done? The author had some suggestions. He recommended having experienced African students give lectures on German life and customs to new arrivals while they were at the Herder Institute, the language-learning center all exchange students attended before continuing to university; setting up a recreation room for African students, where they could contact the eight-member UASA council about any concerns they might have; sponsoring lectures on postcolonial Africa in factories and other venues; compelling the Deutsche Film Aktien-Gesellschaft (German Film Corporation or DEFA) to produce movies on contemporary Africa, since most of what they were currently making reflected only "colonial barbarism"; and, finally, holding meetings with African students to address the serious problems that they all faced. The proposal that universities provide space for an African recreation room came with a subtle dig at the East German state, since the writer claimed a similar step had been taken in the FRG, with notable success.[102]

Both the GDR's Ministry of Foreign Affairs and Ministry of Education took the letter very seriously. In private conversations officials described the situation as one of *Dringlichkeit* (urgency) and in general agreed with the letter's conclusion that violent clashes between East Germans and Africans were on the rise.[103] A Dr. Fischer who worked in the Department of Education talked with colleagues and explained that, after discussion with local police and security, he believed that the opinions expressed in the letter accurately reflected those of the wider African community.[104] Certain concrete measures to combat racism among East Germans were also put in place. For example, a group from the Ministry of Education tasked the Rostock authorities with speaking to the head of the taxi drivers' union, whose drivers frequently directed slurs at Africans, and have him intervene to correct their behavior.[105] More generally, the ministry would send working groups (*Brigaden*) to different unions and have them address the importance of solidarity with the developing world. These groups would "above all explain that international solidarity in the GDR is not limited to donations, but forged through the relationship to Africans in the GDR itself."[106] Along with increased communal engagement on the part of DAFRIG and the FDJ, these steps would form the basis of antiracist education for the public.

Since the GDR tended to brush off accusations of racism, or to see them as exclusively due to Western interference, it is significant that it considered taking these steps to address racism inside the country. This anxiety over the increase in racism, however, was probably grounded in the possibility that stories about confrontation would be leaked to the Western press and undermine the narrative of socialist solidarity that the GDR wanted to project. Officials worried that "right-wing" elements in the UASA might seize the initiative to speak out about their problems in the GDR, damaging the state.[107] Further, despite officials' concerns about the behavior of GDR citizens, they did not believe that African students and workers were blameless. They submitted that it was the UASA's responsibility to monitor the behavior of African students, as well as to teach them about the finer points of the conflict between the GDR and its political opponents. Tired accusations that Africans were likely drinking too much and visiting insalubrious bars were dredged up, and GDR administrators told the UASA to ensure that its members knew about the dangers of alcohol. The UASA was also to educate those students who had a more "delicate" sensibility about adapting to the GDR and, ostensibly, its racism.[108] In other words, those students who had developed a negative opinion of whites over the course of many years under colonialism needed to toughen up and ignore whatever racism they encountered in East Germany.

In the end, the GDR's response to an African protest directed against itself rather than toward the policies of an African state was ambivalent. There was recognition of racism inside its borders, as well as fear about what this racism might mean for the country's international profile. At the same time, the GDR fell back on its more familiar narrative of African responsibility for East German racism, one rooted in beliefs of African backwardness, weakness in the face of temptation, and overt sensitivity.

Conclusion

This chapter has drawn attention to the ways in which African students were able to use their NHG and UASA organizations as vehicles for political protest in a state that tried, often unsuccessfully, to circumscribe political action not reflective of SED-sanctioned policies or narratives. The students challenged not only East German leadership and its attempts to shape their opinions in various venues but also the very governments that had sent them to the GDR in the first place. Daniel Hodgkinson and Luke Melchiorre have argued that in this era, African students generally recognized that university education lent them power to harness nationalist and other political discourses in the same way that their leaders did. This was something that the students in East Germany certainly understood, as they confronted hierarchies of authority at home and abroad.

Student power extended, for instance, to the exposure of hypocrisy. The GDR's cautious approach to Guinea's Touré, whom even passionately Marxist students declared was a fascist, undercut the East German commitment to both Marxist ideology and anti-imperialism. Siding with a dictator in a purely pragmatic move, the SED demonstrated that it was willing to jettison the core principles of the East German state in favor of shoring up already shaky ties with Guinea. The students were able to accentuate the multiple registers in which supposed "allies" operated, and how Marxism-Leninism was unable to become the unifying tool that the GDR believed it would be. Armed with both a complex understanding of Marxism-Leninism and the brutality of recent German history, they brought the viciousness of the Touré regime into the spotlight and revealed the political and moral inconsistencies of East German leadership at the same time.

In the mid- to late 1970s other African student groups became politically active. The student associations of both Somalia and South Africa expressed dissent toward the end of the decade.[109] Such protests demonstrated a continuing engagement with domestic politics in their individual countries and a concomitant resistance to that engagement on the part of the GDR. For example, anxieties surrounded plans by the group from the Republic of Congo—Congo-Brazzaville—to hold a seminar on current events for students from that country in late March 1977. The Office for Study Abroad at the KMU in Leipzig expressed concern about a lecture on the "politics of the USSR and other socialist countries as regards détente and militarization, as well as their attitude toward solidarity with free, independent, and still oppressed nations."[110] The concern was that remarks might be made about the political situation in Congo-

Brazzaville, and such remarks were forbidden.[111] In February, the Congolese ambassador to the GDR had made a speech at the Festival of Congolese Youth in Leipzig, in which he praised his country's stance against the forces of imperialism. However, on March 18 the country's president, Marien Ngouabi, was assassinated.[112] Ngouabi was a socialist and had proclaimed the Republic of Congo Africa's first Marxist-Leninist state when he took power in 1968.[113] The quick changes roiling the country made the SED cautious about supporting the students, even though they were Marxists, and thus supposedly Cold War allies.

African students in the GDR were highly politicized and vocally critical of actions they rejected in their home countries. The GDR was loath to let news of student activism spread beyond its borders and apprehensive about upsetting relations with emergent African states. Indeed, the politics of the state in question—socialist or not—mattered less than the possibility that fragile diplomatic bonds might be broken. This undermined the GDR's narrative of itself as an ardent supporter of those still struggling for independence or working to build new nation states following socialist models. The GDR may have feared alienating groups such as the ANC, with whom it maintained close ties and supported in a variety of ways.[114] When Africans questioned GDR policy in their own states, or challenged the East German antiracist narrative by pointing out the persistence of racism in the country, they demonstrated that their position brought with it the authority to challenge and reprimand their benefactors.

African students indeed had many occasions to dispute the GDR's antiracist assertions. These occasions came up most frequently in instances when African men were chastised—or far worse—for their relationships with East German women. We have seen glimpses of the tensions surrounding interracial romance from the beginning of this book, with the criticism of romantic relationships among the first Nigerian students and the East German women who became their partners. In the next chapter, I will discuss the gendered dimensions of the African student experience, which includes exploring romantic liaisons between African men and East German women more broadly, as well as the varying reactions to them.

CHAPTER 5

African Students at the Intersection of Race and Gender

In 1967, a Zambian official at his country's embassy in Moscow held a meeting with East German diplomats. They discussed the official's concern that there were several Zambian students in the German Democratic Republic who wanted to marry local women, or indeed already had. The Zambian official was unhappy with this development, since "there are still many difficulties to overcome in Zambia, and apart from the effort that it would take their husbands to care for them, the women would have trouble accustoming themselves to the country." He suggested that he would be pleased if the GDR found a way to prevent these marriages. The response of his East German counterparts was swift, decisive, and unequivocal: the GDR would not prevent foreigners from marrying its citizens, nor would it attach any race-based conditions to such marriages.[1]

The East German reaction to the Zambian request echoed the general GDR policy on race that we have encountered throughout this book. The GDR presented itself as a nonracist, anti-imperialist state, and contrasted itself with the West, which the SED depicted as the inheritor of Nazi racism and imperialism.[2] The GDR imagined Africa through the lens of solidarity. This meant that the GDR and its African partner states would work together toward the goal of socialist harmony and economic development. While the GDR was more economically advanced in terms of Marx's historical epochs, the two sides were still equal and would support each other in the struggle to create forward-thinking socialist states.[3]

On the ground, however, East German attitudes toward interracial relationships or marriages were not as liberal as the Zambian official was led to believe. African students who came to the GDR between the 1950s and 1970s found themselves in a place where the professed anticolonial, antiracist dogma of the SED frequently came into conflict with the realities of everyday racism. Racial and sexual stereotypes remained remarkably consistent with those of the pre-1945 era, even as government officials and ordinary citizens struggled to dispel them. The GDR was more a site of inconsistency than tolerance when it came to questions of sex and race. Moreover, the ambivalent attitude toward sex and race at all levels threatened the GDR's status as a brother in anti-imperial solidarity.

The idea of the lascivious African man and his counterpart, the promiscuous German woman, which became prominent in imperial Germany and persisted through the Weimar and Nazi eras, continued to shape perceptions of African-German interactions in the GDR.[4] The SED was committed to demonstrating that its leaders had resisted Nazism; East German doctrine held that while fascism continued to survive in and even defined the neighboring Federal Republic, the GDR had expunged all its traces.[5] The anxiety surrounding African men who consorted with white women makes it clear, however, that even when racial biases were denied on an official level, bigotry endured and complicated efforts to integrate foreigners into the GDR.

The prejudices that African students confronted undercut the GDR's claim to defend international solidarity and racial equality against Western imperialism. Students encountered an East German population that was deeply conflicted about race, which included their professors, administrators, and colleagues at universities, technical schools, and other educational arenas. On the surface, university officials such as those at the KMU were supportive of African students and their right to live and pursue an education in the GDR. At times, however, the private statements that these officials made about African men and their white girlfriends or wives belied their supposedly neutral, antiracist attitudes. African women were not exempt from the racialization that men experienced. The stereotypes adhering to them were not the same—women were imagined as lacking moral discipline rather than being sexually wanton—but they were also subject to an East German "postcolonial gaze" that found them wanting in terms of behavior and hygiene. The cure, as it was for African men, was training in proper manners and East German morality.

At the same time, over the years the presence of African students became routinized. They either lived in the same dormitories as East German students[6] or in international dorms, which housed exchange students from countries around the world.[7] According to Ginga Eichler, an East German who lived in an international dorm during the 1960s, the reason that dorms for international students were established was relatively mundane. During the annual *Leipziger Messe*, or trade fair, Leipzig dormitories were repurposed to house *Messe* guests. While East German students usually went home for the holidays during the *Messe*, international students did not have that option. Thus dormitories where international students could continue to live even during the *Messe* were created.[8] On the flip side, Mac Con Uladh has shown that the conditions in the international student dorms were often poorer than those in dormitories housing primarily East German students.[9]

Archival records also indicate that relationships between African male students and East German women were fairly commonplace. Many personal files from the Karl-Marx-Universität in Leipzig reveal such relationships. Perhaps most indicative of the prevalence of interracial unions was the existence of an illegal "abortion ring" in the 1960s. According to accounts from the Leipzig District Court, a Nigerian student of agriculture was the middleman facilitating contact between African students with pregnant East German girlfriends and a woman who performed abortions for financial compensation. The accounts show that the woman, who was also East German, carried out at least sixty abortions between 1962 and 1965, primarily on women who had been "impregnated by an African student."[10] I will discuss how the case was handled and its more complex implications for the history of Afro-German relationships later in the chapter. What the court case first confirms, however, is that relationships between Africans and Germans were unexceptional. They became points of political debate and were freighted with long-held stereotypes of Black sexuality. Nonetheless, they frequently occurred.

African and German Sexuality in the GDR

There were subtle shifts in how Germans dealt with sexual relationships between white women and Black men over time. In the imperial and Weimar eras, African carnal desires were seen as a threat, and in the Nazi period they were to be expunged through measures such as sterilization. Throughout, however, the notion that African male and German female sexuality constituted an explosive combination remained relatively consistent. Given this consistency in attitudes, it would have been surprising if this belief had not persisted in the GDR.[11] Indeed, a 1959 report concerning international students by the vice rector for student affairs at the KMU suggests how little ideas about the relationship between Black men and white women had changed from the early twentieth century. In a section of the report labeled "the moral situation," the vice rector commented that "from time to time there are some students—especially those from African countries—who make themselves vulnerable to complaints because of their association with questionable women." He continued: "We are convinced that this state of affairs will be improved through the strengthening of our cultural work with these international students."[12] In other words, the vice rector thought that immoral German women were enticing African men, who were unable to control their sexual urges. Moreover, he saw East German, socialist morality as the answer to the problem of sexual impropriety.

Some Africans overstepped the moral bounds of the GDR so completely that they put themselves in danger of being expelled from the country. In 1963, the director of a dormitory in Leipzig complained that a Malian vocational student's promiscuity was causing problems for other residents. The man usually did not come home until at least one in the morning, and he was always with a different woman. He had rejected all attempts to dissuade him from this behavior. The director did not consider him worthy of receiving education in the GDR and recommended sending him back to Mali.[13] The process whereby the GDR would have ejected the student was, however, very dissimilar to a colonial expulsion. Removal could only take place after lengthy examination of an individual case and in consultation with Mali or another African partner state.[14] There was no summary expulsion. Under the political circumstances, the GDR tread cautiously, unwilling to upset relations with African nations.

The East German "corrective" to aberrant African behavior was thus different from that of earlier eras, even if the stereotype was similar. Rather than expelling or deporting perceived offenders, GDR officials hoped to take another tack. They were optimistic that the East German example of morality would save African students from their own worst impulses. To this end, Leipzig's vice rector even recommended that dormitory directors "work patiently and doggedly" on the issue of appropriate sexuality with African students.[15] Sexual conditioning was apparently part and parcel of the general East German goal of Marxist (re)education. A good Marxist not only hewed to a specific ideology; he was also able to exercise self-control over his baser impulses. There were occasional expulsions on moral or sexual grounds, as for example with the Nigerian who helped women procure abortions or a Ghanaian medical student who admitted that he had raped an East German colleague.[16] But students were more commonly allowed to remain, in the belief that they could be "rehabilitated."[17]

The morality that the East German political and educational institutions hoped to impart to their African male and female students closely echoed SED leader Walter Ulbricht's 1958 speech "Ten Commandments of Socialist Morality." As Jennifer V. Evans has argued, while there is a rich historiography on the conservative ethics of the postwar West, including the FRG, there has been less emphasis on the similarly staid morality of the 1950s and 1960s GDR.[18] This conservative, family-centered morality was reflected in Ulbricht's speech, as he urged East German citizens to behave in an upright, virtuous manner. His call to moral decency was also intended as a blow to the FRG, which he depicted as a hotbed of sin completely under the control of the debauched United States.[19] Josie McLellan's work on love and sex in the GDR also shows the extent to which the state remained conventional in its attitudes toward sex and the family at least in the 1950s and 1960s, allowing for some sexual liberation but largely within the framework of traditional heterosexual pairings.[20] In this context, Africa could be viewed not only as a political battleground but also a moral one, where those students who were trained in socialist countries would become models of responsibility, while capitalist Westerners fell deeper into depravity.

Ulbricht envisioned a properly moral GDR, where citizens were decent and hardworking and the state promoted an antiracist, anti-imperial dogma. In reality, though, fear of African sexuality continued. Conflict over racial biases and the extent to which they should be allowed to exist persisted alongside that fear, since it was clear that prejudice weakened the GDR's image as a racially neutral society. In 1963, for example, a bar brawl in Leipzig brought the debate on both African-German relationships and the GDR's antiracist commitment into sharp relief. The manager of the pub where the incident occurred reported that a large group of African students had fought with a handful of Eastern Europeans. The fight began inside the restaurant, surged into the foyer and cloakroom, and ended on the streets of Leipzig. As the brawl moved from place to place, more Africans joined.[21]

The bar manager used the event as a platform to make commentary on the goings-on at his café and his impressions of the general problem with African students and sexually available German women. He claimed that many such women frequented his establishment and lowered its reputation. One of these women had even been the catalyst for the fight. Additionally, the manager maintained that Africans were essentially the only exchange students who caused him difficulties. Indian, Chinese, Japanese, Korean, and Arab students were not disruptive. Neither, he intoned, were *most* Africans; but when troubles did occur, Africans were usually the culprits.[22]

While he denigrated his African clientele, the manager also held himself up as a properly antiracist East German citizen. He said that he and his staff always treated their African clientele in a friendly manner, and that neither his employees nor his other customers had ever made a bigoted remark in their presence. African impropriety only concerned him because of the effect it might have on the broader Leipzig public. When Africans misbehaved in front of Germans, he fretted that they reinforced preexisting "racist, stupid prejudices." The conduct of a minority of African students would harm the entire African community, since Germans would not differentiate between the troublemakers and the larger population. Moreover, if discrimination became rampant, it "would not serve the continuous struggle of honest socialists the world over for the abolition of racial antagonism."[23]

The manager's report on the fight became a general commentary on his African customers. It reflected broader inconsistencies and contradictions in GDR attitudes toward race. He asserted that his staff and patrons were not overtly racist but worried about the overall effect of African aggression on an *already* racist East Germany. The manager's personal prejudices were also on display. He placed himself on the side of international socialists who condemned racism but still assumed that it was the African students, not their Eastern European counterparts, who were responsible for the brawl. Further, he insinuated that Africans upset racialized and gendered orders in the GDR. If anyone shared culpability for the brawl, the manager took for granted that it was immoral white women. Together, African students and libertine German women destabilized a moral hierarchy in which German females were not meant to seduce or form connections with African males.

The manager envisaged a GDR that prized equality and reflected tolerance, but still prohibited African-German unions. He was not alone in conceiving of a GDR that was at once inclusive *and* exclusive. In the mid-1960s, the head of the Malian students' organization in the GDR accused a representative from the KMU's office of international affairs of viciously slandering a fellow Malian. He was charged with telling the man's German wife that her African husband would probably cheat, because he believed that Africans were only in East Germany to have children with as many women as possible.[24] The representative's superior at the KMU upbraided him for making such an uncouth, racist remark, and warned him that he would have to watch his language in the future. Yet the superior also made it clear that he shared his subordinate's suspicion of African men who had relationships with German women. He even agreed that Africans would likely stray from monogamous relationships. However, he confided, he did not want the Malians to know his true opinion.[25] Officially, he hoped to portray the GDR as a paragon of racial equality to its African students, who were esteemed guests. In private, he doubted African morality and fidelity.

The Malians were not the only Africans who remarked on the prejudice that they encountered in the GDR, or its equation with their relationships to white women. The 1965 displeasure of the UASA over the personal experiences of their members in the GDR, addressed in the last chapter, focused to a large extent on issues of interracial sex. The UASA argued that cultural misunderstandings played a role in recent physical altercations between Africans and East Germans, but so too did entrenched racism with regard to African sexuality, which was evident in attitudes toward African men who went out with German women. The drivers of the Leipzig Taxi Association were particularly guilty. The UASA related that "here we see arrogance, jealousy, and perhaps even hatred. Maybe some individuals think it is disgraceful to drive Africans—and there are many who will not serve us at all when they see girls in our company."[26] Discrimination made everyday activities like going out for the evening challenging. The UASA intoned that if something was not done about racism, there would be more conflict. This might reach the Western press and prove embarrassing for all involved.[27]

The government response to UASA complaints, as discussed in the previous chapter, was to send officials from the Ministry of Education to speak with African students in Leipzig and Rostock. In these meetings, the GDR representatives emphasized that the union was responsible for policing the behavior of its members and making sure they were well mannered and did not draw attention to themselves. Among other things, this meant that the UASA should "warn the African students against visiting dubious night clubs and excessive drinking."[28] East German women were not mentioned, but their presence at these venues was implied. Education officials placed the onus for stopping race-based attacks solely on the UASA, and they suggested that African students, not racist East Germans, were the ones who needed to change their behavior.

As the above examples suggest, GDR officials, like their imperial-era forebears, saw African sexuality as something that had to be controlled. Yet if African men became weak around German women, they were not solely accountable. The blame for interracial sex was assigned as much to German women as to African men, if not more so. "Loose" German women and girls often appear at the center of discussions on African sexuality. For example, a woman complained to the KMU in late July 1967 that a Nigerian student had been bothering her granddaughter and her granddaughter's German boyfriend.[29] He often came uninvited to the granddaughter's flat. The KMU's response was terse and to the point. Her granddaughter had willingly entered into the relationship with the Nigerian student. According to him, she had even given him the key to her apartment. Now that the office of international student affairs was aware of the relationship, the representative who wrote to the grandmother told her that he had advised the student to reconsider his bond to her young granddaughter. After all, she already had three children.[30]

The KMU implicitly rebuked the granddaughter for being a single mother, and one who was sexually open enough to give a man continual access to her home. Cold War politics may also have had their part in the KMU siding with the student. The grandmother wrote her letter to the KMU only a few weeks after the start of Nigeria's Biafran War at the beginning of July 1967. Before Biafra, the Soviet Bloc had experienced difficulties gaining a foothold in independent Nigeria, which had rebuffed efforts of aid from the USSR and its partners. The civil war in Nigeria thus provided the Soviets and their allies with an opportunity to support the Nigerian federal government when the West showed reluctance.[31] In this context, it was important for the GDR to proceed gingerly and not offend the Nigerian medical student in question, who was an honored guest. Meanwhile, the woman's granddaughter was dismissed for being sexually available.

The apprehension surrounding African men and German women often fed into another fear, which KMU officials hinted at in their discussions of the Malian man and his East German wife: that Africans and Germans would have children together. The stereotype of the African male held in thrall to sexually available German women or girls was, indeed, complemented by the trope of the *Mischlingskind*. In the wake of the bar brawl in 1963, a local Leipziger wrote several scathing letters to the dean of the KMU concerning German women and their relationships with African men. He made special reference to the "unfortunate children who will now become a burden on our social welfare system."[32] The man railed against what he perceived as the lowering of German women's moral values, as well as against the creation of children who would strain the GDR's social safety net, in language very reminiscent of both the imperial era and the Third Reich.

The majority of stories about the children of African men and German women that emerge from the University of Leipzig Archives, however, make few direct references to race. They focus instead on absent African fathers and unpaid alimony. Of these stories, the most descriptive comes from a man who wrote the department of international student affairs at the KMU in 1973 to request information on a former Cameroonian student. The man's daughter met and had a relationship with the Cameroonian during Leipzig's June 1967 Agricultural Exhibition (Agra) and gave birth to a girl the following March. While the man did refer to his granddaughter as a *Mischling-Tochter*, he seemed less concerned about her African heritage than he did about his own daughter's promiscuity. What upset him most was that at first "she allegedly did not know the father's name." This meant that she could not ask the Cameroonian student for financial support. Five years later, she finally found a notebook with his name and address written inside, and this prompted her father to turn to the KMU. He hoped that if the former student were found, his granddaughter would not only receive alimony but also finally have a father of her own.[33]

This man's account displays some of the contradiction and ambivalence common to GDR narratives on African men and East German women. He chastised his daughter for being loose, sleeping with, and getting pregnant by a man she barely knew. His image of her was not much different from the impression that the restaurant manager had of the German women who waited for African men at the bar, or that of a Leipzig landlady who complained about German girls participating in orgies with the Sudanese men who lived in her building.[34] Even so, he wanted to find his granddaughter's father, for money, to be sure, but also for more personal reasons. He gave no indication that he cared whether his granddaughter's father was African, only that he wanted her to know him.

Family acceptance of an African suitor did not always mean that the East German state would bless the relationship. In the early 1960s, a Togolese man fell in love with an East German law student. Her family warmed to him without reservation and made him feel as though he belonged. They made plans to marry. Initially, the Togolese government refused to give him the necessary papers. When one Togolese regime was replaced by another in 1963, however, the student went home and was able to get the required documents. By that time, he and his fiancée had a child together. Now, however, it was the GDR that stood in the way of the marriage. Local authorities would not issue a permit allowing them to marry when he returned to the country for a three-week visit in 1964. In 1967, he was living in Togo but planning yet another short trip to the GDR, and was still trying to get permission to marry. He wrote to Gerald Götting, at the time vice president of the GDR's privy council, begging him to intercede in the matter.[35]

The records are silent on whether the couple ever married. The Togolese student also gave no reason for why he believed the local authorities in Aue, where his fiancée's family lived, rejected their application for marriage. On the face of it, the case may seem a simple one of small-town officials turning down the appeal of an interracial couple. Considering the highly ambivalent attitude toward African-German relations illustrated above, this may well have been so. However, this is an instance where we must tread carefully. In 1966, the African department of the GDR's Ministry of Foreign Affairs recommended that another young woman not marry her Togolese fiancé. The official who made the recommendation did so on the grounds that the GDR had neither political representation in Togo nor any ties to the state.[36] Additionally, the Togolese student who could not receive permission to marry his fiancée from Aue had complained of the preferential treatment that students from Ghana, Guinea, and Mali received in a different context, while he was enrolled at the FDGB College in Bernau. He protested against their privileged status among the college staff, which contrasted sharply with the poor reception that he claimed greeted Togolese students at the school.[37] The SED viewed Ghana, Guinea, and Mali as friendly, socialist-leaning states, all of which ultimately allowed the GDR to establish trade missions.[38] Togo had no such political connections. With this evidence in mind, the decision may have been motivated as much by politics as questions of race.

Another case from 1972 highlights the difficulty of determining whether political consideration, racial discrimination, or a combination of both were responsible for official attitudes toward interracial relationships. In August of that year a Zairean attaché in Belgrade complained that the GDR was making it difficult for a Zairean student to leave East Germany with his wife. The attaché claimed that the GDR wanted proof that the student would have adequate means to support his wife in Zaire, including an apartment and a job, before they would be allowed to depart.[39] In what seems on the surface to be the polar opposite of the Zambian case, the attaché noted that, per a 1965 law, Zaireans were free to marry whomever they chose, and that no special permission from Zairean authorities was required.[40] Zaire, which is now the Democratic Republic of Congo, was by this point staunchly in the American camp.[41]

These intriguing examples suggest that, while racism was still a serious barrier for interracial couples, the Africans' predicament must be understood within a wider political framework. Where an African came from may have been as important as the fact of his African-ness. Love between capitalists and communists could be taboo. Students from states like Togo and Zaire—who by the mid-1960s were rarities to begin with given the lack of diplomatic connections between their nations and the GDR—may well have been discriminated against on racial bases. At the same time, their position as citizens of Western allies made them undesirable partners for political reasons, too.

Most accounts of absent African fathers are more banal. In 1982, the attorney for a woman in Leipzig wrote to the KMU asking for information on the income of a Tanzanian student, an agricultural engineer who had studied there from 1970 to 1975. He was the father of the woman's child, and she was presumably interested in alimony.[42] Likewise, in 1977 another Cameroonian man, who had studied medicine in Rostock during the 1960s and left for West Germany in 1971, was being sought in connection with a daughter he had fathered in 1966.[43] Moreover, in 1976 the ex-girlfriend of a Mozambican contacted the KMU because he had failed to send his latest alimony payment.[44]

These fragments represent a sampling of the various cases in which East German women petitioned the KMU to locate their husbands and help them get alimony. The stories of these absent African fathers can be compared with the reports on African American men who formed relationships with West German women much earlier, in the 1940s and 1950s, and then returned to the United States leaving their girlfriends or wives and children behind.[45] However, we must be careful not to equate these two groups too closely. In the first place, while some of the racial stereotypes adhering to Africans and African Americans may have been similar, the two groups came from different contexts and traveled to Germany with different goals. The African Americans were mainly soldiers and occupiers, who were confronted with both American and German prejudices a decade or two before most of the African students in question were in the GDR. Indeed, as Fehrenbach and Höhn have both argued, the American prejudice against Blacks was stronger than the German, and African Americans were commonly forced to return to the United States after completing their tours of duty in the Federal Republic even when they wanted to stay. They were compelled to leave because the United States military command frowned upon romantic relations between Black GIs and white German women and was eager to separate couples.[46]

The exact reasons why specific African men left their girlfriends and children in East Germany are often unclear. Since many Africans were sent to the GDR to study by their governments, they were expected to return and use their education to fulfill their duties to the state in fields such as tropical medicine or agriculture. Under such circumstances, they may have had little choice but to leave. Politics may have played a role in other situations, too. Cameroon, like Togo, did not have a political connection with the GDR, though there were also fathers from countries that did have ties, such as Tanzania. Visas to extend stays in the GDR seemed, furthermore, to have been difficult to acquire once exchange students completed their studies. The length of time that often elapsed between the birth of a child and search for absent fathers also indicates that some couples had broken up, and thereafter contact was lost. Finally, because the rates of single motherhood had been rising overall in the GDR since the 1960s, it is possible that the mothers of Afro-German children were considered unremarkable and not in need of special governmental treatment or effort.[47]

Racial difference was not supposed to exist in the GDR, but the attitudes of GDR officials and people on the ground demonstrated that East Germans continued to make race-based assumptions about Africans. Class difference, too, allegedly disappeared under socialism. Yet the stories of relationships between African men and East German women indicate that the concept of morality was closely linked to that of class, and that the moral hierarchy suggested in discussions of interracial liaisons was perhaps standing in for a class hierarchy. The European belief that lower-class women were the only ones who would consort with African men was deep-rooted, stretching back to at least the nineteenth century and only gathering strength in the first half of the twentieth century. For example, Lucy Bland has shown that in colonial Britain the press construed white women who had relationships with non-Western men as either poor or prostitutes; they were assumed only to be with their lovers because of the monetary gain it would bring.[48]

The idea that poor whites were usually the only ones who would form bonds with Black men was thus prevalent in Britain and its empire.[49] It also had a history in Germany, both before and after World War II. With rare exceptions, scholarship on interracial relationships in colonial Germany has tended to focus on connections between white men and Black women in Africa itself.[50] With the influx of African American GIs in the FRG after the war, however, work such as Höhn's and Fehrenbach's has shifted focus to romances between white German women and Black American soldiers. West German women who fraternized with African American GIs were sometimes depicted as economically disadvantaged. Höhn has shown that middle-class German men were disturbed by what they saw as lower-class women breaking sexual and racial taboos when they dated African American men with disposable incomes. American wealth was leading them astray and upsetting previously stable class hierarchies.[51] The "Veronikas" who dated the GIs were, moreover, described as prostitutes, only further reinforcing the sense that they were from the lower class.[52]

The idea that the women who went out with African men were lower class was also present in the GDR. It was, however, couched in terms of morality rather than economics. The women who had relations with Africans were described as "questionable" or "dubious," adjectives that would have been applied to women of blue-collar backgrounds in another time or place.[53] These women showed poor judgment in their actions when they flirted with Africans in bars or at parties, just as the working-class women across the border in the FRG did when they went out with the GIs.

Little is known about the actual class status of the East German women. The women's social standing is obscure, though the single mothers requesting alimony from long-absent partners likely needed it to support their families. But while the economic markers of class are unclear, moral markers as defined by the SED are very evident. Weak morality may, moreover, have been correlated to more than the breaking of racial taboos. The state may have imagined, as McLellan has suggested, that the benefits of an interracial relationship were largely material.[54] Africans were able to traverse the border to the West—and in most cases return across it—whenever they liked. Meanwhile, the GDR forbid its citizens travel outside the Eastern Bloc. Marriage to an African man could allow an East German woman to follow him outside the state. If a woman did so, she would be breaking Ulbricht's second moral commandment, which bid her to love and defend her fatherland.[55] Additionally, in departing for nonaligned or Western-affiliated countries women would enter the capitalist system, in itself a betrayal of the socialist GDR. In the FRG, clergy and politicians condemned the "Veronikas" for seeking out American GIs for the material comforts they could provide.[56] In the GDR, women may well have been chastised along similar lines.

Of course, examples of East German women leaving the GDR with their African partners are rare, with African states sometimes as reluctant to accept East German women migrants as the GDR was to let the same women go. Recall the beginning of this chapter, when I discussed the case of the Zambian ambassador who requested that the GDR prevent East German women from marrying Zambian men. In another instance the Malian government pressed the GDR to find a suitable training opportunity for a student who was married to an East German woman. The government argued that the man and his wife should remain in the GDR because "as a tradesman, he will not be able to support a family with a European wife."[57] Obtaining permission to marry a foreigner was difficult, too, as McClellan notes.[58] And we have seen that the women who requested alimony had obviously neither married their spouses nor left the GDR. Still, GDR officials might well have viewed even the intent to abandon the state as moral treachery.

At the same time, the question of the offspring that might result from interracial relationships, whether or not the relationships ended in marriage, was handled differently than it would have been in earlier eras. The case of the Nigerian student who helped facilitate abortions in the 1960s is illustrative. It encapsulates the confusion over the place of the racialized other in the GDR, as well as the morality surrounding sexual and reproductive politics. The state punished the student with one year in prison and immediate expulsion from the GDR after his release.

Upon delivering its sentence, the district court in Leipzig framed the crime that the Nigerian and his two East German accomplices had committed in expressly moral terms. The verdict commented that "(our) state and its insti tutions pay particular attention to the development of healthy families und happy people in secure material circumstances. The accused have behaved unscrupulously and with disdain for this humanistic goal . . . and in addition to violating socialist law have crudely transgressed against the morality of our workers."[59] The court continued to address the illegal abortions as injurious to the GDR at its core. Drawing on the *Gesetz über den Mutter- und Kinderschutz und die Rechte der Frau* of 1950 (Law for the Protection of Mothers and Children and the Rights of Women), the judgment against the student and his colleagues maintained that the abortions they enabled violated the sanctity of human life and deprived the state of potential contributing citizens. It was an affirmation of the GDR's pronatal politics that McLellan and others have addressed; every individual was valuable, and every destruction of life therefore a crime.[60]

What the case further illuminates is the clear identification of mixed-race children as protected citizens of the East German state. This markedly differentiates it from discussions of cases involving abortion and interracial couples in the immediate postwar FRG. Fehrenbach has spoken to the issue of so-called eugenic abortions in early postwar West Germany. She has shown that in 1945–1946, women who claimed rape by non-Western soldiers were likely to have their petitions for abortion approved.[61] This was true for both the Western and Soviet zones, as abortions on "moral" grounds were allowed in the latter.[62]

Donna Harsch has also demonstrated that "eugenic" abortions were permitted in the GDR in rare instances during the early 1950s. However, it is significant that these were not linked to racial considerations. She describes communist pronatalist policies as not unlike those of the Nazis, with the important distinction that race did not factor into decisions on whether a child was deemed fit for survival.[63] The Leipzig district court certainly did not consider race when it punished the Nigerian student and his two East German associates for performing abortions on women pregnant with mixed-race children; they were prospective citizens, and their destruction was criminal. The incident of the "abortion ring" and its legal treatment thus further highlights East German ambivalence toward race. The women who slept with African men were tramps, but their children were citizens. Marriage was allowed in some cases, but not in others. The GDR's conduct toward racial others was more inconsistent than authors such as McLellan have suggested, and it likely reflected confusion among administrators and citizens over how and whether to integrate non-whites into the GDR's body politic.

African Women in the GDR

Not many African female students surface in the archival records that I have examined, although in some nations there was a keen interest in having them study abroad, as was the case with Zambia, which I discussed in chapter 2. Over the course of East German history, women seem to have constituted only around 10–12 percent of the African student population.[64] Indeed, African women often appear more as an absence than a presence. They are cited as the spouses whom male students left behind when they went to the GDR or the women to whom these men remitted money home each month to cover family expenses. In other cases, they are sometimes visible as spurned wives whose husbands met new girlfriends abroad and left them. Women are, moreover, frequently included among candidates who might have come to the GDR to study, but were ultimately prevented from doing so. Finally, unlike the male African students, who often had relationships with East German women, African women did not appear to have forged similar romantic bonds with East German men.[65]

As with African men, however, women were often discussed in terms of their morality. There was some continuity but also marked difference in how the GDR assessed African women vis-à-vis how Germans had imagined them in the colonial, Weimar, and Nazi eras. Prior to World War II, the attitude toward Black female sexuality was partially determined by a confusion over whether African women were suitable mates for German men, given the lack of German women in the colonies. German authorities permitted "mixed" marriages between German men and African women until the early twentieth century, when the practice was banned.[66] Moreover, African women in the colonies were often discussed in terms of their sexual availability and the violent control white men appropriated over it.[67] In the Weimar Republic, African American jazz singer Josephine Baker epitomized Black female sexuality and the supposed "primitivity" of Black women.[68] By the Nazi era, what few Black women there were inside Germany were subjected to the same brutal treatment as men, which could include sterilization.[69]

In the GDR, women were critiqued less for unbridled sexuality than they were for an inability to comport themselves correctly, in other words to "behave." Sexism and racism intersected and either kept African women out of the country entirely or complicated their lives in it. The SED prided itself on having both antiracist and antisexist policies. Yet in both instances, the policies often had an uneven effect on East German culture at large. As Jane Freeland has pointed out, in the 1950s socialist morality shaped East German under-

Figure 12. "'Smile, please, Adriana!' Adriana Hayford obliged our reporter, who met her in the Berlin City Center at Friedrichstrasse Train Station. Adriana—the friendly girl from Ghana—studies art history and theater in Berlin and enjoys writing home about her interesting classes. Above: (Adriana's) thoughts are with her parents at home." (caption text from Bundesarchiv) Hayford is shown mailing her letter in this highly stylized pose. Contrary to the caption, Hayford is decidedly not smiling. Zentralbild Brüggeman Co., February 8, 1962 (Bundesarchiv).

standing of women's sexuality,[70] much as it did the understanding of African male sexuality. Women's desires had to be controlled in order to fashion a gender-equal, socialist utopia. That female sexual impulses needed to be disciplined while male ones did not undercut the SED's antisexist message. So too did the "double burden" that women were subject to at home; they worked all day just like men, but unlike men, who could relax once they came home, women took on most domestic responsibilities, including meal preparation, cleaning, and childcare, after the workday ended.[71] Women were, as Harsch has demonstrated, very aware of the state's failure to craft the gender equality it touted, and they pressed the SED to make good on its claims.[72]

In terms of racism, on the surface African women's experiences of the

Figure 13. Quedlinburg: view of the city. "Thirty-one young people from Africa are currently learning the secrets of medicine and nursing. The experienced doctors and nurses at Quedlinburg Hospital and other medical establishments in the GDR ensure a high level of education in physical assistance and nursing for students from Mali, Nigeria, Cameroon, and northern Rhodesia." (caption text from Bundesarchiv) Zentralbild Schmidt, May 3, 1963 (Bundesarchiv).

GDR were not that different from those of African men. Both encountered anti-Blackness in their daily lives. East German attitudes toward African women, however, were often expressed in ways that subtly reflected not only racial bias but gender bias. The 1968 story of B.K., a Guinean woman studying at the Deutsche Hochschule für Körperkultur (DHfK)—the German Sports Academy—is illustrative. B.K. was forcibly kicked off a train from Dresden to Leipzig when the conductor alleged that she did not have a ticket. This conductor explicitly told her that he believed Africans were all alike and implied that they were freeloaders and thieves. After the conductor threw B.K. off the train, the security guards at the station took her into their office and attempted to comfort her, patting her shoulder and trying to convince her that not all Germans were "so bad." However, later, in a letter to the DHfK, the Dresden transportation authorities who employed the same guards contended that B.K. had caused an altercation and demanded that the school discipline B.K. for her behavior on the train, although there was no evidence that she had acted inappropriately and she vehemently disputed the charge.[73]

If we look at B.K.'s story closely, as well as at the stories of other African women accused of "inappropriate" behavior, we can find gender-specific tropes embedded within the racism directed at women that were different from those directed at men. Although no overt sexual moves were made, the guards did touch B.K. in an attempt to soothe her, in what may be interpreted as a physically or even sexually transgressive act. Later, however, the transportation authorities claimed that B.K. had been particularly aggressive in her original encounter with the conductor, as well as with them. The DHfK sided with B.K. in the dispute. However, in another context, DHfK officials also described her as belligerent. B.K. was one of four Guinean women attending the DHfK and training to become volleyball coaches. B.K. was described as having an especially contentious relationship with one of the other Guinean women, and reports said that the two sniped at each other and had even come to blows. More generally, the whole group was depicted as slovenly and unladylike, and thus unable to maintain the proper discipline and decorum in their shared quarters. Here there were continuities with earlier eras; as Nancy Reagin has remarked, German women in South West Africa also looked upon their African female counterparts as dirty and unable to create domesticity or impose discipline in their households.[74]

The Guineans were not the only women portrayed as aggressive, disruptive, untidy, and ultimately immoral. A.A., a Nigerian woman studying medicine in the GDR during the late 1960s and early 1970s, was chastised for a lack of discipline in her studies and a failure to behave "appropriately" outside the classroom. Roommates and neighbors at her dorm reported that A.A. was aggressive and unmanageable, as did workers in the office where she picked up her monthly stipend. An East German student named S.D. accused A.A. of slapping her after S.D. stepped on her foot in a streetcar. S.D. did not report the altercation to the police, but she did bring it to the attention of the KMU. As a result, an advisor in the office for exchange student affairs warned A.A. not to become physically violent in future interactions and told her that she needed to "control" (*beherrschen*) herself.[75]

African men were also described as aggressive. However, their aggression was tied to sexual desire and to their supposed inability to constrain themselves around white women. By contrast, African women's aggression was linked to a sense of feminine respectability that they supposedly lacked. In addition,

African women experienced the problem of the GDR's "double burden," though in a somewhat different way than their East German peers. Those African women who were married and, especially, those who had children had limited options if they wanted to study in East Germany. In some cases, they had to leave their children behind because the GDR would not financially accommodate whole African families, and in others they did not come at all if they had children.

African countries also threw up obstacles to women who wanted to study abroad. Such obstacles were related to a colonial legacy of providing more access to Western education for boys than for girls, on the one hand, and on the other to the developmental priorities of most postcolonial states. Women were often ineligible for scholarships because they lacked secondary education, and sometimes even primary education. In chapter 3, we saw how Zambian women, deemed unfit for work in the copper mines, were denied even the rudimentary education offered to men under the British colonial regime. The Zambian experience was not unique. Colonial authorities, missionaries, and African fathers generally all focused on the education of boys to the detriment of girls.[76] In the early postcolonial period, from the late 1950s through the early 1970s, this meant that there were many more men qualified to apply for study abroad than women.

The priorities of postcolonial governments were furthermore oriented in such a way as to make men more appealing candidates for study abroad. These governments were chiefly concerned with national development, that is, with the technological modernization of their countries. The European colonial powers had sorely neglected infrastructure, health care, and advanced agriculture in their respective colonies. Once they were decolonized, these new nations lagged behind the West in terms of development and ability to provide for their populations and compete in a global economy. At the same time, politicians in various African countries wanted to indigenize their professional labor force. Many of the experts available to help build the infrastructure, improve medical treatment, and increase agricultural production were European or American. Dissatisfied with this state of affairs, African leaders saw an urgent need to train their own people in careers such as engineering, medicine, veterinary medicine, or pharmacy. Lacking the resources to do so at home, they often looked abroad for places to send students to earn their degrees.

This preference made it difficult for women, since African governments run by men decided not only which candidates would be chosen for overseas scholarships but also which subjects to prioritize. African women tended to be relegated to "feminine" or "caring" professions. With the exception of medicine, most of the professions that African officials wanted to indigenize were deemed technical and gendered male. In the GDR, African women commonly received training in medicine, biology, nursing, and midwifery—fields that would enable them to enter professions in health care—or German, history, philosophy, and other humanities subjects that would lead to careers in teaching. By contrast, African women rarely studied agriculture, architecture, or engineering, disciplines that were coded as masculine and attracted mainly male students. In addition, they did not enter programs in vocational areas outside the medical arena. There were no women training to become auto mechanics, miners, or truck drivers. This meant that, with the exception of medicine, the kinds of careers that women were likely to follow did not match African governmental priorities of what was needed for development. Women were therefore at a distinct disadvantage when they applied for scholarships.

Forces in the GDR also conspired to keep the number of female students low. Women were often unable to combine motherhood with studies in the GDR and were less likely to become candidates in the first place because they either lacked qualifications or were shunted toward professions that were not deemed national priorities. Nevertheless, African women were part of the story of African students in the GDR from the beginning. Agnes Yetunde Bankole, née Idowu, was the sole woman among the first eleven Nigerians to come to the GDR in 1951. She studied medicine at the KMU and eventually became an obstetrician who practiced in both the GDR and the United Kingdom, becoming intimately involved with East German women's lives through her work in obstetrics.

The exact details of Bankole's life are scant. Compared to most of the ten men who went to Nigeria with her, archival documentation about Bankole is thin. Many of the men's *Lebensläufe*, or curriculum vitae, have been preserved; Bankole's is missing. Nonetheless, it is possible to glean some information about Bankole and her occupation. She was one of the three youngest Nigerian students in the first group that went to the GDR; indeed, Bankole was still a month shy of her fifteenth birthday when she arrived in East Germany in April 1951.[77] She did not begin her medical studies right away, instead entering a German-language course at the Arbeiter- und Bauern Fakultät (ABF) of the university, where she probably took college preparatory classes as well. This was typical. None of the Nigerians spoke much German when they got to Leipzig, and all had to enroll in a basic class. Bankole made excellent progress in the course, and the instructor noted that she had a "musical gift" and "unusually good memory," both of which served her well as she learned the language.[78]

Figure 14. Bankole when she first arrived in Leipzig in 1951 at age fourteen, chatting with young pioneers. ADN-ZB Donath, Vorbereitung zu den III Weltfestspiele der Jugend und Studenten Berlin, July 1951 (Bundesarchiv)

Figure 15. At International Students in the GDR Day: "a friendly chat during a break in the event." Bankole is pictured at right. Zentralbild Bez. Red. Leipzig Naumann, January 23, 1956 (Bundesarchiv).

Bankole stayed at the ABF until 1954, when she graduated from Leipzig's preuniversity program with a grade of "good" (gut).[79] At that point she entered the university's medical school, where she would stay until receiving her medical degree in November 1959. She must have married her husband, the Nigerian student Akintola Bankole, before that, since Bankole and not her maiden name, Idowu, is on her completed dissertation. Between 1953 and 1956, Bankole mostly worked on the practical portion of the dissertation, which was entitled "A Contribution to Causal Research on Perinatal Child Mortality." Bankole conducted her research at the Women's Clinic of Karl-Marx-University. She examined two hundred instances of infants who were either stillborn or died shortly after birth. In looking at the reasons behind their deaths, Bankole took note of the mothers' health and the ways in which treatment of mothers could lead to better outcomes for both mothers and children. She exhorted the medical community to diagnose sexual diseases like syphilis during a pregnancy—since this was eminently possible but not happening frequently—to ensure the health of mother and child. Further, she commented on how a lack of space in the clinic necessitated home births, which had to be attended by either a doctor or experienced midwife. She also recommended expanding the clinic's bed space.[80]

While Bankole's dissertation was sparse and offered few substantive details aside from the ones above, she clearly worked intimately with pregnant and postnatal East German women. After finishing her degree, Bankole moved on to practice medicine at the women's clinic of the Berlin Charité University Hospital.[81] She was also president of the African Women's Union in the GDR,[82] as well as one of the early Nigerian student unions.[83] Documentation of her participation in these organizations beyond the fact that she led them is scant, but what exists evinces Bankole's clear interest in both women's issues and politics.

The fact that Bankole treated patients without complaint, as far as we know, demonstrates another way in which antiracist rhetoric was translating into reality. The presence of a Black female medical student and, later on, doctor may have been unusual for East Germany, as there were not many in the country, but it was also accepted. Moreover, Bankole's later career as an obstetrician in the GDR, Nigeria,[84] and the UK was very much determined by a commitment to treating women—most of whom were probably white.

Like Bankole, many African women students in the GDR were clustered in health-related disciplines, since these were among the fields that African politicians most highly prized. However, while there were other women studying medicine with the goal of becoming doctors, more were grouped in nursing, midwifery, or physiotherapy. Zanzibar, Togo, Mali, Kenya, and Zambia were all eager to have women study to become nurses or midwives abroad. For instance, in 1961 Kenyan politicians James Gichuru and J. K. Koinange sent a letter to Heinrich Eggebrecht, secretary of the GDR's Solidarity Committee, stating, "The world has learnt to day [sic] that (the) training of the people of underdeveloped countries is of paramount importance in order to prepare them for the running of the machineries and operations of Independent States." Gichuru and Koinange continued to say that on the eve of independence Kenya, "only boast(ed) . . . a meagre handful of doctors" and, in addition, "our first two women have (only) recently returned having been qualified in Nursing Midwifery and Health Visiting."[85] The country needed medical professionals in all fields, and Kenyan women fit into the program of national development as nurses and midwives in need of training abroad.

Women going abroad for nursing and midwifery degrees could technically end up anywhere, from other African countries such as Ghana or Tanza-

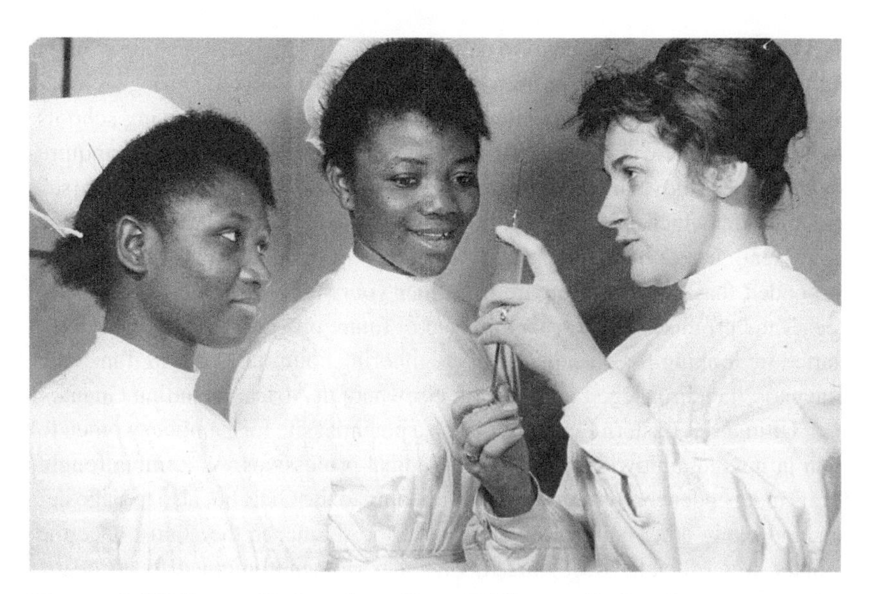

Figure 16. "Malian medical students. Young Malian medical students are currently enrolled at the medical school in Quedlinburg, where they are learning as much as they can about medicine so that, after they graduate, they can return home to contribute to the improvement of public health. 'Here are the true friends of our people,' said the leader of the twenty-person delegation from the young African nation. In the last year the workers of our republic have already sent important medications to Mali. Above: you have to know how to correctly give a shot." (caption text from Bundesarchiv) Zentralbild Schmidt, December 5, 1961 (Bundesarchiv). This image is stylized, with the white East German instructor clearly positioned as having authority over the Black Malian students.

nia, to Western Europe, the United States, or nonaligned nations like India. Nursing and midwifery programs in communist nations were, however, quite highly esteemed. The wife of Abeid Karume, Zanzibar's first president, observed that she had been "very impressed . . . by all that was done for and by women in Russia and East Germany" and was planning to work with their governments to send Zanzibari "girls" to both countries to study for nursing degrees.[86] Meanwhile P. Scher, the general secretary of Togo's Union of Health and Hygiene Workers, hoped to replace "colonial cronies" at the country's Ministry of Health with individuals trained in the GDR. For that purpose, he requested ten scholarships for Togolese women to study nursing and midwifery in East Germany.[87] There was, moreover, a pipeline of Malian nurses going to study in Berlin Buch by the early 1960s.[88]

No country, though, seems to have had as much interest in sending women abroad to become nurses as Zambia, as discussed in chapter 2. During its independence struggle UNIP was intent on finding them spots in nursing schools and colleges wherever it could. In 1961, Beatrice B. wrote to UNIP to inquire about further study, since her "intention (was) to be a state registered nurse" and midwife, which she could not train for at home. She thus requested that the party send her "outside Northern Rhodesia." In Dar es Salaam, Makasa responded that, "keen as you are to further your studies . . . UNIP is equally keen," and promised to keep her apprised of future prospects for study.[89] UNIP started by looking for placements in neighboring countries, such as Tanzania. The party then broadened its search to elsewhere in Africa, including Ghana.

Ultimately, Eastern Europe was also a potential site for Zambian women to train in nursing, midwifery, and other medical professions. As Zambia fought for its independence, women were sent not only to the GDR but also to Yugoslavia, and likely other nations in the Soviet Bloc.[90] Later in the 1960s, once the country was officially decolonized, Zambian women continued to go to the GDR to become nurses or midwives, often in the company of their husbands. Two women whose husbands were concentrating in different subjects started or continued their own studies in East German nursing programs in 1967.[91]

Area of study was not the only domain in which African women experienced East Germany differently from African men. Not surprisingly, their lives were also dramatically impacted by pregnancy and child-rearing. Indeed, while women were rarely discussed in terms of their sexual "appetites," as African men were, their sexuality became salient with regards to reproduction. Women's experiences in the GDR were commonly tied to issues of pregnancy, childbirth, and family, whereas African men were rarely seen in nurturing roles, even when they had children with their East German partners.

To take an example, Gloria I., Bankole's younger sister, came to the GDR in the 1960s to study German literature. Like many African men who studied in East Germany, she had a child during her stay. Unlike the men, she had sole responsibility for childcare. Her husband lived in England, leaving her alone with the baby.[92] Rudolf Große, one of Gloria I.'s professors at the KMU, thought that she was an excellent student with an impeccable knowledge of both English and German who voluntarily gave lectures in linguistics and literature. He made sure to note, however, that Gloria I.'s effort and discipline had begun to slacken after the birth of her child and the additional obligations that maternity entailed.[93]

Gloria I. seems to have been unusual in that her child was allowed to live with her in Leipzig. A.A., whom East German officials criticized for poor "discipline" in her dorm as well as in the classroom, also juggled pregnancy and family alongside her studies. When she arrived in the GDR in the late 1960s, A.A. already had two children and was pregnant with her third. The children did not live with her in the dorms; one was with a foster mother in London, where her husband worked as an engineer, and the other was resident in West Berlin.[94] Even so, while she studied A.A. also took care of her nephew, the son of her brother-in-law E.K., who was a veterinary student in Leipzig.[95] It is not clear whether the mother of E.K.'s child was East German or African, but she was more likely the former, since it was not easy for African wives to accompany their husbands to the GDR. A.A.'s own children did not live with her because the East German government frowned on international students bringing their children while they were at university. This was likely why A.A. concluded arrangements to have her children stay elsewhere. Her workload was obviously substantial and may well have contributed both to the poor grades that ultimately got her expelled from the university and to her violent "outbursts" that her fellow students and dormmates cited. She studied medicine and cared for E.K.'s son, all while being forced to live away from her own children.[96]

Gloria I. and A.A. were not alone in grappling to balance home and work life. K.S., a Malian woman, first came to the GDR to study orthopedics but later switched fields to train as a lab technician. In 1967, K.S., who was married to a Malian engineering student named M.T., was pregnant and already raising their two children in the GDR. The Malian government did not want her to live apart from her husband. Since there was no opportunity to study orthopedics in the same city as M.T., K.S. was compelled to change majors. Her situation was further complicated when she and M.T. asked the East German state department to help them find a new apartment, as theirs was too small for the growing family, along with a place for the baby in a local daycare. GDR authorities responded that they would be unable to continue financing her education unless the couple organized care for their children back in Mali. In other words, they did not want to pay extra to accommodate the couple's children in the country, and K.S. could only keep studying under the condition that they went away.[97] No such condition, however, was placed on her husband.

The unwillingness to allow African children into the GDR with their parents was a key reason that so few female students were in the country. On several occasions, male students requested that their wives and children accompany them to East Germany, so the women could then study. In 1961, Odhiambo Okello, a Kenya African Union representative in Cairo during the era prior to Kenyan independence, met with GDR officials in that city to address various issues related to students. He intoned that several male students wanted to bring their wives and families with them to East Germany. His request was flatly denied; the quota for Kenyan scholarships was set, and the GDR did not have the capacity to bring more people into the country.[98]

A year earlier, in 1960, Grégoire K. Kouessan, secretary of Togo's National Union of Workers, wrote a letter to the chairman of the FDGB that addressed, among other things, the issue of couples going to the GDR. Kouessan knew six Togolese men who wanted to train at the Trade Union College in Bernau. Three of the men were married, and each of them had five or six children. They were all worried about their families and what would happen to them while they were away. One asked whether his wife and children might join him so that she could also go to the college, and another hoped that the GDR might pay for his children to receive their educations in East Germany.[99]

While there was no follow-up to Kouessan's letter, none of the Togolese who actually studied at the Trade Union College in 1960 or 1961 were married or had children, making it likely that none of the married men or their wives actually enrolled. In this case, apprehension about bringing African families to the GDR existed on both the East German and Togolese sides, as Kouessan made clear that even if the GDR were to accept the families, his labor union in Togo would be unable to pay for them.[100]

Economic factors therefore intertwined with sexism to account for why women rarely studied in the GDR. Neither the GDR nor the sending African country was willing or able to fund families, but only single individuals, who were usually men. Further, the GDR really did lack the living space to accommodate them. Apartments were in short supply, and East German families could wait years for larger ones, relegated to ever more cramped living quarters when they added new members.[101] There was a similar lack of student housing. A representative for the GDR's Ministry of Higher and Vocational Education made this clear in a 1973 letter to the East German Embassy in Accra. He explained: "Recently there has been an increase in requests from international students to let their wives and children travel to the GDR with them. Unfortunately, we are not in a position to oblige this demand, as we simply cannot secure enough space in the dormitories." The students' families could visit them in East Germany—at their own expense—but most decidedly could not live there.[102]

In rare instances, Cold War politics played a role in allowing women and their families into the GDR. For example, in the early 1970s the director of international student affairs at the KMU had to negotiate an agreement that would allow the wives and families of Sudanese students to join them in the GDR or risk upsetting an educational agreement with Sudan's government. The situation was critical, because "until now (most) Sudanese students have only gone to imperial (i.e. western) nations, and never had difficulties (bringing their families)."[103] Since the GDR did not want to lose the students or damage relations with Sudan, the director recommended that the women be permitted to come and study in the GDR, even though he worried about the precedent it might set in an environment where family apartments were scarce. Africans had power here: the GDR needed the Sudanese students and had to honor their wishes.

Excluding such rare cases, however, the GDR and African partner nations both made it difficult for women to participate in study abroad programs. Owing to colonial imbalances, fewer African women had the educational background necessary to compete for scholarships than did men. In addition, African governments prized male-dominated occupations that women rarely entered. The East German dictum against African families living in the GDR further complicated women's path to a university or technical school in the country. These roadblocks to study abroad help explain why the number of African women in the GDR was so limited.

Conclusion

In many ways, stereotypes of African men in the GDR were not starkly different from those of previous generations. What had changed was that in the Cold War the GDR preached a policy of socialist openness and tolerance and claimed solidarity with the oppressed peoples of the world. Non-Westerners allegedly came to the country as equals, rather than subjects of a colonial state or hostile prisoners of war. The GDR had to compete with the FRG on any number of levels, and this meant accommodating Africans, even when that included acknowledgment of their sexual relationships with German women.

Contrary visions of the family also contributed to a difference in the reception of interracial relationships in the East. Fehrenbach has shown that in 1950s West Germany mothers of interracial children were commonly urged to give up their offspring. The belief was that they would not fit into German society and would be better off being raised by "their own kind." Afro-German children were consequently sent to orphanages or "repatriated" to the United States to live with adoptive African American families.[104] Nothing similar happened in the East. Indeed, if we take the story of the Zairean student and his family as an example, or that of Aryee-Boi and her mother, the GDR sometimes actively tried to prevent Afro-German children from leaving the country. Moreover, the state definitely considered Afro-Germans to be citizens, as the trial on illegal abortion makes clear.

Africans were still victims of prejudice in the East. The stories above clearly illustrate the continuation of a pernicious anti-Blackness. Further, Peggy Piesche has demonstrated that Afro-German children in the GDR encountered frequent, everyday racism.[105] Nonetheless, there was never an active attempt to remove Afro-German children from East Germany. The doctrine of solidarity mandated their inclusion on an official level, if not in daily life.

While the state may have accepted Afro-German children and possibly Afro-German families, it was distinctly unwelcoming to African children, as it was to African families. Unless it was politically expedient for the GDR to admit African women to study, African women with children found it very difficult to bring them along to East Germany. They were either forced to leave their children with caretakers outside the country or to forgo pursuing an education in the GDR.

Although African women did not enjoy this benefit, the more open attitude toward single motherhood in the GDR may provide another explanation for the greater acceptance of interracial couples and their offspring. As mentioned above, and as Anne Salles and Dagmar Herzog have observed, by the end of communist rule in the East the ratio of children born to single mothers in the GDR was much higher than in the FRG.[106] The banality of single motherhood and the increasing openness toward sexuality in the 1970s and 1980s, which McLellan has noted, would have made the presence of interracial families less shocking in the East than in the West.[107]

The official fiction that racism had been expunged from the East still meant, however, that African students and their children occupied an ambivalent space in the GDR. The students were subject to a "moral" education. This education was based on supposedly "primal" characteristics that had been assigned to Africans much earlier, in the colonial era and even before. It contradicted state claims that race did not matter, as well as state efforts to include Blacks in the body politic. At the same time, the mere presence of African students in East Germany as ambassadors of their countries, ones who might lead the way to solidifying diplomatic relations, was ultimately more critical than their moral character. African students were therefore both welcome for the political benefits they could bring to East Germany and held at arm's length because of the persistent racism that often surfaced in debates over African male sexuality and the immorality of some East German women. African students were not driven out of the GDR; neither were their lovers or their children. But they were never fully integrated into the East German state either.

Conclusion: African Students into the 1970s and 1980s

Geopolitical shifts in the early to mid-1970s fundamentally changed who was coming to East Germany, and from where. The Nigerians were the first African students. They were followed by Kenyans and Cameroonians, and then later by Ghanaians, Guineans, and Malians. Throughout the 1960s, students from socialist-leaning and nonaligned countries like Ghana, Guinea, Mali, and Tanzania would dominate enrollment, while the number of those who came from states affiliated with the United States, including Kenya, Cameroon, and Nigeria, and after 1966, Ghana, would drop. In theory, an African state had to have an educational agreement with the GDR in order to send students there, shutting out or drastically shrinking the numbers from many countries. Some states, such as Senegal, had few students who studied in the GDR before the late 1970s and 1980s. Others, like Malawi, only sent one over the entire course of the GDR's existence.[1]

Political reorientations in Europe and Africa indeed threw previous assumptions and relationships into doubt, and the breaks that occurred in East Germany and throughout Africa in the 1970s marked the end of the first phase in the history of African student exchanges. On the German side, the Hallstein Doctrine was discontinued, greatly easing the GDR's ability to conduct foreign relations with other countries. In 1969, several nonaligned countries had already begun to negotiate and establish diplomatic relations with the GDR, including Iraq, Cambodia, Sudan, and Egypt.[2] Guinea, long one of the principal countries sending students to the GDR, allowed the East Germans to turn their Trade Mission in Conakry into a full-fledged consulate.[3] Officials in nonaligned states realized that with the rise of the SPD and, ultimately, the elevation of Willy Brandt to chancellor of the FRG, the doctrine would likely soon expire. This meant that the FRG would ultimately recognize the GDR, and that withholding their own recognition no longer made sense. For Africa, Asia, and

Latin America, the threat of being cut off from West Germany and its copious aid had dissipated, and the GDR could set up embassies throughout the non-Western world. More countries established relations with the GDR in 1970, including Algeria, Somalia, the Central African Republic,[4] and Congo-Brazzaville. In 1971, there was another sea change: Erich Honecker replaced Walter Ulbricht as general secretary of the SED and leader of the GDR. The Basic Treaty with East Berlin, which inaugurated formal relations between the GDR and FRG, was not signed until 1972, but the writing was on the wall much earlier.[5]

Several African countries were going through major political realignments of their own, and this impacted their Cold War alignments. The fall of Portugal's Estado Novo in 1974, which was a direct consequence of anticolonial uprisings throughout Angola, Mozambique, and Guinea Bissau, ultimately led to the decolonization of all Portuguese territories by 1975. Haile Selassie's Ethiopian monarchy also collapsed in 1974 and was superseded by the Derg, a revolutionary military committee that overthrew Selassie. In 1969, a coup in Somalia had brought in a socialist-leaning government, which was duly backed by the GDR, the USSR, and its other satellites.[6] Meanwhile, the United States was allied with Selassie's Ethiopia. The rise of the Derg, which later proclaimed adherence to Soviet-style Marxism, effectively switched the alliances around; now Ethiopia became affiliated with the Soviets, while the West shifted its allegiance toward Somalia.[7]

The 1970s also spelled the end of another phase of postindependence African history more generally: the era of economic and political promise that had begun with the hopes of decolonization and independence segued into a period of political degeneration and economic collapse. The expectation that development would bring prosperity to a majority of Africans was over, as strongmen across the continent enriched themselves and their inner circles while most of their constituents suffered in poverty.[8] Corruption at the top, mounting debt, and the failure of programs such as import substitution stifled the optimism of the 1960s and gave way to an increasing sense of despair.[9]

The GDR, by contrast, believed that its fortunes in Africa would rise in the 1970s with the advent of socialism in Ethiopia and the former Portuguese colonies. The SED wanted to reinforce its position with the governments of these nations and to intensify its work with the remaining independence movements in Zimbabwe, Namibia, and South Africa. In so doing, the East Germans hoped to lay the foundation for successful relationships once these countries were finally decolonized.[10] Mindful of the increasing economic difficulties at home, the SED also saw economic possibilities through collaboration with various African states, including the North African Libya and its leader Muammar Gaddafi.[11] The problematic aspects of solidarity—such as defense of the Derg, which committed mass atrocities and human rights violations against its own citizens—were largely insignificant to the SED. Indeed, the GDR actively assisted the Derg in its military offensives at home and abroad, providing money, military equipment, and diplomatic support.[12]

These events—the dissolution of the Hallstein Doctrine and formal recognition of the GDR by the FRG, Portuguese decolonization, and the emergence of the Marxist Derg—changed the makeup of the African student population in East Germany. While there had been moments of realignment earlier, such as the coup against Nkrumah in 1966, they did not fundamentally alter student flows. Starting around 1977, Angolans, Mozambicans, and Ethiopians became the most strongly represented student contingents in the GDR, outstripping Tanzanians, who had the largest number earlier in the decade.[13] Further, contract workers from Angola and Mozambique joined the students from those countries, and the number of workers from those nations was consistently higher than the number of students. According to Hans-Joachim Döring, 21,600 contracts were concluded with Mozambican temporary workers,[14] and Schenck has noted that the Mozambican Ministry of Labor estimates that 17,000 Mozambicans went to work in the GDR.[15] The laborers had a very different experience of the GDR than the students—for example, they were housed differently, in separate dormitories, which meant that they had less contact with the East German population.[16]

Those students who were coming were also not necessarily funded as they had been in the past. During the 1950s, students were mostly admitted through arrangements between African trade unions or independence movements. By the 1960s, African students were rarely admitted to study at East German universities or other academic institutions if their countries or political parties did not have official educational exchange agreements with the GDR. The agreements stipulated that the GDR pay for all student expenses other than travel home. Students from states without prearranged agreements—a category into which Nigeria fell by the mid-1960s—were categorically rejected or told to approach their governments about creating an exchange treaty with the GDR. Indeed, in 1966 the Nigerian Breweries African Workers Union and the affiliated Taka Company approached the East German Ministry of Health about training for their members. They were summarily dismissed because no agreements were in place with either the Nigerian government or the union. Since there had just been a coup in Nigeria, it was allowed that a contract might be concluded in the future, but at the time there was no chance.[17] Also in 1966, a

Cameroonian who was studying in the USSR requested that his brother be accepted for study in the GDR and was rebuffed with a similar response: Cameroon had no exchange agreement with the GDR that could facilitate his brother's admission.[18]

By the late 1970s and 1980s, however, declining economic conditions in the GDR compelled East German universities to accept both private, tuition-paying students from abroad,[19] and students delegated from extra-GDR organizations. Agreements between the GDR and other governments no longer appeared necessary, and arrangements for students to attend could be negotiated other ways. In 1979, for example, the Nigerian Student Union in the GDR addressed the falling number of Nigerians studying or working in the GDR and lamented that there was no agreement in place to bring more Nigerians into the country. The students obviously wanted to increase their own numbers. They asked if inquiries to study in the GDR could be processed differently and whether they themselves could form a committee to vet applications.[20] And in 1985 Senegalese-born Karamba Diaby—who would become one of the first Africans elected to the German Parliament in 2013—applied to study in the GDR through an international left-wing student organization in Prague. He was granted a scholarship and went on to study chemistry in Halle.[21]

Racism and Anti-Blackness in the Public Sphere in the 1980s and Postreunification Germany

The multiple stories of racism that have been chronicled throughout this book—ranging from seemingly innocent questions about skin color, to refusal to provide services to Africans, to epithets and name-calling, to outright violence—subverted SED claims that the GDR was the anti-imperial, antiracist Germany, as does the existence of a Radical Right throughout the GDR's existence.[22] It is hard to track the rate of racist incidents in the GDR: not all instances of racist behavior were reported, and the SED did what it could to suppress them and ensure that neither the East German public nor the Western media heard what had happened. East German officials were mortified that the Western press might pick up on stories of racism similar to those of the African student exodus from Bulgaria and the angry protests in the USSR after the death of a Ghanaian student. Their anxiety concerning Aderogba Ajao, George Sapara Arthur, and Gilbert Ofodile, all of whom reported scathingly on their lives in the GDR after leaving for the West, demonstrated that the SED knew their country was not the antiracist paragon they claimed.[23] Whether all the details of these students' stories were accurate—there are questionable aspects in each[24]—their depictions of racism nonetheless presented a GDR that was still very far from conquering it.

The level of open, blatant racism may have risen and fallen throughout the GDR's history. Mohamed Touré, a Malian who began studies in the GDR in 1971 and currently teaches *Afrikanistik* at the University of Cologne, hypothesized that this was the case. He claimed that he encountered virtually no racism during his years in the GDR. This was in sharp contrast to his experiences in the FRG, where he moved in the 1980s. Indeed, when I met with Touré in 2014, he still experienced daily racism in Cologne and mentioned that the day before we met, a man on the subway had told him to "go back to Africa." Touré never thought that the GDR was racism-free, though, speculating that fear of reprisals from the SED had merely driven it underground.[25] Robert Quansah, a Ghanaian student who was in the GDR during the 1980s, similarly remembers little in the way of racism.[26] The same is true for Yvonne Kolagbodi, Mayirue Kolagbodi's daughter. She recalled very positive experiences of the GDR from her student days in the 1980s.[27] Today she still lives in Berlin, where she is a physical therapist.

Yet other stories from the 1970s and 1980s paint a bleaker picture. B., a Senegalese physics professor who studied in the GDR beginning in 1979, had very different experiences from Touré's, to the point that it was rare for him to go a month without having two or three racism-fueled confrontations on the street. On two occasions, B. even took the East German perpetrators to court and won settlements against them. The first happened in the mid-1980s, when a taxi driver refused him as a passenger, saying in English that his cab was "not for niggers," and then sped away. B. noted the license plate number and reported the driver to the police. The second incident occurred sometime later, when he was taking a night train from Dresden to Leipzig. Five or six East Germans, including one woman, entered his compartment and began to shout racial slurs. He started to fight them, and one of the men smashed a beer bottle on his back. The train conductor called ahead to the police at the Dresden train station, and they were able to apprehend one of B.'s attackers. The attacker was tried and found guilty.[28] B.'s experiences mirror those of the Aryee-Bois, with whom this book opened. They are moreover comparable with those of David Tette, who came to study in the former East once it reunified with the West in 1990 and remembers it as a time of upheaval and open racism.[29]

The dual contexts of the Cold War and decolonization played an outsized role in determining how open East Germans could be about their attitudes toward and beliefs about race between 1949 and 1990. Government messaging that the GDR was antiracist likely caused East Germans to push racism to the side as a problem that had already been largely mastered. Others have argued similarly when discussing the issue of race in post-1945 Germany, but with greater attention to the FRG than the GDR.[30] After denazification and concerted attempts to come to grips with the horror of the Holocaust, racism was considered a residue, left over from the Nazi era and only apparent at the margins of West German society. A narrative emerged that Germany had conquered the demons of racism and that the FRG was a postracial state. But as the failure to integrate Turkish guest workers into the West German polity demonstrates, racism was still a potent force. Even when outsiders were invited into the FRG, they were still kept apart, othered.[31]

The similar narrative that the SED produced about the GDR as a postracial state quickly collapsed after the *Wende*, when racism in the former East became apparent and glaring. The far-right Nationaldemokratische Partei Deustchlands (NPD), a neo-Nazi party that was founded in the FRG in 1964, moved rapidly into the region. According to David Art, once it was there, in addition to attacking minorities and burning down asylum centers, the NPD capitalized on crumbling social institutions and the burgeoning hopelessness of young East German men who found themselves unemployed and with few prospects. Art attributed NPD success in part to the SED's Cold War rhetoric of East German antifascism, which absolved GDR citizens from Nazism and largely precluded anti-Nazi education in the East. Moreover, he explains that the NPD also co-opted left-wing language on economics and "social justice" that would have been familiar to former GDR citizens.[32]

Antimigrant or antiforeigner sentiment turned violent in the early 1990s.[33] Outbursts against foreigners included the pogrom against Vietnamese and Mozambican contract workers in Hoyerswerda in 1991,[34] as well as the mob attack on the home of asylum-seekers in Rostock, where one person was killed.[35] It is important to note, however, that these attacks were not limited to the former GDR. Violence against foreigners generally skyrocketed in the first few years following the *Wende* in both the East and the West.[36]

There has been both continuity and change in the ways that race as a concept has been constructed in Germany—and in Europe more broadly—over the course of the twentieth and twenty-first centuries. The idea of race is at once fluid and rigid, so that while negative and positive valuations within categories such as Black and white—or Black and German—shift over time, the external contours of these categories usually do not, and they often continue to be seen as mutually exclusive.[37] In East Germany, Africans were still considered others, marked as different through their skin despite protestations that all were equal under socialism. The SED government denied racism and anti-Blackness, even as it percolated among some of the citizenry, including officials who worked with the African student population. The idea that Blackness and Germanness were incompatible endured.

In post-*Wende* Germany commitments to multiculturalism and pluralism are similarly undercut, as critical race theory and critical whiteness studies have shown, by the continued construction of Germanness as white and the exclusion of nonwhite from that construction. Maureen M. Eggers, Grada Kilomba, Peggy Piesche, and Susan Arndt edited *Mythen und Masken*, the foundational text for critical whiteness studies in Germany, in 2005.[38] This was well after the discipline had gotten its start in other countries, such as the United States and Great Britain.[39] The editors of *Mythen und Masken* argued that whiteness was seen as normative in Germany and that Blackness mainly became visible as its other and opposite, that which was implicitly defined as not German. Debates on multiculturalism before and since have questioned the German commitment to pluralism and raised the issue of who can belong to the German polity or count as "German." The idea of a multicultural Germany is both ambiguous and ambivalent.[40] In this sense, reunified Germany in the twenty-first century has similarities to the GDR, where the SED often invoked an East German antiracism and anti-imperialism that was in direct opposition to the racism that African students encountered in their everyday lives.

Indeed, postracial narratives collapse under scrutiny, whether we are speaking of the GDR or reunified Germany. This is especially apparent in works like Fatima el-Tayeb's *Undeutsch* and *Other Europeans*, which demonstrate the persistence of racialized structures and categories in Europe in general and Germany in particular down through the present. The oft-assumed concept that Europe is postracial (or in el-Tayeb's term, postmigrant) cannot be sustained when European identities are still constructed as white, excluding People of Color from ever completely belonging and at the same time projecting a host of negative qualities, ones that were shaped by a history of colonialism and violence, onto them. The label of "migrant" is not only given to people recently arrived in Germany but to those born there who are not white and thus do not appear to match the German definition of "German"; they constantly have to reassert their belongingness in the German polity. Even German attempts to grapple with the colonial past through museum displays and other educational spaces falter, as Germans of Color are not brought into conversations regarding their creation. Their exclusion means that white scholars and curators construct German colonial and postcolonial narratives without Black or Brown collaboration, subverting the entire purpose of holding such exhibitions in the first place and ensuring that dominant German tropes of colonial encounters endure.[41]

Afro-German scholars, activists, and artists, including el-Tayeb, have made major contributions to the erasure of myths about German pluralism and postracialism. Works by authors such as Noah Sow, Alice Hasters, and Natasha A. Kelly all show that Black or Brown and white experiences of contemporary Germany are drastically divergent. They argue that racism permeates German society, but that this is only immediately apparent to those who are not white, since they are the ones who must continually confront it.[42] The authors speak frankly of their own encounters with racism in Germany, as well as of the underlying stereotypes of Black Germans that have been normalized and essentialized.[43]

In the 2010s, Germany became embroiled in a major refugee crisis that intensified already vexed issues of German identity, culture, and belonging. Fears of the "downfall" of German culture, combined with anxiety about crimes committed by a small minority of migrants, fueled the increasing popularity of far-right parties like the Alternative für Deutschland (AfD) and Islamophobic groups such as the Patriotic Europeans against the Islamicization of the Occident (PEGIDA). The right both in and outside Germany was relentless in its criticism of Chancellor Angela Merkel's proimmigrant and open-borders policy,[44] even as immigration was invigorating an aging German population with a flow of younger asylum seekers.[45]

The influx of Syrian refugees precipitated by the Syrian Civil War, along with the arrival of asylum-seekers from other Middle Eastern and North African countries, also sharpened questions of German "whiteness" and "westness" in both academic and public discourse. Media outlets such as the magazine *Focus* and the *Süddeustche Zeitung* published disturbing, racist images of Black male bodies invading white female ones in the wake of the sexual attacks in Cologne and elsewhere during New Year's Eve 2015–2016.[46] Such images were evocative of the trope of Black men unable to control themselves sexually when confronted with white women, the same trope that had existed since at least the nineteenth century.

The events in Cologne additionally spurred further violence against refugees, as well as their exclusion from public spaces such as swimming pools, bars, and restaurants.[47] In August 2018, two Middle Eastern men were accused of murdering a German in the Eastern city of Chemnitz, the former Karl-Marx-Stadt, and this triggered a wave of violence as Germans chased foreigners through the streets and far-right-wing groups staged demonstrations.[48] In the months that followed, crimes motivated by racism rose sharply in Saxony, where Chemnitz is located.[49]

Hostility toward immigrants and nonwhite Germans is a problem throughout Germany, not just in the *Neue Bundesländer* that were once the GDR. This raises the thorny question of whether racism in the former East is more pronounced than it is in the West, thirty years after reunification. Evidence supports this. The Neo-Nazi National Socialist Underground (NSU) got its start in Jena.[50] Pegida was founded in Dresden in 2014, and its followers have emphasized their proud, Saxon heritage alongside their radical Islamophobic, anti-refugee agenda.[51] A September 2019 analysis in the *Süddeutsche Zeitung*, which charted the popularity of the AfD, called it the "East's new regional party," with statistics showing that the AfD did markedly better in the *Neue Bundesländer* than it did in Western Germany.[52]

AfD popularity in the former East was further reflected in the September 2021 election. The SPD narrowly won that election over the CSU nationwide, with SPD candidate Olaf Scholz succeeding the retiring Merkel as chancellor. In the Eastern German states of Saxony and Thuringia, however, the AfD came in first, capturing 24.6% of the vote in Saxony and 24% in Thuringia. The AfD also had strong showings in other Eastern states where the SPD prevailed.[53]

Brandon Tensley has argued that the very nature/structure of the SED state—which in the 1980s kept Angolan, Mozambican, and Vietnamese contract workers cloistered away from the general East German population in separate housing—reflected a social order in which foreigners were relegated to the bottom rungs. For all of the GDR's antiracist rhetoric, Tensley maintains that racism was institutionalized in structures such as these.[54]

To Tensley's argument, I would say yes—but. The issue is more complex, since class was also a factor. Contract workers did live separately, but African students did not. They more often lived in international student dorms with other exchange students from throughout the world, and in some cases East Germans lived in the dorms with them, as Ginga Eichler has recounted. African students could also live in dorms with the general East German population, as well as in apartment buildings with East Germans. Both race *and* status—i.e., class—were significant to the treatment of contract workers, at least on an official level. Moreover, as we have seen, many students mixed easily with East Germans on a daily basis, suggesting that racism and tolerance coexisted, just as they do today.

Aleksandra Lewicki has, moreover, suggested that in order to understand racism in late twentieth- and early twenty-first-century Germany, we need both to look beyond the East-West German divide *and* address how the history of division contributes to current biases. She says that we must investigate "the *longue durée* of Orientalism," which arcs from the foundation of the German nation-state, through the German colonial era, into the Nazi

Figure 17. "German student Reinhold Keitel enjoys listening to the sounds of his African peers from Ghana. The African students feel very comfortable in the dorms." (caption text from Bundesarchiv) Zentralbild Brüggman Sturm Co.-gi., February 24, 1961 (Bundesarchiv).

period, and then to the Cold War and era of reunification. Seen from this perspective, while there have been "peaks" in racist violence in the East since the *Wende*, these were tied to specific moments of East German experience. In the 1990s, factors such as uncertainty about the future, resentment of Western domination of the reunification process, immediate economic shifts, and upticks in immigration, for example, made the East fertile ground for far-right radicalism. Additionally, Lewicki maintains that "far-right groups instrumentalized narratives of a so-called 'finally united people' to revive German nationalism," which drew on older nationalist tropes of German citizenship as a white construction. This does not, she emphasizes, mean that

Figure 18. "The cook in this (Leipzig) dormitory makes sure that all of our African friends are able to get food that is to their taste. The students are also already accustomed to German cuisine. The boy (sic) from Guinea clearly enjoys it." (caption text from Bundesarchiv) Zentralbild Brüggman Sturm, March 22, 1961 (Bundesarchiv).

East Germans are inherently more racist than their Western counterparts,[55] since both German states and the post-*Wende* FRG have continued to define German citizenship and belongingness as white.[56]

Still, support for far-right parties such as the AfD is stronger in the Eastern part of Germany than it is in the Western, and there has recently been a high level of violence directed against foreigners in the East. There are a number of potential reasons for this, some rooted in the German *longue durée*, some in the history of the GDR, and yet others stemming from experiences of the post-*Wende* era. These include longstanding tropes of nonwhite otherness, stretching back centuries; the fear of state repression in the GDR; the current freedom to express racist opinions; the continuing economic woes of the East thirty years post-*Wende*; the institutional racism that masks policies of multiculturalism and solidarity throughout Germany; the fact that the East did not come to terms with the Nazi past through education in the same way that the West did; and the tendency of police to ignore or downplay episodes of racial violence.

At the same time, counter-protests against neo-Nazis and other far-right groups offer encouraging signs and point to a continuation from the GDR not only of racism but also of solidarity. A week after the attacks in Chemnitz, for example, thousands marched in support of the immigrant community and diversity in Germany.[57] The issues underlying current antirefugee sentiment have a long and very complex history, with many actors involved on both sides: alongside Pegida we have counterdemonstrators who often outnumber Pegida followers. Likewise, there were those who included and excluded Africans and other non-Westerners in the GDR.

Looking backwards at the experience of African students in the GDR can, then, be useful for unpacking debates surrounding what it means to be German in the early twenty-first century. The SED tried to promote the GDR as a tolerant, antiracist society, where the Afro-German children of African and East German students were automatically citizens and the community supported struggles for independence through economic and political solidarity. Antiracist and anti-imperialist policies were, however, undermined by racism on the street as well as institutional racism. Ultimately, once the *Wende* came there were some East Germans who turned to the far-right—perhaps because they had suppressed their racism earlier, felt resurgent German nationalism, or felt economically and politically alienated—with all the resultant consequences.

In contemporary Germany there is a similar embrace of multiculturalism existing in tension with neo-Nazism and xenophobia. But it is important to note that the context is different. During the Cold War, the GDR and FRG were both keen to bring non-Western students, trainees, and interns into their countries as part of an ideological struggle for recently decolonized nations. African governments recognized this and utilized their status as potential allies to garner development aid and provide education for their citizens. The students themselves experienced a newfound mobility that allowed them to cross borders that many Europeans, including most East Germans, could not. Today the number of Africans and Middle Easterners coming to Germany is much larger, and those who arrive are primarily refugees, asylum-seekers, or economic migrants fleeing desperate situations. They hope to stay, which only some Africans did during the Cold War era. Yet both groups encountered not only violence and racism but also acceptance and solidarity. The history of African Students in the Cold War GDR reflects an ambivalence toward nonwhite others, an ambivalence that has only continued into the present despite efforts to combat prejudice and hate.

Notes

INTRODUCTION

1. Author interview with Desmond Aryee-Boi, Accra, Ghana, September 15, 2015.

2. Author interview with Jeannette Aryee-Boi, Accra, Ghana, September 17, 2015.

3. Toni Weis, "The Politics Machine: On the Concept of 'Solidarity' in East German Support for SWAPO," *Journal of Southern African Studies* 37, 2 (June 2011): 351–67.

4. Martin Atangana, *The End of French Rule in Cameroon* (Lanham, MD: University Press of America, 2010), 113.

5. Catherine Theresa Johnson, "The Representation of Blacks in Medieval German Literature and Art," PhD Diss., University of Michigan, 1994, https://deepblue.lib.umich.edu/handle/2027.42/104139; Paul H. D. Kaplan, "The Calenberg Altarpiece: Black African Christians in Renaissance Germany," in Mischa Honeck, Martin Klimke, and Anne Kuhlmann, eds., *Germany and the Black Diaspora: Points of Contact, 1250–1914* (New York: Berghahn, 2013), 21–37.

6. Arne Spohr, "'Mohr und Trompeter': Blackness and Social Status in Early Modern Germany," *Journal of the American Musicological Society* 72, 3 (Fall 2019): 613. *Mohr* was a term that Spohr comments was usually (if not always), used to referred to people from Africa by the seventeenth century.

7. Spohr, "Mohr und Trompeter." Spohr demonstrates that archival documents about the two African musicians whose lives he studies consistently describe them as "moors," whereas their white associates are defined in terms of their position at the court, i.e., trumpeters or drummers. Further, he maintains that "Neither their previous slave status nor their Blackness was erased by their integration into Germany society."

8. Anne Kuhlmann, "Ambiguous Duty: Black Servants at German Ancien Regime Courts," in *Germany and the Black Diaspora*, 57–73.

9. Felix Brahm and Eve Rosenhaft, *Slavery Hinterland: Transatlantic Slavery and Continental Europe, 1680–1850* (Rochester, NY: Boydell & Brewer, 2016), especially Brahm and Rosenhaft, "Towards a Comprehensive European History of Slavery and Abolition," 1–24, and Craig Koslofsky and Roberto Zaugg, "Ship's Surgeon Johann Peter Oettinger: A Hinterlander in the Atlantic Slave Trade, 1682–1696," 25–44. And see also Heike Raphael-Hernandez and Pia Wiegmink, "German Entanglements in Transatlantic Slavery: An Introduction," *Atlantic Studies: Global Currents* 14, 4 (2017), https://doi.org/10.1080/14788810.2017.1366009

10. Dirk Hoerder, "Africans in Europe: A New Perspective," in *Germany and the Black Diaspora*, 231–40.

11. Sara Eigen and Mark Larrimore, eds., *The German Invention of Race* (Binghamton: SUNY Press, 2006), 1.

12. See Eigen and Larrimore, *The German Invention of Race*, especially "Policing Polygeneticism in Germany, 1775 (Kames,), Kant, and Blumenbach," 35–54; Susan Morss-Buck, "Hegel and Haiti," *Critical Inquiry* 26, 4 (Summer 2000): 821–65.

13. John H. Zammito, "Policing Polygeneticism in Germany, 1775 (Kames), Kant, and Blumenbach," in *The German Invention of Race*, 35.

14. Matthew Unangst, "Emin Pasha and Fracturing Imperialist Imaginaries in the Late 1880s," in Sara Pugach, David Pizzo, and Adam A. Blackler, eds., *After the Imperialist Imagination: Two Decades of Research on Global Germany and its Legacies* (Oxford: Peter Lang, 2020), 73–87.

15. See for example Hermann Wittenberg, "Wilhelm Bleek and the Khoisan Imagination: A Study of Censorship, Genocide, and Colonial Science," *Journal of Southern African Studies* 38, 3 (September 2012): 667–79.

16. Andrew Zimmerman, *Alabama in Africa: Booker T. Washington, the German Empire, and the Globalization of the New South* (Princeton, NJ: Princeton University Press, 2010).

17. Sara Pugach, *Africa in Translation: A History of Colonial Linguistics in Africa and Beyond, 1814–1945* (Ann Arbor: University of Michigan Press, 2012), 21–48; Jeremy Best, *Heavenly Fatherland: German Missionary Culture in the Age of Empire* (Toronto: University of Toronto Press, 2020).

18. Pugach, *Africa in Translation*, 43, 95, 160. Missionary research contributed to the cultivation of racial categorization through the application of classificatory hierarchies such as "Hamitic" and "Bantu" to describe both languages and biological characteristics.

19. For instance, Johan Hinrich Schmelen, a German missionary who worked for the London Missionary Society, married a native woman named Zara in the early nineteenth century and together they became patriarch and matriarch of a sizeable, important family in Namibia. Ursula Trüper, *The Invisible Woman: Zara Schmelen, African Mission Assistant at the Cape and in Namaland* (Basel: Basel Afrika Bibliographien, 2008); Kathrin Roller, "Mission und 'Mischehen,' Erinnerung und Körper—geteiltes Gedächtnis an eine afrikanische Vorfahrin. Über die Familie Schmelen-Kleinschmidt-Hegner," in Larissa Förster, Dag Henrichsen, and Michael Böllig, eds., *Namibia-Deutschland. Eine geteilte Geschichte. Widerstand, Gewalt, Erinnerung* (Publikation zur gleichnamigen Ausstellung im Rautenstrauch-Joest-Museum für Völkerkunde Köln und im Deutschen Historischen Museum Berlin 2004/2005) (Wolfratshausen: Editions Minerva Hermann Farnung, 2004), 194–211; and Roller, "Zwischen Rassismus und Frömmigkeit—Biopolitik aus erfahrungsgeschichtlicher Perspektive. Über die Geschwister Hegner, Mathilde Kleinschmidt und Ludwig Baumann als Nachfahren einer deutsch-afrikanischen Missionsfamilie," in Frank Becker, ed., *Rassenmischehen—Mischlinge—Rassentrennung: Zur Politik der Rasse im deutschen Kolonialreich* (Stuttgart: Franz Steiner, 2004), 220–40.

20. Lora Wildenthal, *German Women for Empire, 1884–1945* (Durham: Duke Uni-

versity Press, 2001), 86–87; Felix Axster, "Die Angst vor dem Verkaffern: Politiken der Reiningung im Deutschen Kolonialismus," *Werkstatt Geschichte* 39 (2005): 39–53.

21. Wildenthal, 128.

22. Julia Moses, "From Faith to Race? 'Mixed Marriage' and the Politics of Difference in Imperial Germany," *History of the Family* 24, 3 (July-August 2019): 466–93.

23. Wildenthal, 88.

24. Axster, 43.

25. The term "black peril," referring to the unfounded, baseless fear that Black men will sexually assault white women, is indeed most commonly used in connection with the white settler population in British colonial Southern Africa. See for instance Gareth Cornwell, "George Webb Hardy's *The Black Peril* and the Social Meaning of 'Black Peril' in Early Twentieth Century South Africa," *Journal of Southern African Studies* 22, 3 (September 1996): 441–53; Jock McCulloch, *Black Peril, White Virtue: Sexual Crime in Southern Rhodesia, 1902–1935* (Bloomington: University of Indiana Press, 2000), and others. Krista O'Donnell, "Home, Nation, Empire: Domestic Germanness and Colonial Citizenship," in Krista O'Donnell, Renate Bridenthal, and Nancy Reagin, eds., *The Heimat Abroad: The Boundaries of Germanness* (Ann Arbor: University of Michigan Press, 2005), 40–57, has explored how the concept of Black peril functioned similarly in the German colonial context, and also compared German anxieties about Black sexuality to the French ones discussed by Yael Simpson Fletcher, "Unsettling Settlers: Colonial Migrants and Racialized Sexuality in Interwar Marseilles," in Antoinette Burton, ed., *Gender, Sexuality, and Colonial Modernities* (New York: Routledge, 1999), 79–95.

26. Staatsarchiv Hamburg (StaH), 361–65, I VW Nr. 102, Band I, Heft 6, betr. Seminar für afrikanische Sprachen, Max Förster to School Inspector Professor Dr. Ahlburg, Hamburg, November 16, 1910, "Annahme einer Witbooi-Hottentotten als Sprachgehilfen"; Lora Wildenthal, *German Women for Empire, 1884–1945* (Durham: Duke University Press, 2001), 186–88.

27. Geheimes Staatsarchiv Preußischer Kulturbesitz (GStaPKB), Rep. 208A, Nr. 121, Blatt 1–173, Lektoren des Suaheli, Bd. I, 1899–1909, *Gutachten* of Mtoro bin Mwinyi Bakari, sent from Carl Velten to Eduard Sachau, May 25, 1905; Pugach, *Africa in Translation*, 150–52; Ludger Wimmelbücker, *Mtoro bin Mwinyi Bakari (c.1869–1927): Swahili Lecturer and Author in Germany* (Oxford: African Books Collective, 2009), 41–46.

28. Julia Roos, "Women's Rights, Nationalist Anxiety, and the 'Moral' Agenda in the Early Weimar Republic: Revisiting the 'Black Horror' Campaign against France's African Occupation Troops," *Central European History* 42, 3 (September 2009), 473–508, among others; further, Weimar artist Hannah Hoch shocked German audiences with work that juxtaposed black and white bodies, and implied sexual relations between them. Here see Eric D. Weitz, *Weimar Germany: Promise and Tragedy*, new and expanded edition (Princeton: Princeton University Press, 2013), 290–92.

29. Tina Campt, *Other Germans: Black Germans and the Politics of Race, Gender, and Memory in the Third Reich* (Ann Arbor: University of Michigan Press, 2009), 72ff.

30. Eve Rosenhaft, "Blacks and Gypsies in Nazi Germany: The Limits of the 'Racial State,'" *History Workshop Journal* 72 (Autumn 2011), 161–70.

31. "The Genocide Convention," https://www.un.org/en/genocideprevention/genocide-convention.shtml, accessed May 27, 2020.

32. "The Universal Declaration of Human Rights," https://www.un.org/en/universal-declaration-human-rights/, accessed May 28, 2020.

33. Mark Mazower, *Dark Continent: Europe's Twentieth Century* (New York: Alfred Knopf, 1999).

34. Bonny Ibahwoh, *Imperialism and Human Rights: Colonial Discourses of Rights and Liberties in African History* (Binghamton: SUNY Press, 2007), 161–62. See also Mazower, *No Enchanted Palace: The End of Empire and the Ideological Origins of the United Nations* (Princeton: Princeton University Press, 2009), for discussion of the imperial roots of the UN itself.

35. Woodford McClellan, "Africans and Black Americans in the Comintern Schools, 1925–1934," *International Journal of African Historical Studies* 26, 3 (1993): 371–90; Meredith Roman, *Opposing Jim Crow: African Americans and the Soviet Indictment of US Racism, 1928–1937* (Lincoln: University of Nebraska Press, 2012); Barbara Keys, "An African American Worker in Stalin's Soviet Union: Race and the Soviet Experiment in International Perspective," *Historian* (2009): 32–54; Sophie Lorenz, *"Schwarze Schwester Angela": Die DDR und Angela Davis, Kalter Krieg und Black Power, 1965–1975* (Bielefeld: Transcript, 2020), 60ff.

36. See for instance Jocelyn Alexander and JoAnn McGregor, "African Soldiers in the USSR: Oral Histories of ZAPU Intelligence Cadres' Soviet Training, 1964–1979," *Journal of Southern African Studies* 43, 1 (2017): 49–66.

37. Philip E. Muehlenbeck and Natalia Telepneva, eds., *Warsaw Pact Intervention in the Third World: Aid and Influence in the Cold War* (London: I. B. Tauris, 2018).

38. Woodford McClellan, "Africans and Black Americans in the Comintern Schools, 1925–1934," 372.

39. Julia Hessler, "Death of an African Student in Moscow: Race, Politics, and the Cold War," *Cahiers du Monde Russe* 47, 1 (2006): 33–63; A. J. Kret, "We Unite with Knowledge: The People's Friendship University and Soviet Education for the Third World," *Comparative Studies of South Asia, Africa, and the Middle East* 33, 2 (2013): 239–56.

40. Tanja R. Müller, *Legacies of Socialist Solidarity: East Germany in Mozambique* (Lanham, MD: Lexington Books, 2014), 9, 78.

41. Public Records and Archives Administration Department (PRAAD), Accra, Ghana, JE198, Ministry of Education, Scholarships awarded by other Countries, S. W. Kumah, Ambassador to Yugoslavia, Memorandum on "The Future of African Students in Eastern European Socialist Countries," April 19, 1963.

42. The Political Archive (PAAA) MfAA C327/70, Abt. Afrika, Sektion Mali, Beziehungen auf aussenpolitischen Gebiet sowie auf dem Gebiet des Hoch- und Fachschulwesens, der Volksbildung und des Sports zwischen der DDR und Togo, 1962–1968, J.D. to Gerald Götting, Lome, March 23, 1967.

43. Katherine Pence and Paul Betts, "Introduction," in Pence and Betts., eds., *Socialist Modern: East German Everyday Culture and Politics* (Ann Arbor: University of Michigan Press, 2008), 1–20; Quinn Slobodian, ed., *Comrades of Color: East Germany in the Cold War World* (New York: Berghahn Books, 2015).

44. Eric Burton, "Journeys of Education and Struggle: African Mobility in Times of Decolonization and the Cold War," *Stichproben: Wiener Zeitschrift für kritische Afrikastudiden*, no. 34/2018, vol. 18, 1–17; Meredith Terretta, "Cameroonian Nationalists go Global: From Forest 'Maquis' to a Pan-African Accra," *Journal of African History* 51, 2 (2010): 189–212.

45. Young-sun Hong, *Cold War Germany, the Third World, and the Global Humanitarian Regime* (Cambridge, 2015), 177. Moreover, even prior to the Hallstein Doctrine tension between the two Germanys ensured that the GDR's Africa policy would be defined by its relationship to the FRG; on this point, please see William Glenn Gray, *Germany's Cold War: The Global Campaign to Isolate East Germany, 1949–1969* (Chapel Hill, 2003), 13ff.

46. Jon B. Alterman, "American Aid to Egypt in the 1950s: From Hope to Hostility," *Middle East Journal* 52, 1 (1998): 51–69; David C. Engerman, *The Price of Aid: The Economic Cold War in India* (Cambridge, MA: Harvard University Press, 2018).

47. PRAAD, JE198, Ministry of Education, Scholarships awarded by other Countries, Cabinet Committee on Establishment Matters and Scholarship, Memorandum by the Minister of Economic Affairs, Subject: Offer of Scholarships from East European Countries, 1960.

48. PRAAD, JE198, Extracts from the minutes of a meeting of the Cabinet held on the 11th April 1960, Minute No. 27, Offers of Scholarships from East European Countries. The commitment only to provide scholarships in scientific fields was renewed in 1962; see Extract from the Minutes of a Meeting of the Cabinet Committee on Establishment and Scholarship Matters held on 12 July 1962, concerning Scholarships offered by Eastern European countries.

49. There is debate, however, as to how far South Africa's Communist Party held influence over the ANC members in exile; see for instance Stephen Ellis, *External Mission: The ANC in Exile, 1960–1990* (Oxford: Oxford University Press, 2013), for the idea that the South African Communist Party held substantial sway, and Paul Landau, "Controlled by Communists? (Re)assessing the ANC in its Exilic Decades," *South African Historical Journal* 65, 2 (2015): 222–41, for the view that their influence was not as strong as commonly accepted.

50. Hilary Sapire, "Liberation Movements, Exile, and International Solidarity: An Introduction," *Journal of Southern African Studies* 35, 2 (June 2009), 271–86.

51. Sebastian Pampuch, "Afrikanische *Freedom Fighter* im Exil in der DDR: Dekoloniale Wissensbestände einer 'unerwünschten Deutschen Geschichte,'" in Stephanie Zloch, Lars Müller, and Simone Lässig, eds., *Wissen in Bewegung: Migration und globale Verflechtungen in der Zeitsgeschichte seit 1945* (Berlin: De Gruyter, 2018), 321–48.

52. Simon Stevens, "Bloke Modisane in East Germany," in Quinn Slobodian, ed., *Comrades of Color: East Germany in the Cold War World* (New York: Berghahn, 2015), 124.

53. Ilona Schleicher, "Zur 'Materiellen Solidarität' der DDR mit dem ANC in den 60er Jahren," *Afrika Spectrum* 27, 2 (1992): 213–17.

54. SAPMO-BArch DY/34/27509 (FDGB—Bundesvorstand Büro der Sekretäre für Sozialpolitik ("Büro Tille"), Nr. I 1.21, Afrika/Vorderasien, 1960, Wera Ambitho to W. Perk, 13 July 1960.

55. Stephen Ellis and Tsepo Sechaba, *Comrades against Apartheid: The ANC and the South African Communist Party in Exile* (Bloomington: Indiana University Press, 1992), 88; "Speer in das Herz der Apartheid," http://www.sodi.de/aktuell/nachrichten/news_detail/datum/2017/01/31/speer-in-das-herz-der-apartheid/, January 31, 2017, accessed May 16, 2019.

56. Universitätsarchiv Leipizg (UAL), "Meli, Francis," Lebenslauf, Francis Xhakalegusha Meli, May 1973.

57. Britta Schilling, *Postcolonial Germany: Memories of Empire in a Decolonized Nation* (Oxford: Oxford University Press, 2014), 95.

58. Ilona Schleicher, "Zur Diskussion um die Beteiligung der DDR an Sanktionen gegen Südafrika Anfang der sechziger Jahre," *Afrika Spectrum* 25, 3 (1990): 283–92.

59. For example, Modilim Achufusi's *Lebenslauf* was written with the intent of procuring an assistant position in the African Studies Department of the Oriental Institute at Karl Marx University. He stressed his membership in a revolutionary organization back home in Nigeria, likely to shore up his political bona fides with the vice rector at the university. His primary mentor, the Leipzig historian Markov, and his peers in the FDJ also read it. See UAL PA 4156, Modilim Achufusi, Lebenslauf, n.d.; Markov, recommendation for Achufusi, July 15, 1957, and recommendation from Helmut Biering, FDJ, among others, n.d.

60. Like approximately 620,000 East Germans between 1950 and 1989, Africans and other international students occasionally became IMs. IMs were individuals recruited by the Stasi to inform them of supposed "politically dangerous" activities carried out by their fellow citizens. "Inoffizieller Mitarbeiter" (IM), https://www.bstu.de/mfs-lexikon/detail/inoffizieller-mitarbeiter-im/, accessed May 23, 2020.

61. Universities were established in both of these countries in the postcolonial era; see chapters 2 and 3.

62. After Congolese independence in 1960 the country fell into turmoil with the secession of Katanga, assassination of Patrice Lumumba, and fighting amongst various parties. The situation was dire enough for those abroad to have serious misgivings about returning. On the Congo crisis see Lise Namikas, *Battleground Africa: Cold War in the Congo, 1960–1965* (Stanford: Stanford University Press, 2015).

63. Der Bundesbeauftragte für die Unterlagen des Staatssicherheitsdienstes der ehemaligen Deutschen Demokratischen Republik (BStU), Archiv der Zentralstelle MfS AP, Nr. 2662/67, various on a Ghanaian student who was at the Ing.-Schule Maschinenbau Lichtenberg during the 1960s.

64. See for example UAL, Schriftwechsel Studenten Madagaskar von: 1978 bis: 1985, Nr. 3922b, permission slips for travel to West Berlin, France, etc., between 1977 and 1985.

65. As for example in Helder Adegar Fonseca, Lena Dallywater, and Christopher Saunders, eds., *Southern African Liberation Movements and the Global Cold War 'East': Transnational Activism, 1960–1990* (Berlin: De Gruyter, 2019). In this volume, contributors focus on the microhistorical—here parsed as the biographical or prosopographical—in discussions of Southern African independence movements and their interactions with the Soviet Bloc.

66. Maria Höhn, *GIs and Fräuleins: The German-American Encounter in 1950s West Germany* (Chapel Hill: University of North Carolina Press, 2003); Heide Fehrenbach, *Race after Hitler: Black Occupation Children in Postwar Germany and America* (Princeton: Princeton University Press, 2007).

67. Rita Chin, *The Guestworker Question in Postwar Germany* (Cambridge: Cambridge University Press, 2007); Ruth Mandel, *Cosmopolitan Anxieties: Turkish Challenges to Citizenship and Belonging in Germany* (Durham: Duke University Press, 2008); Nermin Abadan-Unat, *Turks in Europe: From Guestworker to Transnational Citizen* (New York: Berghahn Books, 2005, 2011), Gökçe Yurdakul, *From Guest Workers into Muslims: The Transformation of Turkish Immigrant Associations in Germany* (Newcastle upon Tyne: Cambridge Scholars, 2009); and for a treatment of migrants from multiple areas, see Brittany Lehman, *Teaching Migrant Children in West Germany and Europe, 1949–1992* (New York: Palgrave, 2019).

68. Sem. C. Sutter, "The Fall of the Bibliographic Wall: Libraries and Archives in Unified Germany," *College & Research Libraries*, 55 (1994): 403–11, https://www.dartmouth.edu/~wess/fallwall.html, accessed July 23, 2020.

69. Ulrich Post and Frank Sandvoss, *Die Afrikapolitik der DDR* (Hamburg: Institut für Afrika-Kunde, 1982); Ernst Hillebrand, *Das Afrika-Engagement der DDR* (London: Peter Lang, 1987); Hans-Joachim Spanger and Lothar Brock, *Die Beiden Deutschen Staaten in der dritten Welt* (Wiesbaden: VS Verlag für Sozialwissenschaften, 1987); and Gareth Winrow, *The Foreign Policy of the GDR in Africa* (Cambridge: Cambridge University, 1990).

70. Hans-Georg Schleicher and Ilona Schleicher, *Die DDR im südlichen Afrika: Solidarität und Kalter Krieg* (Hamburg: Institut für Afrika-Kunde, 1997), and *Special Flights to Southern Africa* (Harare: SAPES books, 1998); Ulrich van der Heyden and Ilona Schleicher, *Die DDR und Afrika: Zwischen Klassenkampf und Neuem Denken* (Münster: LIT Verlag, 1993), and *Engagiert für Afrika: Die DDR und Afrika II* (Münster: LIT Verlag, 1994); Hans-Georg Schleicher, *Südafrikas neue Elite: Die Prägung der ANC-Führung durch das Exil* (Hamburg: Institut für Afrika-Kunde, 2004); Ulrich van der Heyden, *Zwischen Solidarität und Wirtschaftsinteresse: Die "geheimen" Beziehungen der DDR zum Südafrikanische Apartheidsregime* (Münster: LIT Verlag, 2005) and *GDR Development Policy in Africa: Doctrine and Strategies between Illusions and Reality, the Example of Southern Africa* (Zurich: LIT Verlag, 2013), among others.

71. Van der Heyden insists, for example, that East German historians' histories of Africa remain relevant today, even if they have a narrowly Marxist-Leninist theoretical focus and are more embedded in the history of European imperialism than the history of Africa; see van der Heyden, "Die Afrika Geschichtsschreibung in der ehemaligen DDR," *Africa Spectrum* 27, 2 (1992): 207–11. He has made the same argument about anthropology and ethnology more recently, in "Afrika im Blick der akademischen Welt der DDR: Ein wissenschaftlicher Überblick afrikabezogene Ethnologie," *Bericht zur Wissenschaftsgeschichte* 42, 1 (March 2019): 83–105. Some of van der Heyden's frustration with the West stems from the justifiable anger that he and other East German scholars of the humanities and social sciences were pushed out of their positions and replaced by Westerners after 1990. See Stefan Bollinger and Ulrich van der Heyden, *Deutsche Einheit und Elitenwechsel in Ostdeutschland* (Berlin: Trafo-Verlag, 2002).

72. See for example Ulrich van der Heyden, "Angedichteter Rassismus," *Ossietsky: Zweiwochenschrift für Politik/Kultur/Wirtschaft* (September 2016), https://www.sopos.org/aufsaetze/57220b74ecdb1/1.phtml.html, accessed July 29, 2020.

73. Quinn Slobodian, ed., *Comrades of Color: East Germany in the Cold War World* (New York: Berghahn, 2015); Young-Sun Hong, *Cold War Germany, the Third World, and the Global Humanitarian Regime* (Cambridge: Cambridge University Press, 2015); Jennifer Hosek, *Sun, Sex, and Socialism: Cuba in the German Imaginary* (Toronto: University of Toronto Press, 2012); and Katherine Pence, "Showcasing Cold War Germany in Cairo: 1954 and 1957 Industrial Exhibitions and the Competition for Arab Partners," *Journal of Contemporary History* 47, 1 (2012): 69–95.

74. And see also Joy Gleason Carew, "Black in the USSR: African Diasporan Pilgrims, Expatriates and Students in Russia, from the 1920s to the first Decade of the twenty-first Century," *African and Black Diaspora: An International Journal* 8, 2 (2015): 202–15, https://doi.org/10.1080/17528631.2015.1027324, accessed August 3, 2020.

75. Marcia Schenck, "Socialist Solidarities and their Afterlives: Histories and Memories of Angolan and Mozambican Migrants in the German Democratic Republic, 1975–2015," PhD Diss., Princeton University, 2017; Eric Burton, "Decolonization, the Cold War, and Africans' Routes to Higher Education Overseas, 1957–1965," *Journal of Global History* 15, 1 (2020): 169–91; Jason Verber, "True to the Politics of FRELIMO? Teaching Socialism and the *Schule der Freundschaft, 1981–1990*," in Quinn Slobodian, ed., *Comrades of Color: East Germany in the Cold War World* (New York: Berghahn, 2015), 188–210; Constantin Katsakioris, "Students from Portuguese Africa in the Soviet Union, 1960–1974: Anti-Colonialism, Education, and the Socialist Alliance," *Journal of Contemporary History*, first published April 3, 2020, https://doi.org/10.1177/0022009419893739, and "The Lumumba University in Moscow: Higher Education for a Soviet-Third World Alliance, 1960–1991," *Journal of Global History* 14, 2 (2019): 281–300; Nedžad Kuč, "Southern African Students in Southeast Europe: Education and Experiences in 1960s Yugoslavia," in Helder Adegar Fonseca, Lena Dallywater, and Christopher Saunders, eds., *Southern African Liberation Movements and the Global Cold War 'East': Transnational Activism, 1960–1990* (Berlin: De Gruyter, 2019), 181–96; and Thom Loyd, "Black in the USSR: African Students, Soviet Empire, and the Politics of Global Education During the Cold War, 1956–1976," PhD Diss., Georgetown University, in progress.

76. Mariya Ivancheva, "Paternalistic Internationalism and (de)colonial Practices of Cold War Higher Education Exchange: Bulgaria's Connections with Cuba and Angola," *Journal of Labor and Society*, first published September 9, 2019, https://doi.org/10.1111/wusa.12444, accessed August 3, 2020; Desislava Pileva, "Images of 'Our Foreign Friends': Representations of Students from the Middle East and Africa in the Bulgarian Newspaper 'Students' Tribune,' 1960s-1970s," *Anthropology Journal for Socio-Cultural Anthropology* 4 (2017), http://anthropology-journal.org/wp/wp-content/uploads/2017/10/Article_Desislava-Pileva.pdf, accessed August 3, 2020; Elena K. Alamgir, "Race is Elsewhere: State Socialist Education and the Racialisation of Vietnamese Workers in Czechoslovakia," *Race and Class*, first published March 28, 2013, https://doi.org/10.1177/0306396813476171, accessed August 3, 2020; Philip Muehlenback, *Czechoslovakia in Africa, 1945–1968* (New York: Palgrave Macmillan, 2016), 157–87 passim; Mihai Dinu Gheorghiu and Adrian Netedu, "African Students and the Transformation Process of Romanian Education, from the Political Issue of Internation-

alism to the Romanian Educational Offer between 1970 and 1990," *Analele Ştiinţifice ale Universităţii »Alexandru Ioan Cuza« din Iaşi. Sociologie şi Asistenţă Socială* 8, 1 (2015): 131–43.

77. Quinn Slobodian, "Introduction," in *Comrades of Color*, 1–19.

78. Burton, "Decolonization, the Cold War, and Africans' Routes to Higher Education Overseas, 1957–1965," 172.

79. Schenck, "From Luanda and Maputo to Berlin: Uncovering Angolan and Mozambican Migrants' Motives to Move to the German Democratic Republic, 1979–1990," *African Economic History* 44 (2016): 202–34.

80. Carol Summers, *Colonial Lessons: Africans' Education in Southern Rhodesia* (Portsmouth, NH: Heinemann, 2002).

81. Here see for instance Julie Ault, "Defending God's Creation? The Environment in State, Church, and Society in the German Democratic Republic, 1975–1989," *German History* https://doi.org/10.1093/gerhis/ghy084, September 2018, who has argued that concerns for the environment brought together East Germans from all aspects of society, and also united them with others who had similar concerns outside the country, such as The World Council of Churches, which was founded in Amsterdam and had branches worldwide. Ault's work is a good example of how East Germans were able to connect beyond their borders despite SED restrictions.

82. See for instance Rita Chin and Heide Fehrenbach, "German Democracy and the Question of Difference, 1945–1995," in Rita Chin, Heide Fehrenbach, Geoff Eley, and Atina Grossman, eds., *After the Nazi Racial State: Difference and Democracy in Germany and Europe* (Ann Arbor: University of Michigan Press, 2010), 127; Daphne Berdahl, "(N)Ostalgie for the Present: Memory, Longing, and East German Things," *Ethnos* 64, 2 (1999): 192–211, https://doi.org/10.1080/00141844.1999.9981598, accessed July 30, 2020, and Gabriele Eckart, "Popkultur, Profit, und das Banale: Stefan Raabs Erfolgsong 'Maschendrahtzaun' und der lächerliche *Ossi*," *German Studies Review* 34, 2 (May 2011): 265–75, for a discussion of the representation of East Germans as uncultured in the West German imagination around the turn of the twenty-first century.

83. Ralph Jessen, "Die Gesellschaft im Staatssozialismus: Probleme einer Sozialgeschichte der DDR," *Geschichte und Gesellschaft* 21 (1995): 96–110, cited in Katherine Pence and Paul Betts, "Introduction," in Katherine Pence and Paul Betts, eds., *Socialist Modern: East German Everyday Culture and Politics* (Ann Arbor: University of Michigan Press, 2007), 5.

84. Pence and Betts, "Introduction," 1–36, and see also Massimiliano Trentin, "Modernization as State Building: The Two Germanies in Syria, 1963–1972," *Diplomatic History* 33, 3 (2009): 487–505, for an example of how both capitalism and socialism were figured as agents of modernization, in this case in Syria.

85. Priya Lal, "Maoism in Tanzania," in Alexander C. Cook, ed., *Mao's Little Red Book* (Cambridge: Cambridge University Press, 2014), 96–116.

86. Radoslav A. Yordanov, *The Soviet Union and the Horn of Africa during the Cold War: Between Ideology and Pragmatism* (Lanham, MD: Lexington Books, 2016); Ana Naomi de Sousa, "Between East and West: The Cold War's Legacy in Africa," *Al Jazeera*, 22 (February 2016), https://www.aljazeera.com/indepth/features/2016/02/east-west-cold-war-legacy-africa-160214113015863.html

87. Ulf Engel and Hans-Georg Schleicher, *Die beiden Deutschen Staaten in Afrika: Zwischen Konkurrenz und Koexistenz 1949–1990* (Hamburg: Institut für Afrika-Kunde, 1998).

88. Pence, "Showcasing Cold War Germany in Cairo."

89. Heike Hartmann and Susann Lewerenz, "Campaigning against Apartheid in East and West Germany," *Radical History Review* 119 (2014): 191–204.

90. Toni Weis, "The Politics Machine: On the Concept of 'Solidarity' in East German Support for SWAPO," *Journal of Southern African Studies* 37, 2 (June 2011): 351–67.

91. See for instance Eric Burton, "Solidarität und ihre Grenzen bei den Brigaden der Freundschaft der FDJ," in Frank Bösch, Caroline Moine, and Stefanie Senger, eds., *Globales Engagement im Kalten Krieg* (Göttingen: Wallstein, 2018); Iris Borowy, "East German Medical Aid to Nicaragua: The Politics of Solidarity between Biomedicine and Primary Health Care," *História, Ciencias, Saúde-Munguinhos* 24, 2 (April–June 2017), http://dx.doi.org/10.1590/s0104-59702017000200006, accessed July 31, 2020; Lothar Fratzke, "Heimat einer FDJ-Freundschaftsbrigade: Das Berufausbildungszentrum in Jinotepe," in Erika Harzer and Willi Volks, eds., *Aufbruch nach Nicaragua: Deutsch-Deutsche Solidarität im Systemwettstreit* (Berlin: Ch. Links Verlag, 2008), 141–43; Inga Emmerling, *Die DDR und Chile: Außenpolitik, Außenhandel, und Solidarität* (Berlin: Ch. Links Verlag, 2013), 78 passim, among others.

92. Hong, *Cold War Germany, the Third World, and the Global Humanitarian Regime*, 155.

93. Hong, *Cold War Germany, the Third World, and the Global Humanitarian Regime*, 155.

94. Hong, 4–5.

95. Hubertus Büschel, *Hilfe zur Selbsthilfe: Deutsche Entwicklungsarbeit in Afrika, 1960–1975* (Frankfurt a.M.: Campus Verlag, 2014).

96. Schenck, "Socialist Solidarities and Their Afterlives"; Eric Burton, "Navigating Global Socialism: Tanzanian Students in and Beyond East Germany," *Cold War History*, https://doi.org/10.1080/14682745.2018.1485146, June 25, 2018.

97. Odd Arne Westad, *The Global Cold War: Third World Interventions and the Making of Our Times* (Cambridge: Cambridge University Press, 2007).

98. Heonik Kwon, *The Other Cold War* (New York: Columbia University Press, 2010).

99. Although it is not the subject of this book, the need for guest workers in both blocs obviously did as well.

100. On Cuban influence in Africa, please see Pierre Gleijeses, *Conflicting Missions: Havana, Washington, and Africa, 1959–1976* (Chapel Hill: University of North Carolina Press, 2013) and Frank Villafana, *Cold War in the Congo: The Confrontation of Cuban Military Forces, 1960–1967* (New York: Routledge, 2017); for China, please see Jamie Monson, *Africa's Freedom Railway: How a Chinese Development Project Changed Lives and Livelihoods in Tanzania* (Bloomington: Indiana University Press, 2011).

101. Elizabeth Schmidt, *Foreign Intervention in Africa: From the Cold War to the War on Terror* (New York: Cambridge University Press, 2013).

102. Matthew Connelly, "Taking off the Cold War Lens: Visions of North-South Conflict during the Algerian War for Independence," *American Historical Review* 105 (June 2000): 739–69.

103. Sue Onslow, "The Cold War in Southern Africa: White Power, Black Nationalism, and External Intervention," in Sue Onslow, ed., *The Cold War in Southern Africa*, 9–34.

104. Chris Saunders, "The Angola/Namibia Crisis of 1988 and its Resolution," in Sue Onslow, ed., *The Cold War in Southern Africa: White Power, Black Nationalism, and External Intervention* (London: Routledge, 2009), 225–40; Gleijeses, *Conflicting Missions: Havana, Washington, and Africa, 1959–1976*.

105. See for instance Slobodian, "Bandung in Divided Germany: Managing Non-Aligned Politics in East and West," *Journal of Imperial and Commonwealth History* 41, 4 (2013): 644–62, who demonstrates that East German officials were leery of Pan-Africanism as it presented an organizing principle for African students that was out of GDR control.

106. Leopold Sédar Senghor, *On African Socialism*, trans. Mercer Cook (New York: Praeger, 1964).

107. William Foltz, *From French West Africa to the Mali Federation* (New Haven: Yale University Press, 1965). And see also Frederick Cooper, *Citizenship between Empire and Nation: Remaking France and French Africa, 1945–1960* (Princeton: Princeton University Press, 2014), for a discussion of attempts to unify not only French Africa but French Africa and France.

108. Priya Lal, *African Socialism in Postcolonial Tanzania: Between the Village and the World* (Cambridge: Cambridge University Press, 2015).

109. Andrew Ivaska, *Cultured States: Youth, Gender, and Modern Style in 1960s Dar es Salaam* (Durham: Duke University Press, 2011).

110. Seth Merkle, *A Motorcycle on Hell Run: Tanzania, Black Power, and the Uncertain Future of Pan-Africanism, 1964–1974* (East Lansing: Michigan State University Press, 2017).

111. Jeffrey Ahlman, *Living with Nkrumahism: Nation, State, and Pan-Africanism in Ghana* (Athens: Ohio University Press, 2017).

112. Jay Straker, *Youth, Nationalism, and the Guinean Revolution* (Bloomington: Indiana University Press, 2009).

113. Torben Gulstörff, "Resetting the Relevance of the Berlin Wall. German Public Diplomacies on the African Continent during the Cold War," in Óscar J. Martin Garcia and Rósa Magnúsdóttir, eds., *Machineries of Persuasion: European Soft Power and Public Diplomacy during the Cold War*, volume 3 of *Rethinking the Cold War* (Berlin: Walter de Gruyter, 2019), 85–104.

114. Winrow, *The Foreign Policy of the GDR in Africa*, 74, 218.

115. Haile Gabriel Dagne, *Das entwicklungspolitische Engagement der DDR in Äthiopien: Eine Studie auf der Basis äthiopischer Quellen*, Spektrum, Berliner Reihe zu Gesellschaft, Wirtschaft, und Politik in Entwicklungsländern, Bd. 87 (Münster: LIT Verlag, 2004), 89.

116. Trond Gilberg, "Eastern European Military Assistance to the Third World," in John F. Copper, ed., *Communist Nations' Military Assistance*, reprint (orig. 1983), (Oxford: Routledge, 2018).

117. Peter Heilmann, "Aspekte des Ausländerstudiums in der DDR," *Asien, Afrika, Lateinamerika* 18 (1990): 798–804.

118. Schenck, "Socialist Solidarities and their Afterlives: Histories and Memories of Angolan and Mozambican Migrants in the German Democratic Republic, 1975–2015"; Hermann W. Schönmeier, "Qualifizierung als Rückkehr Vorbereitung ehemaliger Vertragsarbeiter aus Mosambik," in Almut Zwengel, ed., *Die 'Gastarbeiter' der DDR: politischer Kontext und Lebenswelt*, 205–22 (Münster: LIT Verlag, 2011).

119. Eric Burton, "Navigating Global Socialism: Tanzanian Students in and Beyond East Germany," *Cold War History* 6, https://doi.org/10.1080/14682745.2018.1485146

120. Fehrenbach, *Race after Hitler*; Höhn, *GIs and Fräuleins*; and see also Rosemarie Peña, "From Both Sides of the Atlantic: Black German Adoptee Searches in William Gage's Geborener Deutscher (Born German)," *Geneaology* 2, 40 (2018); doi:10.3390/geneaology2040040, on the experience of Afro-Germans with transnational adoption.

CHAPTER 1

1. This document, along with others that concern British alarm at the prospect of Nigerians studying in the GDR, are housed at the National Archives, UK (TNA), National Scholarships Board, Scholarships in Soviet Zone of Germany, CO 537/5809, "Scholarships Lagos Nigeria, October 9."

2. Damian Mac Con Uladh, "Studium bei Freunden? Ausländische Studierende in der DDR bis 1990," in Christian Th. Müller and Patrice G. Poutrus, eds., *Ankunft, Alltag, Ausreise: Migration und Interkulturelle Begegnung in der DDR-Gesellschaft*(Cologne: Bohlau Verlag, 2005), 175–220.

3. Carolyn Brown, *"We Were All Slaves": African Miners, Culture, and Resistance at the Enugu Government Colliery* (Portsmouth, NH: Heinemann, 2003), chapter 7 passim; see also Toyin Falola, *Colonialism and Violence in Nigeria* (Bloomington: Indiana University Press, 2009), 165f, as well as S. O. Jaja, "The Enugu Colliery Massacre in Retrospect: An Episode in British Administration in Nigeria," *Journal of the Historical Society of Nigeria* 11, 3–4 (December 1982): 186–206. According to Brown, the killings at the colliery marked the end of British colonialism in Nigeria, and galvanized the population to unite behind the nationalist struggle for independence.

4. G. O. Olusanya, "The Zikist Movement—A Study in Political Radicalism, 1946–1950," *Journal of Modern African Studies* 4, 3 (1966): 323–33; Tajudeen Abdulraheem and Adebayo Olukoshi, "The Left in Nigerian Politics and the Struggle for Socialism 1945–1985," *Review of African Political Economy,* no. 37 (December 1986), 64–80; Ehiedu E. G. Iweriebor, "Proletarians and Politics in Colonial and Post-Colonial Nigeria, 1912–1964," *Africa: Rivista Trimestrale di studi e documentazione dell Istituto Italiano per l'Africa e l'Oriente* 41, 1 (March 1986): 29–47. The NCNC, which was founded by Herbery Macaulay in 1944, was a nationalist party that incorporated some socialist ideas. Azikiwe was its first secretary.

5. TNA, National Scholarships Board, Scholarships in Soviet Zone of Germany, CO 537/5809, secret correspondence from the governor of Nigeria to secretary of state Ernest Bevin, July 5, 1950.

6. TNA, National Scholarships Board, C.1. Ed. Scholarships, Germany, National S. Bd., 1950.

7. Odd Arne Westad, *The Global Cold War: Third World Interventions and the Making of Our Times* (Cambridge: Cambridge University Press, 2007).

8. Adelheid von Saldern, *The Challenge of Modernity: German Social and Cultural Studies, 1890–1960* (Ann Arbor: University of Michigan Press, 2004), 3.

9. Christopher Lee, ed., *Making a World after Empire: The Bandung Moment and its Political Afterlives* (Athens: Ohio University Press, 2010); Quinn Slobodian, "Bandung in Divided Germany: Managing Non-Aligned Politics in East and West, 1955–63," *Journal of Imperial and Commonwealth History* 41, 4 (2013): 644–62; and for the 1966 Tricontinental Congress see Isaac Saney, "Tricontinentalism, Anti-Imperialism, and Third World Rebellion," in Elena Fidian-Qasmiyah and Patricia Daley, eds., *Routledge Handbook of South-South Relations* (New York: Routledge, 2019), 153–67; Robert Buzzanco, "Obituary: Fidel Castro (1926–2016) and Global Solidarity," *The Sixties: A Journal of History, Politics, and Culture* 10, 2 (2017): 274–80; and Richard D. Ralston, "Cuba in Africa and Africa in Cuba," *Contemporary Marxism,* no. 7, Revolution in Southern Africa (Fall 1983), 140–53.

10. Steven Pfaff, *Exit-Voice Dynamics and the Collapse of East Germany: The Crisis of Leninism and the Revolution of 1989* (Durham: Duke University Press, 2006), 35.

11. Kristie Macrackis and Dieter Hoffmann, eds., *Science Under Socialism: East Germany in Comparative Perspective* (Cambridge, MA: Harvard University Press, 1999).

12. David C. Engerman and Corinna Unger, "Introduction: Toward a Global History of Modernization," *Diplomatic History* 33, 3 (June 2009): 375–85.

13. Hong, *Cold War Germany, the Third World, and the Global Humanitarian Regime*, 14–15.

14. PAAA MfAA B1263/75, Abt. Afrika, Sektion Gesamtafrikanische Fragen, DAFRIG, Aktennotiz, July 8, 1965.

15. Jeffrey Herf, *Reactionary Modernism: Technology, Culture, and Politics in Weimar and the Third Reich* (Cambridge: Cambridge University Press, 1984).

16. See Paul Steege, Andrew Stuart Bergerson, Maureen Healy, and Pamela E. Swett, "The History of Everyday Life: A Second Chapter," *Journal of Modern History* 80, 2 (June 2008) for a good description of the history of *Alltagsgeschichte* methodology.

17. Damian Mac Con Uladh, "Guests of the Socialist Nation? Foreign Students and Workers in the GDR" (M.A. Thesis, University of London, 2005), 4, explains that while a handful of foreign students studied in East Germany before 1949, the Nigerians were the first to study in the country once it was actually founded as a separate state.

18. Damian Mac Con Uladh, "Guests of the Socialist Nation? Foreign Students and Workers in the GDR" (M.A. Thesis, University of London, 2005), North Korean students, for example, only started to come in 1956

19. Those that do exist are housed at the archives of the UL or the TUD.

20. M. E. Kolagbodi, *Dr. M.E. Kolagbodi: Collected Speeches* (Lagos: Malthouse Press, 1995).

21. Interview with Yvonne Kolagbodi, Berlin, September 10, 2014.

22. A. E. Ohiaeri, *Behind the Iron Curtain*, 2nd ed. (Enugu: Fourth Dimension Publishing Co., 2000), 2.

23. "OHIAERI, (DR) Anyanjo Ejisimekwu," Biographical Legacy and Research Foundation, Nigeria, last modified February 6, 2017, accessed June 21, 2018, https://blerf.org/index.php/biography/ohiaeri-dr-anyanjo-ejisimekwu/

24. Ohiaeri, *Behind the Iron Curtain*.

25. MfAA A 14601, Ausbildung Nigerianischer Studenten und Facharbeiter in der DDR, 1958–1963, letter from A.E. Ohiaeri, August 27, 1959. At this point Ohiaeri had already finished his studies and was a practicing physician in Leipzig.

26. Ohiaeri, 2, 5.

27. Tijani, 127; Ohiaeri, 5ff.

28. Tijani.

29. Tijani; see also TNA, National Scholarships Board, Scholarships in Soviet Zone of Germany, CO 537/5809. Reuters report, October 9, 1950.

30. University of Leipzig Archives (hereafter referred to as UAL), Stu A55321, biographical data, n.d., and Dresden University of Technology Archives (hereafter referred to as UAD) Prorektorat für Studienangelegenheiten, 10 794 Bauwesen Abg./1960 VIII/Nr/ 8251, Aufnahmeantrag, July 18, 1953; UAD VIII/6002, Aufnahmeantrag, June 7, 1953.

31. Ohiaeri, 5.

32. Tijani, chapter 4.

33. Abdulraheem and Olukoshi, "The Left in Nigerian Politics and the Struggle for Socialism, 1945–1985," 64–69.

34. TNA, National Scholarships Board, Scholarships in Soviet Zone of Germany, CO 537/5809, advertisement, *West African Pilot*, August 16, 1950; notation of the Reuters report, October 9, 1950, by Mr Vile.

35. Sam O. Idemli, "What the West African Pilot did in the Movement for Nigerian Nationalism between 1937 and 1957," *Black American Literature Forum* 12, 3 (Autumn 1978): 84–91.

36. TNA, National Scholarships Board, Scholarships in Soviet Zone of Germany, CO 537/5809, C.1. Ed. Scholarships, Germany, National S. Bd., c. July 1950.

37. TNA, National Scholarships Board, Scholarships in Soviet Zone of Germany, CO 537/5809, J. Griffiths to Reverend R. W. Sorensen, M.P., August 1, 1950.

38. TNA, National Scholarships Board, Scholarships in Soviet Zone of Germany, CO 537/5809, Macpherson to Griffiths, July 1, 1950. This could be done with the rationale that a GDR education would not prepare them for careers in Nigeria.

39. UAD, Prorektorat für Studienangelegenheiten, Betreff: O.C., VIII Nr. 6986, Lebenslauf, n.d., c. 1953; Tijani, 124ff.

40. Ohiaeri, 22–23.

41. UAL ABF 077, "Gesamtanalyse der Vorbildung der Kolonialstudenten in der deutschen Sprache bei Eintreffen in Leipzig," May 15, 1951.

42. UAD, Prorektorat für Studienangelegenheiten A., A., 10–794 Bauwesen, Abg./1960, VIII/Nr/ 8251, "Mein Lebenslauf," May 20, 1953

43. Hakeem Tijani, "Britain and the Development of Leftist Ideology and Organisa-

tions in West Africa: The Nigerian Experience, 1945–1965" (PhD Diss., UNISA, Pretoria, 2005),124ff.

44. UAL Stu A 8854, A., I., Lebenslauf, April 11, 1954.

45. Federal Commissioner for the Records of the State Security Service of the Former German Democratic Republic (Hereafter known as BStU) MfS, AS 182/66, Band 7, list of African participants in the 1951 *Weltfestspiele*.

46. UAL ABF 77, Besprechung zwischen der Abteilungsleiterin des Staatssekretariats, Frau Erdmann, dem Direktor der Arbeiter- und Bauernfakultät, Herrn Ebschbach, dem Studiendirektor, Herrn Kurlenski, dem Betreuer, Herrn G.P., und dem Betreuer H., April 27, 1951.

47. O. Delano-Oriaran, "Diversifying the Professions: Gender Inequity and Female Career Aspirations in Nigeria," in Michael A. Burayidi, ed., *Multiculturalism in a Cross-National Perspective* (Lanham, MD: University Press of America, 1997), 355. Until 1955, school attendance was not compulsory in colonial Nigeria, and everyone had to pay fees.

48. UAD Prorektorat für Studienangelegenheiten, A.A. 10794, Lebenslauf, May 20, 1953; UAL PA 4156 M.A., Lebenslauf, n.d., c. 1954; and UAD VIII/6002, O.,C., "Kurze Lebensbeschreibung," March 6, 1953.

49. UAD, A.A., Lebenslauf, May 20, 1953; UAL, M.A., Lebenslauf, n.d., c. 1954; UAD, O.C., "Kurze Lebensbeschreibung," March 6, 1953.

50. UAD VIII/6002, O.,C., "Kurze Lebensbeschreibung."

51. UAD, Prorektorat für Studienangelegenheiten A., A., 10–794 Bauwesen, Abg./1960, VIII/Nr/ 8251, "Mein Lebenslauf," May 20, 1953

52. UAD VIII/6002, O.C., "Kurze Lebensbeschreibung."

53. UAL ABF 077, Recommendations on courses of further study, October 13, 1954.

54. UAL, Student Registration Card Catalogue, 1951–1990. A sample of 265 students who came from throughout sub-Saharan Africa, and who studied at the Karl-Marx-Universität and TUD between 1951 and 1990, shows that 174, or 65 percent, studied scientific subjects such as medicine, veterinary medicine, engineering, or tropical agriculture.

55. See for example PAAA MfAA 14396, Ausbildung von ghanesischen Facharbeiter und Fachschulern in der DDR, 1957–1962, Educational Agreement between Ghana and the GDR, September 16, 1959, among others.

56. UAD, Prorektorat für Studienangelegenheiten, Betreff: C.O, VIII Nr. 6986, Lebenslauf, n.d., c. 1953.

57. Young-Sun Hong, "'The Benefits of Health Must Spread Among All': International Solidarity, Health, and Race in the East German Encounter with the Third World," in Katherine Pence and Paul Betts, eds., *Socialist Modern: East German Everyday Culture and Politics* (Ann Arbor: University of Michigan Press, 2008), 183–210. Such students came from countries like Zanzibar prior to its unification with Tanganyika and incorporation into Tanzania.

58. UAL, Med. Fak. Prom. Bd. 26 (1957–1959). Bankole completed her dissertation on perinatal mortality after months examining and interviewing obstetric patients at a women's clinic in Leipzig

59. UAL ABF 077, G.P., "Bericht über die Entwicklung der westafrikanischen Studentengruppe an der ABF der Universität Leipzig," May 13, 1952.

60. UAL ABF 077, G.P.

61. See both Johannes Fabian, *Time and the Other: How Anthropology makes its Object*, 2nd ed. (New York: Columbia University Press, 2014), and Keletso Atkins, *The Moon is Dead! Give Us Our Money! The Cultural Origins of an African Work Ethic, Natal, South Africa, 1840–1900* (Portsmouth, NH: Heinemann, 1995), whose research demonstrates that, far from being idle, Africans had an extremely sophisticated understanding of time that Europeans perceived negatively because it deviated from their own.

62. There is copious evidence of this European view; for a specifically German expression of it, see among others Sabine Wilke, "Romantic Images of Africa: Paradigms of German Colonial Paintings," *German Studies Review* 29, 2 (May 2006): 285–98, and Birgit Meyer, "Christianity and the Ewe Nation: German Pietist Missionaries, Ewe Converts, and the Politics of Culture," *Journal of Religion in Africa* 32, 2, "The Politics of Mission" (May 2002): 167–99.

63. UAL ABF 077, G.P., "Bericht über die Entwicklung der westafrikanischen Studentengruppe an der ABF der Universität Leipzig," May 13, 1952. The student further commented that the British educational system had raised them this way purposefully, so that they would regard themselves as better than their uneducated compatriots

64. UAL ABF 077, G.P., "Bericht über die Entwicklung der westafrikanischen Studentengruppe an der ABF der Universität Leipzig," May 13, 1952.

65. UAL Stu A 55321, U.-O., L.I., "Beurteilung des nigerianischen Studenten I. U.-O.," April 12, 1954.

66. Sara Pugach, "African Students and the Politics of Race and Gender in the German Democratic Republic, 1957–1990," in Quinn Slobodian, ed., *Comrades of Color: East Germany in the Cold War World* (New York: Berghahn Books, 2015).

67. UAL ABF 077, Fritz Kurlenski, komm. Direktor der Arbeiter-u.-Bauern-Fakultät der Universität Leipzig, "Unser Verhalten zu unseren Auslandsstudenten," n.d.

68. Ulrich Herbert, Dirk van Laak, and Lutz Niethammer, eds., *Deutschland Danach* (Bonn: Dietz, 1999); Brigitte Schulz, "The Politics of East-South Relations: The GDR and Southern Africa," in Thomas A. Bayliss, David Childs, Erwin L. Collier, and Marilyn Rueschemeyer, eds., *East Germany in Comparative Perspective* (New York: Routledge, 2002), 159; Katrina Hagen, "Ambivalence and Desire in the East German 'Free Angela Davis' Campaign," in Quinn Slobodian, ed., *Comrades of Color: East Germany in the Cold War World* (New York: Berghahn, 2015), 158.

69. UAL ABF 077, Fritz Kurlenski, komm. Direktor der Arbeiter-u.-Bauern-Fakultät der Universität Leipzig, "Unser Verhalten zu unseren Auslandsstudenten," n.d

70. Wildenthal, *German Women for Empire*, 111–18; Wimmelbücker, *Mtoro bin Mwinyi Bakari*, 41–43; Moses, "From Faith to Race?"

71. Birthe Kundrus, "'Weiß und Herrlich': Überlegungen zu einer Geschlechtergeschichte des Kolonialismus," in Annegret Friedrich, Birgit Haehnel, Viktoria Schmidt-Linsenhoff, and Christina Threuter, eds., *Projektionen: Rassismus und Sexismus in der visuellen Kultur*, 41–50 (Marburg: Jonas Verlag, 1997); Axster, "Die Angst vor dem Verkaffern: Politiken der Reiningung im Deutschen Kolonialismus."

72. UAL ABF 077, Interpreter's Report.

73. The exception was a student from Kano, a city in northern Nigeria. See TUD VIII/6002, O.C., Lebenslauf, June 18, 1953.

74. "Nigeria," Harvard Divinity School, Religious Literacy Project, accessed June 21, 2018, https://rlp.hds.harvard.edu/nigeria-overview. The north, by contrast, is primarily Muslim, though as the author of this page also points out, the situation is complex, as there are Christian communities in the north and Muslim ones in the south.

75. UAL ABF 077, "Bericht der nigerianischen Studenten C. und A. vor der Direktion am 13.5.53 (mit anwesend war A.A.)."

76. BStU Leipzig AIM 103/54, Bd. 1–2 (O., C.), "Betr.: Persönliche Rücksprache mit dem Negerstudenten O., C.," von der ABF Leipzig, Schnabel, Bezirksverwaltung Leipzig, Abteilung VI, Leipzig, September 12, 1953.

77. BStU Leipzig AIM 103/54, Bd. 1–2 (O., C.).

78. Even at this early stage, the Protestant Church was under considerable pressure from the East German state, which was antireligion. There were many Christians among the 3.5 million people who left the GDR for the FRG before the Berlin Wall went up in 1961, although there were calls for pastors and other believers to stay in the East and strengthen the faith there. See Wendy Tyndale, *Protestants in Communist East Germany: In the Storm of the World* (London: Routledge, 2010), 21.

79. BStU Leipzig AIM 103/54, Bd. 1–2 (O., C.), "Betr.: Persönliche Rücksprache mit dem Negerstudenten O., C.," von der ABF Leipzig, Schnabel, Bezirksverwaltung Leipzig, Abteilung VI, Leipzig, September 12, 1953.

80. There was one other, later negative account by a Nigerian student who was in the GDR in the 1960s; this is Gilbert Ofodile, *I Shall Never Return: Eight Months in Communist East Germany, A Nigerian Student of Journalism Reports* (Esslingen am Neckar: Bechtle Verlag, 1967).

81. John M. Crewdson, "Worldwide Propaganda Network Built by the CIA," *New York Times*, December 26, 1977. This article alleged that *On the Tiger's Back* was funded by the CIA as U.S. propaganda against the USSR and its satellites.

82. Crewdson, "Worldwide Propaganda Network Built by the CIA."

83. Aderogba Ajao, *On the Tiger's Back: Six Years under Communism by a Nigerian* (London: Allen and Unwin, 1962), 35, 44.

84. Ajao, *On the Tiger's Back,* 50ff.

85. Ajao, *On the Tiger's Back,* 68.

86. Ajao, *On the Tiger's Back,* 29.

87. Ajao, *On the Tiger's Back,*70.

88. Ajao, *On the Tiger's Back,* 73.

89. Ajao, *On the Tiger's Back,* 114.

90. Ajao, *On the Tiger's Back,* 62ff.

91. Ajao, *On the Tiger's Back,* 83.

92. Ajao, *On the Tiger's Back,* 88.

93. Ajao, *On the Tiger's Back,* 128.

94. Ajao, *On the Tiger's Back,* 130.

95. SAPMO-BArch, DY/24/6822, Zentralrat der FDJ, Zentralarchiv, Bestand: Intern. Verbindungen, 1958–1962, "Die Schauermärchen von Aderogba Ajao alias

'Adelani' und die Wahrheit," von O.O., Aspirant der Wirtschaftswissenschaften der Karl-Marx-Universität Leipzig, n.d., c. 1958.

96. SAPMO-BArch, DY/24/6822, Zentralrat der FDJ, Zentralarchiv, Bestand: Intern. Verbindungen, 1958–1962, "Die Schauermärchen von Aderogba Ajao alias 'Adelani' und die Wahrheit," von O.O., Aspirant der Wirtschaftswissenschaften der Karl-Marx-Universität Leipzig, n.d., c. 1958.

97. SAPMO-BArch, DY/24/6822, Zentralrat der FDJ, Zentralarchiv, Bestand: Intern. Verbindungen, 1958–1962, "Die Schauermärchen von Aderogba Ajao alias 'Adelani' und die Wahrheit," von O.O., Aspirant der Wirtschaftswissenschaften der Karl-Marx-Universität Leipzig, n.d., c. 1958.

98. Peter Köpf, *Wo ist Lieutenant Adkins? Das Schicksal desertierter Nato-Soldaten in der DDR* (Berlin: Ch. Links Verlag, 2013), 185–86; Köpf, "Flucht nach Bautzen: Go West? Nicht nur im kalten Krieg liefen Hunderte NATO-Soldaten in den Osten über. Eine Villa in der Lausitz war ihr Auffanglager," *Die Zeit,* no. 10 (2013), http://www.zeit.de/2013/10/Nato-Deserteure-DDR-Bautzen, accessed October 13, 2014.

99. SAPMO-BArch, DY/24/6822, Zentralrat der FDJ, Zentralarchiv, Bestand: Intern. Verbindungen, 1958–1962, "Die Schauermärchen von Aderogba Ajao alias 'Adelani' und die Wahrheit," von O.O., Aspirant der Wirtschaftswissenschaften der Karl-Marx-Universität Leipzig, n.d., c. 1958.

100. BStU MfS AP 4954/73, Vermerk zu "Olga," September 2, 1968; O., "Problemen der wirtschaftlichen Zusammenarbeit zwischen den ostafrikanischen Staaten Kenia, Uganda, und Tansania im Prozeß ihrer Industrialisierung," (Ph.D. diss., Berlin-Karlshorst, 1970).

101. SAPMO-BArch DY/34 24618, Büro des Präsidiums, Protokollbüro Präsidiums-u. Sekretariatsbeschlüsse des Bundesvorstands betr. Afrika allg., 1960–1963, "Bericht über die Aussprachen mit Afrikanern in Cairo," April 17, 1961.

102. Ohiaeri's biography at blerf.org states that he was a resident medical officer at the University of Nigeria in Nsukka between 1962 and 1966. This contradicts the MfAA sources, which clearly place him in the GDR in 1965, and indicate that he was probably also there earlier in the 1960s.

103. This is confirmed in the *Federal Republic of Nigeria, Official Gazette*, Lagos, (No. 10, Vol. 62): February 13, 1965, 266, which shows that Ohiaeri registered as a physician in Nigeria on June 27, 1960, and practiced at General Hospital, Enugu.

104. PAAA MfAA B1263/75, Abt. Afrika, Sektion Gesamtafrikanische Fragen, DAFRIG, Aktennotiz, July 8, 1965.

105. UAD Prorektorat für Studienangelegenheiten, A.A. 10 794 Bauwesen Abg./1960, VIII/Nr/ 8251, A.A., Western Nigeria Water Corporation, to Referent Herr W., TUD, December 15, 1969.

106. UAL ABF 077, "Bericht über die Entwicklung der westafrikanischen Studentengruppe an der ABF der Universität Leipzig."

107. "Political Penetration through 'Friendship,'" *East-West Contacts: A Monthly Review* V, 9 (September 1971): 49–50. The journal *East-West Contacts* also referred to a "Dr. Bankole"—in this case probably Yetunde Bankole's husband, Akintola Bankole—as also being a member of the Nigerian GDR Friendship Society. It also alleged he was the head of a Nigerian Marxist group in East Germany. However, since

East-West Contacts was an International Documentation Centre (Interdoc) journal, and Interdoc was an anticommunist organization headquartered in The Hague and dedicated to fighting communism through cultural diplomacy and propaganda, its information is not necessarily reliable. On Interdoc please see Giles Scott-Smith, *Western Anti-Communism and the Interdoc Network: Cold War Internationale* (London: Palgrave Macmillan), 212.

108. Interview with Yvonne Kolagbodi, Berlin, September 10, 2014.

109. Mayirue Kolagbodi, "Trade Unions, Philosophy, and Leadership," in *Dr. M.E. Kolagbodi: Collected Speeches*, 50–57.

110. Modilim Achufusi, Untitled Essay in Walter Markov, ed., *Geschichte und Geschichtsbild Afrikas: Beiträge der Arbeitstagung für Neuere und Neueste Geschichte Afrikas am 17. und 18. April 1959 in Leipzig* (Berlin: Akademie Verlag 1960), cited in Walter Z. Laqueur, "Communism and Nationalism in Tropical Africa," *Foreign Affairs* 39, 4 (July 1961): 610–21.

111. Harald v. Sicard, "XXV. Internationaler Orientalistenkongreß, Moskau," *Anthropos* Bd. 56, H. 1&2 (1961): 271–73.

112. Walter Markov and Fausto Codino, "Appunti sulla storiografia Africa," *Studi Storici*, 4, 4 (October–December 1963): 759–82.

113. See https://cies.org/grantee/modilim-achufusi, accessed July 21, 2021.

114. https://cies.org/grantee/modilim-achufusi, accessed July 21, 2021.

115. Abdulraheem and Olukoshi, "The Left in Nigerian Politics and the Struggle for Socialism, 1945–1985," 64–69.

116. G. O. Olusanya, "The Zikist Movement—A Study in Political Radicalism, 1946–1950," 330.

117. PAAA MfAA C411 Studienplätze in der DDR für afrikanische Bürger, 1966–1967, Ministry of Foreign Affairs to the Department of Health, n.d., c. 1966.

118. As Eric Burton has highlighted in his discussion of students from Tanzania. See Eric Burton, "Navigating Global Socialism: Tanzanian Students in and Beyond East Germany," *Cold War History* https:// 10.1080/14682745.2018.1485146.

CHAPTER 2

1. British Library Endangered Archives Programme: United National Independence Party of Zambia, 1949–1988 (2008), EAP121/2/7/1/21 Tanganyika Representative, Correspondence [1961–1963], J. M. Chapoloko, Secretary for Deputy National President and UNIP Cairo Representative to M.C.B., October 3, 1961.

2. EAP121/2/7/1/21 Tanganyika Representative, Correspondence [1961–1963], M.B. to R.S. Makasa, UNIP Representative, Dar es Salam, January 7, 1962.

3. EAP121/2/7/1/21 Tanganyika Representative, Correspondence [1961–1963], M.B. Lebenslauf, August 10, 1961.

4. EAP121/2/7/1/41, R.S. Makasa to the UNIP Representative, Cairo, June 6, 1962.

5. Burton, "Hubs of Decolonization," 26, 28.

6. Ghanaian student George Sapara-Arthur, discussed further later in the book,

was one student who decried East German racism in the Western press; see PAAA MfAA 14396, Ausbildung von ghanesischen Facharbeiter und Fachschulern in der DDR, 1957–1962, letter from Neidhardt, Sektorleiter, Abt. Berufsbildung, Sektor Aus- und Weiterbildung ausländischen Bürger, to the Office of the high commissioner für Ghana, Technical Education Section, London, June 29, 1961, and "African Student Disillusioned with East Germany," *Windward Islands' Opinion*, Saturday, July 1, 1961: 10. Nigerian journalist and student Gilbert Ofodile was another; see "Nigerian Attacks Reds' Education: Disillusionment of Students from African Reported," *New York Times*, May 31, 1964, as well as Ofodile, *I Shall Never Return: Eight Months in Communist Germany, a Nigerian Student of Journalism Reports* (Esslingen: Bechtle Verlag, 1967).

7. Indeed, African students usually considered the GDR a better place to be than its Eastern European neighbors. This is even suggested in the article "Preference for the West by Foreign Students," *London Times*, Thursday, June 5, 1967, p. 5, which addresses "racial prejudice" in the communist bloc but mentions that "Those students who have studied in east (sic) Gernany . . . have normally returned (home) in a much better frame of mind than those from other east (sic) European countries."

8. SAPMO-BArch DY/24/6827, Intern. Verbindungen 1960/61, Aktenvermerk: Aussprache mit den Freunden Sam Nujoma, Präsident der South West African Peoples Organisation und Emil Appolus aus SW-Afrika, der zu einem Journalistenlehrgang in der DDR weilte am 11.1.1962, January 22, 1962.

9. Sebastian Conrad, *What is Global History?* (Princeton: Princeton University Press, 2016), 120–22.

10. Daniel Branch, "Political Traffic: Kenyan Students in Eastern and Central Europe, 1958–1969," *Journal of Contemporary History*, July 23, 2018, https://doi.org/10.1177/0022009418761194

11. Eric Burton, "Introduction: Journeys of Education and Struggle: African Mobility in Times of Decolonization and the Cold War," *Stichproben: Wiener Zeitschrift für kritische Afrika-Studien* 18, 34 (2018): 1–17.

12. Burton, "Decolonization, the Cold War, and Africans' Routes to Higher Education Overseas," 172.

13. Burton, "Decolonization," 176–77.

14. Burton, "Decolonization," 172; 182–83. Burton says that women were present in another route he discusses, that associated with the "airlift" that took East African students to the United States. Moreover, in "Hubs," 52, he briefly discusses female members of the South African ANC receiving military training in various African countries, as well as in Eastern Europe. For the most part, though, gender is not the focus in either of these works.

15. EAP121/2/7/1/7 Tanganyika Office, Correspondence [1961] (2008), Part II, E.W.D. C., for the Education Secretary, to Makasa, October 26, 1961. This letter to Makasa detailed a short list of possible contenders, but dismissed most of them for various reasons

16. EAP121/2/7/1/14 Tanganyika Office, Correspondence [1961–1962] (2008), Parts I-IV, Makasa to Monica C., October 28, 1961.

17. EAP121/2/7/1/14 Tanganyika Office, Correspondence [1961–1962] (2008), Parts I-IV, Makasa to Catherine P., October 28, 1961.

18. For the Zambian case, please see Fay Gadsden, "Patriarchal Attitudes: Male Control over and Policies towards Female Education in Northern Rhodesia, 1924–1963," *Zambia Journal of History* 6 (1993): 25–45, and Karin Tranberg Hansen, "Negotiating Sex and Gender in Urban Zambia," *Journal of Southern African Studies* 10, 2 (April 1984): 219–38.

19. EAP121/2/7/1/41pt2b, A.Z. Banda to J.C., August 29, 1962.

20. EAP121/2/7/1/41pt2b A.Z. Banda to F.C, Far East, Pyongyang, August 17, 1962.

21. See chapter 5 below for greater detail.

22. Elena Torreguitar, *National Liberation Movements in Office: Forging Democracy with African Adjectives in Namibia* (Oxford: Peter Lang, 2009), 112; Johann A. Müller, *The Inevitable Pipeline into Exile: Botswana's Role in the Namibian Liberation Struggle* (Basel: Basler Afrika Bibliographien, 2012).

23. http://nvdatabase.swarthmore.edu/content/zambians-campaign-independence-1944-1964

24. Kenya National Archives (hereafter referred to as KNA) ED-3–467, German University Scholarships for Kenya Students (West) Federal Republic (Western), Curriculum Vitae of Hassan Wani Ali Kamau, April 5, 1963.

25. KNA ED-3–2958, B.F.F. Oluande K'Odoul, Secretary to Jaramogi Oginga Odinga, Answers (Daniel arap) Moi, August 8, 1962.

26. SAPMO-BArch DY/79/613 Briefwechsel mit ehemaligen Studenten aus Afrika und Asien vom 1.1.1961–30.6.1964, Wachira to the President of DAFRIG, January 9, 1964.

27. SAPMO-BArch DY 6/2551, Nationalrat der Nationalen Front der DDR, Sekretariat, Abt. Internationale Verbindungen, Solidarität mit den Völkern Ostafrikas—u.a. Kenia 1958–1961, M.G., Lumumba Str. 5, Leipzig, to the President, Kenya Office, Cairo, December 11, 1961, Re: K.I.!

28. Burton, "Hubs of Decolonization," 33, notes that as of 1962 there were fifteen African independence movements or opposition parties with a foothold in Cairo, and that more came later.

29. Burton, "Hubs of Decolonization," 32.

30. Harvey Glickman, "Dar es Salaam: Where Exiles Plan—And Wait," *Africa Report* (July 1963): 3–6; and see also Burton, "Hubs," 47ff, for a discussion of Dar-es-Salaam as a meeting point for key political figures from across Africa.

31. In my own research, Addis Ababa never appeared as a way station on the route north.

32. Glickman, "Dar es Salaam: Where Exiles Plan—And Wait."

33. EAP121/2/7/1/7 Tanganyika Office, Correspondence [1961] (2008), Part III, as for instance with Makasa's letter to the secretary of education, August 4, 1961, in which he asked that no further students be sent to Cairo until the ticket situation was addressed.

34. EAP121/2/7/1/10 Tanganyika Office, Correspondence [1961], as for example in Simon Kapwepwe to Nicholas K., Trinity College School, Port Hope, Ontario, Canada, September 8, 1961, where Kapwepwe reached out to solicit bursaries from Canada.

35. EAP121/2/7/1/22 Refugees Committee Tanganyika, Correspondence [1961–1963], Minutes of the Refugee Committee Meeting Held in the A.N.C. (S.A.) Office, 15 Arab Street, Dar es Salaam, January 3, 1963, 2:30 p.m..

36. Meredith Terretta, "Cameroonian Nationalists Go Global: From Forest *Maquis* to a Pan-African Accra," *Journal of African History* 51 (2010): 189–212.

37. Terretta, "Cameroonian Nationalists Go Global," 198.

38. Interview with Jeannette Aryee-Boi, Accra, September 2015.

39. SAPMO-BArch DY/24/6827, Intern. Verbindungen 1960/61, Aloys-Marie Njog, Demokratischen Jugend Kamerun Exekutiv-Komitee in Ausland, Cairo, to the FDJ, Berlin July 10, 1961.

40. SAPMO-BArch DY/6/2404, Über eine Aussprache mit Posse François, Intérim-Bevollmächtiger des B.C.D der UPC in Conakry und Nkwalla Robert, Sekretär des C.G.E.T., Conakry, July 23, 1961, among others.

41. Thomas Deltombe, "The Forgotten Cameroon War," *Jacobin Magazine*, October 12, 2016, https://www.jacobinmag.com/2016/12/cameroon-france-colonialism-war-resistance/, accessed September 13, 2017.

42. SAPMO-BArch DY/6/2404, Nationalrat der Nationalen Front der DDR, Abt. Internationale Verbindungen, Sekretariat des Büros des Präsidiums, Zusammenarbeit mit der UPC, "Bericht auf Einladung des Präsident der UPC in der DDR," Berlin, October 23, 1961.

43. UAL DHfK VWA 203, "Aussprache mit den 3 Togolesen, die am Afrika-Lehrgang teilnehmen, am 6.6.1961 15.00 Uhr."

44. Benjamin N. Lawrance, *Locality, Mobility, and "Nation": Periurban Colonialism in Togo's Eweland, 1900–1960* (Rochester, NY: University of Rochester Press, 2007), 179.

45. UAL DHfK VWA 203, "Aussprache mit den 3 Togolesen."

46. Burton, "Hubs," 41ff; Jean Allman, "Kwame Nkrumah, African Studies, and the Politics of Knowledge Production in the Black Star of Africa," *International Journal of African Historical Studies* 46, 2 (2013): 113–37; and Jeffrey S. Ahlman, "Road to Ghana: Nkrumah, Southern Africa, and the Eclipse of a Decolonizing Africa," *Kronos*, no. 37 (November 2011): 23–40.

47. EAP121/2/5/5/7, Socialist Students, Correspondence (1960–1962), Kalulu to M. Sipalo, January 23, 1962.

48. EAP121/2/7/1/23, letter from M. Sipalo to S. Kalulu, January 22, 1962. Mary N. was in Ghana with a male UNIP official, and she was to study at the Institute while he was being sent on "mission."

49. Gerardo Serra and Frank Gerrits, "The Politics of Socialist Education in Ghana: The Kwame Nkrumah Ideological Institute, 1961–6," *Journal of African History* 60, 3 (November 2019): 407–28.

50. Kristen Ghodsee, *Second World, Second Sex: Socialist Women's Activism and Global Solidarity during the Cold War* (Durham: Duke University Press, 2018), 127.

51. Kenneth Kaunda, "Address, Introducing Zambian Humanism, UNIP National Council, October 26, 1967, cited in Hugo F. Hinfelaar, *Bemba Speaking Women of Zambia in a Century of Religious Change* (Leiden: Brill, 1988), 151.

52. Ghodsee, 125.

53. Burton, "Introduction: Journeys of Education and Struggle," 3.

54. SAPMO-BArch DY/6/3183 (Nationalrat der Nationalen Front der DDR) Abt. Internationale Verbindungen, Kenia, 1960–1964, "Beurteilung der Delegationsmitglieder," concerning a Kenyan student delegation visiting from London, August 18, 1960.

55. SAPMO-BArch DY/6/3183, Nationalrat der Nationalen Front der DDR, Abt. Internationale Verbindungen, Kenia 1960–1964, Bericht Koll. Kern MfAA, Korrespondent, about a meeting between Odinga and his associates and the Nationalrat; Gespräch mit Mr. Paul Naboth Mwok, (Sekretär des Vizepräsidenten der KANU, Oginga Odinga), am. 15.5.1961, 9.00 Uhr, Solidaritätskomitee.

56. PAAA MfAA A14325, Ausbildung guinesicher Facharbeiter und Studenten in der DDR, 1959–1962, Kürze Darstellung der Vorgänge, die mit der zeitweiligen Rückberufung eines Teiles der guineischen Studenten in der DDR im Zusammenhang stehen, March 14, 1962.

57. Indeed, such supranational organizations had existed in the United Kingdom and France from the 1910s and 1920s; see Stefan Goodwin, *Africa in Europe: Interdependencies, Relocations, and Globalization* (Lanham, MD: Lexington Books, 2009), 187, 215. By the 1960s, there were more organizations linking not only students in Europe but those in the United States, too; see Immanuel Wallerstein, *The Politics of Independence and Unity* (Lincoln: University of Nebraska Press, 2005), 215, and also Goodwin.

58. Andrew Dunlop Roberts, "Northern Rhodesia: The Post-War Background, 1945–1953," in Jan-Bart Gewald et al., eds., *Living the End of Empire: Politics and Society in Late Colonial Zambia* (Leiden: Brill, 2011), 15–24.

59. Daniel Speich, "The Kenyan Style of African Socialism," *Diplomatic History* 33, 3 (2009): 449–66.

60. EAP121/2/10/1/21, Zambian Students in Poland, "Declaration on the need for more scholarships to study in Eastern Europe," May 18, 1964.

61. PAAA MfAA C402 Vol. 2, Gurke, MfAA, to Reisenweber, DAfriG, 26 January 1966, in conversation about Kenyan student organizations.

62. Peter Anyang Nyong'o, "Profiles of Courage: Ramogi Achieng' Oneko," *Review of African Political Economy* 34, 113 (September 2007): 531–35, and many others (this may not be the best example).

63. David M. Anderson, "'Yours in Struggle for Majimbo': Nationalism and the Party Politics of Decolonization in Kenya, 1955–1964," *Journal of Contemporary History* 40, 3 (July 2005): 547–64.

64. SAPMO-BArch DY/6/3183, Nationalrat der Nationalen Front der DDR, Abt. Internationale Verbindungen, Kenia 1960–1964, Bericht Koll. Kern MfAA, Korrespondent, about a meeting between Odinga and his associates and the Nationalrat, n.d..

65. See for instance Kevin Sieff, "Who Are the Men Competing to Be President of Kenya?" *Washington Post*, August 9, 2017, https://www.washingtonpost.com/news/worldviews/wp/2017/08/08/who-are-the-two-men-competing-to-be-president-of-kenya/, accessed August 13, 2019.

66. Burton, "Decolonization, the Cold War, and Africans' Routes to Higher Education Overseas," 181f.

67. Miles Larmer, *Rethinking African Politics: A History of Opposition in Zambia* (London: Ashgate, 2013).

68. EAP121/2/7/1/22 Refugees Committee Tanganyika, Correspondence [1961–1963], Particulars and Purpose of Visitor form, Joseph M., April 17, 1962, documents how Joseph M. needed to flee Northern Rhodesia on suspicion of having communist literature at his house.

69. EAP121/2/7/1/22 Refugees Committee Tanganyika, Correspondence [1961–1963], Particulars and Purpose of Visitor form, Henry, April 17, 1962.

70. EAP121/2/7/1/22 Refugees Committee Tanganyika, Correspondence [1961–1963], Particulars and Purpose of Visitor form, Edward, April 17, 1962.

71. David Gordon, "Rebellion or Massacre? The UNIP-Lumpa Conflict Revisited," in Jan-Bart Gewald, Marja Hinfelaar, and Giacomo Macola, eds., *One Zambia, Many Histories: Towards a History of Postcolonial Zambia* (Leiden: Brill, 2008), 45–97. This violence was orchestrated not only by colonial forces but also by UNIP members, especially in clashes with adherents of the Christian Lumpa movement.

72. As well as to the West, since Kaunda's Zambia was a nonaligned state that straddled the Cold War divide; see Andy DeRoche, *Kenneth Kaunda, the United States, and Southern Africa* (London: Bloomsbury, 2016).

73. Milton Nkosi, "The Airlift Education Scholarship that Changed the World," https://www.bbc.com/news/world-africa-33629577, July 23, 2015.

74. EAP121/2/7/1/41pt2b, Makasa to The Party Representative, UNIP, Mbeya, August 18, 1962.

75. EAP121/2/7/1/13 Mbeya Office, Correspondence [1961–1962], Letter from UNIP's Mbeya Representative to the TANU Provincial Secretary, December 12, 1961.

76. Kenneth Kaunda, "Installation Address by the Chancellor," in *The University of Zambia: Inauguration Ceremony* (Lusaka: Government Printer, 1966), cited in Gatian F. Lungu, "Educational Policy-Making in Colonial Zambia: The Case of Higher Education for Africans from 1924–1964," *Journal of Negro History* 78, 4 (1993): 207–32.

77. Kaunda, "Installation Address by the Chancellor."

78. Gadsden, "Patriarchal Attitudes," and Hansen, "Negotiating Sex and Gender in Urban Zambia."

79. EAP121/2/7/1/6 Tanganyika Office, Correspondence [1961], R.S. Makasa to The Divisional President, Northern Division, P.O. Box 17, Mpika, December 29, 1961.

80. EAP121/2/7/1/13 Mbeya Office, Correspondence [1961–1962], Masaiti to Makasa, November 12, 1961.

81. EAP 121/2/7/1/42pt2a, M. Sokoni to all Branch Secretaries of UNIP and TANU, April 15, 1962.

82. EAP121/2/7/1/41pt2b, Makasa to The Party Representative, UNIP, Mbeya, August 18, 1962.

83. EAP121/2/7/1/22 Refugees Committee Tanganyika, Correspondence [1961–1963], Makasa to the UNIP Representative, Mbeya, October 9, 1961.

84. EAP121/2/7/1/26 Tanganyika Office, Correspondence [1961–1964], Part III, UNIP, NR, Freedom House, to "Comrade Applicants and Regional Secretaries, UNIP, NR," June 28, 1962.

85. EAP121/2/7/1/41pt2b, A.Z. Banda to Comrade Mubanga, August 25, 1962

86. EAP121/2/7/1/7 Tanganyika Office, Correspondence [1961] (2008), Part II, Simon Kapwepwe, National Treasurer, to the National Chairman/Education Committee Chairman, Lusaka, November 25, 1961.

87. EAP121/2/7/1/7 Tanganyika Office, Correspondence [1961] (2008), Part I, S. Kalulu to Simon Kapwepwe, December 6, 1961.

88. EAP121/2/7/1/83a, Wilted Phiri to R.M. Kapangala, May 7, 1964.

89. EAP121/2/7/1/7 Tanganyika Office, Correspondence [1961] (2008) (Part I), Jonah S. to the National Treasurer, September 6, 1960, and Jonah S., c/o Dr. F.J. Bennett, Makerere College, P.O. Box 262, Kampala, to Simon Kapepwe, December 23, 1960.

90. EAP121/2/7/1/14pt1b, Tanganyika Office, Correspondence [1961–1962], Makasa to Jonah S., November 14, 1961.

91. PAAA MfAA A15060, Aufnahme nordrhodesischer bzw. sambischer Studenten und Facharbeiter zur Ausbildung in der DDR, 1962–1966, Application of Jonah S., c. August 1962.

92. EAP121/2/10/1/21, letter of Jonah S., Rostock-Südstadt, to the UNIP General Secretary, Freedom House, Lusaka, August 17, 1964.

93. EAP121/2/7/1/23, Mulemba to Makasa, circa April 1963.

94. EAP121/2/7/1/23, Makasa to Oliver Chama, student in Yugoslavia, April 1, 1963.

95. Burton, "Decolonization," 184–89, discusses the "exodus" of African students from Eastern Europe to West Germany and other Western countries. While he does mention racism as a factor driving the students to leave, he says that other considerations, such as the inability to choose their own course of education and track records of poor performance at their Eastern European universities, were more definitive in compelling the students to go.

96. EAP121/2/7/1/26 Tanganyika Office, Correspondence [1961–1964] Part I, Masaiti to William M., February 2, 1963.

97. EAP121/2/7/1/7 Tanganyika Office, Correspondence [1961] (2008), Part II, E.W.D. Chalabesah, for the Education Secretary, to Makasa, October 26, 1961.

98. EAP121/2/7/1/6 Tanganyika Office, Correspondence [1961] (2008), Makasa to the Education Secretary, Lusaka, November 14, 1961.

99. EAP121_2_7_1_14pt2B, aka Part IV, Makasa to Mama Mulenga-Mukuka, January 16, 1962.

100. EAP121/2/7/1/7 Tanganyika Office, Correspondence [1961] (2008), Part II, E.W.D. Chalabesah, for the Education Secretary, to Makasa, October 26, 1961.

101. EAP121/2/7/1/26 Tanganyika Office, Correspondence [1961–1964] (2008), Part III, Agnes M. to Robert Makasa, September 21, 1961, and EAP121/2/7/1/7 Tanganyika Office, Correspondence [1961] (2008), Part III, Makasa to UNIP Education Secretary, Lusaka, October 6, 1961. Interestingly enough, Sabrina M. was the one who replaced Agnes M. for the nursing scholarship in the GDR.

102. EAP121/2/7/1/7 Tanganyika Office, Correspondence [1961] (2008), Part III, Makasa to Education Secretary, Lusaka, cc'ed to Reverend M., UNIP, Broken Hill, September 13, 1961, and Makasa to UNIP Accountant, Lusaka, October 12, 1961.

103. EAP 121/2/7/1/6, Tanganyika Office, Correspondence [1961](2008), Emmanuel, Dar-es-Salaam, to S. Kalulu, Lusaka, n.d., ca. November 1961.

104. Tsitsi Dangarembga, *Nervous Conditions* (London: The Women's Press, 1988).

105. EAP121/2/7/1/7 Tanganyika Office, Correspondence [1961] (2008), Kalulu to Makasa, August 10, 1961.

106. EAP121/2/7/1/55, Students, Circulars (1962–1963), M. Sokoni to ALL STUDENTS IN THE G.D.R., April 21, 1962.

107. Jane L. Parpart, "Sexuality and Power on the Zambian Copperbelt, 1926–1964," in Jane L. Parpart and Sharon B. Stichter, eds., *Patriarchy and Class: African Women in the Home and the Workforce* (New York: Routledge, reprint, 2019), 115–38.

108. Gisela Geisler, "Troubled Sisterhood: Women and Politics in Southern African Case Studies from Zambia, Zimbabwe, and Botswana," *African Affairs* 94, 377 (October 1995): 545–78.

109. EAP121/2/7/1/10 Tanganyika Office, Correspondence [1961] (2008), Part II, Makasa to the Deputy National President, UNIP, Cairo, September 20, 1961.

110. EAP121/2/7/1/14pt2a, Kapepwe to the UNIP Representative, Los Angeles, December 20, 1961.

111. Matthew Hughes, "Fighting for White Rule in Africa: The Central African Federation, Katanga, and the Congo Crisis, 1958–1965," *International History Review* 25, 3 (September 2003): 592–615, discusses the interest of Rhodesian white settlers in preserving white hegemony not only in the Federation of Rhodesia and Nyasaland/Central African Federation but also in the Congo's mineral-rich province of Katanga, where they envisioned forming an alliance with Belgian settlers. Cold War politics collided with a regional crisis, with Roy Welensky, prime minister of the Federation, considering the situation in Congo critical to the Federation's political survival and to its preservation of white rule. Maintaining white rule was also seen as key to preventing the spread of communism. Here see Stephen M. Saideman, *The Ties that Divide: Ethnic Politics, Foreign Policy, and International Conflict* (New York: Columbia University Press, 2001), 36–69.

112. Kay Sifuniso, "What happens to African Students in Eastern Europe?" *Mail*, Zambian Edition, February 7, 1964; EAP121/2/7/1/23, Mulemba to Makasa, circa April 1963.

113. Julie Hessler, "Death of an African Student in Moscow: Race, Politics, and the Cold War," *Cahiers du Monde Russe* 47, 1/2 (2006): 33–63; Maxim Matusevich, "Black in the USSR," *Transition,* no. 100 (2008): 56–75; Sean Guillory, "Culture Clash in the Socialist Paradise: Soviet Patronage and African Students' Urbanity in the Soviet Union, 1960–1965," *Diplomatic History* 38, 2 (2014): 271–81; Jordan Bonfante, "African Students at Iron Curtain Schools flee a Hateful Epithet: 'Cherni Maimuni,'" *Life*, March 15, 1963.

114. EAP121_2_7_1_14pt2a, Kapwepwe to unnamed German official, December 1, 1961.

115. Amos Ndyamba, "Former Berlin Student Replies to Kay Sifuniso: Eastern Europe Is Not That Bad," *Mail*, February 28, 1964.

116. EAP121_2_7_1_14pt1b, Kapwepwe to "Dear Brothers and Sisters" in the GDR, November 25, 1961.

117. EAP121/2/7/1/55, Students, Circulars (1962–1963), M. Sokoni to ALL STUDENTS IN THE G.D.R., April 21, 1962.

118. EAP121/2/7/1/71, Cairo Correspondence, Wilted Phiri, UNIP Representative, Cairo, to the UNIP Representative, Dar-es-Salaam, confirming tickets for the two scholarship holders, n.d..

119. https://www.geni.com/projects/Rhodesia-and-Nyasaland-Zambia-Zimbabwe-Malawi-Timeline/14576, accessed August 14, 2017.

120. EAP121/2/7/1/71, Cairo Correspondence, D.M. Lisulo to Wilted Phiri, April 19, 1963.

121. DeRoche, "Kenneth Kaunda, the United States, and Southern Africa."

122. Susan Aurelia Gitelson, "Policy Options for Small States: Kenya and Tanzania Reconsidered," *Studies in Comparative International Development* 12, 2 (Summer 1977): 28–58; "PARM: Annual Policy and Resource Assessment, Part I," March 31, 1977, http://www.princeton.edu/~achaney/capsule/doc/1977NAIROB04101, accessed August 16, 2017.

123. SAPMO-BArch DY 6/2551 (DY 6 Nationalrat der Nationalen Front der DDR, Sekretariat), Abt. Internationale Verbindungen, Solidarität mit den Völkern Ostafrikas—- u.a. Kenia, 1958–1961, Aktenvermerk über den Zwischenaufenthalt des Präsidenten der KANU, Jomo Kenyatta, im Kairo am 15.11.61, 02 Uhr.

124. This included a woman named Joanna M., who was likely married to a Christopher M. who arrived in Dresden in 1960. Joanna M. only came to the GDR in 1965. Similarly, Jane O., who was in East Germany as of 1963, studied education in Dresden and then medicine in Leipzig, may have been married to the male Kenyan student Oscar O., who was in the country by 1959. While there is no definitive evidence here, the timing of their arrivals and where they lived in the GDR make it seem probable. See MfS C-SKS 12713, notes on Christopher M. and Joanna M., notes on Jane O. and Oscar O., and Studentenkartei Ausländer, c. 1965–1990. I am not sure why Kenyan women did not "go on the road" as Zambian women did; perhaps it is because the Zambians rarely walked long distances overland, even though they did ride in trucks, and the Kenyans did not want women to make the more arduous trek.

125. KNA ED-3–467, German University Scholarships for Kenya Students (West) Federal Republic (Western), Curriculum Vitae of Hassan Wani Ali Kamau, April 5, 1963

126. Murumbi's memory of when the office opened contradicts Burton, "Decolonization," 177, who claims that the office was only opened in 1959.

127. Anne Thurston et al., *A Path not Taken: The Story of Joseph Murumbi, Africa's Greatest Private Culture Collector and Kenya's Second Vice President* (Nairobi: The Murumbi Trust, 2015), 72–74. Murumbi further claimed that there were students who walked even further, from Nairobi to Liberia, and from Nairobi to Ghana.

128. Thurston et al., 73.

129. Catherine Atieno Jimbo Odari, "A Blessing or Curse? The Mboya-Kennedy Students' Airlift and its Implications," M.A. Thesis, Oxford, OH: Miami University, 2011, 31 passim.

130. Thurston et al., 73.

131. SAPMO-BArch DY/6/3183 (Nationalrat der Nationalen Front der DDR) Abt. Internationale Verbindungen, Kenia, 1960–1964, "Beurteiling der Delegationsmitglieder."

132. SAPMO-BArch DY 6/2551 (DY 6 Nationalrat der Nationalen Front der DDR, Sekretariat), Abt. Internationale Verbindungen, Solidarität mit den Völkern Ostafrikas—- u.a. Kenia, 1958–1961, Letter of N. Njururi, London, to H. Eggebrecht, Berlin, March 7, 1961.

133. SAPMO-BArch DY 6/2551, Letter from Norman N. to Eggebrecht, May 25, 1961.

134. SAPMO-BArch DY 6/2551, Thomas G. to Eggebrecht, April 15, 1961.

135. SAPMO-BArch DY 6/2551, Thomas G. to Oliver O., June 21, 1961.

136. SAPMO-BArch DY 6/2551, Thomas G. to Eggebrecht, December 11, 1961.

137. SAPMO-BArch DY 6/2551, Oliver O. to Eggebrecht, December 23, 1961.

138. East Africa Living Encyclopedia, https://www.africa.upenn.edu/NEH/kethnic.htm, accessed October 19, 2018.

139. Rok Ajulu, "Politicised Ethnicity, Competitive Politics and Conflict in Kenya: A Historical Perspective," *African Studies* 61, 2 (2002): 251–67.

140. SAPMO-BArch DY/6/3183, Nationalrat der Nationalen Front der DDR, Abt. Internationale Verbindungen, Kenia 1960–1964, Bericht Koll. Kern MfAA, Korrespondent, n.d..

141. Branch, "Political Traffic"; Burton, "Decolonization."

142. KNA ED-3–2958, KOSAC Subcommittee Meetings, 1962, "Moi Challenges Odinga and Kenya Office Cairo on Student Affairs," extracts from the *Daily Nation* of November 8, 1962, Nairobi.

143. KNA ED-3–2958, KOSAC Subcommittee Meetings, 1962, "B.F.F. Oluande K'Oduol, Secretary to Jaramogi Oginga Odinga, answers Moi," November 8, 1962.

144. Anderson, "Yours in the Struggle for Majimbo."

145. KNA ED-3–2958, KOSAC Subcommittee Meetings, 1962, "B.F.F. Oluande K'Oduol, Secretary to Jaramogi Oginga Odinga, answers Moi," November 8, 1962.

146. KNA MAC-RED-215–3, "Kenya Students 'Stranded' in Cairo," November 15, 1962.

CHAPTER 3

1. PRAAD JE198, Ministry of Education, Scholarships Awards by Other Countries, I.R.O. Neequaye, "Passports and Exit Permits for Ghanaian Students Proceeding Overseas," July 19, 1965.

2. Sometimes also written as Nkrumahism.

3. Matteo Grilli, *Nkrumaism and African Nationalism: Ghana's Pan-African Foreign Policy in the Age of Decolonization* (New York: Springer, 2018), 13–14; David E. Apter, "Ghana's Independence: Triumph and Paradox," *Transition*, no. 98 (2008): 6–22.

4. In 1960, for instance, the GDR offered "30 Vocational Training Awards" and "20 University Scholarships." See PRAAD JE198, Ministry of Education, Scholarships Awards by Other Countries, Cabinet Committee on Establishment and Scholarship Issues, The Registrar of Scholarships, "Offer of Scholarships from East European Countries," c. April 1960.

5. "Interview—Walter Mignolo/Part II: Key Concepts," https://www.e-ir.info/2017/01/21/interview-walter-mignolopart-2-key-concepts/, accessed December 29, 2020, explains that according to Walter Mignolo the decolonization processes of the post-1945 era did not succeed because they remained grounded in a Western episteme that organized knowledge according to Eurocentric principles. Ergo, Mignolo says that "[d]ecoloniality means first to delink (to detach) from that overall structure of knowledge in order to engage in an epistemic reconstitution. . . . Of ways of thinking, lan-

guages, ways of life and being in the world that the rhetoric of modernity disavowed and the logic of coloniality implement." The concept "decolonial" also implies that decolonization is an ongoing process and not a complete, finished event. This process is one that started well before any "official" process of decolonization and involves active resistance to and rejection of discourses of white supremacy. Here see for instance Brittany Lehman, "West German Involvement in North African Decolonization in the 1950s and 1960s," in Sara Pugach, David Pizzo, and Adam Blackler, eds., *After the Imperialist Imagination: Two Decades of Research on Global Germany and its Legacies* (Oxford: Peter Lang, 2020), 261–84.

6. Seymour M. Hersh, "CIA Said to Have Aided Plotters Who Overthrew Nkrumah in Ghana," *New York Times*, May 19, 1978.

7. Governments, moreover, did not necessarily need to shift; political priorities could be rearranged within the same government, as we will see in the next chapter with the case of Guinea.

8. PRAAD JE198, letter from Aaron N. to the State Enterprise Secretariat, Office of the President, December 9, 1964.

9. PAAA MfAA 14396 Ausbildung von ghanesischen Facharbeiter und Fachschulern in der DDR, 1957–1962, Simons, MfAA, to Noelle, Handelsvetretung, Khartoum, July 17, 1957, addressing the five scholarships on offer to Ghana, and requesting that Noelle inform the Ghanaian Handelsvertretung of the same, and Scharfenberg, MfAA, Aktenvermerk, September 5, 1957, discussing Acquah and his recommendation to bypass the British and approach the Minister of Education directly.

10. PAAA MfAA 14396, Aktenvermerk, Kupferschmidt to the MfAA, November 7, 1957.

11. Naaborko Sackeyfio-Lenoch, "The Ghana Trades Union Congress and the Politics of International Labor Alliances, 1957–1971," *International Review of Social History* 62, 2 (August 2017): 191–213.

12. Rod Alence, "Colonial Government, Social Conflict, and State Involvement in Africa's Open Economies: The Origins of the Ghana Cocoa Marketing Board, 1939–1946," *Journal of African History* 42 (2001): 397–416.

13. PAAA MfAA 14396, letter from Gerald O. to Herr Krause of the Abteilung Internationale Organisationen, September 18, 1957.

14. PAAA MfAA 14396 Ausbildung von ghanesischen Facharbeiter und Fachschulern in der DDR, 1957–1962, Vereinbarung GDR-Ghana, September 20, 1958.

15. PAAA MfAA 14396 Ausbildung von ghanesischen Facharbeiter und Fachschulern in der DDR, 1957–1962, Muhlmann, MfAA, to Eckloff, Stellvertretender des Ministers für Aussenhandel und Innerdeutschen Handel der DDR, March 11, 1959.

16. PAAA MfAA 14396, Fritsch, MfAA, Aktenvermerk concerning a discussion with Dowuona Hammond, Staatssekretär im Ministerium für Erziehung und Information, December 22, 1959, where the latter told him that British influences in the government would not allow any more scholarships from the GDR to be utilized.

17. PRAAD JE198, Letter to the Registrar of Scholarships, May 4, 1960.

18. PAAA MfAA 14396, Allassani/Muhlmann.

19. PAAA MfAA 14396, "Realisierung des Studentenabkommens von 16.9.59," Fritsch, October 10, 1960.

20. PAAA MfAA 14396, "Realisierung des Studentenabkommens von 16.9.59," Fritsch, October 10, 1960.

21. PAAA MfAA 15975, Aufnahme ghanesischer Bürger zum Studium und zur Facharbeiterausbildung in der DDR, 1962–1966.

22. PRAAD JE 198, Scholarships Awarded by other Countries, discussion of "GDR Scientific and Technical Training" scheme, 1959, and "East German Vocational Scholarships: Minutes of Meetings of the U.K. Selections Board," November 11, 1959.

23. TNA DO35/10874 East Germany, Relations with Ghana, 6-7-59 to 16-8-60, Ghana Fortnightly Summary, 27th May–9th June, 1960, Accra, June 14, 1960.

24. TNA DO35/10874 East Germany, Relations with Ghana, 6-7-59 to 16-8-60, Ghana Fortnightly Summary, 27th May–9th June, 1960, Accra, June 14, 1960, British Embassy in Bonn, Chancery, to the African Department, Foreign Office, July 15, 1960.

25. David Ernest Apter, *Ghana in Transition*, 2nd ed. (Princeton: Princeton University Press, 2015), 344.

26. TNA DO35/10874 East Germany, Relations with Ghana, 6-7-59 to 16-8-60, Confidential Inward Telegram from Accra to Commonwealth Relations Office, July 27, 1960, July 28, 1960, No. 100 Saving, Confidential, Ghana Fortnightly Summary, 8th July, 1960–24th July, 1960, Part II, I., Internal, East German Visitors to Ghana.

27. Why were there Ghanaian students already waiting in England in the first place? The answer is fairly simple: by the time the GDR attempted to bring Africans to East German universities and vocational schools, there was already a long tradition of Africans from elite families studying in the British metropole. Hakim Adi has shown that there was a significant West African student presence from the early twentieth century, and that this grew exponentially after World War II. This population briefly included Nkrumah, who studied in London from 1945 to 1947. There was thus a sizable pool of eligible study abroad candidates in England by the late 1950s, which seems to have been comprised of both students and workers in various industrial fields. See Adi, *West Africans in Britain, 1900–1960* (London: Lawrence and Wishart, 1998).

28. PRAAD JE198, Ministry of Education, Scholarships Awards by Other Countries, Minutes of Meetings of the UK Selection Board held at 13 Belgrave Square, London, Tuesday and Wednesday, November 11–12, 1959.

29. For instance, "Scholarships Offered by the Governments of Yugoslavia, Poland, German Democratic Republic, Rumania, Czechoslovakia, and Union of Soviet Socialist Republic for 1964–5," *Daily Graphic*, April 5, 1964, p. 11.

30. PRAAD JE198, Ministry of Education, Scholarships Awards by Other Countries, Minutes of Meetings of the UK Selection Board held at 13 Belgrave Square, London, Tuesday and Wednesday, November 11–12, 1959.

31. PRAAD EP151, 17/8/56–5/6/59, Parliamentary Questions on Education answered by General and Tech Education Divisions, "Fourth Meeting of the First Session of the First National Assembly, 11 October 1957."

32. PRAAD EP151, Second Meeting of the Second Session of the First National Assembly, December 11, 1958.

33. PRAAD EP151. These particular overseas scholarships were likely for spots at British universities, considering that they were discussed in the context of a scholarship "scheme" that had existed since 1952. However, it seems likely that the same held true for the scholarships from Soviet Bloc nations.

34. PAAA MfAA A14396, Realisierung des Studenten und Facharbeiterabkommens für das Studienjahr 1961/1962, June 1, 1961.

35. PAAA MfAA 14396, Ernest O. to the MfAA, June 15, 1959.

36. PAAA MfAA 14396, Charlie A. to the MfAA, March 30, 1960.

37. Samuel Atwi Darkwah and Nahanga Verter, "An Empirical Analysis of Cocoa Bean Production in Ghana," *European Scientific Journal* 10, 16 (June 2014), http://citeseerx.ist.psu.edu/viewdoc/download?doi=10.1.1.841.146&rep=rep1&type=pdf, accessed April 29, 2019.

38. PRAAD EP151, 17/8/56–5/6/59, Parliamentary Question, Meeting of the First National Assembly, August 6, 1957.

39. PRAAD EP151, Fritsch, HV Accra, to the MfAA, March 1960.

40. PRAAD EP151, Samuel A..

41. PRAAD JE198, 'Appendix B': Minutes of Meeting of a Selection Committee Held at the Civil Service Training Center on 24th July–2nd August 1963 to Interview Candidates in Connection with the Governments (*sic*) Czechoslovakia, German Democratic Republic, Poland, U.S.S.R. and Yugoslavia Awards.

42. Minutes of Meetings of the UK Selection Board held at 13 Belgrave Square, London, Tuesday and Wednesday, November 11–12, 1959.

43. PRAAD JE198, Telegram concerning "Report of Selection Committee for East German Vocational Training," May 11, 1960.

44. PRAAD JE198, R.K.O. Djang, Executive Secretary, Office of the Planning Commission, Memo on Foreign Government Scholarships 1966, December 10, 1965

45. PAAA MfAA A14396, Hasler, MfAA, to Seidel, HV, March 23, 1961.

46. PAAA MfAA A14396, Hasler, MfAA, to Seidel, HV, March 23, 1961.

47. PRAAD JE198, Ministry of Education, Scholarships Awards by Other Countries, "Supplementary to the East German Vocational Scholarships," November 12, 1959.

48. PRAAD JE198, Ministry of Education, Scholarships Awards by Other Countries, "Supplementary to the East German Vocational Scholarships," November 12, 1959.

49. Exact statistics are not available, but since this was before the number of African students in the Soviet Bloc began to increase with the wave of decolonizations that started in 1960, it seems unlikely that there would have been as many Afro-German children as there were in West Germany, which had a substantial African American presence from the immediate postwar period.

50. For discussion of family separations in the GDR with applicability to foreign workers, see Mac con Uladh, "Guests of the Socialist Nation?" 71, 97.

51. PRAAD JE198, Ministry of Education, Scholarships Awards by Other Countries, S.W. K., "The Future of African Students in Eastern European Countries: Summary," Embassy of the Republic of Ghana, YUGOSLAVIA, April 19, 1963.

52. "*Bulgaria* Exodus: NCNC Calls for Inquiry," *West African Pilot*, February 19, 1963; "African Students Bulgaria," HC Deb February 21, 1963, vol 672 c614, https://api.parliament.uk/historic-hansard/commons/1963/feb/21/african-students-bulgaria; Robert Kotey, "Ghanaian Students Beaten, Arrested in Bulgarian Restaurant Incident," *Stanford Daily* 143, 17 (February 27, 1963), among others.

53. "The Future of African Students in Eastern European Countries: Summary."

54. "The Future of African Students in Eastern European Countries: Summary." In fact, Kumah told the following remarkable story about Africans arriving in Belgrade one winter's night: "On February this last year, I was at the Belgrade International Airport when some twenty African students disembarked an Ilysion Aircraft in a heavy snowfall. The airport was 3–4 feet deep in snow and the temperature was about minus 15 degrees centigrade. The students were in light tropical clothes and not one of them had a winter coat on. In order to help them endure the bleak cold weather while walking a distance of about 150 yards from the Aircraft to the Airport Terminal, they were given blankets to wrap themselves from head to waist. This presented a very funny spectacle. Their queer appearance attracted a lot of attention and camera men rushed to take pictures. When the students finally entered the terminal I approached them to find out where they came from and what was their destination. I was in fact ashamed to learn that they were Ghanaians, on their way to Moscow on scholarships offered by the Russian Government. This is one example of what happens nearly every month in some of these Eastern European countries." S. W. Kumah said that while the Eastern European governments did keep their promises to buy the students clothing, when they went to the store they were accompanied by a "huge number of on-lookers," making the shopping trip into what he termed "a degrading show of love." Finally, he opined that the lack of decent clothing might be expected for students from countries that were not yet independent and lacked funds, but were embarrassing for students from an independent state such as Ghana.

55. "The Future of African Students in Eastern European Countries: Summary."

56. "The Future of African Students in Eastern European Countries: Summary."

57. PAAA MfAA 14396, Protest, das Komitee der Afro-Asiatischen Studenten in Leipzig, June 15, 1961.

58. PAAA MfAA 14396, Protest, das Komitee der Afro-Asiatischen Studenten in Leipzig, June 15, 1961.

59. PAAA MfAA 14396, Protest, das Komitee der Afro-Asiatischen Studenten in Leipzig, June 15, 1961.

60. PAAA MfAA 14396, Protest, das Komitee der Afro-Asiatischen Studenten in Leipzig, June 15, 1961.

61. PRAAD JE198, Ministry of Education, Scholarships Awards by Other Countries, E. Ako Nai, Warsaw, to Ako Adjei, Minister of Foreign Affairs, Accra, Ghana, March 29, 1962.

62. Slobodian, "Bandung in Divided Germany."

63. SAPMO-BArch DC 4/1558, Bericht ueber die Reise einer Delegation des Zentralrats der FDJ in die westafrikanischen Republiken Mali, Guinea, und Ghana, January 3, 1963.

64. Grilli, 16, 226.

65. PRAAD JE198, Kodwo Addison, Director, Kwame Nkrumah Ideological Institute, to the Registrar, The Scholarship Secretariat, regarding "Scholarships awarded to students from the Kwame Nkrumah Ideological Institute," August 1965.

66. PAAA MfAA 14396, Vermerk zur Notenbank, March 15, 1961.

67. PAAA MfAA 14396, Vermerk zur Notenbank, March 15, 1961, CV of Alex E. K. Ashiabor. Once again, it is difficult to tell whether any Ghanaian students did come

to study banking in the GDR. There were evidently internal governmental disputes over the issue, and as of early 1962 only two students had been delegated to study banking in East Germany, one who had already spent time studying the banking system in Israel. That student, Alex Ashiabor, went on to become a governor of the Bank of Ghana.

68. Grilli, 226.

69. PAAA MfAA 14396, C. C. Nunoo, Registrar of Scholarships, to the Economic and Trade Mission of Ghana, Berlin, August 26, 1965.

70. PAAA MfAA 15975.

71. PAAA MfAA 14396, Felix M. and Edmund T., "For and on behalf of the Scholarship Holders in the GDR," copied to the Ghanaian Government, the GDR's Ministry of Foreign Affairs, and the GDR's Trade Mission in Accra, September 26, 1960.

72. PAAA MfAA 14396,, Drionel.

73. He would later take the same position in Tanzania.

74. PAAA MfAA 14396, Fritsch, HV Accra, to Büttner, MfAA, July 30, 1960.

75. PAAA MfAA 14396, Fritsch, HV Accra, to Büttner, MfAA, July 30, 1960, Fritsch, "Realisierung des Studentenabkommens von 16.9.59," October 10, 1960.

76. "Afrikanische Studenten in der Zone unzufrieden," *Die Welt*, June 21, 1961.

77. PAAA MfAA 14396, Ausbildung von ghanesischen Facharbeiter und Fachschulern in der DDR, 1957–1962, letter from Neidhardt, Sektorleiter, Abt. Berufsbildung, Sektor Aus- und Weiterbildung ausländischen Bürger, to the Office of the high commissioner für Ghana, Technical Education Section, London, June 29, 1961.

78. U.K.I.O., "African Student Disillusioned with East Germany," *Windward Islands' Opinion*, Saturday, July 1, 1961: 10.

79. PAAA MfAA 14396, Ausbildung von ghanesischen Facharbeiter und Fachschulern in der DDR, 1957–1962, letter of Hasler, MfAA, to Rolf Seidel, Handelsvertretung der DDR in Ghana, March 23, 1961, concerning the continued career training of Ghanaian citizens.

80. PRAAD JE198, Daniel Woods, Education Attaché, to the Scholarships Secretariat, March 15, 1961.

81. PAAA MfAA 15975, "Übertritt ghanesischer Studenten nach Westdeutschland," February 1, 1963.

82. PAAA MfAA 15975, "Übertritt ghanesischer Studenten nach Westdeutschland," February 1, 1963.

83. PAAA MfAA 15975, "Übertritt ghanesischer Studenten nach Westdeutschland," February 1, 1963.

84. UAD, Jeffrey B., HS-Nr. 27731, Bauwesen, Abg. 31.3.65, Archivsignatur IX/ Nr. 8533.

85. Samuel Adu-Gyamfi, Wilhelmina Joselyn Donkoh, and Anim Adinkrah Addo, "Educational Reforms in Ghana: Past and Present," *Journal of Education and Human Development* 5, 3 (September 2016): 158–72. See also Graham on Higher Education in Ghana.

86. Apollos O. Nwauwa, "The British Establishment of Universities in Tropical Africa, 1920–1948: A Reaction against the Spread of American 'Radical' Influence," *Cahiers d'Études Africaines* 33, 30 (1993): 247–74. Nwauwa has noted that the National Congress of British West Africa (NCBWA) had been pressuring the British for addi-

tional higher education options in the 1920s. The British saw Achimota, along with similar colleges in Nigeria and Sierra Leone, as schools for the education of low-level civil servants who would later assist the British colonial government. Nwauwa has argued that the British ultimately allowed these institutions to be transformed into universities because they feared the radicalization of those Africans who, lacking opportunities to go to school in the United Kingdom or Ghana, decided to earn their degrees in the United States. Further, as nationalist movements grew across the colonies in the 1930s and 1940s, the British began to believe that reforms to the colonial system, including its education, might be the only way to hold on to their empire. And see also https://www.eaumf.org/ejm-blog/2018/1/29/january-28-1927-achimota-prince-of-wales-college-opened, accessed April 22, 2019.

87. G. F. Daniel, "The Universities in Ghana," *Commonwealth Universities Year Book* 1 (1997–1998): 649–56, http://www.users.globalnet.co.uk/~univghana/ghanahed.htm, accessed July 24, 2019.

88. Daniel, "The Universities in Ghana."

89. Adu-Gyamfi, Donkoh, and Addo, "Educational Reforms in Ghana"; Jean Allman, "Kwame Nkrumah, African Studies, and the Politics of Knowledge Production in the Black Star of Africa," *International Journal of African Historical Studies* 46, 2 (2013): 181–203.

90. Kojo Botsio, speech to the Ghanaian Parliament, July 1961, cited in Wilton S. Dillon, *Journal of Modern African Studies* 1, 1 (March 1963): 75–89.

91. Jean Allman, "Kwame Nkrumah, African Studies, and the Politics of Knowledge Production in the Black Star of Africa," *International Journal of African Historical Studies* 46, 2 (2013): 181–203, and see also Takyiwaa Manuh, "Building Institutions for the New Africa: The Institute of African Studies at the University of Ghana," in Peter J. Bloom, Stephen F. Miescher, and Takyiwaa Munah, eds., *Modernization as Spectacle in Africa* (Bloomington: Indiana University Press, 2014), 268–84, as well as A. Biney, *The Political and Social Thought of Kwame Nkrumah* (New York: Palgrave Macmillan, 2011).

92. EAP121/2/5/5/18, Ghana UNIP Office Correspondence (1963), letter of Jacques C. Chiwale to National Secretary, UNIP, December 30, 1963; Bureau of African Affairs, Accra, to Humphrey Mulemba, UNIP Representative, Bureau of African Affairs, Accra, February 15, 1963, discussing a potential scholarship scheme that would be directed at students from across Africa.

93. Grilli, 138.

94. PRAAD EP151, 17/8/56–5/6/59, Parliamentary Questions on Education answered by General and Tech Education Divisions, Parliamentary Question, Second Meeting of the Second Session of the First National Assembly, December 11, 1958.

95. PRAAD JE198, K. Frempong, "Publication of Foreign Governments Scholarships Awards 1965–1966," December 1, 1964, and "Scholarships Offered by the Governments of the Federal Republic of Germany, German Democratic Republic, Hungary, Poland, Rumania, Czechoslovakia, Yugoslavia, and Union of Soviet Socialist Republics," n.d., c. December 1964.

96. PRAAD JE198, 'Appendix B': Minutes of Meeting of a Selection Committee Held at the Civil Service Training Center on 24th July–2nd August 1963 to Interview

Candidates in Connection with the Governments (sic) Czechoslovakia, German Democratic Republic, Poland, U.S.S.R. and Yugoslavia Awards.

97. PRAAD JE198, Appendix A, "Foreign Governments Awards—1965/66."

98. Kersuze Simeon-Jones, "The Pan-African Philosophy and Movement: Social and Educational Praxis of Multiculturalism," in Luis Cordeiro-Rodrigues and Marko Simendic, eds., *Philosophies of Multiculturalism: Beyond Liberalism* (New York: Routledge, 2016), 217.

99. http://gil.edu.gh/about.html, accessed May 6, 2019.

100. PRAAD JE198, Edwin P. letter requesting admissions at the University of Cape Coast, June 22, 1966. More generally, Neequaye sent a letter to the Institute inquiring about whether he could have a report on the performance or results of tests of those students heading to the GDR. See Neequaye to the Principal, Ghana Institute of Languages, August 2, 1965.

101. PRAAD JE198, Ministry of Education, Scholarships Awards by Other Countries, Memorandum for the National Liberation Council by the Principal Secretary, Higher Education Division, Ministry of Education (E. K. Minta), Review of Cultural Agreements, June 17, 1966.

102. Kevin K. Gaines, *African Americans in Ghana: Black Expatriates and the Civil Rights Era* (Chapel Hill: University of North Carolina Press, 2012), 238.

103. PRAAD JE198, Ministry of Education, Scholarships Awards by Other Countries, Neequaye, Scholarships Secretariat, writing to the Registrar, University College of Cape Coast, concerning Emmanuel S., whose scholarship had been withdrawn, April 22, 1966; Neequaye to the Registrar concerning Emmanuel P., who was in a similar situation, July 22, 1966; Neequaye to the Registrar on Benjamin K., the same, August 8, 1966; Neequaye to the Registrar on Ernie O., the same, August 8, 1966.

104. PRAAD JE198, Volta River Authority to the Registrar of Scholarships, Scholarships Secretariat, May 11, 1966.

105.PRAAD JE198, Modern Ghana Builders Ltd. to the Registrar of Scholarships, Scholarships Secretariat, May 12, 1966.

106. See for instance PRAAD JE198, Ministry of Education, Scholarships Awards by Other Countries, Director of Sound Broadcasting, Ghana Broadcasting Corporation, to the Scholarships Secretariat, concerning Edwin P., June 16, 1966, and see also Ghana Broadcasting Corporation, to the Registrar, Scholarships Secretariat, May 25, 1966, in regards to setting up interviews for Ghanaians whose scholarships were canceled.

107. PRAAD JE198, Ministry of Education, Scholarships Awards by Other Countries, Paul O. to the Chairman, National Liberation Council, April 29, 1966.

108. PRAAD JE198, Ministry of Education, Scholarships Awards by Other Countries, Scholarships Secretariat to Paul O., November 28, 1966, commenting that there were no available scholarships for him at the time.

109. UAL ZM 3916a, Scholz, Leiter des Referats Ausländerstudium, February 1966.

110. UAL ZM 3916a, Scholz, Leiter des Referats Ausländerstudium, February 1966, Statement by Kassian Guruli, President of UASA.

111. Mac con Uladh, "Guests of the Socialist Nation," 53. News of students fleeing the East—primarily from the USSR—and ending up in Wickrath was also reported in the West German press; see "Neger-Exodus," *Der Spiegel*, February 12, 1964. More-

over, Nkrumah's government certainly knew about Wickrath, as it housed several defectors from Moscow and Kiev in 1964. See PRAAD JE198, G.E.K. Doe, Ambassador of the Republic of Ghana in the Federal Republic of Germany, Bad Gödesberg, to Enoch Okoh, Secretary of the Cabinet, President's Office, Accra, concerning "Defective Students from the Soviet Union and Eastern European Countries," March 13, 1964.

112. BStU MfS AP 9161/80, Seiler, Treffbericht with Ali of September 7, 1966.

113. BStU MfS AP 9161/80, Seiler, Treffbericht with Ali of September 7, 1966, Seiler, Treffbericht with Ali of August 3, 1966.

114.BStU MfS AP 9161/80, Seiler, Treffbericht with Ali of September 7, 1966, Seiler, Treffbericht with Ali of August 17, 1966, submitted on August 22, 1966.

115. Seiler, Treffbericht, September 7, 1966.

116. BStU MfS AP 9161/80, "Bericht über die Reise 'Alis' nach Bonn und Wickrath," Berlin, 8 September 1966, Seiler, BVA III/05.

117. https://www.mdr.de/zeitreise/ddr-aussenhandel-die-aussenhacndler in-afrika100.html, accessed May 6, 2019.

118. PAAA MfAA C1361/74, Educational Exchange Agreement between the GDR and Ghana, March 12, 1973.

119. The new agreement was indeed oddly biologized, with the GDR now requiring x-rays of each student, which would be taken in Ghana. The students would have to undergo a more extensive medical examination, too, in order to certify that they were in good health and able to withstand East Germany's harsh winter climate. They would be tested for infectious diseases, and if found to be sick would not be able to enter the GDR. See PAAA MfAA C1361/74, Forster, Ministry of Higher and Technical education, to the Botschaft of the DDR in Accra, March 12, 1973. The East German government's demands here that Ghanaians submit to bodily inspection could be interpreted as a simple attempt to keep certain diseases out of the country, but it can also be seen as extending a discourse about the suitability of certain "races" to inhabit specific areas dating back to at least the eighteenth century. See Londa Schiebinger, "The Anatomy of Difference: Race and Sex in Eighteenth Century Science," *Eighteenth-Century Studies* 23, 4 (Summer 1990): 387–405.

120. BStU MfS AP 4941/73, Schmidt, Bericht über einen Treff mit der KP Präsident am 21 Juli 1969 von 13.00–14.30 Uhr.

121. Bericht über einen Treff mit der KP Präsident, September 2, 1969.

122. David Leith Crum, "Mali and the U.M.O.A.: A Case Study of Economic Integration," *Journal of Modern African Studies* 22, 3 (September 1984): 469–86.

CHAPER 4

1. Mac Con Uladh, "Guests of the Socialist Nation?" refers to these groups as *National Studentenvereinigungen* (NSV), but files at the University of Leipzig Archives consistently refer to them as *National Hochschulgruppen (NHG)*. It is possible that the term NHG was used primarily in individual universities, and that NSV was the name for overarching national organizations. Here see "Ausländer in der DDR – Geholt, Gekommen, und Gewollt?" https://www.auslaender-in-der-ddr.com/home/studenten/situation-an-hoch-und-fachschulen/, accessed July 22, 2020.

2. UAL FDJ 894, Rektor, KMU, Richtlinien zur Würdigung von Feiertagen ausländischer Studierender, n.d., after 1973.

3. UAL ZM 3965, Mali 1975–1985, plans for the "Tag der Malinesischen," 1977.

4. Marcia Schenck, "Negotiating the German Democratic Republic: Angolan student migration during the Cold War, 1976–90," *Africa* 89 (January 2019): 5144–66.

5. UAL ZM 3962, 'Discourse prononcé par S. E. Eyemi Richard, Ambassadeur du Congo à l'occasion de la fête de la Jeunesse Congolais à Leipzig,' February 8, 1977; BStU Archiv der Zentralstelle MfS-HA XX Nr. 3209, Böttger, Major, Stellv. Leiter der Abt. XX, report on the annual meeting of the Studenten aus Südafrika in der DDR/Union der Südafrikanischen Studenten in der DDR, May 15, 1976.

6. Slobodian, *Foreign Front*, 62ff.

7. Slobodian, *Foreign Front*, 62ff.

8. "Walter Ulbricht an Pauline Lumumba," *Neues Deutschland*, February 16, 1961.

9. "Pauline Lumumba beendet Aufenthalt in unserer Republik," *Neues Deutschland*, March 20, 1965.

10. PAAA MfAA B290.79, Studium von Kongolesischen Studenten in der DDR und Bewerbungen, 1963–1972, Schmid, III Sekretär in Cairo, to the MFAA, August 28, 1966, concerning Pauline Lumumba.

11. Winrow, 60.

12. Stephen Ellis, *External Mission: The ANC in Exile, 1960–1990* (Oxford: Oxford University Press, 2013), 243–44.

13. Ellis, 95, 152.

14. Slobodian, "Bandung in Divided Germany: Managing Non-Aligned Politics in East and West, 1955–1963," *Journal of Imperial and Commonwealth History* 41, 4 (2013): 644–62.

15. Slobodian, *Foreign Front*, 32 passim.

16. SAPMO-BArch DY/24/6822, Zentralrat der FDJ, Zentralarchiv, Bestand: Intern. Verbindungen, 1958–1962, L.I. Jarju, Kulturleiter der Vereinigten Afrikanischen Studenten in der DDR to the Sekretär der Gruppe der Nigeria Studenten in der DDR, May 26, 1958. It is not clear whether this organization emerged in cooperation with the FDJ or on its own; Mac Con Uladh has argued that the FDJ had little involvement with these early national groups, though the evidence I have found suggests that the FDJ had a much more active, prominent role, as mentioned above. See Mac Con Uladh, "Guests of the Socialist Nation?" 59–60.

17. Guinea decolonized later that year, in October.

18. SAPMO-BArch DY/24/6822, Zentralrat der FDJ, Zentralarchiv, Bestand: Intern. Verbindungen, 1958–1962, L.I. Jarju, Kulturleiter der Vereinigten Afrikanischen Studenten in der DDR to the Sekretär der Gruppe der Nigeria Studenten in der DDR, May 26, 1958.

19. SAPMO-BArch DY/24/6822, Zentralrat der FDJ, Zentralarchiv, Bestand: Intern. Verbindungen, 1958–1962, Sekretär der Gruppe der Nigeria Studenten in der DDR to Herr M., May 28, 1958.

20. SAPMO-BArch DY/24/6822, Zentralrat der FDJ, Zentralarchiv, Bestand: Intern. Verbindungen, 1958–1962, "Verfassung," n.d.

21. Slobodian, "Bandung in Divided Germany," 652–55. There was also a certain

wariness that Pan-Africanism might supersede Marxism-Leninism as the regnant ideology among African students; here see SAPMO-BArch DY 24/6707, Intern. Verbindungen (FDJ) 1962–1963 letter from the Stellv. Schulleiter at the Jugendhochschule Wilhelm Pieck, Intern. Lehrgänge, to Werner Lamberz, Sekretär des ZR der FDJ, February 19, 1962.

22. Slobodian, "Bandung," 652–55.

23. UAL Pror Stu A 17, Einschätzung einzelner Landsmannschaften, May 3, 1960. It is possible that they thought the UASA lacked structure and organization.

24. SAPMO-BArch DY34/378, Herbert Warnke, correspondence, letter from the Nigeria Union of Students, Leipzig, President was Frau Dr. med. Y. Bankole to Warnke, September 10, 60.

25. SAPMO-BArch DY34/378, Report betr. Ausländische Studierende, January 20, 1959.

26. SAPMO-BArch DY34/378, "Niederschrift über die erste Beratung mit den Betreuern der Auslandsstudenten," February 12, 1959.

27. SAPMO-BArch DY34/378, Einschätzung einzelner Landsmannschaften, May 3, 1960.

28. PAAA MfAA C720.74, Aufnahme malinesischer Studentem in der DDR, 1967–1972, letter from Ernst, MfAA, to Herr Gaebelein, April 29, 1971.

29. Dale Tatum, *Who Influenced Whom? Lessons from the Cold War* (Lanham, MD: University Press of America, 2002), 83ff; Jay Straker, *Youth, Nationalism, and the Guinean Revolution* (Bloomington: Indiana University Press, 2009), 48–55 passim.

30. PAAA MfAA A14325 Ausbildung guinesicher Facharbeiter und Studenten in der DDR, 1959–1962, Recording of a Meeting of Guinean Students in the GDR (Anlage 2), "Auf Tonband gesprochen von Dozentin Renate Harnisch," January 6, 1962.

31. PAAA MfAA A14325 Ausbildung guinesicher Facharbeiter und Studenten in der DDR, 1959–1962, Büttner, MfAA, to the Handelsvertretung, Conakry, October 14, 1960, as well as Aktenvermerk, November 8, 1960.

32. PAAA MfAA A14325, Aktenvermerk, November 8, 1960.

33. PAAA MfAA A14325, Ausbildung guinesicher Facharbeiter und Studenten in der DDR, 1959–1962, "Kürze Darstellung der Vorgänge, die mit der zeitweiligen Rückberufung eines Teiles der guineischen Studenten in der DDR im Zusammenhang stehen," March 14, 1962.

34. PAAA MfAA A14325, Report on a meeting with the Guinean Ambassador to Prague, January 1, 1962.

35. PAAA MfAA A14325, Recording of a Meeting of Guinean Students in the GDR (Anlage 2), "Auf Tonband gesprochen von Dozentin Renate Harnisch," January 6, 1962.

36. PAAA MfAA A14325, "Kurze Information: Streng Vertraulich," January 10, 1962.

37. PAAA MfAA A14325, Recording of a Meeting of Guinean Students in the GDR (Anlage 2), "Auf Tonband gesprochen von Dozentin Renate Harnisch," January 6, 1962.

38. PAAA MfAA A14325, "Auf Tonband gesprochen von Dozentin Renate Harnisch.".

39. "Amnesty International Briefing: Guinea, June 1978," 6. For more on Camp Boiro, please see Suzanne Lehn, "Guinea: A Memorial for the Camp Boiro Victims," April 2, 2009, https://globalvoices.org/2009/04/02/guinea-a-memorial-for-the-camp-boiro-victims/, accessed July 30, 2019.

40. PAAA MfAA A14325, Ausbildung guinesicher Facharbeiter und Studenten in der DDR, 1959–1962, Recording of a Meeting of Guinean Students in the GDR (Anlage 2), "Auf Tonband gesprochen von Dozentin Renate Harnisch," January 6, 1962.

41. PAAA MfAA A14325, Kath. Harig, Bericht des Herder-Instituts der Karl-Marx-Universität Leipzig über die Vorgänge in der nationalen Hochschulgruppe Guinea, January 10, 1962.

42. PAAA MfAA A14325, Kath. Harig, Bericht des Herder-Instituts der Karl-Marx-Universität Leipzig über die Vorgänge in der nationalen Hochschulgruppe Guinea, January 10, 1962.

43. PAAA MfAA A14325, Ausbildung guinesicher Facharbeiter und Studenten in der DDR, 1959–1962, "Kurze Information: Streng Vertraulich," January 10, 1962.

44. As Straker shows, this was untrue. The strike did occur, as did the bloody crackdown.

45. PAAA MfAA A14325, Ausbildung guinesicher Facharbeiter und Studenten in der DDR, 1959–1962, "Kurze Information: Streng Vertraulich," January 10, 1962.

46. But as we have seen, African governments were almost always the ones who made the selections, and not only in the Guinean case.

47. PAAA MfAA A14325, Ausbildung guinesicher Facharbeiter und Studenten in der DDR, 1959–1962, Report on meetings of the Guinean NHG, January 5, 1962.

48. Schmidt, *Cold War and Decolonization in Guinea, 1946–1958*.

49. UAL ZM 3931/Ia, Schriftwechsel Studenten Nigeria von: 1960 bis: 1968, Y. Bankole, Präsidentin der Gruppe der Nigerianische Studenten in der DDR, 1960.

50. UAL ZM 3931/IIa-IIIa, Correspondence from The Nigerian Union of Students in the German Democratic Republic to the Rector of the KMU, International Student Division, February 13, 1968; "Appeal for Mass Branch Meeting," from Nigerian students C., I., and J., to "The Branch Chairmain," NUS/GDR, June 8, 1968.

51. UAL ZM 3931/IIa-IIIa, Correspondence from The Nigerian Union of Students in the German Democratic Republic to the Rector of the KMU, International Student Division, February 13, 1968.

52. UAL ZM 3931/IIa-IIIa, Aufstelling der Vorkommnisse mit dem nigerianischen Studenten M., May 8, 1968.

53. UAL ZM 3931/IIa-IIIa, Correspondence from The Nigerian Union of Students in the German Democratic Republic to the Rector of the KMU, International Student Division, February 13, 1968.

54. UAL ZM 3931/IIa-IIIa, Correspondence from The Nigerian Union of Students in the German Democratic Republic to the Rector of the KMU, International Student Division, February 13, 1968.

55. BStU MfS-HA XXNr. 3206, P. Heilmann, Aktennotiz zu Nigeria, April 5, 1979.

56. PAAA MfAA C402 Vol. 2, Gurke, MfAA, to Riesenweber, DAfriG, January 26, 1966.

57. BStU MfS AP 4954/73 Olwa, Owilla Ouma, informant report of September 17, 1963.

58. PAAA MfAA C402 Vol. 2, Gurke, MfAA, to Riesenweber, DAfriG, January 26, 1966; MfS AP 4954/73 Olwa, Owilla Ouma, informant report, n.d.

59. BStU MfS AP 4954/73 Olwa, Owilla Ouma, informant report, n.d.

60. PAAA MfAA C402 Vol. 2, Gurke, MfAA, to Riesenweber, DAfriG, January 26, 1966.

61. G. B. Lamb, "The Political Crisis in Kenya," *World Today* 25, 12 (December 1969): 537–44.

62. Kiprono was first an MP, and served as speaker from 1988–1991. See Wanyiri Kihoro, *Politics and Parliamentarians in Kenya, 1944–2007* (Nairobi: Centre for Multiparty Democracy, 2007), 92.

63. The Kipsigis are the largest subgroup of Kalenjin speakers.

64. PAAA MfAA C402 Vol. 2, Gurke, MfAA, to Riesenweber, DAfriG, January 26, 1966.

65. Charles Hornsby, *Kenya: A History since Independence* (London: I. B. Tauris, 2012), 8, 547.

66. BStU MfS AP 4954/73 Olwa, Owilla Ouma, Vermerk über 2 weitere Gespräche mit Herrn Ouma OLWA/Kenya, Ende März und Anfang April 1966.

67. Timothy Parsons, "The Lanet Incident, 2–25 January 1964: Military Unrest and National Amnesia in Kenya," *International Journal of African Historical Studies* 40, 1 (2007): 51–70.

68. BStU MfS AP 4954/73 Olwa, Owilla Ouma, Vermerk über 2 weitere Gespräche mit Herrn Ouma OLWA/Kenya, Ende März und Anfang April 1966.

69. Hornsby, 72, 79, 105.

70. PAAA MfAA C402 Vol. 2, Gurke, MfAA, to Riesenweber, DAfriG, January 26, 1966.

71. PAAA MfAA C402 Vol. 2, Gurke, MfAA, to Riesenweber, DAfriG, January 26, 1966.

72. PAAA MfAA C402 Vol. 2, Gurke, MfAA, to Riesenweber, DAfriG, January 26, 1966; Oginga Odinga, *Not yet Uhuru* (London: Heinemann, 1967).

73. Robert M. Maxon and Thomas P. Ofcansky, *Historical Dictionary of Kenya* (Lanham, MD: Rowman and Littlefield, 2014), 319–20.

74. BStU MfS AP 4954/73 Olwa, Owilla Ouma, "Einschätzung der KP 'Olga' und ihrer erfolgten Aufklärung," Keller, Berlin, November 18, 1968.

75. Upon independence, Mali initially entered into a short-lived federation with Senegal before becoming independent as a separate, nonfederated nation-state. See Claude E. Welch, Jr., *Dream of Unity: Pan-Africanism and Political Unity in West Africa* (Ithaca: Cornell University Press, 1966), 264–66.

76. PAAA MfAA A14452, Ausbildung malinesischer Facharbeiter und Studenten in der DDR, 1961–1964, Evaluation of Omar P., Malian citizen, student in geology at Humboldt University, Prorektor für Studienangelegenheiten, Ausländerstudium, Humboldt Universität, Staatssekretariat für Hoch- und Fachschulwesen, September 1, 1961.

77. PAAA MfAA A14452, Ausbildung malinesischer Facharbeiter und Studenten in der DDR, 1961–1964, Schedlich of the MfAA to Lange at the Staatssekretariat für Hoch- und Fachschulwesen, May 15, 1961.

78. "Von Dr. Homann empfangen," *Neues Deutschland*, November 13, 1969.

79. PAAA MfAA C720.74, Aufnahme malinesischer Studenten in der DDR, 1967, 192, Vermerk über ein Gespräch des Genossen Ronald Weidemann mit dem Leiter der WHM der Republik Mali in der DDR, Tidiani Kante, October 24, 1970.

80. PAAA MfAA C720.74, Aufnahme malinesischer Studenten in der DDR, 1967, 192, Vermerk über ein Gespräch am 16.10.70 in der Abteilung Konsularische Angelegenheiten (von 10 bis 10:30 Uhr).

81. PAAA MfAA C720.74, Aufnahme malinesischer Studentem in der DDR, 1967–1972, "Politische Entschließung," December 21–23, 1970.

82. This was true even as the country shifted from a military to a civilian regime in 1979. See 24. Mali (1960–present), https://uca.edu/politicalscience/dadm-project/sub-saharan-africa-region/mali-1960-present/

83. PAAA MfAA C720.74, Aufnahme malinesischer Studentem in der DDR, 1967–1972, "Politische Entschließung," December 21–23, 1970.

84. PAAA MfAA C720.74, Aufnahme malinesischer Studentem in der DDR, 1967–1972, "Politische Entschließung," December 21–23, 1970.

85. PAAA MfAA C720.74, Aufnahme malinesischer Studentem in der DDR, 1967–1972, "Politische Entschließung," December 21–23, 1970.

86. PAAA MfAA C720.74, Aufnahme malinesischer Studentem in der DDR, 1967–1972, "Politische Entschließung," December 21–23, 1970, internal memo from Ernst to Gaebelein, April 29, 1971.

87. PAAA MfAA C720.74, Aufnahme malinesischer Studentem in der DDR, 1967–1972, "Politische Entschließung," December 21–23, 1970, internal memo from Kiesewetter of the MfAA to Schoeche, April 27, 1971

88. PAAA MfAA C720.74, Aufnahme malinesischer Studentem in der DDR, 1967–1972, "Politische Entschließung," December 21–23, 1970, internal memo from Schoeche to Kiesewetter, June 4, 1971.

89. PAAA MfAA C718.74, Beziehungen zwischen der DDR und Mali auf dem Gebiet des Hoch- und Fachschulwesens, 1967–71. Hinweise für ein Gespräch des Genossen Dr. Kiesewetters mit dem Leiter der Kulturabteilung des MfAA Malis, June 7, 1971.

90. PAAA MfAA B1263/75 Abt. Afrika, Sektion Gesamtafrikanische Fragen, Aufteilung des Studentenkontingents f. Afrikanischen Staaten, 1972–73, "Information über die in Zusammenhang mit dem Brief der Union afrikanischer Studenten in der DDR festgelegten Maßnahmen vom 12. März 1965."

91. Tanja Müller, *Legacies of Socialist Solidarity*, 86.

92. SAPMO-BArch, DY/24/8752, "Zentralrat der FDJ, Zentralarchiv, Bestand: Intern. Verbindungen, 1961–1965. Einschätzung der Aussprachen mit den Delegationen des II. Internationalen Halbjahreslehrganges—Afrika—1962," August 14, 1962. This report suggests that Western influence on East Germany was one of the primary reasons for the existence of any lingering racism in the country.

93. W. Frindte, "Sozialpolitische Anmerkungen zur Entwicklung Rechstradikaler Tendenzen in der DDR," in H. Butterwegge and C. Isola, eds., *Rechstextremismus im Vereinten Deutschland: Randerscheinung oder Gefahr für die Demokratie* (Berlin: Links-Druck, 1990), 88–96.

94. PAAA MfAA B1263/75 Abt. Afrika, Sektion Gesamtafrikanische Fragen,

Aufteilung des Studentenkontingents f. Afrikanischen Staaten, 1972–73, "Besorgnisse der afrikanischen Studenten und Arbeiter in der DDR," February 1965.

95. Diop was a multifaceted Senegalese scholar who was accomplished in such areas as history, anthropology, archaeology, and physics; Fanon was a Martinican psychiatrist and philosopher; and Césaire was a Martinican poet and politician.

96. The interest in Diop, Fanon, and Césaire reflected many students' embrace of Pan-Africanist principles, as well as those of its French cousin Négritude, which Césaire had cofounded with Léopold Sédar Senghor, the first president of independent Senegal.

97. Cheikh Anta Diop, *Nations Négres et Culture* (Paris: Présence Africain, 1999 [1955]).

98. Frantz Fanon, *Black Skin, White Masks* (New York: Grove Press, 2008 [1952]).

99. Aimé Césaire, "Culture and colonization," *Social Text* 28 (2/103) (2010): 127–44.

100. Aimé Césaire, "Culture and colonization."

101. PAAA MfAA B1263/75Abt. Afrika, Sektion Gesamtafrikanische Fragen, Aufteilung des Studentenkontingents f. Afrikanischen Staaten, 1972–1973; Union afrikanischer Studenten in der DDR to Walter Ulbricht, "Besorgnisse der afrikanischen Studenten und Arbeiter in der DDR," February–March 1965.

102. PAAA MfAA B1263/75, Union afrikanischer Studenten in der DDR to Walter Ulbricht, "Besorgnisse der afrikanischen Studenten und Arbeiter in der DDR," February–March 1965.

103. PAAA MfAA B1263/75, "Aktenvermerk über ein Gespräch mit Dr. Joachimi, Staatssekretariat für das Hoch und Fachschulwesen, am 2. März 1965, 10:00 bis 11:20," March 3, 1965.

104. PAAA MfAA B1263/75, "Auszug aus einem Aktenvermerk über eine am 11.3.65 stattgefundene Beratung des Staatssekretariats für das Hoch- und Fachschulwesen mit Vertretern zentraler Dienststellen, die für die Ausbildung und Betreuung von Auslandsstudenten zuständig sind."

105. PAAA MfAA B1263/75, "Information über die in Zusammenhang mit dem Brief der Union afrikanischer Studenten in der DDR festgelegten Maßnahmen vom 12. März 1965."

106. PAAA MfAA B1263/75, "Auszug aus einem Aktenvermerk über eine am 11.3.65 stattgefundene Beratung des Staatssekretariats für das Hoch- und Fachschulwesen mit Vertretern zentraler Dienststellen."

107. PAAA MfAA B1263/75, "Information über die in Zusammenhang mit dem Brief der Union afrikanischer Studenten in der DDR festgelegten Maßnahmen vom 12. März 1965."

108.. PAAA MfAA B1263/75, "Information über die in Zusammenhang mit dem Brief der Union afrikanischer Studenten in der DDR festgelegten Maßnahmen vom 12. März 1965."

109. BStU Archiv der Zentralstelle MfS-HA II Nr. 28723, report on the Situation in der "Union der somalischen Studierenden in der DDR, November 17, 1977; BStU Archiv der Zentralstelle MfS HA XX Nr 3209, Böttger, Major, Stellv. Leiter der Abt. XX, report on the annual meeting of the Studenten aus Südafrika in der DDR/Union der Südafrikanischen Studenten in der DDR, May 15, 1976."

110. UAL, ZM 3962, Discourse prononcé par S. E. Eyemi Richard, Ambassadeur du Congo à l'occasion de la fête de la Jeunesse Congolais à Leipzig,' February 8, 1977, and Letter from Dr M. Schmidt to Professor Voight, Direktor der Sektion Afrika- und Nahostwissenschaften, KMU, 11 March 1977.

111. UAL, ZM 3962, "Aktennotiz," March 30, 1977.

112. Apolinaire Ngolongolo, *L'Assassinat de Marien Ngouabi* (Paris: L'Harmattan, 1988).

113. John F. Clark, "Socio-Political Change in the Republic of Congo: Political Dilemmas of Economic Reforms," *Journal of Third World Studies* 10, 1 (Spring 1993): 52–77.

114. S. M. Thomas, *The Diplomacy of Liberation: The Foreign Relations of the ANC since 1960* (London: I. B. Tauris, 1995).

CHAPTER 5

1. PAAA MfAA, C409, Studienplatz-Kontingent und Studienangelegenheiten sambischer Bürger in der DDR, letter from the Embassy of the GDR, Moscow, to the MfAA, March 10, 1967.

2. Katrina Hagen, "Internationalism in Cold War Germany" (PhD Diss., University of Washington, 2008), 352.

3. Toni Weis, "The Politics Machine: On the Concept of 'Solidarity' in East German Support for SWAPO," *Journal of Southern African Studies* 2 (June 2011): 351–67.

4. On the imperial context see Lora Wildenthal, *German Women for Empire, 1884–1945* (Durham: Duke University Press, 2001), 186–88; Sara Pugach, *Africa in Translation: A History of Colonial Linguistics in Germany and Beyond, 1814–1945* (Ann Arbor: University of Michigan Press, 2012), 150–52.

5. Cynthia Miller-Idriss, *Blood and Culture: Youth, Right-Wing Extremism, and National Belonging in Contemporary Germany* (Durham: Duke University Press, 2009), 55.

6. Lutz Basse, "Das Ausländerstudium an Universitäten, Hoch- und Fachschulen der DDR," auslaender-in-der-ddr.com, http://www.auslaender-in-der-ddr.com/home/studenten/situation-an-hoch-und-fachschulen/, accessed November 12, 2014. Exchange students did not always welcome the chance to live with Germans, though. For instance, around 1976 Fräulein E., a Nigerian pharmacy student at the Ingenieurschule für Pharmazie in Leipzig, wrote to the head of the school complaining that she was the only foreign student living among Germans, and she wanted to live with other African students instead if possible. See UAL ZM 3931IIa, Schriftwechsel Studenten Nigeria, von 1974 bis 1981, letter of Fräulein E. to the *Ingenieurschule*, n.d., ca. 1976.

7. Damian Mac Con Uladh, "Studium bei Freunden? Ausländische Studierende in der DDR bis 1970," in Christian Th. Müller and Patrice G. Poutrus, *eds., Ankunft, Alltag, Ausreise: Migration und interkulturelle Begegnung in der DDR-Gesellschaft* (Cologne: Böhlau, 2003), 175–219, 83.

8. Ginga Eichler, Personal Interview, August 1, 2014.

9. Mac Con Uladh, "Studium bei Freunden?"

10. UAL StuA 114791, Bezirksgericht Leipzig, "Urteil im Namen des Volkes!," n.d., ca. 1965.

11. As well as in the neighboring FRG.

12. UAL Pror. Stud. 17, Report, Dr. Moehle, Prorektor für Studienangelegenheiten, to the Regierung der DDR, Staatssekretariat für das Hoch- und Fachschulwesen, Sektor Ausland, Auslandsstudium, Betr.: Ausländische Studierende, January 20, 1959.

13. PAAA MfAA A14452, Ausbildung malinesischer Facharbeiter und Studenten in der DDR, 1961–1964, undated letter, approximately October 1963, from Heimleiter P., griechischen Internat "unbezwingbares Athen," Leipzig, to the MfAA, Berlin.

14. PAAA MfAA A14452, Fritsch, MfAA Berlin, to Gross, Trade Mission in Bamako, December 13, 1963, u.a.

15. UAL Pror. Stud. 17, Report, Dr. Moehle, Prorektor für Studienangelegenheiten, to the Regierung der DDR, Staatssekretariat für das Hoch- und Fachschulwesen, Sektor Ausland, Auslandsstudium, Betr.: Ausländische Studierende, January 20, 1959.

16. BStU MfS AP 9161/80, Ausfertigung, Bezirksgericht Dresden, 2 BSB 104/1969, "Urteil Im Namen des Volkes," April 3, 1969.

17. UAL StuA 114791, "Urteil im Namen des Volkes!"; Der Bundesbeauftrage für die Unterlagen des Staatssicherheitsdienstes der ehemaligen Deutschen Demokratischen Republik, Ministerium für Staatssicherheit (hereafter referred to as BStU, MfS) AP 9161/80, Abschlußvermerk, III/C/301, Berlin, March 20, 1970.

18. Jennifer V. Evans, "The Moral State: Men, Mining, and Masculinity in the Early GDR," *German History* 23, no. 3 (2005): 355–70.

19. Eric D. Weitz, *Creating German Communism, 1890–1990: From Popular Protests to Socialist State* (Princeton: Princeton University Press, 1997), 372.

20. Josie McLellan, *Love in the Time of Communism: Intimacy and Sexuality in the GDR* (New York: Cambridge University Press, 2011), 14ff.

21. UAL Pror. Stud. 17, letter from the Restaurant- und Stellv. Objektleiter des HO-Objekts "Burgkeller" to die Volkspolizei, Abteilung Ausländerswesen, April 12, 1963.

22. UAL Pror. Stud. 17, letter from the Restaurant- und Stellv. Objektleiter des HO-Objekts "Burgkeller" to die Volkspolizei, Abteilung Ausländerswesen, April 12, 1963. There was some implication in his report that Arabs may have occasionally caused issues, but much more rarely than Africans.

23. UAL Pror. Stud. 17, letter from the Restaurant- und Stellv. Objektleiter des HO-Objekts "Burgkeller" to die Volkspolizei, Abteilung Ausländerswesen, April 12, 1963.

24. UAL ZM 3923b, Schriftwechsel Studenten Mali von 1963 bis 1985, Y.D., Generalssekretär of the Verband der Malinesischen Studenten und Praktikanten in der DDR, Sektion der JUSRDA, to Ernst-Joachim Gießmann, Staatssekretär für das Hoch- und Fachschulwesen der DDR, December 17, 1966.

25. UAL ZM 3923B, Schriftwechsel Studenten Mali von 1963 bis 1985, Dr. P. to Horst Joachimi, Ministerrat der Deutschen Demokratischen Republik, Staatssekretariat für das Hoch- und Fachschulwesen, Abt. Ausländerstudium, February 10, 1967.

26. PAAA MfAA B1263/75 Abt. Afrika, Sektion Gesamtafrikanische Fragen, Aufteilung des Studentenkontingents f. Afrikanischen Staaten, 1972–1973; Union afrikanischer Studenten in der DDR to Walter Ulbricht, "Besorgnisse der afrikanischen Studenten und Arbeiter in der DDR," February–March 1965.

27. PAAA MfAA B1263/75, Union afrikanischer Studenten in der DDR to Walter Ulbricht, "Besorgnisse der afrikanischen Studenten und Arbeiter in der DDR," February–March 1965..

28. PAAA MfAA B1263/75, report concerning "Information über die in Zusammenhang mit dem Brief der Union afrikanischer Studenten in der DDR festgelegten Maßnahmen vom 12. März 1965," April 7, 1965.

29. UAL ZM 3931/IIa, Schriftwechsel Studenten Nigeria, 1960–1968, letter from Mrs. L. to the KMU, July 26, 1967.

30. UAL ZM 3931/IIa, Schriftwechsel Studenten Nigeria, 1960–1968, July 28, 1967.

31. Maxim Matusevich, *No Easy Row for a Russian Hoe: Ideology and Pragmatism in Nigerian-Soviet Relations, 1960–1991* (Trenton, NJ: Africa World Press, 2003), 105ff.

32. UAL Pror. Stud. 17, letter of Mr. W.B. to the Dean of the Universof Leipzig, n.d., ca. 1963.

33. UAL ZM 3314b, Schriftwechsel Studenten Kamerun, 1964 bis 1984, letter of Mr. S. to the Abt. Ausländerstudium, KMU, March 12, 1973.

34. UAL, ZM 3944/Ia, Schriftwechsel Studenten Sudan, 1965 bis 1974, Sandke, Oberleutnant der Volkspolizei-Kreisamt Leipzig, to the Karl-Marx-Universität, Direktorat Ausländerstudium, concerning "Information über die Verhaltensweise eines Studenten Ihrer Universität," January 26, 1974.

35. PAAA MfAA C327/70, Abt. Afrika, Sektion Mali, Beziehungen auf aussenpolitischen Gebiet sowie auf dem Gebiet des Hoch- und Fachschulwesens, der Volksbildung und des Sports zwischen der DDR und Togo, 1962–1968, J.D. to Gerald Götting, Lome, March 23, 1967.

36. PAAA MfAA, Abt. Afrika, Sektion Mali, Beziehungen auf aussenpolitischen Gebiet sowie auf dem Gebiet des Hoch- und Fachschulwesens, der Volksbildung und des Sports zwischen der DDR und Togo, 1962–1968, Mr. P of the Abteilung Afrika, Ministerium für Auswärtige Angelegenheiten, Berlin, to Ms. B., August 3, 1966.

37. SAPMO-BArch DY/34/24698, FDGB—Bundesvorstand, Büro des Präsidiums, Protokollbüro, Sekretariatsbeschlüsse des Bundesvorstandes betr. Gewerschaftshochschule, 1961–1963, "Denkschrift des Kollegen J.D., Togo, z. Zt. Student am Ausländerinstitut der Hochschule der Deutschen Gewerkschaften 'Fritz Heckert,'" June 5, 1961.

38. Winrow, *The Foreign Policy of the GDR in Africa*, 41, 55.

39. PAAA MfAA B290.79, Studium von Kongolesischen Studenten in der DDR und Bewerbungen, 1963–1972, letter from the Zairean Embassy in Belgrade to the Ministry of Foreign Affairs, September 1, 1972.

40. PAAA MfAA B290.79, Studium von Kongolesischen Studenten in der DDR und Bewerbungen, 1963–1972, Proclamation of August 9, 1972, stating that the 1965 law gave Zaireans license to marry the partners of their choice.

41. Ch. Didier Gondola, *The History of Congo* (Westport, CT: Greenwood Press, 2002), 127. As stated earlier in this book, after Congolese independence in 1960, the West had feared that its first president, Patrice Lumumba, was getting too close to the Soviet Union. Once Lumumba was assassinated with Western help, the country had turned away from the USSR and received American aid and military support through the end of the Cold War in 1990.

42. UAL ZM 3947a, Schriftwechsel Studenten Tansania, 1968–1985, letter from the Kriegsgericht Leipzig, Stadtbezirk West, to the Direktorat für Internationale Beziehungen, KMU, February 10, 1982.

43. UAL ZM 3914b, Schriftwechsel Studenten Kamerun, 1964 bis 1984, Studienrat Hass, Leiter des Referates Jugendhilfe, Rat der Stadt Rostock, to the Karl-Marx-Universität, April 27, 1977, and response of Dr. Jünger, KMU, to Hass, May 9, 1977.

44. UAL ZM 3926b, Schriftwechsel Studenten Mocambique, 1974 bis 1985, letter from Frau Z. to the Direktorat Internationale Beziehungen, Abt. Ausländerstudium, October 18, 1976, and Bescheinigung that the student had returned to Mozambique, November 30, 1976.

45. On this point see Fehrenbach, *Race After Hitler*, and Höhn, *GIs and Fräuleins*.

46. Fehrenbach, *Race After Hitler*, 17; Höhn, *GIs and Fräuleins*, 85.

47. Anne Salles, "The Effects of Family Policy in the GDR on Nuptiality and Births outside Marriage," *Population* 61, 1–2 (January–April 2006): 141–51; Elizabeth D. Heinemann, *What Difference Does a Husband Make? Women and Marital Status in Nazi and Postwar Germany* (Berkeley: University of California Press, 2003), 228.

48. Lucy Bland, "White Women and Men of Colour: Miscegenation Fears in Britain after the Great War," *Gender & History* 17, 1 (2005): 29–61.

49. See for instance Will Jackson, "Bad Blood: Poverty, Psychopathy and the Politics of Transgression in Kenya Colony, 1939–59," *Journal of Imperial and Commonwealth History* 39, 1 (2011): 73–94, or Carina E. Ray, "'The White Wife Problem': Sex, Race and the Contested Politics of Repatriation to Interwar British West Africa," *Gender & History* 21, 3 (2009): 628–46.

50. Krista O'Donnell, "Home, Nation, Empire: Domestic Germanness and Colonial Citizenship," in Krista O'Donnell, Renate Bridenthal, and Nancy Ruth Reagin, eds., *The Heimat Abroad: The Boundaries of Germanness* (Ann Arbor: University of Michigan Press, 2005), 40–58, among others, discusses the issue of the importation of German women to the colony of South West Africa, where fear of miscegenation between German men and native women was rife.

51. Höhn, *GIs and Fräuleins*, 172.

52. Höhn, *GIs and Fräuleins*, 118–20.

53. UAL Pror. Stud. 17, Report, 20 January 1959; UAL ZM 3944/Ia, Schriftwechsel Studenten Sudan, 1965 bis 1974, Sandke, "Information über die Verhaltensweise eines Studenten Ihrer Universität," 25 January 1974.

54. McLellan, *Love in the Time of Communism*, 108.

55. Walter Ulbricht, "Zur Geschichte der deutschen Arbeiterbewegung," in Walter Ulbricht, ed., *Zur Geschichte der deutschen Arbeiterbewegung* (Berlin: Dietz, 1964), 376–78.

56. Höhn, *GIs and Fräuleins*, 126ff.

57. PAAA MfAA A16972, Studium malinesischer Studenten an Hoch- und Fachschulen der DDR, 1964–1966, Schöche, Third Secretary to the Economic and Trade Mission of the GDR in Bamako to the Ministry of Foreign Affairs, Berlin, September 23, 1965.

58. McLellan, *Love in the Time of Communism*, 109–10.

59. UAL StuA 114791, "Urteil im Namen des Volkes!"

60. McLellan, *Love in the Time of Communism*, 6; Michael Schwartz, "Emanzipation zur sozialen Nutzlichkeit: Bedingungen und Grenzen von Frauenpolitik in der DDR," in Dierk Hoffmann and Michael Schwartz, eds., *Sozialstaatlichkeit in der DDR: Sozialpolitische Entwicklungen im Spannungsfeld von Diktatur und Gesellschaft, 1945/49–1989* (Munich: Oldenbourg, 2005), 47–88, 68.

61. Fehrenbach, *Race After Hitler*, 59ff.

62. Fehrenbach, *Race After Hitler*, 211–12.

63. Donna Harsch, *Revenge of the Domestic: Women, the Family, and Communism in the German Democratic Republic* (Princeton: Princeton University Press, 2007), 152–53.

64. From a sampling of 432 students from throughout the African continent who were in the GDR sometime between 1951 and 1990.

65. Indeed, I have only found one possible instance of an African woman in a relationship with an East German man, and even this case is uncertain, given that the ethnicity of the woman's partner is never explicitly stated. See SAPMO-BArch DY 31, Demokratischer Frauenbund Deutschlands, Internationale Verbindungen, Aktenvermerk, February 1, 1972, concerning the pregnancy of a South African trainee in Plauen.

66. Michael Berenbaum and Abraham J. Peck, *The Holocaust and History: The Known, the Unknown, the Disputed, and the Reexamined* (Bloomington: Indiana University Press, 2002), 123.

67. See among others Daniel Walther, "Sex and Control in Germany's Overseas Possessions: Venereal Disease and Indigenous Agency," in Nina Berman, Klaus Mühlhahn, and Patrice Nganang, eds., *German Colonialism Revisited: African, Asian, and Oceanic Experiences* (Ann Arbor: University of Michigan Press, 2014), 71–84; Krista O'Donnell, "Home, Nation, Empire: Domestic Germanness and Colonial Citizenship," in Krista O'Donnell, Renate Bridenthal, and Nancy Reagin, eds., *The Heimat Abroad: The Boundaries of Germanness* (Ann Arbor: University of Michigan Press, 2010), 40–57; Lora Wildenthal, *German Women for Empire, 1884–1945* (Durham: Duke University Press, 2001), 73–74; and Marcia Klotz, "Memoirs from a German Colony: What do White Women Want?" *Genders* 19 (June 30, 1994): 154.

68. Nancy Nenno, "Femininity, the Primitive, and Modern Urban Space: Josephine Baker in Berlin," in Katharina Von Ankum, ed., *Women in the Metropolis: Gender and Modernity in Weimar Culture* (Berkeley: University of California Press, 1997), 89–105.

69. Tina Campt, *Other Germans: Black Germans and the Politics of Race, Gender, and Memory in the Third Reich* (Ann Arbor: University of Michigan Press, 2004), 20.

70. Jane Freeland, "Creating Good Socialist Women: Continuities, Desire, and Degeneration in Slatan Dudow's 'The Destinies of Women,'" *Journal of Women's History* 29, 1 (Spring 2017): 87–110.

71. Irmtraud Morgner, "Third Fruit of Bitterfeld: The Tightrope," in Nancy Lukens and Dorothy Rosenberg, trans. and eds., *Daughters of Eve: Women's Writing from the German Democratic Republic* (Lincoln: University of Nebraska Press, 1993), 137ff.

72. Harsch, *Revenge of the Domestic*.

73. UAL DHfK VWA 545, Sonderlehrgang 4 Frauen Guinea, 1966–1968.

74. Nancy R. Reagin, "German *Brigadoon*? Domesticity and Metropolitan Ger-

mans' Perceptions of *Auslandsdeustchen* in Southwest Africa and Eastern Europe," in O'Donnell, Reagin, and Bridenthal, eds., *The Heimat Abroad: The Boundaries of Germanness*, 248–66.

75. UAL StuA 17398, A.A., Aktennotiz, July 10, 1969.

76. Joseph M. Hodge, Gerald Hödl, and Martina Kopf, *Developing Africa: Concepts and Practices in Twentieth-Century Colonialism* (Oxford: Oxford University Press, 2017), 273.

77. BStU MfS AS 182/66, Bd. 7, list of West African students attending the *Weltfestspiele* in Leipzig, 1951; UAL ABF 077, Gernot Pflugk, Gesamtanalyse der Vorbildung der Kolonialstudenten in der deutschen Sprache bei Eintreffen in Leipzig, May 22, 1951.

78. UAL ABF 077, Pflugk, Gesamtanalyse.

79. UAL ABF 077, Pflugk, Gesamtanalyse, Betreuung der nigerianischen Studenten an der Arbeiter- und Bauern-Fakultät der Karl-Marx-Universität Leipzig, July 2, 1954.

80. UAL Med. Fak. Prom. 5162, Agnes Yetunde Bankole aus Lagos/Nigeria, "Ein Beitrag zur Ursachenuntersuchung der perinatalen Kindersterblichkeit," submitted to the Hohen medizinischen Fakultät der Universität Leipzig zur Erlangung der medizinischen Doktorwürde, Leipzig, 1959.

81. UAL StuA 10511, Frau Agnes Yetunde Bankole.

82. Mac Con Uladh, "Guests of the Socialist Nation?" 59, footnote 78. The only evidence of this union that I have found is in this footnote.

83. SAPMO-BArch DY34/378, letter from the Nigeria (*sic*) Students Union to Herbert Warnke, Chairman of the FDGB, inviting him to a celebration in honor of Nigerian independence, September 10, 1960.

84. Bankole registered as a medical doctor in Yaba, Nigeria, on September 3, 1965. See "List of Medical Practitioners in Nigeria," *Republic of Nigeria, Official Gazette* 53, 60 (June 16, 1966): 1080. It is unclear how long she stayed in Nigeria after returning, though.

85. SAPMO -BArch DY 6/2551, Abt. Internationale Verbindungen, Solidarität mit den Völkern Ostafrikas, u.a. Kenia, Gichuru and Koinange to Heinrich Eggebrecht, Solikomite, May 1961.

86. TNA DO 214/118, East German Aid to Zanzibar, D.F.B. Le Breton of the British High Commission, Vuga, Zanzibar, June 12, 1964, to R. de Burlet, Esq., East Africa Political Department, Commonwealth Relations Office, London.

87. PAAA MfAA A15907 Togo, P. Scher, Generalsekretär der Gewerkschaft Gesundheit und Hygiene Togos, to the Minister für Gesundheitswesen in the DDR, September 5, 1962. Scher's request was ultimately rejected.

88. PAAA MfAA A14429, Mali, Unterbeck, Leiter des Büros der Wirtschaft und Handelsmission in der Republik Mali, to the GDR's Ministries of Education and Foreign Affairs, Betr. Ausbildung von Krankenpflegern, September 9, 1961.

89. EAP121/2/7/1/26 Tanganyika Office, Correspondence (1961–1964), Makasa to Beatrice B., August 9, 1961.

90. EAP121/2/7/1/42 Tanganyika Office, Correspondence (1962), 83b, Makasa to Tembo, February 27, 1963.

91. PAAA MfAA C409, Zambia, 1967 list of students.

92. UAL StuA 10511, Fichtner, Referent, VPKA, Abt. Ausländerwesen, approving travel for Joda to visit her husband in England, March 1969.

93. UAL StuA 10511, Fichtner, Referent, VPKA, Abt. Ausländerwesen, Beurteilung, July 31, 1968.

94. UAL StuA 17398, Lebenslauf.

95. UAL StuA 17398, Lebenslauf, and UAL PA-A 59279, E.K.

96. UAL StuA 17398, Lebenslauf.

97. PAAA MfAA C401, Aufnahme malinesischer Studenten in der DDR, Jan.-Dezember 1967, May 1967.

98. SAPMO-BArch DY 6/2551, Aktenvermerk, February 10, 1961.

99. SAPMO-BArch DY34 27509, FDGB—Bundesvorstand/Büro der Sekretäre für Sozialpolitik, Nr. I 1.21, Afrika/Vorderasien, 1960, G.K. Kouessan, Generalssekretär of the Nationale Union der Werktätigen Togos, to the Vorsitzenden of the FDGB Berlin, July 18, 1960.

100. SAPMO-BArch DY34 27509, G.K. Kouessan, Generalssekretär of the Nationale Union der Werktätigen Togos, to the Vorsitzenden of the FDGB Berlin, July 18, 1960..

101. C. Bradley Scharf, *Politics and Change in East Germany: An Evaluation of Socialist Democracy* (New York: Routledge, 2019); Eli Rubin, *Amnesiopolis: Modernity, Space, and Memory in East Germany* (Oxford: Oxford University Press, 2016), 21, 31.

102. PAAA MfAA C1361–74, part II, Forster, Ministry of Higher and Technical Education, to the Embassy of the GDR in Accra, Ghana, March 12, 1973.

103. UAL ZM 3944/Ia, Schriftwechsel Studenten Sudan, 1965 bis 1974, letter from the Director of International Student Affairs, KMU, to the representative of the Minister for Higher Education in the GDR, March 9, 1971.

104. *Race After Hitler*, 132ff.

105. Peggy Piesche, "Black and German? East German Adolescents Before 1989: A Retrospective View of a 'Non-Existent Issue' in the GDR," in Leslie Adelson, ed., *The Cultural After-Life of East Germany: New Transnational Perspectives* (Washington, DC: AICGS Humanities, 2002).

106. Salles, "The Effects of Family Policy in the GDR on Nuptiality and Births outside Marriage"; Dagmar Herzog, *Sex after Fascism: Memory and Morality in Twentieth-century Germany* (Princeton: Princeton University Press, 2005), 215. Herzog states that one in three children were born out of wedlock in the GDR by the time the Berlin Wall fell; in the FRG, it was one in ten.

107. McLellan, *Love in the Time of Communism*, 94.

CONCLUSION

1. Sebastian Pampuch, "Afrikanische Migrationserfahrungen mit zwei Deutschen Staaten: Rekonstruktion eines migratorischen Lebensweges über die Grenze zweier deutscher Staaten hinweg," Magisterarbeit, Humboldt Universität zu Berlin, 2008.

2. William Glenn Grey, *Germany's Cold War: The Global Campaign to Isolate*

East Germany, 1949–1969 (Chapel Hill: University of North Carolina Press, 2003), 229ff.

3. Grey, 232.

4. But only briefly; see Hermann Wentker, *Außenpolitik in engen Grenzen, die DDR im internationalen System* (Munich: Oldenbourg Wissenschaftsverlag, 2007), 352ff.

5. Grey, 235.

6. Wentker, 352.

7. Maxim Matusevich, "Revisiting the Soviet Moment in Sub-Saharan Africa," *History Compass* 7, 9 (September 2009), 1259–68.

8. Frederick Cooper, *Africa Since 1940: The Past of the Present* (Cambridge: Cambridge University Press, 2002), 156.

9. Mojeed Adekunle Animashaun, "State Failure, Crisis of Government, and Disengagement from the State in Africa," *African Development/Afrique et Développement* 34, 3–4 (2009): 47–63.

10. Wentker, 467.

11. Wentker, 460–61.

12. Wentker, 464–65.

13. Eric Burton, "Navigating Global Socialism: Tanzanian Students in and beyond East Germany," *Cold War History,* https://doi.org/10.1080/14682745.2018.1485146, June 25, 2018. Moreover, Haile Gabriel Dagne has pointed out that when reunification occurred in 1990, there were officially 529 Ethiopian students in the GDR. See Dagne, *Das entwicklungspolitische Engagement der DDR in Äthiopien: Eine Studie auf der Basis äthiopische Quellen* (Münster: LIT Verlag, 2004), 82.

14. Hans-Joachim Döring, *"Es geht um unsere Existenz": Die Politik der DDR gegenüber der Dritten Welt am Beispiel von Mosambik und Äthiopien* (Berlin: Ch. Links Verlag, 1999), 143.

15. Marcia Schenck, "From Luanda and Maputo to Berlin: Uncovering Angolan and Mozambican Migrants' Motives to Move to the German Democratic Republic, 1979–1990," *African Economic History* 44 (2016): 202–34.

16. "Schon nahe am Pogrom," *Der Spiegel*, April 4, 1990; Wolfgang Kil and Hilary Silver, "From Kreuzberg to Marzahn: New Migrant Communities in Berlin," *German Politics and Society* 24, 4 (Winter 2006): 95–121.

17. PAAA MfAA C411, Studienplätze in der DDR für afrikanische Bürger, 1966–1967, Nigerian Breweries African Workers Union and the Taka (Nigeria) Company to the Ministry of Health, 1966.

18. PAAA MfAA C411, Studienplätze in der DDR für afrikanische Bürger, 1966–1967, J.D.I. to the East German Ministry of Foreign Affairs, 1966.

19. Hans Mathias Müller, *Die Bildungshilfe der Deutschen Demokratischen Republik* (London: Peter Lang, 1995); Burton, *Navigating Global Socialism*, 6.

20. BStU MfS-HA XX Nr. 3206, P. Heilmann, "Aktennotiz zu Nigeria," April 5, 1979.

21. Chris Cottrell, "German from Senegal Vies to Break Bundestag Barrier," *New York Times*, May 31, 2013, https://www.nytimes.com/2013/06/01/world/europe/german-from-senegal-vies-for-bundestag-and-a-first.html?pagewanted=all&_r=0, and

Cottrell, "Two Black Lawmakers voted to Parliament in Germany," *New York Times*, September 23, 2013, https://www.nytimes.com/2013/09/24/world/europe/2-black-lawmakers-voted-to-parliament-in-germany.html

22. Bernd Wagner, "Vertuschte Gefahr: Die Stasi und Neonazis," Bundeszentrale für politische Bildung, http://www.bpb.de/geschichte/deutsche-geschichte/stasi/218421/neonazis, accessed January 31, 2019.

23. Gilbert Ofodile, *I Shall Never Return: Eight Months in Communist Germany, a Nigerian Student of Journalism Reports* (Esslingen: Bechtle Verlag, 1967).

24. These questionable aspects mainly emerge from archival evidence and the conflicting recording of the details surrounding the men's experiences in their retellings versus the accounts found in the archives. On the unreliability of Ajao's account, please see chapter 1; for the questionability of Sapara-Arthur, please see chapter 3. Ofodile's claims are harder to refute. There is a Stasi file on Ofodile, a journalism student, BStU MfS ZAIG Nr. 868, which demonstrates that he was under surveillance, as was his friend and fellow journalism student Raphael Omenye. This would not have been unusual, since many African students had Stasi files. The file largely concerned their carousing and partying and claimed that Omenye was under Ofodile's bad influence. The trope of African "bad behavior" was common and usually involved drinking, relationships with women, etc., and embedded in the racialized belief that Africans were more likely to succumb to temptations than whites. Yet some of Ofodile's contentions in the memoir, especially those about Omenye, are problematic. Ofodile claimed that Omenye had been attacked and badly beaten by some East German men, and then forced to publicly lie about the attack and say it had occurred in West Berlin, not East. The two of them fled the country under dire circumstances, but apparently Omenye returned soon after they left in 1966, or perhaps did not leave at all—the files on Omenye from the UAL are unclear on this point and show that he transferred between faculties twice in the summer and fall of 1966, from journalism to economics, and then from economics to mathematical statistics. Thereafter, Omenye remained in the GDR through 1972. While he may have returned despite having experienced violence in the East, it may also be that his circumstances were not exactly what Ofodile had indicated. See Ofodile, *I shall never Return*, 67, for discussion of the attack on Omenye. For details on Omenye's student career in 1966–1967, see UAL, StuA 30562, Omenye, Raphael, Verband der Journalisten der DDR, Horst Voigt, 1. Sekretät, to Rößler, concerning Raphael Omenye, May 6, 1966, and note from Dr. Schweiger, Leiter des Studiums, Wirtschaftswissenschaftliche Fakultät, also concerning Omenye, September 14, 1966; and UAL, StuA 12259, Omenye, Raphael, Aufnahmeantrag für Studienbewerber KMU, Wirtschaftswissenschaftliche Fakultät, Mathemathische Statistik, admission 1966/7, graduation 1972.

25. Interview with Mohamed Touré, Cologne, August 11, 2014.

26. Interview with Robert Quansah, Accra, October 28, 2015.

27. Interview with Yvonne Kolagbodi, Berlin, September 10, 2014.

28. Interview with B., Dakar, January 11, 2019.

29. Interview with David Tette, Accra, September 17, 2015.

30. As has been argued forcefully throughout Rita Chin, Heide Fehrenbach, Geoff Eley, and Atina Grossman, *After the Nazi Racial State: Difference and Democracy in Germany and Europe* (Ann Arbor: University of Michigan Press, 2010).

31. Chin and Fehrenbach, "German Democracy and the Question of Difference, 1945–1995," in *After the Nazi Racial State*.

32. David Art, "The Wild, Wild East: Why the DVU Doesn't Matter and the NPD Does," *German Politics and Society* 22, 4 (Winter 2004), 122–33. Art comments that additionally the lack of a 1968 left-wing groundswell and the weakness of civil society organizations to combat racism contributed to the NPD's success in Eastern Germany.

33. Julian O'Halloran, "The March of History," *Fortnight,* no. 301 (December 1991): 18–19, details some of the earlier eruptions against asylum seekers and contract workers in the East.

34. This may have been rooted in the specific history of Hoyerswerda and the economic ills it was experiencing in the early 1990s, as Panikos Panayi argued not long after the events themselves; he said that this was also likely the case in Rostock, which had seen a sharp rise in unemployment after the *Wende*. See Panayi, "Racial Violence in the New Germany, 1990–1993," *Contemporary European History* 3, 3 (November 1994): 265–87.

35. See Sara Lennox, "Antiracist Feminism in Germany: An Introduction to Ika Hügel and Dagmar Schultz," *Women in German Yearbook* 9 (1994): 225–29; Denijal Jegic "How East Germany became a stronghold of the Far-Right," https://www.aljazeera.com/indepth/opinion/east-germany-stronghold-180914121858728.html, September 29, 2018, accessed May 15, 2019, and Astrid Prange, "Rostock Riots Revealed 'the Dark Side of Humanity," https://www.dw.com/en/rostock-riots-revealed-the-dark-side-of-humanity/a-18673369, August 26, 2015, accessed May 15, 2019.

36. Panayi, "Racial Violence in the New Germany."

37. Lara Day and Oliver Haag, "Introduction," in Lara Day and Oliver Haag, eds., *The Persistence of Race: Continuity and Change in Germany from the Wilhelmine Empire to National Socialism* (New York: Berghahn Books, 2017), 13, make a similar argument with regard to the changing parameters of race as a concept in the period covered by their volume. One can certainly maintain that racialized categories remain largely rigid, even as some parts of society become more receptive to the idea that a person can be both Black and German.

38. Maureen M. Eggers, Grada Kilomba, Peggy Piesche, and Susan Arndt, eds., *Mythen, Masken, und Subjekten: Kritische Weißseinforschung in Deutschland*, 4th ed. (Münster: Unrast Verlag), 2017, is considered a classic in critical whiteness studies in Germany. Its first edition appeared in 2005 and opened the field to a German audience.

39. David R. Roediger, "Critical Studies of Whiteness, USA: Origins and Arguments," *Theoria: A Journal of Social and Political Theory*, no 98 (December 2001): 72–98.

40. For example, Maria Stehle and Beverly M. Weber have pointed out that an ethnically diverse 2010 World Cup team was celebrated at the same time as Theo Sarrazin's popular anti-immigrant treatise stoked fear of white German demise. They argue that as Germans applauded the team as evidence that Germany and Europe had finally become antiracist or postracial, media discussions of team members in racialized terms demonstrated a continuing reification of racial difference. See Stehle and Weber, "German Soccer, the 2010 World Cup, and Multicultural Belonging," *German Studies Review* 36,

1 (February 2013): 103–24. For more on the Sarrazin controversy, see Michael Meng, "Silences about Sarrazin's Racism in Contemporary Germany," *Journal of Modern History* 87, 1 (March 2015): 102–35.

41. Fatima el-Tayeb, *Undeutsch: Die Konstruktion des Anderen in der postmigrantischen Gesellschaft* (Transcript: Bielefeld, 2016), and *European Others: Queering Ethnicity in Postnational Europe* (Minneapolis: University of Minnesota Press, 2011).

42. Noah Sow, *Deutschland Schwarz Weiss: der alltäglichen Rassismus* (Gütersloh: Bertelsmann, 2008); Alice Hasters, *Was weisse Menschen nicht über Rassismus hören wollen—aber wissen sollten* (Munich: Hanserblau, 2019); Natasha A. Kelly, *Afroism: Zur Situation einer ethnischen Minderheit in Deutschland* (Saarbrücken: VDM Verlag Dr. Müller, 2008); Kelly, *Millis Erwachen: Schwarze Frauen, Kunst und Wiederstand* (Berlin: Orlanda Frauenverlag, 2019); Fatima Aydemir and Hengameh Yaghoobifarah, *Eure Heimat ist unser Albtraum* (Berlin: Ullstein, 2019).

43. Sow, 91; Hasters, 80.

44. Gouri Sharma, "Angela Merkel's Mixed Legacy: Open-Door Policy, Rise of Far-Right," https://www.aljazeera.com/news/2018/12/angela-merkel-mixed-legacy-open-door-policy-rise-181208085144548.html, December 8, 2018, accessed May 15, 2019.

45. Griff Witte and Luisa Beck, "Angela Merkel Welcomed Refugees to Germany. They're Starting to Help the Economy," https://www.washingtonpost.com/world/europe/angela-merkel-welcomed-refugees-to-germany-theyre-starting-to-help-the-economy/2019/05/03/4bafa36e-6b60-11e9-bbe7-1c798fb80536_story.html?utm_term=.e05bf23d38a0, May 5, 2015, accessed May 15, 2019.

46. "Der Focus zu den Kölner Übergriffen: Titel der Schande," https://taz.de/Der-Focus-zu-den-Koelner-Uebergriffen/!5267901/, January 9, 2016, accessed October 23, 2020; "Süddeutsche entschuldigt sich, Focus nicht," https://www.spiegel.de/kultur/gesellschaft/focus-und-sueddeutsche-zeitung-eine-entschuldigung-eine-rechtfertigung-fuer-titel-a-1071334.html, January 10, 2016, accessed October 23, 2020.

47. Yermi Brenner and Katrin Ohlendorf, "Time for the Facts. What Do We Know about Cologne Four Months Later?" de Correspondent, May 2, 2016, https://thecorrespondent.com/4401/time-for-the-facts-what-do-we-know-about-cologne-four-months-later/1073698080444-e20ada1b, accessed May 15, 2019.

48. "German Police Criticised as Country Reels from Far-Right Violence," https://www.theguardian.com/world/2018/aug/28/german-police-criticised-as-country-reels-from-far-right-violence, August 28, 2018, accessed May 15, 2019.

49. "Racist Crime up Sharply in East Germany's Saxony State," https://www.france24.com/en/20190307-racist-crime-sharply-east-germanys-saxony-state, July 3, 2019, accessed October 23, 2020.

50. Denijal Jegic, "How East Germany Became a Stronghold of the Far-Right," https://www.aljazeera.com/opinions/2018/9/29/how-east-germany-became-a-stronghold-of-the-far-right/, September 29, 2018, accessed October 23, 2020.

51. Jegic, "How East Germany Became a Stronghold of the Far-Right," 3

52. Hanna Eiden, Vanessa Wormer, and Wolfgang Jaschensky, "Wo die AfD erfolgeich ist," https://www.sueddeutsche.de/politik/afd-wahl-auswertung-bundeslaender-1.4585616, September 3, 2019, accessed October 23, 2020. Other sources from the late

2010s also reflect the relative strength of the AfD in the East as opposed to in the West, including Frank Decker, "Wahlergebnisse und Wählerschaft der AfD," https://www.bpb.de/politik/grundfragen/parteien-in-deutschland/afd/273131/wahlergebnisse-und-waehlerschaft, July 16, 2018, and Timo Lehmann, "Im Osten hilflos gegen die AfD: Zusammen sind wir schwach." https://www.spiegel.de/politik/deutschland/thueringen-sachsen-und-brandenburg-was-die-landtagswahlen-gebracht-haben-a-1296301.html, November 26, 2019.

53. Amy Walker, "AfD und SPD sind Wahlsieger im Osten: Ist die AfD die Volkspartei in Ostdeutschland?", Moz.de, September 28, 2021, accessed February 28, 2022, https://www.moz.de/nachrichten/brandenburg/bundestagswahl-wahl-osten-ostdeutschland-prognosen-hochrechnungen-ergebnisse-umfragen-ergebnis-sachsen-anhalt-thueringen-brandenburg-berlin-mecklenburg-vorpommern-mv-59498421.html.

54. Brandon Tensley, "It's Been 25 Years Since German Reunification. Why Are Former East Germans Responsible for so Much Xenophobic Violence?" https://www.washingtonpost.com/news/monkey-cage/wp/2015/10/02/its-been-25-years-since-german-reunification-why-are-former-east-germans-responsible-for-so-much-xenophobic-violence/?utm_term=.c69d61bfda82, October 2, 2015, accessed May 15, 2019.

55. Aleksandra Lewicki, "Race, Islamophobia and the Politics of Citizenship in Post-Unification Germany," *Patterns of Prejudice* 52 (2018), https://doi.org/10.1080/0031322X.2018.1502236. To complicate the idea of the East as especially racist vis á vis the West, she points to surveys on attitudes toward asylum seekers that posed questions to both East and West Germans in the early 1990s. These surveys showed that East Germans were sometimes more sympathetic to refugees than Westerners, and that both groups of Germans had similarly negative opinions about migrant ability to assimilate to German culture.

56. Lewicki, "Race, Islamophobia, and the Politics of Citizenship in Post-Unification Germany." Lewicki indeed argues that the state in both German nations engaged in a politics of citizenship that was grounded in white German identity and excluded migrants of Color. In West Germany, this played out in the invitation of guest workers from the Middle East and North Africa with no expectations that they would, or could, eventually become German citizens. Meanwhile, in the East the policing of citizenship also played out through a separation of white Germans from Black contract workers, who were not eligible for citizenship. To this I would add African students, who were encouraged to return to their homelands with no sense that they could achieve citizenship. However, the fact that citizenship was not only open but assumed for their children with East German women does complicate the issue and question of who could or could not belong in the GDR in terms of citizenship, if not of social acceptance.

57. "In Chemnitz, Anti-Fascists Stand Up to the Nazi Salutes of Germany's Far-Right," https://www.theguardian.com/world/2018/sep/01/chemnitz-protests-germany-migration, September 2, 2018, accessed May 15, 2019.

Works Cited

ARCHIVES

BArch	Bundesarchiv (Federal Archives), Berlin
BStU	Stasi Unterlagen Archiv (Stasi Records Archive), Berlin
EAP	Endangered Archives Programme, The British Library
KNA	Kenya National Archives, Nairobi
PAAA	Politisches Archiv des Auswärtigen Amtes (Political Archives of the Foreign Office), Berlin
PRAAD	Public Records and Archives Administration Department, Accra
SAPMO-B	Arch Archiv der Partein und Massenorganisationen der DDR im Bundesarchiv
TNA	The National Archives, London
UAD	Universitätsarchiv (University Archives), Technische Universität, Dresden
UAL	Universitätsarchiv (University Archives), Leipzig

INTERVIEWS

Aryee-Boi, Desmond. Accra, September 15, 2015
Aryee-Boi, Jeanette. Accra, September 17, 2015
B. (Anonymous). Dakar, January 11, 2019
Bondzie, Kobina. Accra, September 16, 2015
Eichler, Ginga. Berlin, August 5, 2014
Kolagbodi, Yvonne. Berlin, September 10, 2014
Quansah, Robert. Accra, September 28, 2015
Quaysah, Alfred. Accra, September 16, 2015
Tette, David. Accra, September 17, 2015
Touré, Mohamed. Cologne, August 11, 2014

PRIMARY SOURCES

Ajao, Aderogba. *On the Tiger's Back: Six Years under Communism by a Nigerian*. London: George Allen and Unwin, 1962.

Api.Parliament.uk. "African Students Bulgaria." HC Deb 21 February 1963 vol 672 c614. https://api.parliament.uk/historic-hansard/commons/1963/feb/21/african-students-bulgaria

Arbeitstagung über Neuere und Neueste Geschichte Afrikas, ed. *Geschichte und Geschichtsbild Afrikas; Beiträge der Arbeitstagung für Neuere und Neueste Geschichte Afrikas am 17. und 18. April 1959 in Leipzig*. Berlin: Akademie-Verlag, 1960.

Bonfante, Jordan. "African Students at Iron Curtain Schools flee a Hateful Epithet: 'Cherni Maimuni.'" *Life*, March 15, 1963.

Botsio, Kojo. Speech to the Ghanaian Parliament, July 1961. Cited in Wilton S. Dillon, "Universities and Nation Building." *Journal of Modern African Studies* 1, no. 1 (March 1963): 75–89.

Césaire, Aimé. *Culture and Colonization*. Yaoundé, Cameroon: University of Yaoundé, 1978.

Crewdson, John M. "Worldwide Propaganda Network Built by the CIA." *New York Times*, December 26, 1977.

Diop, Cheikh Anta. *Nations negres et culture: De l'antiquité nègre égyptienne aux problems culturels de l'Afrique Nord d'aujourd'hui*. Paris: Présence Africaine, 2000.

East-West Contacts: A Monthly Review. "Political Penetration through 'Friendship.'" Vol. V, no. 9 (September 1971): 49–50.

Fanon, Frantz. *Black Skin, White Masks*. New York: Grove Press, 1967.

Glickman, Harvey. "Dar es Salaam: Where Exiles Plan—And Wait." *Africa Report* (July 1963): 3–6.

Hersh, Seymour M. "CIA said to have Aided Plotters who Overthrew Nkrumah in Ghana." *New York Times*, May 19, 1978.

Kaunda, Kenneth. "Installation Address by the Chancellor." In *The University of Zambia: Inauguration Ceremony*. Lusaka: Government Printer, 1966.

Kolagbodi, M. E. *Collected Speeches*. Lagos, Nigeria: Malthouse Press, 1995.

Kotey, Robert. "Ghanaian Students Beaten, Arrested in Bulgarian Restaurant Incident." *Stanford Daily* 143, no. 17 (February 27, 1963).

Lamb, Geoffrey B. "The Political Crisis in Kenya." *World Today: Chatham House Review* 25, no. 12 (1969): 537–44.

London Times. "Preference for the West by Foreign Students." June 5, 1967.

Markov, Walter, and Fausto Codino. "Appunti sulla storiografia Africa." *Studi Storici* 4, no. 4 (October–December 1963): 759–82.

Ndyamba, Amos. "Former Berlin Student Replies to Kay Sifuniso: Eastern Europe is not that bad." *Mail (Zambian Edition)*, February 28, 1964.

Neues Deutschland. "Pauline Lumumba beendet Aufenthalt in unserer Republik." March 20, 1965.

Neues Deutschland. "Von Dr. Homann empfangen." November 13, 1969.

Neues Deutschland. "Walter Ulbricht an Pauline Lumumba." February 16, 1961.

New York Times. "Nigerian Attacks Reds' Education: Disillusionment of Students from Africa Reported." May [illegible]

Ofodile, Gilbert. *I Shall Never Return; Eight Months in Communist Germany, a Nigerian Student of Journalism Reports*. Esslingen am Neckar: Bechtle Verlag, 1967.

O'Halloran, Julian. "The March of History." *Fortnight* No. 301 (December 1991): 18–19.
Ohiaeri, A. E. *Behind the Iron Curtain*. Enugu, Nigeria: Fourth dimension publ., 2002.
Senghor, Léopold Sédar. *On African Socialism*. New York: Praeger, 1964.
Sicard, Harald V. "XXV. Internationaler Orientalistenkongreß, Moskau." *Anthropos* 56, no. 1–2 (1961): 271–73.
Sifuniso, Kay. "What happens to African Students in Eastern Europe?" *Mail* (Zambian Edition), February 7, 1964.
Der Spiegel. "Neger-Exodus." February 12, 1964.
Der Spiegel. "Schon nahe am Pogrom." April 4, 1990.
Ulbricht, Walter. *Zur Geschichte der deutschen Arbeiterbewegung*. Berlin: Dietz, 1964.
Die Welt. "Afrikanische Studenten in der Zone unzufrieden." June 21, 1961.
West African Pilot. "*Bulgaria* Exodus: NCNC Calls for Inquiry." February 19, 1963.
Windward Islands' Opinion. "African Student Disillusioned with East Germany." July 1, 1961: 10.

SECONDARY SOURCES

Bibliography (Secondary Sources)

Abadan-Unat, Nermin. *Turks in Europe: From Guestworker to Transnational Citizen*. Oxford: Berghahn, 2011.
Abdulraheem, Tajudeen, and Adebayo O. Olukoshi. "The Left in Nigerian Politics and the Struggle for Socialism: 1945–1985." *Review of African Political Economy*, no. 37 (1986): 64–80.
Adi, Hakim. *West Africans in Britain, 1900–1960: Nationalism, Pan-Africanism, and Communism*. London: Lawrence & Wishart, 1998.
Adu-Gyamfi, Samuel, Wilhelmina Joselyn Donkoh, and Anim Adinkrah Addo. "Educational Reforms in Ghana: Past and Present." *Journal of Education and Human Development* 5, no. 3 (September 2016): 158–72.
Ahlman, Jeffrey S. *Living with Nkrumahism: Nation, State, and Pan-Africanism in Ghana*. Athens: Ohio University Press, 2017.
Ahlman, Jeffrey S. "Road to Ghana: Nkrumah, Southern Africa and the Eclipse of a Decolonizing Africa." *Kronos*, no. 37 (2011): 23–40.
Aitken, Robbie, John Macvicar, and Eve Rosenhaft. *Black Germany: The Making and Unmaking of a Diaspora Community, 1884–1960*. Cambridge: Cambridge University Press, 2013.
Ajulu, Rok. "Politicised Ethnicity, Competitive Politics and Conflict in Kenya: A Historical Perspective." *African Studies* 61, no. 2 (2002): 251–68.
Alamgir, Alena K. "Race Is Elsewhere: State-Socialist Ideology and the Racialisation of Vietnamese Workers in Czechoslovakia." *Race & Class* 54, no. 4 (April 1, 2013): 67–85. https://doi.org/10.1177/0306396813476171
Alence, Rod. "Colonial Government, Social Conflict and State Involvement in Africa's Open Economies: The Origins of the Ghana Cocoa Marketing Board, 1939–46." *Journal of African History* 42, no. 3 (2001): 397–416.

Alexander, Jocelyn, and JoAnn McGregor. "African Soldiers in the USSR: Oral Histories of ZAPU Intelligence Cadres' Soviet Training, 1964–1979." *Journal of Southern African Studies* 43, no. 1 (January 2, 2017): 49–66. https://doi.org/10.1080/03057070.2017.1272299

Allman, Jean. "Kwame Nkrumah, African Studies, and the Politics of Knowledge Production in the Black Star of Africa." *International Journal of African Historical Studies* 46, no. 2 (2013): 181–203.

Alterman, Jon B. "American Aid to Egypt in the 1950s: From Hope to Hostility." *Middle East Journal* 52, no. 1 (1998).

Aminzade, Ronald. *Race, Nation, and Citizenship in Postcolonial Africa: The Case of Tanzania*. New York: Cambridge University Press, 2013.

Amnesty International. "Amnesty International Briefing: Guinea, June 1978." Accessed July 30, 2019.

Anderson, David. "'Yours in Struggle for Majimbo.' Nationalism and the Party Politics of Decolonization in Kenya, 1955–64." *Journal of Contemporary History* 40, no. 3 (2005): 547–64.

Animashaun, Mojeed Adekunle. "State Failure, Crisis of Governance and Disengagement from the State in Africa." *Africa Development / Afrique et Développement* 34, no. 3–4 (2009): 47–63.

Apter, David E. *Ghana in Transition*. Princeton: Princeton University Press, 2019.

Apter, David E. "Ghana's Independence: Triumph and Paradox." *Transition*, no. 98 (2008): 6–22.

Arndt, Susan, Maureen Maisha Eggers, Grada Kilomba, and Peggy Piesche, eds. *Mythen, Masken und Subjekte: Kritische Weißseinforschung in Deutschland*. 4th ed. Berlin: Unrast, 2017.

Art, David. "The Wild, Wild East: Why the DVU Doesn't Matter and Why the NPD Does." *German Politics and Society* 22, no. 4 (2004): 122–33.

Atangana, Martin-René. *The End of French Rule in Cameroon*. Lanham, MD: University Press of America, 2010.

Atkins, Keletso E. *The Moon Is Dead! Give Us Our Money!: The Cultural Origins of an African Work Ethic, Natal, South Africa, 1843–1900*. Cambridge: Boydell & Brewer, 1993.

Ault, J. E. "Defending God's Creation? The Environment in State, Church and Society in the German Democratic Republic, 1975–1989." *German History* 37, no. 2 (2019): 205–26.

Ausländer in der DDR. "Ausländer in der DDR—Geholt, Gekommen, und Gewollt?" https://www.auslaender-in-der-ddr.com/home/studenten/situation-an-hoch-und-fachschulen/

Axster, Felix. "Die Angst vor dem Verkaffern: Rassenreinheit und Identität im deutschen Kolonialismus." *Werkstatt Geschichte* 14 (2005): 39–54.

Aydemir, Fatma, and Hengameh Yaghoobifarah. *Eure Heimat ist unser Albtraum*. Berlin: Ullstein, 2020.

Basse, Lutz. "Das Ausländerstudium an Universitäten, Hoch- und Fachschulen der DDR." http://www.auslaender-in-der-ddr.com/home/studenten/situation-an-hoch-und-fachschulen

Becker, Frank, and Franz-Hitze-Haus. *Rassenmischehen—Mischlinge—Rassentrennung: zur Politik der Rasse im deutschen Kolonialreich*. Stuttgart: Steiner, 2004.

Berdahl, Daphne. "'(N)Ostalgie' for the Present: Memory, Longing and East German Things." *Ethnos* 64, no. 3 (1999): 192–211.

Berenbaum, Michael, and Abraham J. Peck. *The Holocaust and History: The Known, the Unknown, the Disputed, and the Reexamined*. Bloomington: Indiana University Press, 2002.

Best, Jeremy. *Heavenly Fatherland: German Missionary Culture and Globalization in the Age of Empire*. Toronto: University of Toronto Press, 2021.

Biney, Ama. *The Political and Social Thought of Kwame Nkrumah*. London: Palgrave, 2016.

Biographical Legacy and Research Foundation, Nigeria. "OHIAERI, (DR) Anyanjo Ejisimekwu." Accessed June 21, 2018. https://blerf.org/index.php/biography/ohiaeri-dr-anyanjo-ejisimekwu/

Bland, Lucy. "White Women and Men of Colour: Miscegenation Fears in Britain after the Great War." *Gender & History Gender History* 17, no. 1 (2005): 29–61.

Bollinger, Stefan, and Ulrich van der Heyden. *Deutsche Einheit und Elitenwechsel in Ostdeutschland*. Berlin: Trafo-Verlag, 2002.

Borowy, Iris. "East German Medical Aid to Nicaragua: The Politics of Solidarity between Biomedicine and Primary Health Care." *História, Ciências, Saúde-Manguinhos* 24, no. 2 (2017): 411–28.

Brahm, Felix, and Eve Rosenhaft. *Slavery Hinterland: Transatlantic Slavery and Continental Europe, 1680–1850*. London: Boydell and Brewer, 2016.

Branch D. "Political Traffic: Kenyan Students in Eastern and Central Europe, 1958–69." *Journal of Contemporary History* 53, no. 4 (2018): 811–31.

Brenner, Yermi, and Katrin Ohlendorf. "Time for the Facts. What do we know about Cologne four Months later?" *The Correspondent*, May 2, 2016. Accessed May 15, 2019. https://thecorrespondent.com/4401/time-for-the-facts-what-do-we-know-about-cologne-four-months-later/1073698080444-e20ada1b

Brown, Carolyn A. *We Were All Slaves: African Miners, Culture, and Resistance at the Enugu Government Colliery*. Portsmouth, NH: Heinemann, 2003.

Buck-Morss, Susan. "Hegel and Haiti." *Critical Inquiry* 26, no. 4 (2000): 821–65.

Burton, Eric. "Decolonization, the Cold War, and Africans' Routes to Higher Education Overseas, 1957–65." *Journal of Global History* 15, no. 1 (March 2020): 169–91. https://doi.org/10.1017/S174002281900038X

Burton, Eric. "Hubs of Decolonization: African Liberation Movements and Eastern Connections in Cairo, Accra, and Dar es Salaam." In *Southern African Liberation Movements and the Global Cold War "East": Transnational Activism, 1960–1990*, edited by Lena Dallywater, Helder A. Fonseca, and Chris Saunders, 25–68. Berlin: De Gruyter, 2019.

Burton, Eric. "Introduction: Journeys of Higher Education and Struggle: African Mobility in Times of Decolonization and the Cold War." *Stichproben: Wiener Zeitschrift für kritische Afrikastudien* 18, no. 34 (2018). https://stichproben.univie.ac.at/alle-ausgaben/stichproben-nr-342018/

Burton, Eric. "More than a Cold War Scholarship: East-Central African Anticolonial

Activists, the International Union of Socialist Youth, and the Evasion of the Colonial State, 1955–1965." *Stichproben: Wiener Zeitschrift für kritische Afrikastudien* 18, no. 34 (2018). https://stichproben.univie.ac.at/alle-ausgaben/stichproben-nr-342018/

Burton, Eric. "Navigating Global Socialism: Tanzanian Students in and beyond East Germany." *Cold War History* 19, no. 1 (2019): 63–83.

Burton, Eric. "Solidarität und ihre Grenzen bei den Brigaden der Freundschaft der FDJ." In *Globales Engagement im Kalten Krieg*, edited by Frank Bösch, Caroline Moine, and Stefanie Senger. Göttingen: Wallstein, 2018.

Büschel, Hubertus. *Hilfe zur Selbsthilfe: deutsche Entwicklungsarbeit in Afrika 1960–1975*. Frankfurt am Main; New York: Campus, 2014.

Buzzanco, Robert. "Fidel Castro (1926–2016) and Global Solidarity." *The Sixties* 10, no. 2 (2017): 274–80.

Campt, Tina. *Other Germans: Black Germans and the Politics of Race, Gender, and Memory in the Third Reich*. Ann Arbor: University of Michigan Press, 2003.

Carew, Joy Gleason. "Black in the USSR: African Diasporan Pilgrims, Expatriates and Students in Russia, from the 1920s to the First Decade of the Twenty-First Century." *African and Black Diaspora: An International Journal* 8, no. 2 (2015): 202–15.

Childs, David, Thomas A. Baylis, and Marilyn Rueschemeyer. *East Germany in Comparative Perspective*. London: Routledge, 2003.

Chin, Rita C-K. *The Guest Worker Question in Postwar Germany*. New York: Cambridge University Press, 2009.

Clark, John F. "Socio-Political Change in the Republic of Congo: Political Dilemmas of Economic Reform." *Journal of Third World Studies* 10, no. 1 (1993): 52–77.

Connelly, Matthew. "Taking Off the Cold War Lens: Visions of North-South Conflict during the Algerian War for Independence." *American Historical Review* 105, no. 3 (June 2000): 739–69.

Conrad, Sebastian. *What Is Global History?* Princeton: Princeton University Press, 2017.

Cook, Alexander C. *Mao's Little Red Book: A Global History*. Cambridge: Cambridge University Press, 2016.

Cooper, Frederick. *Africa since 1940: The Past of the Present*. Cambridge: Cambridge University Press, 2019.

Cooper, Frederick. *Citizenship between Empire and Nation: Remaking France and French Africa, 1945–1960*. Princeton: Princeton University Press, 2014.

Copper, John F. *Communist Nations' Military Assistance*. Milton Park, United Kingdom: Routledge, 2019.

Cornwell, Gareth. "George Webb Hardy's the Black Peril and the Social Meaning of 'Black Peril' in Early Twentieth-century South Africa." *Journal of Southern African Studies* 22, no. 3 (September 1, 1996): 441–53. https://doi.org/10.1080/03057079608708504

Cottrell, Chris. "German from Senegal vies to break Bundestag Barrier." *New York Times*, May 31, 2013. https://www.nytimes.com/2013/06/01/world/europe/german-from-senegal-vies-for-bundestag-and-a-first.html?pagewanted=all&_r=0

Cottrell, Chris. "Two Black Lawmakers voted to Parliament in Germany." *New York*

Times, September 23, 2013. https://www.nytimes.com/2013/09/24/world/europe/2-black-lawmakers-voted-to-parliament-in-germany.html

Crum, David Leith. "Mali and the U.M.O.A.: A Case-Study of Economic Integration." *Journal of Modern African Studies* 22, no. 3 (1984): 469–86.

Dagne, Haile Gabriel. *Das entwicklungspolitische Engagement der DDR in Äthiopien: eine Studie auf der Basis äthiopischer Quellen*. Münster: Lit, 2004.

Dallywater, Lena, Chris Saunders, and Helder Adegar Fonseca. *Southern African Liberation Movements and the Global Cold War "East": Transnational Activism 1960–1990*. Oldenbourg: De Gruyter, 2019.

Dangarembga, Tsitsi. *Nervous Conditions*. Banbury: Ayebia Clarke, 2004.

Daniel, G. F. "The Universities in Ghana." *Commonwealth Universities Year Book* 1 (1997–1998): 649–56. Accessed July 24, 2019. http://www.users.globalnet.co.uk/~univghana/ghanahed.htm

Darkwah, Samuel Antwi, and Nahanga Verter. "An Empirical Analysis of Cocoa Bean Production in Ghana." *European Scientific Journal* 10, no. 16 (2014): 295–306.

Day, Lara, and Oliver Haag, eds. *The Persistence of Race: Continuity and Change in Germany from the Wilhelmine Empire to National Socialism*. New York: Berghahn, 2017.

Decker, Frank. "Wahlergebnisse und Wählerschaft der AfD." *Bundeszentrale für politische Bildung*, October 26, 2020. https://www.bpb.de/politik/grundfragen/parteien-in-deutschland/afd/273131/wahlergebnisse-und-waehlerschaft

Delano-Oriaran, Omobolade. "Diversifying the Professions: Gender Inequity and Female Career Aspirations in Nigeria." In *Multiculturalism in a Cross-National Perspective*, edited by Michael A. Burayidi, 353–66. Lanham, MD: University Press of America, 1997.

Deltombe, Thomas. "The Forgotten Cameroon War." *Jacobin Magazine*, October 12, 2016. https://www.jacobinmag.com/2016/12/cameroon-france-colonialism-war-resistance/

DeRoche, Andy. *Kenneth Kaunda, the United States and Southern Africa*. London: Bloomsbury, 2017.

De Sousa, Ana Naomi. "Between East and West: The Cold War's Legacy in Africa." *Al Jazeera*, February 22, 2016. https://www.aljazeera.com/indepth/features/2016/02/east-west-cold-war-legacy-africa-160214113015863.html

Döring, Hans-Joachim. *"Es geht um unsere Existenz": die Politik der DDR gegenüber der Dritten Welt am Beispiel von Mosambik und Äthiopien*. Berlin: Links, 2001.

East Africa Living Encyclopedia. Accessed October 19, 2018. https://www.africa.upenn.edu/NEH/kethnic.htm

Eckart, Gabriele. "Popkultur, Profit und das Banale: Stefan Raabs Erfolgssong 'Maschendrahtzaun' und der lächerliche 'Ossi.'" *German Studies Review* 34, no. 2 (2011): 365–75.

Edward A. Ulzen Memorial Foundation. "January 28, 1927, Achimota (Prince of Wales) College Opened." January 29, 2018. https://www.eaumf.org/ejm-blog/2018/1/29/january-28–1927-achimota-prince-of-wales-college-opened

Eiden, Hanna, Vanessa Wormer, and Wolfgang Jaschensky. "Wo die AfD erfolgeich ist." *Süddeutsche Zeitung*, September 3, 2019. Accessed October 23, 2020. https://www.sueddeutsche.de/politik/afd-wahl-auswertung-bundeslaender-1.4585616

E-International Relations. "Interview—Walter Mignolo/Part II: Key Concepts." Accessed December 29, 2020. https://www.e-ir.info/2017/01/21/interview-walter-mignolopart-2-key-concepts/

Ellis, Stephen. *External Mission—the ANC in Exile, 1960–1990*. Oxford: Oxford University Press, 2015.

Ellis, Stephen, and Tsepo Sechaba. *Comrades against Apartheid: The ANC and the South African Communist Party in Exile*. London: Currey, 1992.

El-Tayeb, Fatima. *European Others: Queering Ethnicity in Postnational Europe*. Minneapolis: University of Minnesota Press, 2011.

El-Tayeb, Fatima. *Undeutsch: Die Konstruktion des Anderen in der postmigrantischen Gesellschaft*. Berlin: Transcript, 2016.

Emmerling, Inga. *Die DDR und Chile (1960–1989): Aussenpolitik, Aussenhandel und Solidarität*. Berlin: Ch. Links Verlag, 2013.

Engel, Ulf, Hans-Georg Schleicher, and Inga-Dorothee Rost. *Die beiden deutschen Staaten in Afrika: zwischen Konkurrenz und Koexistenz, 1949–1990*. Hamburg: Institut für Afrika-Kunde im Verbund der Stiftung Deutsches Übersee-Institut, 1998.

Engerman, David C. *Price of Aid: The Economic Cold War in India*. Cambridge, MA: Harvard University Press, 2019.

Engerman, David C, and Corinna R Unger. "Introduction: Towards a Global History of Modernization." *Diplomatic History* 33, no. 3 (2009): 375–85.

Evans, Jennifer V. "The Moral State: Men, Mining, and Masculinity in the Early GDR." *German History* 23, no. 3 (2005): 355–70.

Fabian, Johannes. *Time and the Other: How Anthropology Makes Its Object*. New York: Columbia University Press, 2014.

Fehrenbach, Heide. *Race after Hitler: Black Occupation Children in Postwar Germany and America*. Princeton: Princeton University Press, 2005.

Fehrenbach, Heide, and Rita Chin, eds. *After the Nazi Racial State*. Ann Arbor: University of Michigan Press, 2010.

Fiddian-Qasmiyeh, Elena, and Patricia Daley. *Routledge Handbook of South-South Relations*. London: Routledge, 2019.

Foltz, William J. *From French West Africa to the Mali Federation*. New Haven: Yale University Press, 1965.

Fonseca, Ana Monica, and Daniel Marcos. "Cold War Constraints: France, West Germany and Portuguese Decolonization." *Portuguese Studies* 29, no. 2 (2013): 209–26. https://doi.org/10.5699/portstudies.29.2.0209

Förster, Larissa, Dag Henrichsen, and Michael Bollig, eds. *Namibia-Deutschland, eine geteilte Geschichte: Widerstand, Gewalt, Erinnerung*. Wolfratshausen: Edition Minerva, 2004.

France 24. "Racist Crime up Sharply in East Germany's Saxony State." July 3, 2019. Accessed October 23, 2020. https://www.france24.com/en/20190307-racist-crime-sharply-east-germanys-saxony-state

Fratzke, Lothar. "Heimat einer FDJ-Freundschaftsbrigade: Das Berufausbildungszentrum in Jinotepe." In *Aufbruch nach Nicaragua: Deutsch-Deutsche Solidarität im Systemwettstreit*, edited by Erika Harzer and Willi Volks, 141–44. Berlin: Ch. Links Verlag, 2008.

Freeland, Jane. "Creating Good Socialist Women: Continuities, Desire, and Degeneration in Slatan Dudow's 'The Destinies of Women.'" *Journal of Women's History* 29, no. 1 (2017): 87–110.

Frindte, W. "Sozialpolitische Anmerkungen zur Entwicklung Rechstradikaler Tendenzen in der DDR." *Rechstextremismus im Vereinten Deutschland: Randerscheinung oder Gefahr für die Demokratie*, edited by H. Butterwegge and C. Isola, 88–96. Berlin: Links-Druck, 1990.

Gadsden, Fay. "Patriarchal Attitudes: Male Control over and Policies towards Female Education in Northern Rhodesia, 1924–1963." *Zambia Journal of History*, no. 6/7 (1994): 25–45.

Gaines, Kevin Kelly. *American Africans in Ghana: Black Expatriates and the Civil Rights Era*. Chapel Hill: University of North Carolina Press, 2012.

Gallus, Alexander, Axel Schildt, and Detlef Siegfried, eds. *Deutsche Zeitgeschichte—Transnational*. Göttingen: Wallstein, 2015.

Geisler, Gisela. "Troubled Sisterhood: Women and Politics in Southern Africa : Case Studies from Zambia, Zimbabwe and Botswana." *African Affairs* 94 (1995): 545–78.

Geni. "Rhodesia and Nyasaland (Zambia, Zimbabwe, Malawi—Timeline." Accessed August 14, 2017. https://www.geni.com/projects/Rhodesia-and-Nyasaland-Zambia-Zimbabwe-Malawi-Timeline/14576

Gewald, Jan-Bart, ed. *Living the End of Empire: Politics and Society in Late Colonial Zambia*. Leiden: Brill, 2011.

Gewald, J. B., M. Hinfelaar, and G. Macola, eds. *One Zambia, Many Histories: Towards a History of Post-Colonial Zambia*. Leiden: Brill, 2008.

Gheorghiu, Mihai Dinu, and Adrian Netedu. "African Students and the Transformation Process of Romanian Education, from the Political Issue of Internationalism to the Romanian Educational Offer between 1970 and 1990." *Analele Ştiinţifice ale Universităţii »Alexandru Ioan Cuza« din Iaşi. Sociologie şi Asistenţă Socială* 8, no. 1 (2015): 131–43.

Ghodsee, Kristen. *Second World, Second Sex. Socialist Women's Activism and Global Solidarity during the Cold War*. Durham: Duke University Press, 2019.

Gitelson, Susan Aurelia. "Policy Options for Small States: Kenya and Tanzania Reconsidered." *Studies in Comparative International Development* 12, no. 2 (1977): 29–57.

Gleijeses, Piero. *Conflicting Missions: Havana, Washington, and Africa, 1959–1976*. Chapel Hill: University of North Carolina Press, 2011.

Global Non-Violent Action Database. *Zambians Campaign for Independence, 1944–1964*. http://nvdatabase.swarthmore.edu/content/zambians-campaign-independence-1944-1964

Gondola, Didier. *The History of Congo*. Westport, CT: Greenwood Press, 2003.

Goodwin, Stefan. *Interdependencies, Relocations, and Globalization*. Lanham, MD: Lexington Books, 2009.

Gordon, David. "Rebellion or Massacre?: The UNIP-Lumpa Conflict Revisited." In *One Zambia, Many Histories: Towards a History of Postcolonial Zambia*, edited by Jan-Bart Gewald, Marja Hinfelaar, and Giacomo Macola, 45–97. Leiden: Brill, 2008.

Gray, William Glenn. *Germany's Cold War: The Global Campaign to Isolate East Germany, 1949–1969*. Chapel Hill: University of North Carolina Press, 2014.

Grilli, Matteo. *Nkrumaism and African Nationalism: Ghana's Pan-African Foreign Policy in the Age of Decolonization*. London: Palgrave Macmillan, 2019.

The Guardian. "In Chemnitz, anti-Fascists stand up to the Nazi Salutes of Germany's Far-Right." September 2, 2018. Accessed May 15, 2019. https://www.theguardian.com/world/2018/sep/01/chemnitz-protests-germany-migration

The Guardian. "German Police Criticised as Country Reels from Far-Right Violence." August 28, 2018. Accessed May 15, 2019. https://www.theguardian.com/world/2018/aug/28/german-police-criticised-as-country-reels-from-far-right-violence

Guillory, S. "Culture Clash in the Socialist Paradise: Soviet Patronage and African Students' Urbanity in the Soviet Union, 1960–1965." *Diplomatic History* 38, no. 2 (2014): 271–81.

Gülstorff, Torben. "Resetting the Relevance of the Berlin Wall. German Public Diplomacies on the African Continent During the Cold War." In *Machineries of Persuasion: European Soft Power and Public Diplomacy during the Cold War*, edited by Óscar J. Martín García and Rósa Magnúsdóttir, 85–104. Berlin: De Gruyter, 2019.

Hagen, Katrina M. "Internationalism in Cold War Germany." PhD Diss., University of Washington, 2008.

Hansen, Karen Tranberg. "Negotiating Sex and Gender in Urban Zambia." *Journal of Southern African Studies* 10, no. 2 (April 1984): 219–38.

Harsch, Donna. *Revenge of the Domestic: Women, the Family, and Communism in the German Democratic Republic*. Princeton: Princeton University Press, 2006.

Hartmann, Heike, and Lewerenz Susann. "Campaigning against Apartheid in East and West Germany." *Radical History Review*, no. 119 (2014): 191–204.

Harvard Divinity School Religious Literacy Project. "Nigeria." Accessed June 21, 2018. https://rlp.hds.harvard.edu/nigeria-overview

Hasters, Alice. *Was weiße Menschen nicht über Rassismus hören wollen, aber wissen sollten*. Munich: Carl Hansen Verlag, 2020.

Heilmann, Peter. "Aspekte des Ausländerstudiums in der DDR." *Asien, Afrika, Lateinamerika* 18 (1990): 798–804.

Heineman, Elizabeth D. *What Difference Does a Husband Make? Women and Marital Status in Nazi and Postwar Germany*. Berkeley: University of California Press, 2003.

Herf, Jeffrey. *Reactionary Modernism: Technology, Culture, and Politics in Weimar and the Third Reich*. Cambridge: Cambridge University Press, 2003.

Herzog, Dagmar. *Sex after Fascism: Memory and Morality in Twentieth-Century Germany*. Princeton: Princeton University Press, 2007.

Hessler, Julie. "Death of an African Student in Moscow." *Cahiers du monde russe* 47, no. 1 (2006): 33–63.

Hillebrand, Ernst. *Das Afrika-Engagement der DDR*. Bern: Peter Lang, 1987.

Hinfelaar, Hugo F. *Bemba-Speaking Women of Zambia in a Century of Religious Change (1892–1992)*. Leiden: Brill, 1994.

Hodge, Joseph Morgan, Gerald Hödl, and Martina Kopf, eds. *Developing Africa: Concepts and Practices in Twentieth-Century Colonialism*. Manchester: Manchester University Press, 2017.

Hodgkinson, Dan, and Luke Melchiorre. "Introduction: Student Activism in an Era of Decolonization." *Africa: The Journal of the International African Institute* 89, no. 5 (2019): S1–14.

Höhn, Maria. *GIs and Fräuleins: The German-American Encounter in 1950s West Germany*. Chapel Hill: University of North Carolina Press, 2003.

Honeck, Mischa, Martin Klimke, and Anne Kuhlmann-Smirnov. *Germany and the Black Diaspora: Points of Contact, 1250–1914*. New York: Berghahn, 2013.

Hong, Young-Sun. "'The Benefits of Health Must Spread Among All': International Solidarity, Health, and Race in the East German Encounter with the Third World." In *Socialist Modern: East German Everyday Culture and Politics*, edited by Katherine Pence and Paul Betts, 183–210. Ann Arbor: University of Michigan Press, 2008.

Hong, Young-Sun. *Cold War Germany, the Third World, and the Global Humanitarian Regime*. Cambridge: Cambridge University Press, 2017.

Hornsby, Charles. *Kenya: A History since Independence*. London: I. B. Tauris, 2013.

Hosek, Jennifer Ruth. *Sun, Sex, and Socialism: Cuba in the German Imaginary*. Toronto: University of Toronto Press, 2012.

Hughes, Matthew. "Fighting for White Rule in Africa: The Central African Federation, Katanga, and the Congo Crisis, 1958–1965." *International History Review* 25, no. 3 (2003): 592–615.

Ibhawoh, Bonny. *Imperialism and Human Rights: Colonial Discourses of Rights and Liberties in African History*. Albany: SUNY Press, 2008.

Idemili, Sam O. "What the 'West African Pilot' Did in the Movement for Nigerian Nationalism between 1937 and 1957." *Black American Literature Forum* 12, no. 3 (1978): 84–91.

Ivancheva, Mariya. "Paternalistic Internationalism and (de)Colonial Practices of Cold War Higher Education Exchange: Bulgaria's Connections with Cuba and Angola." *Journal of Labor and Society* 22, no. 4 (2019): 733–48. https://doi.org/10.1111/wusa.12444

Ivaska, Andrew M. *Cultured States: Youth, Gender, and Modern Style in 1960s Dar Es Salaam*. Durham: Duke University Press, 2011.

Iweriebor, Ehiedu E. G. "Proletarians and Politics in Colonial and Post-Colonial Nigeria, 1912–1964." *Africa: Rivista Trimestrale Di Studi e Documentazione Dell'Istituto Italiano per l'Africa e l'Oriente* 41, no. 1 (1986): 29–47.

Jackson, Will. "Bad Blood: Poverty, Psychopathy and the Politics of Transgression in Kenya Colony, 1939–59." *Journal of Imperial and Commonwealth History* 39, no. 1 (2011): 73–94.

Jaja, S. O. "The Enugu Colliery Massacre in Retrospect: An Episode in British Administration of Nigeria." *Journal of the Historical Society of Nigeria* 11, no. 3–4 (1982): 86–106.

Jegic, Denijal. "How East Germany Became a Stronghold of the Far-Right." *Al Jazeera*, September 29, 2018. https://www.aljazeera.com/indepth/opinion/east-germany-stronghold-180914121858728.html

Jessen, Ralph. "Die Gesellschaft im Staatssozialismus. Probleme einer Sozialgeschichte der DDR." *Geschichte und Gesellschaft* 21, no. 1 (1995): 96–110.

Johnson, Catherine T. "The Representation of Blacks in Medieval German Literature and Art." PhD Diss., University of Michigan, 1994.

Katsakioris, Constantin. "The Lumumba University in Moscow: Higher Education for a Soviet-Third World Alliance, 1960–91." *Journal of Global History* 14, no. 2 (July 2019): 281–300. https://doi.org/10.1017/S174002281900007X

Katsakioris, Constantin. "Students from Portuguese Africa in the Soviet Union, 1960–1974: Anti-Colonialism, Education, and the Socialist Alliance." *Journal of Contemporary History*, April 2020. https://doi.org/10.15495/EPub_UBT_00004976

Kelly, Natasha A. *Afroism: Zur Situation einer ethnischen Minderheit in Deutschland.* Saarbrücken: VDM-Verl. Müller, 2008.

Kelly, Natasha A. *Millis Erwachen: Schwarze Frauen, Kunst Und Widerstand = Milli's Awakening: Black Woman, Art and Resistance.* Berlin: Orlanda, 2018.

Keys, Barbara. "An African-American Worker in Stalin's Soviet Union: Race and the Soviet Experiment in International Perspective." *Historian* 71, no. 1 (2009): 31–54.

Kil, Wolfgang, and Hilary Silver. "From Kreuzberg to Marzahn: New Migrant Communities in Berlin." *German Politics & Society* 24, no. 4 (2006): 95–121.

Klotz, M. "Memoirs from a German Colony: What Do White Women Want?" *Genders,* no. 20 (1994): 154–87.

Köpf, Peter. "Flucht nach Bautzen: Go West? Nicht nur im kalten Krieg liefen Hunderte NATO-Soldaten in den Osten über. Eine Villa in der Lausitz war ihr Auffanglager." *Die Zeit,* no. 10/2013. http://www.zeit.de/2013/10/Nato-Deserteure-DDR-Bautzen

Köpf, Peter. *Wo ist Lieutenant Adkins? Das Schicksal desertierter Nato-Soldaten in der DDR.* Berlin: Ch. Links Verlag, 2013.

Kret, Abigail Judge. "'We Unite with Knowledge' The Peoples' Friendship University and Soviet Education for the Third World." *Journal of Global History* 33, no. 2 (2013): 239–56.

Kundrus, Birte. "'Weiß und Herrlich': Überlegungen zu einer Geschlechtergeschichte des Kolonialismus." In *Projektionen: Rassismus und Sexismus in der visuellen Kultur*, edited by Annegret Friedrich, Birgit Haehnel, Viktoria Schmidt-Linsenhoff, and Christina Threuter, 41–50. Marburg: Jonas Verlag, 1997.

Kwon, Heonik. *The Other Cold War.* New York: Columbia University Press, 2010.

Lal, Priya. *African Socialism in Postcolonial Tanzania: Between the Village and the World.* Cambridge: Cambridge University Press, 2017.

Lal, Priya. "Maoism in Tanzania." In *Mao's Little Red Book: A Global History*, edited by Alexander C. Cook, 96–116. Cambridge: Cambridge University Press, 2016.

Landau, Paul Stuart. "Controlled by Communists? (Re)Assessing the ANC in Its Exilic Decades: Review Essay Devoted to *The External Mission: The ANC in Exile* by Stephen Ellis." *South African Historical Journal* 67, no. 2 (2015): 222–41.

Laqueur, Walter Z. "Communism and Nationalism in Tropical Africa." *Foreign Affairs* 39, no. 4 (1961): 610–21.

Larmer, Miles. *Rethinking African Politics: A History of Opposition in Zambia.* London: Routledge, 2016.

Larrimore, Mark J., and Sara Eigen, eds. *The German Invention of Race.* Albany: State University of New York Press, 2006.

Lawrance, Benjamin Nicholas. *Locality, Mobility, and "Nation": Periurban Colonialism in Togo's Eweland, 1900–1960.* Rochester, NY: University of Rochester Press, 2007.

Lee, Christopher J., ed. *Making a World after Empire: The Bandung Moment and Its Political Afterlives*. Athens: Ohio University Press, 2019.

Lehman, Brittany. *Teaching Migrant Children in West Germany and Europe, 1949–1992*. London: Palgrave, 2019.

Lehmann, Timo. "Im Osten hilflos gegen die AfD: Zusammen sind wir schwach." *Der Spiegel*, November 26, 2019. https://www.spiegel.de/politik/deutschland/thueringen-sachsen-und-brandenburg-was-die-landtagswahlen-gebracht-haben-a-1296301.html

Lehn, Suzanne. "Guinea: A Memorial for the Camp Boiro Victims." April 2, 2009. Accessed July 30, 2019. https://globalvoices.org/2009/04/02/guinea-a-memorial-for-the-camp-boiro-victims/

Lennox, Sara. "Antiracist Feminism in Germany: Introduction to Dagmar Schultz and Ika Hügel." *Women in German Yearbook* 9 (1993): 225–29.

Lewicki, Aleksandra. "Race, Islamophobia and the Politics of Citizenship in Post-Unification Germany." *Patterns of Prejudice* 52, no. 5 (2018): 496–512.

Lorenz, Sophie. *"Schwarze Schwester Angela"- Die DDR und Angela Davis Kalter Krieg, Rassissmus und Black Power 1965–1975*. Bielefeld: Transcript, 2020.

Lungu, Gatian F. "Educational Policy-Making in Colonial Zambia: The Case of Higher Education for Africans from 1924 to 1964." *Journal of Negro History* 78, no. 4 (1993): 207–32.

Lüthi, Lorenz M. "The Non-Aligned Movement and the Cold War, 1961–1973." *Journal of Cold War Studies* 18, no. 4 (October 2016): 98–147. https://doi.org/10.1162/JCWS_a_00682

MacClellan, Woodford. "Africans and Black Americans in the Comintern Schools, 1925–1934." *International Journal of African Historical Studies* 26, no. 2 (1993): 371–90.

Mac Con Uladh, Damian Henry Tone. "Guests of the Socialist Nation? Foreign Students and Workers in the GDR, 1949–1990." MA Thesis, University of London, 2005.

Mac Con Uladh, Damian Henry Tone. "Studium bei Freunden? Ausländische Studierende in der DDR bis 1990." In *Ankunft, Alltag, Ausreise: Migration und Interkulturelle Begegnung in der DDR-Gesellschaft*, edited by Christian Th. Müller and Patrice G. Poutrus, 175–220. Cologne: Bohlau, 2005

Macrakis, Kristie, and Dieter Hoffmann. *Science under Socialism: East Germany in Comparative Perspective*. Cambridge, MA: Harvard University Press, 1999.

Mandel, Ruth Ellen. *Cosmopolitan Anxieties: Turkish Challenges to Citizenship and Belonging in Germany*. Durham: Duke University Press, 2008.

Manuh, Takyiwaa. "Building Institutions for the New Africa: The Institute of African Studies at the University of Ghana." In *Modernization as Spectacle in Africa*, edited by Peter J. Bloom, Stephen F. Miescher, and Takyiwaa Manuh, 268–84. Bloomington: Indiana University Press, 2014.

Markle, Seth M. *A Motorcycle on Hell Run Tanzania, Black Power, and the Uncertain Future of Pan-Africanism, 1964–1974*. East Lansing: Michigan State University Press, 2017.

Matusevich, Maxim. "Black in the USSR: Africans, African Americans, and the Soviet Society." *Transition,* no. 100 (2008): 56–75.

Matusevich, Maxim. *No Easy Row for a Russian Hoe: Ideology and Pragmatism in Nigerian-Soviet Relations, 1960–1991*. Trenton, NJ: Africa World Press, 2003.

Matusevich, Maxim. "'Revisiting the Soviet Moment in Sub-Saharan Africa.'" *History Compass* 7, no. 5 (2009): 1259–68.

Mazower, Mark. *Dark Continent: Europe's Twentieth Century*. New York: Vintage, 2018.

Mazower, Mark. *No Enchanted Palace: The End of Empire and the Ideological Origins of the United Nations*. Princeton: Princeton University Press, 2013.

McCulloch, Jock. *Black Peril, White Virtue: Sexual Crime in Southern Rhodesia, 1902–1935*. Bloomington: Indiana University Press, 2000.

McLellan, Josie. *Love in the Time of Communism: Intimacy and Sexuality in the GDR*. Cambridge: Cambridge University Press, 2011.

Meaker, Morgan. "How Two Cities Encapsulate the Battle for Germany's Identity." *Atlantic*, September 23, 2017. Accessed October 23, 2020. https://www.theatlantic.com/international/archive/2017/09/leipzig-versus-dresden-and-the-battle-for-east-german-identity/540831/

Meng, Michael. "Silences about Sarrazin's Racism in Contemporary Germany." *Journal of Modern History* 87, no. 1 (2015): 102–35.

Meyer, B. "Christianity and the Ewe Nation. German Pietist Missionaries, Ewe Converts and the Politics of Culture." *Journal of Religion in Africa* 32, no. 2 (January 2002): 167–99. https://doi.org/10.1163/157006602320292906

Miller-Idriss, Cynthia. *Blood and Culture Youth, Right-Wing Extremism, and National Belonging in Contemporary Germany*. Durham: Duke University Press, 2009.

Mitteldeutscher Rundfunk. "Afrika war für die DDR-Außenpolitik Wichtig." https://www.mdr.de/zeitreise/ddr-aussenhandel-die-aussenhaendler-in-afrika100.html

Monson, Jamie. *Africa's Freedom Railway: How a Chinese Development Project Changed Lives and Livelihoods in Tanzania*. Bloomington: Indiana University Press, 2011.

Morgner, Irmtraud. "Third Fruit of Bitterfeld: The Tightrope." In *Daughters of Eve: Women's Writing from the German Democratic Republic*, edited and translated by Nancy Lukens and Dorothy Rosenberg, 137–42. Lincoln: University of Nebraska Press, 1993.

Moses, Julia. "From Faith to Race? 'Mixed Marriage' and the Politics of Difference in Imperial Germany." *History of the Family* 24, no. 3 (July 3, 2019): 466–93. https://doi.org/10.1080/1081602X.2019.1598461

Muehlenbeck, Philip E. *Czechoslovakia in Africa, 1945–1968*. London: Palgrave, 2016.

Muehlenbeck, Philip E., Natalia Telepneva, and Bloomsbury Publishing. *Warsaw Pact Intervention in the Third World: Aid and Influence in the Cold War*. London: Bloomsbury, 2020.

Müller, Alexander. *The Inevitable Pipeline into Exile: Botswana's Role in the Namibian Liberation Struggle*. Basel: Basler Afrika Bibliographien, 2012.

Müller, Tanja R. *Legacies of Socialist Solidarity: East Germany in Mozambique*. Lanham, MD: Lexington Books, 2014.

Namikas, Lise. *Battleground Africa: Cold War in the Congo, 1960–1965*. Redwood City, CA: Stanford University Press, 2015.

Nenno, Nancy. "Femininity, the Primitive, and Modern Urban Space: Josephine Baker in Berlin." In *Women in the Metropolis: Gender and Modernity in Weimar Culture*, edited by Katharina Von Ankum, 89–105. Berkeley: University of California Press, 1997.

Ngolongolo, Appolinaire. *L'assassinat de Marien Ngouabai: ou, L'histoire d'un pays ensanglanté*. Self-published, 1988.

Niethammer, Lutz. *Deutschland danach postfaschistische Gesellschaft und nationales Gedächtnis*. Bonn: Dietz 1999.

Nkosi, Milton. "The Airlift Education Scholarship that Changed the World." BBC, July 23, 2015. https://www.bbc.com/news/world-africa-33629577

Nwaubani, Ebere. *The United States and Decolonization in West Africa, 1950–1960*. Rochester, NY: University of Rochester Press, 2001.

Nwauwa, A. O. "The British Establishment of Universities in Tropical Africa, 1920–1948: A Reaction against the Spread of American 'Radical' Influence." *Cahiers d'études Africaines* 33 (1993): 247–74.

Nyong'o, Peter Anyang'. "Profiles of Courage: Ramogi Achieng' Oneko." *Review of African Political Economy* 34, no. 113 (2007): 531–35.

Odari, Catherine J. "A Blessing or Curse? The Mboya-Kennedy Students' Airlift and Its Implications." MA Thesis, Miami University, 2011.

Odinga, Oginga. *Not yet Uhuru: The Autobiography of Oginga Odinga*. London: Heinemann, 1968.

O'Donnell, K. Molly, Renate Bridenthal, and Nancy Reagin, eds. *The Heimat Abroad: The Boundaries of Germanness*. Ann Arbor: University of Michigan Press, 2010.

Ofcansky, Thomas P., and Robert M. Maxon. *Historical Dictionary of Kenya*. London: Rowman & Littlefield, 2014.

Olusanya, G. O. "The Zikist Movement: A Study in Political Radicalism, 1946–50." *Journal of Modern African Studies* 4, no. 3 (1966): 323–33.

Onslow, Sue, ed. *Cold War in Southern Africa: White Power, Black Liberation*. London: Routledge, 2012.

Pampuch, Sebastian. "Afrikanische Freedom Fighter im Exil der DDR." In *Wissen in Bewegung: Migration und globale Verflechtungen in der Zeitgeschichte seit 1945*, edited by Stephanie Zloch, Lars Müller, and Simone Lässig, 321–48. Berlin: De Gruyter, 2018.

Pampuch, Sebastian. "Afrikanische Migrationserfahrungen mit zwei Deutschen Staaten: Rekonstruktion eines migratorischen Lebensweges über die Grenze zweier deutscher Staaten hinweg." MA Thesis, Humboldt Universität zu Berlin, 2008.

Panayi, Panikos. "Racial Violence in the New Germany 1990–93." *Contemporary European History* 3, no. 3 (1994): 265–88.

Parpart, Jane L. "Sexuality and Power on the Zambian Copperbelt, 1926–1964." In *Patriarchy and Class: African Women in the Home and the Workforce*, edited by Jane L. Parpart and Sharon B. Stichter, 115–38. Reprint. New York: Routledge, 2019.

Parsons, Timothy. "The Lanet Incident, 2–25 January 1964: Military Unrest and National Amnesia in Kenya." *International Journal of African Historical Studies* 40, no. 1 (2007): 51–70.

Peña, Rosemarie. "From Both Sides of the Atlantic: Black German Adoptee Searches in William Gage's Geborener Deutscher (Born German)." *Genealogy* 2, no. 4 (2018): 40.

Pence, Katherine. "Showcasing Cold War Germany in Cairo: 1954 and 1957 Industrial Exhibitions and the Competition for Arab Partners." *Journal of Contemporary History* 47, no. 1 (2012): 69–95.

Pence, Katherine, and Paul Betts. *Socialist Modern: East German Everyday Culture and Politics*. Ann Arbor: University of Michigan Press, 2011.

Pfaff, Steven. *Exit-Voice Dynamics and the Collapse of East Germany: The Crisis of Leninism and the Revolution of 1989*. Durham: Duke University Press, 2006.

Piesche, Peggy. "Black and German? East German Adolescents Before 1989: A Retrospective View of a 'Non-Existent Issue' in the GDR." In *The Cultural After-Life of East Germany: New Transnational Perspectives*, edited by Leslie Adelson, 38–44. Washington, DC: AICGS Humanities, 2002.

Pileva, Desislava. "Images of our 'Foreign Friends': Representations of Students from the Middle East and Africa in the Bulgarian Students' *Tribune* Newspaper (1960s–1970s)." *Anthropology: Journal for Socio-Cultural Anthropology* 4 (2017). Accessed December 19, 2020. http://anthropology-journal.org/wp/author/pileva

Post, Ulrich, and Frank Sandvoss. *Die Afrikapolitik der DDR*. Hamburg: Institut für Afrika-Kunde, 1982.

Prange, Astrid. "Rostock Riots Revealed 'the Dark Side of Humanity." *Deutsche Welle*, August 26, 2015. https://www.dw.com/en/rostock-riots-revealed-the-dark-side-of-humanity/a-18673369

Pugach, Sara. *Africa in Translation: A History of Colonial Linguistics in Germany and beyond, 1814–1945*. Ann Arbor: University of Michigan Press, 2012.

Pugach, Sara, Elizabeth Berg, David Pizzo, and Adam A. Blackler, eds. *After the Imperialist Imagination: Two Decades of Research on Global Germany and Its Legacies*. Oxford: Peter Lang, 2020.

Ralston, Richard D. "Cuba in Africa and Africa in Cuba." *Contemporary Marxism*, no. 7 (1983): 140–53.

Raphael-Hernandez, Heike, and Pia Wiegmink. "German Entanglements in Transatlantic Slavery: An Introduction." *Atlantic Studies* 14, no. 4 (2017): 419–35.

Ray, Carina E. "'The White Wife Problem': Sex, Race and the Contested Politics of Repatriation to Interwar British West Africa." *Gender & History* 21, no. 3 (2009): 628–46.

Roberts, Andrew D. "Northern Rhodesia: The Post-War Background, 1945–1953." In *Living the End of Empire: Politics and Society in Late Colonial Zambia*, edited by Jan-Bart Gewald, Marja Hinfelaar, and Giacomo Macola, 15–26. Leiden: Brill, 2011.

Roediger, D. R. "Critical Studies of Whiteness, USA: Origins and Arguments." *Theoria*, no. 98 (2001): 72–98.

Roller, Kathrin. "Zwischen Rassismus und Frömmigkeit—Biopolitik aus erfahrungsgeschichtlicher Perspektive Über die Geschwister Hegner, Mathilde Kleinschmidt und

Ludwig Baumann als Nachfahren einer deutsch-afrikanischen Missionarsfamilie." In *Rassenmischehen—Mischlinge—Rassentrennung: Zur Politik der Rasse im Deutschen Kolonialreich*, edited by Frank Becker, 210–53. Stuttgert: Franz Steiner, 2004.

Roman, Meredith L. *Opposing Jim Crow African Americans and the Soviet Indictment of U.S. Racism, 1928–1937*. Lincoln: University of Nebraska Press, 2012.

Roos, Julia. "Women's Rights, Nationalist Anxiety, and the 'Moral' Agenda in the Early Weimar Republic: Revisiting the 'Black Horror' Campaign against France's African Occupation Troops." *Central European History* 42, no. 3 (2009): 473–508.

Rosenhaft, Eve. "Blacks and Gypsies in Nazi Germany: The Limits of the 'Racial State.'" *History Workshop Journal* 72, no. 1 (2011): 161–70.

Rubin, Eli. *Amnesiopolis Modernity, Space, and Memory in East Germany*. Oxford: Oxford University Press, 2016.

Sackeyfio-Lenoch, Naaborko. "The Ghana Trades Union Congress and the Politics of International Labor Alliances, 1957–1971." *International Review of Social History* 62, no. 2 (2017): 191–213.

Saideman, Stephen M. *The Ties That Divide: Ethnic Politics, Foreign Policy, and International Conflict*. New York: Columbia University Press, 2001.

Saldern, Adelheid von. *The Challenge of Modernity: German Social and Cultural Studies, 1890–1960*. Ann Arbor: University of Michigan Press, 2005.

Salles, Anne. "The Effects of Family Policy in the Former GDR on Nuptiality and Births Outside Marriage." *Population* 61, no. 1–2 (2006): 141–51.

Saney, Isaac. "Tricontinentalism, Anti-Imperialism, and Third World Rebellion." In *Routledge Handbook of South-South Relations*, edited Elena Fidian Qasmiyah and Patricia Daley, 153–67. New York: Routledge, 2019.

Sapire, Hilary. "Liberation Movements, Exile, and International Solidarity: An Introduction." *Journal of Southern African Studies* 35, no. 2 (2009): 271–86.

Scharf, C. Bradley. *Politics and Change in East Germany: An Evaluation of Socialist Democracy*. London: Routledge, 2019.

Schenck, Marcia Catherine, "From Luanda and Maputo to Berlin: Uncovering Angolan and Mozambican Migrants' Motives to Move to the German Democratic Republic (1979–1990)." *African Economic History* 44 (2016): 202–34.

Schenck, Marcia Catherine, "Negotiating the German Democratic Republic: Angolan Student Migration during the Cold War, 1976–90." *Africa* 89, no. S1 (2019): S144–66.

Schenck, Marcia Catherine. "Socialist Solidarities and Their Afterlives: Histories and Memories of Angolan and Mozambican Migrants in the German Democratic Republic, 1975–2015." PhD Diss., Princeton University, 2017.

Schilling, Britta. *Postcolonial Germany: Memories of Empire in a Decolonized Nation*. Oxford: Oxford University Press, 2014.

Schleicher, Hans-Georg. *Südafrikas neue Elite: die Prägung der ANC-Führung durch das Exil*. Hamburg: Institut für Afrika-Kunde im Verbund Deutsches Übersee Institut, 2004.

Schleicher, Hans-Georg, and Ilona Schleicher. *Die DDR Im Südlichen Afrika: Solidarität Und Kalter Krieg*. Hamburg: Institut für Afrika-Kunde, 1997.

Schleicher, Hans-Georg, and Ilona Schleicher. *Special Flights to Southern Africa [the GDR and Liberation Movements in Southern Africa]*. Harare: SAPES Books, 1998.

Schleicher, Ilona. "Zur Diskussion um die Beteiligung der DDR an Sanktionen gegen Südafrika Anfang der sechziger Jahre." *Africa Spectrum* 25, no. 3 (1990): 283–92.

Schleicher, Ilona. "Zur 'materiellen Solidarität' der DDR mit dem ANC in den 60er Jahren." *Afrika Spectrum* (1992): 213–17.

Schmidt, Elizabeth. *Cold War and Decolonization in Guinea, 1946–1958*. Athens: Ohio University Press, 2007.

Schmidt, Elizabeth. *Foreign Intervention in Africa: From the Cold War to the War on Terror*. Cambridge: Cambridge University Press, 2013.

Schönmeier, Hermann W. "Qualifizierung als Rückkehr Vorbereitung ehemaliger Vertragsarbeiter aus Mosambik." In *Die 'Gastarbeiter' der DDR: politischer Kontext und Lebenswelt*, edited by Almut Zwengel, 205–22. Münster: LIT Verlag, 2011.

Schulz, Brigitte. *Development Policy in the Cold War Era: The Two Germanies and Sub-Saharan Africa, 1960–1985*. Münster: Lit, 1995.

Schulz, Brigitte. "The Politics of East-South Relations: The GDR and Southern Africa." In *East Germany in Comparative Perspective*, edited by Thomas A. Bayliss, David Childs, Erwin L. Collier, and Marilyn Rueschemeyer, 156–72. New York: Routledge, 2002.

Schwartz, Michael. "Emanzipation zur sozialen Nutzlichkeit: Bedingungen und Grenzen von Frauenpolitik in der DDR." In *Sozialstaatlichkeit in der DDR: Sozialpolitische Entwicklungen im Spannungsfeld von Diktatur und Gesellschaft, 1945/49–1989*, edited by Dierk Hoffmann and Michael Schwartz, 47–88. Munich: Oldenbourg, 2005.

Scott-Smith, G. *Western Anti-Communism and the Interdoc Network: Cold War Internationale*. London: Palgrave Macmillan, 2014.

Serra, Gerardo, and Frank Gerits. "The Politics of Socialist Education in Ghana: The Kwame Nkrumah Ideological Institute, 1961–6." *Journal of African History* 60, no. 3 (2019): 407–28.

Sharma, Gouri. "Angela Merkel's Mixed Legacy: Open-Door Policy, Rise of Far-Right." *Al Jazeera*, December 8, 2018. https://www.aljazeera.com/news/2018/12/angela-merkel-mixed-legacy-open-door-policy-rise-181208085144548.html

Sieff, Kevin. "Who Are the Men Competing to be President of Kenya?" *Washington Post*, August 9, 2017. https://www.washingtonpost.com/news/worldviews/wp/2017/08/08/who-are-the-two-men-competing-to-be-president-of-kenya/

Simeon-Jones, Kersuze. "The Pan-African Philosophy and Movement: Social and Educational Praxis of Multiculturalism." In *Philosophies of Multiculturalism: Beyond Liberalism*, edited by Luis Cordeiro-Rodrigues and Marko Simendic, 217–32. New York: Routledge, 2016.

Slobodian, Quinn. "Bandung in Divided Germany: Managing Non-Aligned Politics in East and West, 1955–63." *Journal of Imperial and Commonwealth History* 41, no. 4 (2013): 644–62.

Slobodian, Quinn, ed. *Comrades of Color: East Germany in the Cold War World*. New York: Berghahn, 2017.

Slobodian, Quinn. *Foreign Front Third World Politics in Sixties West Germany*. Durham: Duke University Press, 2012.

Sow, Noah. *Deutschland Schwarz Weiss: Der Alltägliche Rassismus*. 2nd. ed. Gütersloh: Bertelsmann, 2018.

Spanger, Hans-Joachim, and Lothar Brock. *Die beiden deutschen Staaten in der Dritten Welt: Die Entwicklungspolitik der DDR—eine Herausforderung für die Bundesrepublik Deutschland?* Wiesebaden: Springer VS, 1987.

Speich, D. "The Kenyan Style of 'African Socialism': Developmental Knowledge Claims and the Explanatory Limits of the Cold War." *Diplomatic History* 33, no. 3 (2009): 449–66.

Der Spiegel. "Süddeutsche entschuldigt sich, Focus nicht." January 10, 2016. Accessed October 23, 2020. https://www.spiegel.de/kultur/gesellschaft/focus-und-sueddeutsche-zeitung-eine-entschuldigung-eine-rechtfertigung-fuer-titel-a-1071334.html

Spohr, Arne. "'Mohr Und Trompeter': Blackness and Social Status in Early Modern Germany." *Journal of the American Musicological Society* 72, no. 3 (2019): 613–63.

Steege, Paul, Andrew S. Bergerson, Maureen Healy, and Pamela E. Swett. "The History of Everyday Life: A Second Chapter." *Journal of Modern History* 80, no. 2 (2008): 358–78.

Stehle, Maria, and Beverly M. Weber. "German Soccer, the 2010 World Cup, and Multicultural Belonging." *German Studies Review* 36, no. 1 (2013): 103–24.

Straker, Jay. *Youth, Nationalism, and the Guinean Revolution*. Bloomington: Indiana University Press, 2009.

Summers, Carol. *Colonial Lessons: Africans' Education in Southern Rhodesia, 1918–1940*. Portsmouth, NH: Heinemann, 2002.

Sutter, S. C. "The Fall of the Bibliographic Wall: Libraries and Archives in Unified Germany." *College and Research Libraries* 55, no. 5 (1994): 403.

Tatum, Dale C. *Who Influenced Whom? Lessons from the Cold War*. Lanham, MD: University Press of America, 2002.

Taz. "Der Focus zu den Kölner Übergriffen: Titel der Schande." January 9, 2016. Accessed October 23, 2020. https://taz.de/Der-Focus-zu-den-Koelner-Uebergriffen/!5267901/

Tensley, Brandon. "It's Been 25 Years Since German Reunification. Why Are Former East Germans Responsible for So Much Xenophobic Violence?" *Washington Post*, October 2, 2015. Accessed May 15, 2019. https://www.washingtonpost.com/news/monkey-cage/wp/2015/10/02/its-been-25-years-since-german-reunification-why-are-former-east-germans-responsible-for-so-much-xenophobic-violence/?utm_term=.c69d61bfda82

Terretta, Meredith. "Cameroonian Nationalists Go Global: From Forest 'Maquis' to a Pan-African Accra." *Journal of African History* 51, no. 2 (2010): 189–212.

Thomas, Scott. *The Diplomacy of Liberation: The Foreign Relations of the African National Congress since 1960*. London: Tauris Academic Studies, 1996.

Thurston, Anne. *A Path Not Taken: The Story of Joseph Murumbi: Africa's Greatest Private Cultural Collector and Kenya's Second Vice-President*. Nairobi: Franciscan Kolbe Press, 2015.

Tijani, Hakeem Ibikunle. "Britain and the Development of Leftist Ideology and Organisations in West Africa: The Nigerian Experience, 1945–1965." PhD Diss., University of South Africa, 2005.

Tijani, Hakeem Ibikunle. *Union Education in Nigeria: Labor, Empire, and Decolonization since 1945*. Basingstoke: Palgrave Macmillan, 2012.

Torreguitar, Elena. *National Liberation Movements in Office: Forging Democracy with African Adjectives in Namibia*. Frankfurt am Main: Peter Lang, 2009.

Trentin, Massimiliano. "Modernization as State Building: The Two Germanies in Syria, 1963–1972." *Diplomatic History* 33, no. 3 (2009): 487–505.

Tyndale, Wendy. *Protestants in Communist East Germany: In the Storm of the World.* London: Routledge, 2016.

University of Central Arkansas. "Mali (1960-present)." Accessed December 29, 2020. https://uca.edu/politicalscience/dadm-project/sub-saharan-africa-region/mali-1960-present/

Van der Heyden, Ulrich. "Afrika im Blick der akademischen Welt der DDR. Ein wissenschaftsgeschichtlicher Überblick der afrikabezogenen Ethnographie." *BEWI Berichte zur Wissenschaftsgeschichte* 42, no. 1 (2019): 83–105.

Van der Heyden, Ulrich. *Die Afrikawissenschaften in der DDR: eine akademische Disziplin zwischen Exotik und Exempel : eine wissenschaftsgeschichtliche Untersuchung*. Münster: Lit, 1999.

Van der Heyden, Ulrich. "Die Afrika-Geschichtsschreibung in der ehemaligen DDR: Versuch einer kritischen Aufarbeitung (Africa Historical Research in the Former GDR: Attempt of a Critical Evaluation)." *Africa Spectrum* 27, no. 2 (1992): 207–11.

Van der Heyden, Ulrich. "Angedichteter Rassismus." Accessed December 19, 2020. https://www.sopos.org/aufsaetze/57220b74ecdb1/1.phtml.html

Van der Heyden, Ulrich. *Die DDR und der Handel mit dem Apartheidregime in Südafrika*, 2004.

Van der Heyden, Ulrich. *Engagiert für Afrika: die DDR und Afrika II*. Münster: LIT, 1994.

Van der Heyden, Ulrich. *Kalter Krieg in Ostafrika? Die Beziehungen der DDR zu Sansibar und Tansania*, 2009.

Van der Heyden, Ulrich. *Zwischen Solidarität und Wirtschaftsinteressen: Die "geheimen" Beziehungen der DDR zum südafrikanischen Apartheidregime*, 2005.

Van der Heyden, Ulrich, Wolfgang Semmler, and Ralf Strassburg. *Mosambikanische Vertragsarbeiter in der DDR-Wirtschaft: Hintergründe, Verlauf, Folgen*, 2014.

Van der Heyden, Ulrich, Ilona Schleicher, and Hans-Georg Schleicher. *Die DDR und Afrika [1]: Zwischen Klassenkampf und neuem Denkung*. Münster: LIT, 1993.

Villadaata, Frank R. *Cold War in the Congo: The Confrontation of Cuban Military Forces, 1960–1967*. London: Routledge, 2012.

Wagner, Bernd. "Vertuschte Gefahr: Die Stasi und Neonazis." *Bundeszentrale für politische Bildung*, January 2, 2018. http://www.bpb.de/geschichte/deutsche-geschichte/stasi/218421/neonazis

Walker, Amy. "AfD und SPD sind Wahlsieger im Osten: Ist die AfD die Volkspartei in Ostdeutschland?" Moz.de, September 28, 2021, accessed February 28, 2022, https://www.moz.de/nachrichten/brandenburg/bundestagswahl-wahl-osten-ostdeutschland-prognosen-hochrechnungen-ergebnisse-umfragen-ergebnis-sachsen-anhalt-thueringen-brandenburg-berlin-mecklenburg-vorpommern-mv-59498421.html.

Wallerstein, Immanuel Maurice. *Africa: The Politics of Independence and Unity*. Lincoln: University of Nebraska Press, 2006.

Walther, Daniel. "Sex and Control in Germany's Overseas Possessions: Venereal Disease and Indigenous Agency." In *German Colonialism Revisited: African, Asian, and Oceanic Experiences*, edited by Nina Berman, Klaus Mühlhahn, and Patrice Nganang, 71–84. Ann Arbor: University of Michigan Press, 2014.

Weis, Toni. "The Politics Machine: On the Concept of 'Solidarity' in East German Support for SWAPO." *Journal of Southern African Studies* 37, no. 2 (2011): 351–67. https://doi.org/10.1080/03057070.2011.579443

Weitz, Eric D. *Creating German Communism, 1890–1990: From Popular Protests to Socialist State*. Princeton: Princeton University Press, 1997.

Weitz, Eric D. *Weimar Germany: Promise and Tragedy*. Princeton: Princeton University Press, 2018.

Welch, Claude E. *Dream of Unity: Pan-Africanism and Political Unification in West Africa*. Ithaca: Cornell University Press, 1972.

Wentker, Hermann. *Außenpolitik in engen Grenzen: Die DDR im internationalen System 1949–1989*. Berlin: De Gruyter, 2012. https://doi.org/10.1524/9783486707380

Westad, Odd Arne. *The Global Cold War: Third World Interventions and the Making of Our Times*. Cambridge: Cambridge University Press, 2005.

Wildenthal, Lora. *German Women for Empire, 1884–1945*. Durham: Duke University Press, 2002.

Wilke, Sabine. "Romantic Images of Africa: Paradigms of German Colonial Paintings." *German Studies Review* 29, no. 2 (2006): 285–98.

Wimmelbücker, Ludger. *Mtoro Bin Mwinyi Bakari: Swahili Lecturer and Author in Germany*. Dar es Salaam: Mkuki na Nyota Publishers, 2009.

Winrow, Gareth M. *The Foreign Policy of the GDR in Africa*. Cambridge: Cambridge University Press, 2009.

Witte, Griff, and Luisa Beck. "Angela Merkel Welcomed Refugees to Germany. They're Starting to Help the Economy." *Washington Post*, May 5, 2015. Accessed May 15, 2019. https://www.washingtonpost.com/world/europe/angela-merkel-welcomed-refugees-to-germany-theyre-starting-to-help-the-economy/2019/05/03/4bafa36e-6b60-11e9-bbe7-1c798fb80536_story.html?utm_term=.e05bf23d38a0

Wittenberg, Hermann. "Wilhelm Bleek and the Khoisan Imagination: A Study of Censorship, Genocide and Colonial Science." *Journal of Southern African Studies* 38, no. 3 (2012): 667–79.

Yordanov, Radoslav A. *The Soviet Union and the Horn of Africa during the Cold War: Between Ideology and Pragmatism*. Reprint. Lanham, MD: Lexington Books, 2017.

Yurdakul, Gokce. *From Guest Workers into Muslims the Transformation of Turkish Immigrant Associations in Germany*. Newcastle upon Tyne: Cambridge Scholars, 2009.

Zimmerman, Andrew. *Alabama in Africa: Booker T. Washington, the German Empire, and the Globalization of the New South*. Princeton: Princeton University Press, 2012.

Zloch, Stephanie, Lars Müller, and Simone Lässig. *Wissen in Bewegung: Migration und globale Verflechtungen in der Zeitgeschichte seit 1945*. Berlin: De Gruyter, 2018.

Zwengel, Almut. *Die "Gastarbeiter" der DDR politischer Kontext und Lebenswelt*. Münster: LIT Verlag, 2011.

Index

Note: Page numbers in italics indicate figures.

Printed and bound by CPI Group (UK) Ltd, Croydon, CR0 4YY

09/06/2025

14685670-0004